"This wonderfully rich collection of essays by psychoanalyst and historian David James Fisher provides a beautiful integration of psychoanalytic thinking and thinking about psychoanalysis. As an intellectual immersed in European Cultural History who followed his passion for the self-knowledge that psychoanalysis uniquely affords, Fisher makes short work of orthodoxy and convention, while sifting lovingly through inherited tradition for its remaining jewels. An act of love and erudition, *The Subversive Edge of Psychoanalysis* follows the path psychoanalysis has taken over the decades, while inviting outsiders a rare chance to savor and learn from the intimate knowledge and innovations of a vibrant psychoanalytic community."

– **Jessica Benjamin,** *psychoanalyst and social theorist; author, The Bonds of Love and Beyond Doer and Done To: Recognition Theory, Intersubjectivity, and the Third*

"WHEN SCHOLARSHIP IS A PAGE-TURNER: This collection of brilliant essays reads like a fascinating novel that addresses a remarkably rich tapestry of ideas and realms of experience in ways that we don't even notice how much we are learning. Fisher takes us on an exciting, always questing, and often moving, journey as he variously critiques and admires psychoanalysis, its applications, and the thinking of many of its luminaries and critics in a strikingly balanced way. We read how psychoanalytic ideas and the vicissitudes of its institutions past and present struggle to maintain significance in a world that is changing so rapidly in mass psychological, cultural, judicial, and institutional ways. Fisher's book left me wishing it would never end and, indeed, it may not insofar as psychoanalysis retains, as Fisher does, an attitude of 'subversive vitality'."

– **Howard A. Bacal,** *MD, Training and Supervising Analyst, The New Center for Psychoanalysis and the Institute of Contemporary Psychoanalysis, Los Angeles*

"David James Fisher's *The Subversive Edge of Psychoanalysis* is a wonderful and worthwhile contribution to our psychoanalytic thought collective. Many of the chapters are devoted to distinguished psychoanalysts with whom Fisher has had direct, sometimes extensive, contact. He offers serious and valuable critiques of their work, but the critiques never overshadow his high esteem for their significant contributions. His writing style is clear and illuminating, giving the reader the opportunity of feeling warmly accompanied on an intellectual exploration. We meet Fisher's mentors, colleagues, and then in subsequent sections, his special areas of interest, including psychoanalytic history, anti-Semitism, French psychoanalysis, US politics, his reflections on his father's dementia, and even his psychoanalytic reflections of being on a jury. It is like an intellectual memoir. Throughout all of it, one has the feeling that Fisher, in an almost intimate fashion, is explaining all that he saw and was thinking about in relation to the topics he presents. And when he writes about mentors and colleagues, it is almost like sitting at a coffee table listening in on their conversation. We've all read collections of essays before, but this one is unique in my mind, as there is a clear unifying thread of a first-rate psychoanalyst and historian serving as guide to each area

he addresses. And that unifying thread is made up of cultivated critical thinking and a subversive vision of psychoanalysis. I highly recommend Fisher's selected essays and can guarantee that you will come away from it having learned something new."
– **Daniel S. Benveniste,** *PhD; clinical psychologist, Sammamish, Washington; author, Libido, Culture, and Consciousness: Revisiting Freud's Totem and Taboo*

"This book is a psychoanalytic *tour de force* and a labor of love for the author. It presents an account of the history of psychoanalytic developments at the cutting edge of recent decades. It includes in-depth accounts of the important players, many with whom Dr. Fisher established deep personal relationships. I ended one of my papers with the comment that psychoanalysis was a subversive discipline. Dr. Fisher's book firmly establishes that this is indeed the case."
– **Arnold Richards,** *M.D., former Editor, The Journal of the American Psychoanalytic Association (1994–2003); publisher, internationalpsychoanalysis.net; author, Unorthodox: My Life In and Outside of Psychoanalysis*

"This is an elegant work that will withstand time. Readers will be grateful to Dr. Fisher's thoughtful and clear 'subversive' study of our discipline. Listen to what a great sweep of psychoanalysis Jimmy Fisher covers here. First, the idea of subversion and psychoanalysis. His perspective is provocative and engaging. We learn in psychoanalysis how we live covert lives, often undermining our own pleasure in life. What does psychoanalysis subvert: how it is both non-elitist, yet non-conforming. The subversiveness of psychoanalysis permits us to listen to the *covert*, then *convert* it to something useful to lead us to richer lives. Dr. Fisher understands how the unease of psychoanalysis and the psychoanalyst helps us to come to terms with our own unease. Read this. You will get wiser."
– **Nathan Szajnberg,** *M.D.; retired Freud Professor of Psychoanalysis, The Hebrew University*

"David James Fisher's collection could well have been entitled 'Illuminations'. It shines a bright light not only on many aspects of psychoanalysis but also diverse topics from Vichy France to Donald Trump. The expertise Dr. Fisher brings to so many diverse topics is extraordinary. He insightfully employs his knowledge as a practicing psychoanalyst with his doctorate in history. Crossing boundaries is home territory for him. On psychoanalysis, he finds the field needs to recover its subversive vitality. Psychoanalytic goals are not to make the unconscious conscious, or to fortify the ego, but to enable the person to resonate with his or her sense of inner authenticity. The book exemplifies this psychoanalytic exploration of the authentic. Particularly resonant is Dr. David James Fisher's poignant encounter with another Dr. Fisher, his own father, not long before his elder's death. This book is an enriching experience that will remain after reading the whole volume."
– **Ken Fuchsman,** *emeritus faculty and administrator, University of Connecticut; past President, International Psychohistorical Association; author, Freud, Movies, Rock & Roll and What It is To Be Human*

The Subversive Edge of Psychoanalysis

The Subversive Edge of Psychoanalysis examines the radical and non-conformist perspectives of both classical and contemporary psychoanalysis.

The chapters included in this book span the course of David James Fisher's career. They contextualize significant cases from the recent history of psychoanalysis, critically analyze key aspects of psychoanalytic work, consider the role of psychoanalysis in the history of the twentieth century, and provide biographical sketches of major figures in the field. The book concludes with a cogent interview of the author by a distinguished psychohistorian, depicting how subjectivity, family themes, politics, and cultural affinities marked his choice of subject matter and methodology, his identifications, and his antipathies.

The Subversive Edge of Psychoanalysis will appeal to mental health professionals and students with an interest in psychoanalytic practice and theory and academics and researchers who are fascinated by the subversive, non-conforming aspects of both classical and contemporary psychoanalysis.

David James Fisher is Senior Faculty at the New Center for Psychoanalysis and Training and Supervising Analyst at the Institute of Contemporary Psychoanalysis. He specializes in the history of psychoanalysis, the convergence of cultural history with psychoanalysis, and psychoanalytic applications to politics, movies, literature, and works of art. His background is in European Cultural and Intellectual History. He has been practicing psychoanalysis and psychotherapy in Los Angeles for 45 years.

History of Psychoanalysis
Series Editor
Peter L. Rudnytsky

This series seeks to present outstanding new books that illuminate any aspect of the history of psychoanalysis from its earliest days to the present and to reintroduce classic texts to contemporary readers.

Other titles in the series:

A Brief Apocalyptic History of Psychoanalysis
Erasing Trauma
Carlo Bonomi

Theories and Practices of Psychoanalysis in Central Europe
Narrative Assemblages of Self Analysis, Life Writing, and Fiction
Agnieszka Sobolewska

Sigmund Freud and his Patient Margarethe Csonka
A Case of Homosexuality in a Woman in Modern Vienna
Michal Shapira

Sigmund Freud, 1856-1939
A Biographical Compendium
Christfried Toegel

The Marquis de Puysegur and Artificial Somnambulism
Memoirs to Contribute to the History and Establishment of Animal Magnetism
Edited and translated by Adam Crabtree and Sarah Osei-Bonsu

The Subversive Edge of Psychoanalysis
David James Fisher

For further information about this series, please visit https://www.routledge.com/The-History-of-Psychoanalysis-Series/book-series/KARNHIPSY

The Subversive Edge
of Psychoanalysis

David James Fisher

LONDON AND NEW YORK

Designed cover image: © 2024 Estate of Pablo Picasso/Artists Rights Society (ARS), New York

First published 2025
by Routledge
4 Park Square, Milton Park, Abingdon, Oxon OX14 4RN

and by Routledge
605 Third Avenue, New York, NY 10158

Routledge is an imprint of the Taylor & Francis Group, an informa business

© 2025 David James Fisher

The right of David James Fisher to be identified as author of this work has been asserted in accordance with sections 77 and 78 of the Copyright, Designs and Patents Act 1988.

All rights reserved. No part of this book may be reprinted or reproduced or utilised in any form or by any electronic, mechanical, or other means, now known or hereafter invented, including photocopying and recording, or in any information storage or retrieval system, without permission in writing from the publishers.

Trademark notice: Product or corporate names may be trademarks or registered trademarks, and are used only for identification and explanation without intent to infringe.

British Library Cataloguing-in-Publication Data
A catalogue record for this book is available from the British Library

ISBN: 9781032785509 (hbk)
ISBN: 9781032785493 (pbk)
ISBN: 9781003488439 (ebk)

DOI: 10.4324/9781003488439

Typeset in Times New Roman
by KnowledgeWorks Global Ltd.

Pour Sherry

Comme toujours et pour toujours

Contents

Acknowledgments   *xi*
Introduction   *xii*

PART I
Erotics, Transitional Objects, and Dreamwork   1

1. Stoller, Erotics, Sexual Excitement   3
2. Transitional Objects and Generativity: Ekstein's Blending of Erikson and Winnicott   21
3. Concerning the Life Cycle of the Transitional Object (by Rudolf Ekstein)   26
4. A Conversation with Adam Phillips   31
5. Comments on James S. Grotstein's Dreambook   52

PART II
The History of Psychoanalysis   59

6. Sartre's Freud: Dimensions of Intersubjectivity in *The Freud Scenario*   61
7. Reflections on the Psychoanalytic Free Clinics   85
8. A Power Structure Analysis of Psychoanalytic Institutes (Followed by an Interview with Douglas Kirsner)   98
9. On the History of Lacanian Psychoanalysis in France   114
10. What Was Revolutionary about the Psychoanalytic Revolution in Mind?   124

x Contents

11 Discovering Wounded Healers in *A Dangerous Method*   130

12 Peter Loewenberg's Contribution to Psychohistory
 and Psychoanalysis   142

PART III
**Toward a Psychological Understanding of Resistance
and Collaboration during Vichy France**   147

13 Reflections on the Collaboration and the Jewish Question   149

14 To Resist and to Protect: A Critical Analysis of *Weapons
 of the Spirit*   159

PART IV
Funeral Orations   163

15 Father's Day   165

16 Remembering Robert J. Stoller (1924–1991)   171

17 Eulogy for Joseph Natterson, M.D. (1923–2023)   178

PART V
Psychoanalysis and Political Engagement   181

18 Trump as Symptom   183

19 Against the Separation of Children from Parents
 at the U.S. Border (with Van DeGolia)   190

20 A Manifesto for Psychoanalytic Education
 with Sixteen Suggestions   192

21 A Psychoanalyst Serves on a Jury   198

PART VI
Epilogue   215

22 The Intellectual Itinerary of a Psychoanalyst: David James
 Fisher Interviewed by Paul Elovitz   217

Index   *228*

Acknowledgments

I have profited from extensive discussions with friends and colleagues on the themes of this book. I would like to acknowledge Peter Loewenberg, Robert Nye, Mary Jo Nye, Robert Rosenstone, Russell Jacoby, Paul Elovitz, Ken Fuchsman, Nathan Szajnberg, Arnold Richards, Elena Bezzubova, Josh Hoffs, Sherry Rodriguez, Jacques Szaluta, Daniel Benveniste, Roland Kaufhold, Howard Bacal, Jessica Benjamin, Laurie Baron, Elyn Saks, Charles Levin, Richard Levine, Mort Shane, Michelle Moreau-Ricaud, Adam Phillips, Charles Levin, Robert Goldstein, Michael Kibler, Douglas Kirsner, Ken Rasmussen, Andrew Samuels, and Bart Blinder. I also want to express my gratitude to deceased friends and mentors: George L. Mosse, Germaine Bree, Alain de Mijolla, Gerry Aronson, Mike Leavitt, Mel Mandel, Jim Grotstein, Albert Mason, Joseph Natterson, and John Forrester. I want to thank Peter L. Rudnytsky for facilitating the publishing of this book in his series on the History of Psychoanalysis with Routledge Publishers. Susannah Frearson from Routledge was encouraging and helpful throughout the process. Dr. Vladimir Melamed did an excellent job as a copy editor, making many pertinent suggestions along the way.

Introduction

I distinguish the concept of subversive from revolutionary or destructive. By subversive, I mean an attempt to undermine conventional ideas of psychology, morality, education, social allegiances, and attachments based on faith. It is a radical form of teaching and applying psychoanalytic principles to transmit analytic forms of knowledge. At its best, psychoanalysis is neither an ideology nor a utopia, even if it leans toward the possibility of personal emancipation. Psychoanalysis is not a fully formed worldview or *Weltanschauung*. Psychoanalysis can liberate individuals suffering from crippling inhibitions, maladaptive anxieties, persistent depression, severe self-criticism, self-attacks, and recurring challenges to positive self-esteem and self-regard. Psychoanalytic therapy can overthrow stifling patterns of repetition and of stalemate, leading to individual transformation and modes of creative and expansive fulfillment. Psychoanalytic practice relies on subversive ethics, a way of establishing connections and assigning meaning that yield powerful forms of understanding – at times unwanted insights, impressions, and revelations.

Psychoanalysis blurred the distinction between normalcy and pathology. It shifted the stance of the analyst being moralistic, self-righteous, scientific, neutral, and objective, or soft and sentimental. It provided a tough-minded and hard-earned humanism by radically differentiating between reality and fantasy, an understanding of finite possibilities versus magical thinking and infantile illusions, and a capacity to accept the individual as he was in his conflicted state, without a well-defined and universal notion of what defined adulthood, maturity, or ethics.

Psychoanalysis was never meant to be popular or mainstream. It is best served by being marginal. Because of its emphasis on the unconscious, on the persistent force of sexuality and aggression, and on the pressures and reversals of intimate relationships, psychoanalysis continues to be socially and culturally corrosive. It will never be widely accepted because of its attunement to ambiguity, paradox, and complexity. Contemporary analysts have become more comfortable in acknowledging not-knowing and uncertainty, over-determination, and the persistence of complementarity in explaining psychic phenomena. Psychoanalysis generates pathways to the unruly and the ungovernable in terms of how our inner worlds are structured. It creates a porous membrane between life and death, understanding that old age and death may illuminate aspects of life. It enables individuals to live more fully rich lives because it allows them to mourn and grieve.

Both psychoanalytic theory and practice, including the application of psychoanalysis to cultural artifacts, call into question the identity of victimhood.

Similarly, its understanding of external and internal forms of aggression does not permit a hijacking of thought through blunting of mankind's destructive, even genocidal, potential. Mindlessness, or the multiple varieties of dissociation encountered in the clinical realm, is no longer an option; it is best understood as a symptom permitting the analyst to "stand between the spaces" to reverse the psychic numbness and to work through aspects of psychic splitting. It also includes the analysts' ability to acknowledge his anger, resentments, and aggression, the varieties of his countertransference hatred. This may renew the individual's emotional and intellectual capacity to perceive outward messages and receive internal cues. Psychoanalysts also appreciate the ways in which contradictions work within us as ambivalence and can surround us externally with precarious and at times absurd choices, choices that are often the lesser of two evils.

Psychoanalysis permits us to grasp a mind in flight, understanding internal conflict, splits in the personality, and the conflict of the self with the external world, often deriving from the family, religion, the State, institutions, and hierarchies, and the self in conflict with itself. In working with patients and in deciphering texts psychoanalytically, we understand the persistent role of projection and displacements, of condensation and symbolic representation. The dynamic conflicts help us to approach individuals attempting to flee or disguise pain, or to obscure the multiple meanings of intense trauma and loss. It does so without eliminating ambiguity and subtlety, without simplifying or reifying realms of mental production. If authenticity is to be profoundly valued and sought after, it does not imply an embrace of soft thinking, or the mystifying principles of the New Age, or strictly intuitive modes of operation.

Because the analyst works as a participant-observer, he understands the roles of his own affectivity and subjectivity in determining the accuracy of his observations and the "truth" and efficacy of his interpretations. Operating from a unique position of trust and suspicion, the analyst undermines definitive forms of understanding by skeptically acknowledging that his own insights might be provisional, relative, situational, and open to further revision or elaboration. He may be wrong or misguided. He needs to be honest about his own biases, including his bias about bias. Just as there is no single truth about human nature, so too is there no single unified theory capable of explaining personality structure or psychopathology; nor does a single theory of technique exist that guarantees a complete understanding of individuals and their emergence from family systems with specific deficits or defenses, as well as with their capacity for cure, for mindful adaptation, as well as for creativity, spontaneity, and playfulness. It embraces the "Yes, and" in the world of improvisation, while tolerating the messiness and often confusing nature of psychic reality.

Psychoanalysis also injures our narcissistic sense about ourselves, our perfectionism, and desire to frame ourselves as poised, autonomous, and independent.

It brings to light disturbing and dark things we don't want to think about, themes that give rise to shame, guilt, and disavowal of feelings, generating self-protective maneuvers and cover-ups. For those of us searching for meaning and coherence in our lives, psychoanalysis permits us to clear out of the way assorted dissociative and defensive strategies. These diminish our mental faculties and limit our engagement with intimate relationships, including our capacity to interact with the external world. Last, but not least, psychoanalysis subverts attempts to scapegoat the other by working against binary oppositions, mechanistic explanations, and essentialism, whether biological or theological. It encourages us to look at ourselves in the project of constructing or co-constructing meaning with another, including thinking about things we don't particularly want to think about.

The Subversive Edge of Psychoanalysis unites 22 chapters I have written over the past 20 years.

Chapter 1 focuses on Robert Stoller's inclusion of his subjective and bodily states in his long case history of Belle, one of the finest and most complex in the clinical literature. It makes major advances in this genre of presenting clinical work. Stoller's contribution to our understanding of sexuality and gender is second only to Freud's. As someone who was an initiator of discourse on erotics and the concept of primary femininity, Stoller's method shows his recognition and creative use of erotic countertransference. The analyst's susceptibility to erotic stimulation from the patient was omitted or avoided in most previous psychoanalytic case histories, considered by some as an impediment to treatment and as an indication that the analyst needed further analysis. Stoller never suggested that sexual enactments with a patient were appropriate forms of doing analysis. By arguing that aggression was at the root of sexual arousal, Stoller subverted conventional analytic approaches and romantic notions about sexual life and fantasy. It helped him to explore the persistent themes of sadomasochism and sexual dissatisfaction in the patients he treated. The hostility toward the other operated dialectically, engendering excitement and also an attempt to master or triumph over previous traumatic sexual experiences. Stoller also proposed that case histories ought to be read and approved of by patients before publication, a stance he justified both ethically and scientifically. He thought it would encourage more analytic humility about being correct, working against arrogance about definitive interpretations. He argued that the truths of the analytic relationship were shared truths, mutually constructed and validated.

Chapter 2 contextualizes and introduces Rudolf Ekstein's essay on the life cycle of the transitional object. By bridging two previous schools in psychoanalytic psychology thought to be antithetical, the ego psychological views of Erikson and the British object relations Middle School of Winnicott, Ekstein shows how the two can be blended creatively. In this intermediate area of theorizing, he argues that transitional objects operate throughout the life cycle of the individual, not just in early childhood. They are present during every stage of the life span as outlined by Erikson. The chapter draws on anecdotes from his own life and observations of his own children, which indicate his sensitivity to developmental themes and to ways in which children, adolescents, and adults have to navigate difficult moments of change and uncertainty in their lives. We use transitional objects throughout the life span to calm anxieties and to help navigate life's often precarious rites of passage. Ekstein's essay is also an astute version of self-reflection, an essay which reverberates because of its evocative and rewarding legacy even though written in his late seventies. Lastly, the first publication of this essay became a transitional moment in my own relationship with Ekstein as my former training analyst. Now we were both being published in the institute's official Bulletin, both proud contributors to the psychoanalytic literature.

Chapter 3 consists of Rudolf Ekstein's charming and wise essay on the life cycle of the transitional object which astutely blends the ego psychological theories of Erikson and the relational theories of Winnicott into a coherent whole. By looking at transitional objects and transitional phenomena, Ekstein shows how individuals cope with potentially traumatic rites of passage throughout the life cycle, not just in the period of early childhood development. The use of transitional objects also occurs in adolescence, early middle age, middle age, and old age, helping individuals deal with separation anxieties and uncertainty. In drawing on his own memory of his transit from Europe to America as a refugee from the Nazis in 1938, Ekstein explains that each individual in his cohort of four carried different transitional objects, connecting to the past, containing hope for the future, and promoting some semblance of security in an unsafe, chaotic, dangerous world. Ekstein also provides anecdotes from his children's experiences, showing how difficult it is to navigate developmental shifts in life. His essay lightly and engagingly draws on his vast clinical experience, including his work with children and adolescents, fused into a coherent developmental perspective, which he added to his philosophical and linguistic background. This fertile blend of Erikson and Winnicott promotes further pathways of research, as well as serving as a marvelous example of self-analysis.

Chapter 4 is a probing conversation with Adam Phillips, perhaps the world's most widely read psychoanalytic writer and public intellectual. Phillips is a contemporary spokesman for the English object relations school, closest to the spirit of Winnicott's work. In answering questions about his psychoanalytic education and supervision, his analysis with Masud Khan, his relationship to his Jewishness and to British anti-Semitism, his biographical writings on Freud and Winnicott, his insistence on Winnicott's grasp of the intensity of the dyadic relationship, including sexuality and aggression, Phillips reveals a refreshing candor and brilliance that both delight and stimulate deeper thinking. He has much to say about Winnicott's books, *Playing and Reality*, as well as subtle and illuminating ideas about his elusive article "The Uses of an Object." Phillips answers questions about his books on kindness, monogamy, the translation of Freud, therapeutic zeal, the need for open-minded and experimental psychoanalysis, and the rejection of essentialist points of view and so-called definitive interpretations. Just as his critique of establishment psychoanalysis is useful, contentious, and refreshing to contemplate, so too it is subversive of the establishment's norms and pieties. Phillips joins hands with Winnicott in his pleasure in surprise, astonishment, playfulness, intellectual dexterity, and love of paradox. As a reader of great literature, he also exemplifies a joy in writing, having an ability to engage with his readers in productive dialogue.

Chapter 5 is a critical analysis of James Grotstein's book, *Who Is the Dreamer Who Dreams the Dream?* (2000). It points out the potentially liberating, insightful, and even inspiring aspects of how he deals with the dream work, reverie, and mystical forms of knowledge. It also questions the obscurantist nature of his Kleinian/Bionian approach to technique and its theoretical language, indicating how his attachment to this theory may obfuscate the consciousness of his readers. The chapter discusses Grotsein's specimen dream, at once an evocative narrative about a dramatic moment in his life, a moment of mourning and of self-revelation, and also one that captures the structure and essence of the dreaming process. In discussing his dual-track approach, one that alternates between a one-person and two-person psychology, Grotstein remains open to multiple perspectives on psychic phenomena, including symptoms, and aspects of the transference/countertransference matrix. His approach avoids reductionism and a narrow form of determinism. It is also receptive to mystical and intuitive forms of knowing. Grotstein the clinician and supervisor worked in a more direct and plain-spoken manner than appears in this text, avoiding some of the confusions and mystifications that appear in his writings. Depth does not have to be the enemy of clarity; nor does convoluted prose always promote profundity of understanding and clinical acumen.

Chapter 6 provides a detailed historical and textual explication of Sartre's underestimated screenplay, *The Freud Scenario*. Sartre temporarily reversed his longstanding opposition to psychoanalytic theory and practice, becoming a son to the founder of psychoanalysis, while elaborating an original, intersubjective Freud. Sartre accomplished his innovative work despite his conflictual relationship with the film director John Huston on the movie "*Freud*" and despite the rupturing of their relations. This chapter explores the conflictual, dialectical relationships between Austrian anti-Semites and Jews, doctors and patients, fathers and sons, showing how these oppressive and dominating relationships can be worked through and resolved through analytic forms of self-reflection. Only after his extensive self-analysis is Freud able to establish deeper and more trusting bonds with his patients. Working analytically with his patients helps him to understand himself. Sartre's emancipatory story about the early origins of Freud's discoveries about the unconscious, his patients, and himself focuses less on an understanding of sexual desire and its repression than on how Freud recognized and mastered his own anger and aggression. Before his self-analysis, Freud related to his patients with contempt, repugnance, shame and guilt, and authoritarian attitudes. After his self-analysis and his understanding of his relationship with his father, he was able to be caring, sensitive, collaborative, and empathic, able to work in a co-constructed and co-created analytic dyad.

Chapter 7 discusses the historical origins of the free clinic movement, which sprang up above all in Central Europe, but also internationally in the period between the two world wars. It shows that during the interwar period the radically progressive second generation of psychoanalysts, namely, Wilhelm Reich, Otto

Fenichel, Erich Fromm, and Siegfried Bernfeld experimented with synthesizing Marx and Freud. The free clinics offered free or low fee mental health treatment to poor people, artists, under-employed, and unemployed, in short to underserved sectors of the population excluded from analytic practice. The movement provided analytic candidates and junior graduates of psychoanalytic institutes with exposure to a broad spectrum of psychopathology and included free supervision. It broke with the elitism and privileged class and educational status of individuals who could come into therapy. This chapter shows that Wilhelm Reich was a major leader in the free clinic movement. The free clinics were opposed by reactionary psychiatrists, Catholics, and members of conservative religious associations, who postured against psychoanalysis for its supposed pan-sexualism. Eventually, the movement was destroyed by the Nazi takeover in Germany in 1933 and in Austria by 1938, where the clinics were shut down and Jewish clinicians excluded.

Chapter 8 provides an internal power structure analysis of contemporary psychoanalytic institutes, showing how these institutions are fundamentally "unfree," anti-democratic, and oligarchical in nature. It demonstrates that the transmission of psychoanalytic education in America has been distorted into various paranoid structures, enforcing conformism, accommodation, a religious cult-like mentality, and discipleship. Simultaneously, these institutes have punished dissenters, marginalizing those experimenting with different theoretical and clinical approaches to their patients. With a detailed investigation of the Los Angeles Psychoanalytic Society and Institute, the author's home institute, we explore many of Douglas Kirsner's perspectives, including their strengths and weaknesses, and uses and abuses. The author concludes with an incisive interview of Kirsner, shortly after his book *Unfree Associations* appeared.

Chapter 9 explicates and contextualizes Roudinesco's history of the Lacanian movement in France, highlighting both her brilliance and blind spots as a historian and witness to this fascinating and baroque history. Roudinesco underscores the subversive aspects of Lacan's theory and his creation of a major psychoanalytic school. Lacan synthesized the valid aspects of Hegel's philosophy, surrealism, textual analysis of Freud's writings, and the conceptual apparatus of French structuralism, organizing them into a coherent whole. There were some wildness and non-transmissible aspects of Lacan's mode of working, including the short sessions, boundary violations with his patients, and disregard for the patient-analyst's vows of confidentiality. Lacan also conducted polemics against ego psychology and the International Psychoanalytic Association, while remaining critical of the English object relations school. Lacan practiced an unconventional and problematic mode of training candidates, including the imperative for candidates to be self-authorizing. He disavowed the exploration of meaning and the task of understanding his analysand's content. Instead, he focused on their spoken words, on puns, slips of the tongue, lapses, pauses, and punctuation of their utterances. Late in life, some of Lacan's innovations hardened into incoherent discourse, the mimicry of the master's pronouncements, and the creation of a cult around him with loyal lieutenants and obedient disciples.

Chapter 10 critically examines George Makari's impressive *Revolution in Mind*, especially his arguments about Freud's construction of a powerful synthesis by 1940. This synthesis consisted of integrating the findings of nineteenth-century French academic psychology centered on psychopathology, the tradition of German psychophysics, the postulation of a threshold between unconscious and conscious phenomena, and the perspectives of English and Viennese sexology. Makari's command of the literature in German, French, and English opens a conversation about what was revolutionary about early psychoanalysis and what aspects of that mental or internal revolution have been co-opted or muted by the discipline's professionalization, medicalization, and its penetration and diffusion into different cultures and cities. Psychoanalysis' success may paradoxically have blunted its subversive thrust, turning it into another soothing and conformist instrument of social adjustment and domination by powerful sectors of privilege in the mental health community. Within the encyclopedic framework of the book, there is a well-articulated argument and a conducting thread, namely, that after Freud's grand synthesis, psychoanalysis became professionalized in the 1920s. Despite persistent conflicts in the psychoanalytic field and a history of splits and acrimonious struggles, psychoanalysis triumphed with the emergence of American ego psychology during and after World War II. Makari's work will continue to be a useful and accurate guide to those concerned with the emergence of psychoanalysis in the first half of the twentieth century. His volume contains fundamental nuggets of knowledge for intellectual historians, historians of science, and mental health practitioners. Methodologically, he is able to draw on the strengths of both history and psychoanalysis in telling his story and constructing his argument, while deciphering the underlying subtexts.

Chapter 11 is an extended discussion of the brilliant, artistic film by David Cronenberg, *A Dangerous Method*. It examines the triangular relationship between Freud, Jung, and Sabina Spielrein. In exploring how Jung's relationship with Spielrein liberated her from a disabling mental disorder, Jung's treatment of her was at times exploitative, sadistic, selfish, and callous. By portraying the early pioneers of psychoanalysis as wounded healers, the movie humanizes the major characters, making them less mythological, less heroic and exalted. We are allowed to see them as vulnerable and real, making them comprehensible to contemporary audiences. The movie artistically moves beyond a typical Hollywood venture by enabling the viewers to experience transference and countertransference to its leading figures, including ambivalence and charged feelings of love and hatred toward these personalities. Audiences are swept away by the film's visual images, the exquisite Wagnerian music, and the accuracy of detail in the office and dress of Freud, Jung, and Spielrein. While watching the film, temporarily we become psychoanalysts, trying to figure out the truths and fallacies of their words and the contradictions of their behavior.

Chapter 12 is a brief biographical account of Peter Loewenberg's life and legacy as a psychohistorian and psychoanalyst. It points out unities in his work, including an early experience in China, where his parents emigrated to Shanghai to escape from Nazi Germany. Currently, he is involved in disseminating psychoanalysis in contemporary China, responding to a fascination by the Chinese with psychoanalytic perspectives. Loewenberg's work in psychohistory unseated the naïve and shallow psychological approaches to leaders and followers, by privileging underlying psychodynamic understanding and his cogent decoding of unconscious material. He was a pioneer in psychoanalytic biography in his studies of Theodor Herzl, Walter Rathenau, and Karl Renner. Peter helped to establish psychohistory as a legitimate sub-specialty in the historical profession and in academia. His advocacy of Research Psychoanalysis, the training of academics from the humanities and social sciences, was far in advance of other developments throughout the country. The presence of Research psychoanalysts at the New Center for Psychoanalysis and on the faculty has added scholarly rigor, distinction, and diversity. Loewenberg made it possible for lay analysts from other disciplines to receive full psychoanalytic clinical training, subsequently to be able to practice, teach, and write with clinical expertise about psychoanalysis.

Chapter 13 targets the ideology and politics of Vichy France, especially regarding its dehumanizing behavior toward Jews and members of the French Resistance. To grasp the Collaboration, we must understand the psychological dynamics of French supporters of the Vichy government in the context of the early and middle 1940s in France. The Collaboration objectified, denigrated, and pathologized Jews in this era without pressure from Nazi Germany, leading ultimately to roundups, deportation, and genocide, to clear crimes against humanity. Over 76,000 Jews were deported and exterminated because of Vichy's anti-Semitic sentiments and policies. Implementing a hostile and militaristic ethic of surpassing Nazi Germany, of being "more German than the Germans," the collaboration reveals the murderous mix of racism, cultural nationalism, and xenophobia placed into action. These attitudes and prejudices were superimposed on unconscious feelings of envy, resentment, rage, and inadequacy projected onto an unarmed civilian population and Jewish minority. Jews were often despised for their talents, brilliant achievements, and cultural and economic privileges. Vilified as foreign, sick, cancerous, venomous, grotesque, and plague ridden, Jews were debased and dehumanized. Yet the period of Vichy cannot be understood unless we grasp the pockets of resistance to the regime from large sectors of the population, from intellectuals and artists, and from those who those who resisted a fascistic, anti-Semitic, German-dominated France.

Chapter 14 interprets and explicates the documentary film by Pierre Sauvage, *Weapons of the Spirit*. We examine the historical, cultural, and psychological causes of why this small, provincial town in south-eastern France hid and safeguarded the lives of over five thousand Jews during the period of Vichy France. To do so was an existential danger; it meant risking one's life. It is historically elusive to understand from the inside the altruism and moral decency of the proud villagers of this mostly Protestant community. While resisting the murderous policies and hideous ideology of Vichy France and its collaborators, the village protected the highly vulnerable population of French and foreign-born Jews who came there seeking shelter. We understand far better the dynamics of sadism and cruelty than we do the psychology of care and decency, which this community demonstrated. Camus, perhaps not accidentally, lived in this town while completing a draft of his novel *The Plague*, a novel that underscores the necessity to fight the plague from within and without; it is a novel that some regard as the greatest statement of anti-fascist resistance ever written. Many of its themes apply to the villagers of Le Chambon during this era.

Chapter 15, "Father's Day" is the intimate record of my last visit to my sick and ailing father at the Hebrew Home for the Aged. It would be the last time I saw him alive, the last time we would converse, and the last time we would share some time together. I tried to make the writing as emotionally honest as possible. In it, the feelings of grief, sadness, and miscomprehension surface as I observed my father in a state of depression and dementia after having suffered a stroke. The sub-text of the essay is an expression of guilt about not taking my father in to live with my family and me. This coexisted with the contemplation of the sad end of his existence, his utter dependence on caretakers, and his retreat into a zone of transition somewhere between consciousness and dissociation, between living and dying. Experiencing the decline and death of a parent may help to prepare me and others for the inevitable final chapters of our own lives.

Chapter 16 is a memorial tribute combining clinical, intellectual, and personal memories of Stoller over the years of our friendship. It highlights Stoller's brilliance and ordinality in his writing on gender, erotics, and the dynamics of aggression in the psychopathology of perversions and the understanding of the complex roots of sexual excitement and fantasies related to sexual arousal. Stoller pioneered and strongly advocated against the pathologizing of homosexuality and the treatment of sexually active women; he approached most of his homophobic profession with an emphasis on the plural nature of homosexuality; it could not be reduced to one cause or one etiology. The eulogy recalls his strong support of research and creative thinking by younger colleagues in the psychoanalytic profession. It makes a case for seeing him as a psychoanalytic stylist and original thinker of the first rank. It was written with an attitude of both gratitude and grief for having known and collaborated with him, even if his life was abruptly cut off by an absurd automobile accident.

Chapter 17 eulogizes about the role of Joseph Natterson as friend, mentor, intellectual comrade, and clinical consultant over the past forty-five years. It provides an overview of his life and work, including his commitments to social justice, to socioeconomic inequalities, and his care and concerns about the future of the planet in the face of climate changes and global warming. It emphasizes his understanding of love and the emergence of the loving self in the clinical context of therapy. It traces his understanding of intersubjectivity and his evolution into a contemporary relational analyst. It celebrates his outstanding contributions to the analytic literature and his intellectual and relational vitality until the last months of his life. As a family man, teacher, supervisor, and analyst, Joe Natterson served his community well. He remained receptive to new emancipatory approaches to the mind and to society. He loved to write, to exchange ideas, and to engage in passionate dialogue. As a friend, he could be relied upon in a crisis and in more normal times.

Chapter 18 analyzes Trump's political appeal into four overlapping categories: misogyny, racism, xenophobia, and the repudiation of political correctness. These attitudes and emotional messages resonate with a large sector of the American population that has been neglected or vilified by elites for many decades. Trump's supporters are threatened economically by globalization and respond emotionally to aspects of the cultural wars – to antiabortion positions, to the appointment of conservative Supreme Court justices, and to the distrust of ethnic and racial minorities. Trump taps into the politics of resentment, where one group attributes basic problems that are repugnant and antithetical to their value system. They see themselves as victims, as overlooked, disregarded, and treated unfairly by residents of cities, coastal elites, and university educated, secular citizens of America. The chapter uses and revises Hofstadter's writings on the "paranoid style in American politics" to grasp the dimensions of projection, identification with the aggressor, and simplistic versions of black and white thinking now dominating the political landscape. Empathy for Trump's supporters may open possibilities of a deeper understanding of their grievances and resentments. It may also allow progressives and liberals to design a more effective political and messaging campaign to defeat Trump and the Trumpians in the next election.

Chapter 19 is a protest against a recent Trump policy of separating children from their parents at the Southern Border of the United States, of incarcerating immigrant children in cages, and of not permitting families to be reunited. It employs psychoanalytic concepts of moral injury and of intense reactions to trauma to indicate the harm done both to the children and the parents by such inhumane policies. In stepping into the social and political arena, it shows that psychoanalysts have something valuable and insightful to contribute to our understanding of dehumanizing policies which can and will create debilitating symptoms of PTSD, including dissociation and feelings of fragmentation, potentially both in the children and the parents.

Chapter 20 is a two-part chapter where the author discusses the seminal influence of his encounter with Joseph Kepecs, M.D. during an early part of his graduate studies at the University of Wisconsin. Kepecs was a psychoanalyst trained at the Chicago Psychoanalytic Institute; he was poised, conversant with Freudian theory, and deeply immersed in the clinical application of Freudian and post-Freudian perspectives. His teaching method was free associational and non-authoritarian. Kepecs functioned as a solid alternative to learning from charismatic and entertaining lecturers, who provided highly structured approaches to education. In issuing a manifesto for psychoanalytic education, the author underscores the importance of constructing and sustaining a safe space for dialogue and debate around issues of importance. These discussions can be free wheeling, irreverent, iconoclastic, and expansive. The psychoanalytic educator is invited to never be boring, to be open to surprise and critique, to be process oriented but interested in the content, to beware of intellectualization but never be anti-intellectual, and to be playful, ironic, and present but never to trivialize or debunk the exchange. Such an instructor would be receptive to alternative theories and techniques of psychoanalysis while being cognizant of the subversive nature of classical modes of thinking. Blending new and old, the spontaneous and the traditional, optimizes the psychoanalytic seminar. This stance will assist the student to understand what questions really matter while promoting experimental approaches to clinical practice and encouraging research into advances in psychoanalytic theory and its application to forms of high and popular culture.

Chapter 21 is a detailed report of the author's experiences as a juror during a particularly gruesome case of rape, sodomy, kidnapping, and armed robbery. He conducted a thought experiment during the trial: he did his civic duty, followed the facts of the case and the rule of law but simultaneously functioned as a psychoanalyst. In the latter role, he observed his own subjective and mood states, the roles of transference and countertransference, assessing the various psychologies and credibility of the perpetrator, victim, attorney, and presiding judge, including the temptation to dissociate and to be numbed off to the horrific aspects of the case. The author's awareness of systemic racism and sexism compounded the emotional conflicts and dilemma of judgment faced by the analyst-juror. It also added another dimension of complexity. Within the essay, there is a comparison of how "truth" is assessed during the judicial process and how it works in the analytic framework. The author explores the trauma and guilt of witnessing and evaluating human violence. He realizes that the carriage of justice can be brutal and brutalizing. The purpose of the essay was to help him work through some of the secondary trauma he experienced as a juror and to restore "normalcy" after nine days in this trial bubble. He proposes that the legal system offer other jurors assistance in the form of psychotherapy, allowing them to process their horrendous jury experiences and to help restore a disrupted sense of self.

Chapter 22 presents a probing analytic interview by the distinguished psychohistorian Paul Elovitz; the conversation reconstructs the author's intellectual itinerary. His earliest interests in psychohistory derived from the writings of Erik Erikson, Frank Manuel, and Peter Loewenberg, inspiring him to think psychologically about history and to study depth psychology critically and contextually. In declaring himself primarily a psychoanalyst, the author discusses the strengths and weakness, uses and abuses, of psychohistory; he argues that serious psychohistorians ought to be psychoanalyzed, or preferably trained in psychoanalytic institutes – to provide them with the lived experience of being a patient, and of working in an empathic and attuned way with patients. He explores his interest in Romain Rolland, an early anti-war writer, pacifist, and Gandhian, and how those forms of commitment appealed to him because of his own opposition to the United States' politically miscalculated and immoral involvement in the War in Vietnam. He discusses his complicated friendship with Bruno Bettelheim and the ways he was touched by Bettelheim's writings and overwhelmed and puzzled by his suicide. The author discusses his lucky but diligently pursued search for male mentors and the ways in which the idealization of the father may interfere with the emergence of a unique, playful, creative voice of his own. He concludes by mentioning his earliest fascination with the "Boys of Summer," the Brooklyn Dodgers of the 1950s, and his intense identification with Duke Snider, Jackie Robinson, Gil Hodges, Roy Campanella, and Sandy Koufax.

I have used Picasso's 1937 painting "Woman Sitting with Crossed Arms" for my cover. Not only is it a beautiful and evocative image, but also it captures artistically the ways we see the face and body, and aspects of reality, from multiple and often contradictory perspectives simultaneously. Picasso expresses the Surrealist idea that external reality may conceal a mysterious and powerful inner reality, often operating from different principles and motives. In the painting, Picasso demonstrates the subversive method of psychoanalysis at its best. He takes us on a journey away from conventional reality into the unknown (and possibly the unknowable) capturing life moving into abstraction.

Part I

Erotics, Transitional Objects, and Dreamwork

Chapter 1

Stoller, Erotics, Sexual Excitement

In revisiting the case history of Belle, the centerpiece of Robert Stoller's 1979 book, *Sexual Excitement: Dynamics of Erotic Life*, I will present three vignettes.

First, twinkling thighs: on the couch during her analytic hours, Belle would manipulate the bottom of her skirt so that it moved up and down her thighs. Sometimes her skirt would be hiked up high enough that her bottom, as she called it, would be seen. In Stoller's words, "I would gradually become aware that first her knees and then an inch more of her thigh were twinkling at me while at the same time she chattered away" (p. 131). Belle sometimes came to analysis wearing no underpants.

Second, the Erotic Daydream, sometimes referred to as the Director's Fantasy:

A cruel man, the Director, a Nazi type, is directing the activity. It consists of Belle being raped by a stallion, which has been aroused to a frenzy by a mare held off at a distance beyond where Belle is placed. In a circle around the periphery stand vaguely perceived men, expressionless, masturbating while ignoring each other, the Director, and Belle. She is there for the delectation of these men, including the Director, who, although he has an erection, makes no contact with her: her function is to be forced to unbearable sexual excitement and pleasure, thereby making a fool of herself before these men. She has been enslaved in this obscene exhibition of humiliation because it creates erections in these otherwise feelingless men; they stand there in phallic, brutal indifference. All that, however, is foreplay, setting the scene. What sends her excitement up and almost immediately to orgasm as she masturbates is not this scene alone, for obviously, if it were really happening, she would experience horror, not pleasure. Rather, what excites her is the addition of some detail that exacerbates her humiliation, e.g., the horse is replaced by a disreputable, ugly old man; or her excitement makes her so wild that she is now making a dreadful scene; or her palpitating genitals are spotlighted to show that she has lost control of her physiology. And, behind the scenes, a part of herself permits the excitement because it (she) knows that she, who is masturbating in the real world, is not literally the same as 'she' who is the suffering woman in the story. In the story, she is humiliated; in reality, she is safe (p. 68).

Third, the Underground Fantasy:

All action takes place in a city below ground, with numerous levels – artificially lighted, without natural landscaping. The feeling is one of great coziness. There is no danger, no uneasiness, no excitement, sexual or otherwise. All is quiet though not silent, for the city is populated and busy with people going about their activities. Nothing special happens. Instead Belle wanders through the streets and on different levels, looking at people and buildings. She is under no strain; there are no obligations; nothing to be accomplished, nothing will happen. She is always alone. She knows none of the many people who populate the town, has never talked with them. The outstanding qualities are calm and aloneness without feeling lonely. Associated with this daydream were firehouses. Since childhood, whenever she had passed one in the evening, the same tranquil feeling had come up in her, accompanied by the urge to move her bowels ... Firemen gave her a calm feeling, because although they were fully men – unquestionably male – she categorized them as less educated than she, from a different class, with different expectations from society, without ambition; in other words, non-penetrating, non-sadistic but still masculine men who caused her no anxiety and no sexual excitement. They were not castrated but rather neuter: categorially male but non-inflammatory (pp. 88–89).

When Belle began her analysis, "she was young, lively, intelligent, sensual, attractive, stylish, educated, and nice" (p. 61). Note Stoller's love of lists in descriptions, implying that one road to truth is additive, with truth residing in the accurate accumulation of facts. Note also the simple word "nice," which indicates how much he liked her, that is, that he had a high regard for her intelligence, creativity, prettiness, femininity, courage, and desire to know the truth about herself. Finding one or more things to like in our analytic patients certainly opens up pathways to success in the treatment. "At the start of her analysis, she was twenty-four, a quiet, intelligent, attractive, well-groomed, feminine woman, white, American, Southern, middle-class, college educated, single, Baptist ..." (p. 59). Again, the recourse to lists, the attention to surface, the hint that methodologically he will move from surface to depth, investigating the mediations between the external world and her internal world, following standard analytic practice, emulating the principles set by Freud, Fenichel, and Greenson, and most probably practiced by his own analyst, Hanna Fenichel.

Belle was an only child whose parents separated when she was six years old. Her father, considerably older than her mother and a former professional athlete, had run off with a teenage lover and died the following year. A man of muscle and not of culture, he was unreliable, hypochondriacal, and unable to relate affectively to his daughter. At best, he was a rather inadequate, uncaring dad. As for her mother, she is described as a superficial and self-absorbed person who perceived her daughter to be an object of display, a token of her grandiose feat of having produced a baby. Stoller evocatively refers to Belle's mother as a "milk-less breast." Belle's mother was incapable of sustaining contact with her infant and for long periods of her daughter's childhood, sometimes for months at a time, left her in the care of an aunt, known as the Caretaker. In short, Belle had been traumatically abandoned by both parents, suffering deeply from these losses with persistent anxiety, bordering on terror, about being deserted yet again.

Her presenting complaints revolved around a vague sense of distress, a feeling that she was wasting her life, that her wishes to be a wife and mother would be thwarted, and a confused notion that her sexuality was somehow impaired. There is a marked ambivalence toward the caretaking aunt: she could be intermittently loving and soothing toward Belle, yet she also conveyed her dislike of sensuality and her own defenses against erotic pleasure. She had a particular concentration on Belle's bowel movements, which were a recurring source of inspection and discussion, crossing over into invasion. The Caretaker administered long-lasting, strong enemas to Belle, generating great pain and horror. Belle surrendered to these multiple violations of her rear end. There is no doubt that the enemas inflicted pain and confusion on this little girl. Stoller will demonstrate in the case history how the enemas functioned both to symbolize danger and to organize excitement around Belle's anus. If she did not comply with the Caretaker's intrusions, she might be abandoned; once again, this anxiety was countered by the Underground Fantasy. Belle's ass, then, became the site of sensations, traumas, and fantasies that had originally been put into the little girl's rear end.

Several aspects of Belle's life history were intentionally omitted from Stoller's account. We learn little about her professional activities, except to know that she was self-employed. We are told she was musical and had an artistic sensibility, but these significant traits are not elaborated. Because the focus is on the theme of sexual excitement, Stoller omitted many salient features of her personality and her specialness as a human being. If these omissions work to protect anonymity and confidentiality, they work against accuracy and provide a fuller portrait of Belle, a fact openly acknowledged and regretted by Stoller. Despite Belle's poignant psychological issues, specifically around the heightened terror of abandonment, and because of the magnified focus around the bizarre and complex nature of her sexual fantasies, he insisted that she not be perceived as neurotic by the world or seen by his readers as a highly pathological specimen. A unique and unhappy person, she was a good candidate for analysis. By calling her Belle, perhaps he was alerting the reader to something fundamentally healthy charming, and beautiful about her inner world. It appears that her interior beauty was always apparent to him, making him relatively optimistic about her prognosis throughout the treatment.

The case study of Belle is vintage Stoller. In the researching and writing of the book, we see him at the top of his game – knowing, confident, erudite, lightly cynical, and playfully ironic. He wrote with verve, versatility, and imagination, taking on a big topic, about which he has much to contribute. Ten years beyond his breakthrough study, *Sex and Gender: The Development of Masculinity and Femininity* (1968), and six years after a complementary volume, *Splitting: A Case of Female Masculinity* (1974), Stoller was prepared to display his clinical skills, fearlessness, and knowledge as applied to the study of erotics. For all its epistemological shortcomings (to which I will return), the case of Belle becomes a stimulating vehicle of conceptual thinking about the hidden dimensions of sexuality. By stressing the primacy of the clinical, by allowing the patient to speak as freely as possible, and by clearing away the obstacles blocking access to the patient's unconscious dynamics, Stoller was also demonstrating the intellectual power and generative potential of resistance analysis.

In writing this case history, Stoller was making a contribution to erotics, which he thought had been insufficiently studied. By erotics he meant the subjective state of sexuality, how sexuality is organized intrapsychically and interpersonally. For the sake of clarity, he divided erotics into the study of gender identity and erotic desire. The two are merged within us. The case history of Belle was designed to explore erotic desire, for neither Belle nor members of her family had gender identity disturbances. Stoller would conduct his research within the framework of the analytic situation by exploring contents and forms, wishes and defenses, memories, and secrets, and especially those recollections that were affectively loaded. He would investigate those scripts, which in condensed form generated sexual excitement.

If Stoller insisted on the primacy of the clinical, he did so in a polemical way. He urged clinicians to speak and write in plain English, refusing all forms of technical language; good clinical writing must eschew jargon, resist the temptations of theory, and the seductive – sometimes mystifying – vocabulary of the metapsychologists. If the practitioner uses metaphors and analogies, he would do so with self-awareness. For Stoller, staying close to the clinical material as it emerges in the analytic encounter meant opting for a language that is earthy, raucous, and exuberant, one that resists intellectualization and scholastic discourse; in brief, it meant speaking an interpersonal idiom, one that avoids euphemisms, pretense, and clichés. Just as Stoller had no use for technical terms that obscure intellectual weaknesses or cover over pseudoscientific posturing, so too did he oppose the use of ill-defined terms such as narcissism, cathexis, and psychic energy (Fisher, 1996). Since the analyst is the primary instrument in the analytic situation, he intended to reveal himself in the case study, following Freud's own self-disclosures in his famous case studies. Making himself visible became part of his method in order to legitimize analytic research, remain consistent with scientific methods, and test the limits of the discipline's explanatory possibilities. He was particularly concerned about confirming data once it was accurately collected and reported. I will return later to the issues of Stoller's visibility, wishing that he had revealed even more of his subjectivity in doing the analysis with Belle.

Stoller's narrative is grounded in material culled from the analytic experience itself. Within the analysis, he clearly prioritizes the tracking and explication of fantasy as the crucial point of entry into the understanding of sexual excitement. Interpreting fantasy is his royal road to the understanding of erotic life. To comprehend Belle's Erotic Daydream and the Underground Fantasy is to understand her paradigmatic erotic scenarios; it is simultaneously a fundamental way of understanding the person. These scripts, scenarios, daydreams, and stories – synonymous terms in Stoller's lexicon – are in effect highly condensed fantasies, with disguised meanings, conflictual tensions, paradoxes, and twists, that create a problem to be solved by the analyst and analysand. Analytic exploration and working through dissolve the fantasy, thereby potentially softening the desire that underlay Belle's erotic narrative life and lived experience of sex.

Stoller argues that Belle's scripts both reproduce and repair the precise traumas, frustrations, and debasements of her childhood, including her anxiety about abandonment. His chapters on her exhibitionism, anal erotism, sadomasochism, her femaleness and its oscillations between loveliness and dirtiness, and her need for danger and humiliation all revolve around the interpretation of the meaning of her fantasies. Fantasy was integral to her ability to feel aroused. In effect, Belle's scripts recapitulate in disguised ways the history of her psychic life. To put it another way, the script is an elaborate and beautiful condensation that constitutes the buried meanings of Belle's subjective life. Fantasies need to be analyzed in order to discover their internal coherence and deeper meanings. Fantasy, Stoller reminds us, can combine conscious, preconscious, and unconscious elements. Psychoanalytic forms of deciphering can unearth its hiding places; fantasy also plays a decisive role in character structure and symptoms, sexual behavior, posture, clothing, and humor (Stoller, 1985). Through the close and sensitive reading of these stories, analysts and patients assign private and intense affective significance to their subjective lives. Stoller explicitly joins forces with hermeneutic psychoanalysts who focus on meaning as the essence of subjective functioning; he rejects thinking in terms of the energy model, stating that "sex is not cathexis" (p. xiv). Yet, at the same time, he tends not to speak the language of the relational analysts, who privilege inner objects and the interpersonal connections between self and others.

From his intricate, detailed, and at times stunning decoding of these scripts, Stoller concludes that sexual excitement is always a dialectic, a rapid oscillation between risk and possibility, pleasure and pain, relief and trauma, success and failure, danger and safety. Sexual excitement is by implication enacted by the individual to undo childhood trauma or overcome frustration. It is a construct. The daydream synthesizes these oppositions into a script. With each script, hostility and mystery operate to generate arousal. By hostility, Stoller means the hidden or overt desire to harm or be harmed by another person. The absence of hostility leads to a waning of sexual desire, resulting in indifference or boredom. Unsurprisingly, he underscores how fetishization and dehumanization of the love object occur in sexual practice, including acts of cruelty and revenge. Always recognizing the degree of hostility at work, he presents a nuanced understanding of how arousal combines and displaces multiple elements to create its story. Sexual fantasies function to transform the victim into an erotically successful victor. They help to undo and master trauma. The "writer" of sexual scenarios becomes excited by these mental products, which have a discernible structure and trajectory, with a hero, tension, risks, and drama, in addition to a happy ending celebrated by orgasm.

Stoller refuses to sentimentalize or romanticize sexual excitement; he states that the thorough examination of sexual scenarios shows that nonhostile qualities, qualities such as tenderness, affection, generosity, and concern for the other, infrequently contribute to arousal (p. 33). Likewise, he dismisses exuberance and irrepressible lust, putting them at the bottom of the list in generating excitement, disagreeing with the versions of sex to be found in romantic love songs, romances, and idealized works of fiction (p. 6).

For Stoller, sexual excitement can be conceptualized as a defense against anxiety, a transformation of anxiety into something more bearable – namely, a melodrama in which safety and danger oscillate. The ultimate danger in sexual excitement is the degree to which one's sense of maleness or femaleness may be threatened. Hostility functions to dissolve the threat, to dehumanize the other.

Mystery is the second component of sexual excitement in Stoller's schema. Here he draws some analogies between sexual arousal and fashion. Fashion takes the nude body and creates an illusion to maintain the mystery. In both, there is a need for secrecy, for veiling. Dangers and fears are reduced in sexual excitement by the creation of scripts that produce illusions of danger, sometimes in theatrical ways. Why are men turned on by tantalizing women? Or women by bullying men? Stoller argues that such mysteries as sexual attraction work by establishing contrasts between knowing and not knowing, seeing and not seeing, and safety and danger. Excitement can be created by stealing the other's secrets. Mystery functions as a way of possessing what one's sexual object will not yield (Kernberg 1995, p. 60).

In Stoller's analysis of the twinkling thighs explodes, he refers to Belle's display of her legs as odd – her "willingness to be seen to be behaving grotesquely" (p. 144). With Belle as an exhibitionist, Stoller found himself in a voyeuristic position; it became a double pleasure for him, enjoying the spectacle, admitting candidly that "she had nice legs." But he was also pleased that her willingness to be seen in this manner actually opened up a possibility for analytic exploration of behavior that otherwise may have remained latent and inaccessible to investigation. Belle's display combined some elements of reality with a great deal of fantasy.

Although Belle knew realistically that her legs were just legs, she still felt that she "could blast me out of my senses with the view" (p. 145). Throughout this case history, Stoller switches positions between the voyeur who gazes and the visual who truly sees and who achieves insight.

Belle's repeated enactments of hiking up her skirt on the couch became part of an ongoing analytic performance, gradually making manifest aspects of her exhibitionism, sadomasochism, and anal erotism. Belle also was easily excited and easily humiliated on the couch. Adhering to an analytic stance of tact and reserve, Stoller acknowledges how painful it is for masochistic patients to endure analytic treatment and how big a "headache" it becomes for the analyst in the countertransference. Stoller deploys a rather considerable armamentarium in response to this situation, including a continual analysis of Belle's defensive maneuvers (which he refers to as tricks, forms of self-deception). He draws heavily on his intuition, bodily sensations, and sublimated stimulation. He speaks of "the interchanges between us tumbling head over heels, making available the next stage of confusion" (p. 98).

Not surprisingly, Stoller's sustained curiosity and attention regarding Belle's erotic fantasies, in addition to her intense, sadomasochistic erotic transference to him, often resulted in her becoming sexually excited on the couch. Stoller describes her stretched out on the couch, feeling exposed on humiliating display, being watched in her mind by a cold, distant, phallic, sadistic analyst, sitting behind her, not touching her, refusing to sleep with her, reenacting the Director's Fantasy. Yet intense sexual arousal created difficulties for him. Because it was actually experienced, because it carried intense bodily sensations ("the truth of the body"), Belle's erotic stimulation contained a piece of reality in it. For Belle, Stoller became an omnipotent Henry Miller in the transference, with a detached, calculating, pornographic interest in her sexual body parts and a desire to debase her: "I am Godlike but frozen as a stone phallic carving, raunchy Henry Miller and his fetishistic interest in women's genitals and smells" (p. 95). She may have intuited that like Henry Miller, Stoller may have wished to write about her and the story of their analytic adventure.

An important component of Belle's transference to Stoller revolved around her experiencing him as the Director, a torturer sitting quietly and erect behind the couch, ready to pounce, an uncaring and insensitive "hard-on." She viewed him as obsessive-compulsive, as someone who was wedded to a mechanical technique, who disavowed his feelings for her, especially his anger. Stoller's calm and apparent lack of passion proved to Belle that he was cowardly and a liar. She slowly articulated her intense, provocative, self-victimizing sexual excitement toward him. Transferentially, Stoller became someone who was arrogant, aloof, disgusting, hateful, and indifferent to her tender aspirations. Sitting up behind her and interpreting relentlessly, he occupied a dominating position over both her mind and her body. Belle often expressed feelings of being penetrated, flayed, and humiliated during her analytic sessions, specifically after analytic interpretations of her erotic daydreams. When Belle experienced him more positively, Stoller was transformed into a Dalmatian, the fireman's dog, quiet, competent, trustworthy, and nondangerous (p. 89). Only after years of analysis, work that was often messy and chaotic, where for long periods Stoller felt "chronically confused," did Belle's daydream begin to crack, yielding its meanings, resulting in a more coherent understanding. As its power diminished, she became genuinely closer to and more revealing with Stoller. By the end of the treatment, he reports loving and quiet moments with Belle, the emergency of a true self. Only late in the analysis did she manage to develop relatively loving and stable relationships with caring men. Only late in the analysis did she reach profound, genital orgasms as a result of consensual loving sex with men during intercourse (p. 90).

Transference, Stoller reminds us, contains drama and conflict, taking on "its own passionate life" during the course of an analysis (p. 110). Transference love is authentic love, marked by an intensity, power, and duration that is quite extraordinary. Resistance served as a device to protect the patient from an imagined attack by the analyst; strategically, it was an attempt to reverse victimhood into victory. At times this meant making the analyst suffer by thwarting him (p. 110). If analysis of the transference is combined with the analyst's consistent and reliable availability, what Stoller calls his "real presence," then the patient will eventually achieve a deeper understanding of their relationship. "The therapeutic effect came as much from her knowing the two of us shared the insight as from the power of the insight itself" (p. 112). Reciprocity of insight, then, within an intimate relationship produced a healing effect. Despite fostering regressions in the patient through the methodical application of the analytic technique, Stoller refused to infantilize the patient by treating her like an ignorant child or condescending to her as if he were her teacher. Eschewing arrogance and didacticism, good-enough analysis permitted Belle to learn what she had always known (p. 107). This included the understanding that she was the inventor of her own sexual excitement; it was her construct, flowing out of her life history and family constellation.

As part of the story of Belle's case history, Stoller recorded a number of his own impressions, reactions, feelings, and expectations about how the treatment affected him. These glosses of his subjective states bring a texture and aliveness to the text that traditionally is not found in case studies. In the face of Belle's masochistic dynamics, he mentioned that he was "hanging on by the fingertips" (p. 62), attempting to ward off for both of them her sense of imminent disaster. Because her regression oscillated between stages between postpuberty and her current age and did not plunge into dangerous earlier developmental phases, Stoller felt better about her prognosis (p. 63). Working with one of Belle's dreams made him feel alarmed, unanchored, like he was "stepping into empty space"; he speculated that the dream may have represented her profound sense of infantile aloneness, of being "unsupported" in her early childhood, and was being reenacted in the countertransference (p. 64).

When Stoller functions as the Dalmatian in the transference, Belle could tolerate being with him (or any gentle, nonthreatening man) only for short durations; she would drift off, dissociate, and disrupt the intimacy. He reports that after an hour in which she felt close to him, Belle became "so distant that her dullness almost decorticated me." Here Stoller's humanity suddenly interrupts the text, where he wisely and compassionately comments on the tragedy of self-sabotaging individuals: "This is the sadness of neurosis and the devastation of masochism: people prefer their defenses to the lost, original desires" (p. 81).

Belle repeatedly experienced Stoller's interpretation and confrontations as intrusions into her bowels, as acts of violation experienced as enemas (p. 103). She developed a pattern of resistance by diverting insight through the misrepresentation or misrecognition of his intentions. Aware of the dynamics of domination and submission, Stoller had to resist playing a sadistic role with her, persisting in his desire to analyze and understand. "During most of this analysis, Belle did all she could – which was plenty – to drive me crazy with her sadomasochistic tricks, to get me to hit back as she distorted my words, meanings, and motives" (p. 104). It took years for them to work through this defensiveness on her part.

Stoller candidly admits being stymied by Belle for long periods while analyzing the transference. He speaks of her "pestering" him with her no-win position, her need to transform the analysis into a battlefield with sexual attackers and victims, the repetition of which was a "headache" for the analyst. This entailed staging the Director's Fantasy with her, making the analysis palpable in the here and now and simultaneously heightening the analysis with "its own passionate life" (p. 116). Conscious of the inevitability of a reversal in working with sadomasochistic patients, Stoller voices his frustrations regarding the cycle of turnaround. He underscored Belle's paradoxical desire to protect herself and her chronic vulnerability by defeating him and causing him pain. "Perhaps, generalizing about resistance, one can say it not only functions to ward off the analyst and thus to protect the patient from attack, but also is a secret way to reversing the situation so that the apparent victim – the patient – becomes the victor and, by thwarting the analyst, makes him suffer" (p. 116 n).

Stoller ultimately opted for a position of analytic self-reflection and restraint with regard to her "masochistic shenanigans." Assuming a difficult, paradoxical stance, hard to sustain over long durations, he would serve as a victim of her masochism without feeling himself a victim and without assuming the posture of a cruel sadist (p. 118).

Regarding his erotic countertransference, Stoller speaks of one session in which Belle's "lovely" dominated the hour. It was an hour marked by an intensity of exhibitionism on Belle's part, including a vast spectrum of sensuous display encompassing the affects and sensations of sight, touch, smell, and, most prominently, taste (Hughes, 1999, pp. 113–115). It was also a session of heightened sexual excitement for Belle, eliciting the following "delicious" reactions from her analyst in response to his ripe and tasty analysand: "She was so edible that I wondered to her if the couch was not functioning as a table in which she was serving herself up ... the kneeling position, she said, let her offer herself up as a 'bounteous Renoir woman'" (pp. 154, 155).

Finally, Stoller includes a brief vignette documenting the eruption of his annoyance with Belle. Unfortunately, he does not include the specific context and process of his exasperation, omitting his precise words and her reactions to his anger. While he argues that his intervention opened things up in the analysis, he speculates with lists of questions about the various meanings of his countertransference intrusion into the process, leaving it undecided if his irritable intervention was harmful or unnecessary. Stoller raises here a critically important methodological and epistemological issue, without venturing a definitive answer. By keeping the issues open-ended and ambiguous, he invites readers to deepen their research, prompting them to become more rigorous about the analytic process: "After several years, I got genuinely, uncomplicatedly exasperated with Belle one day and told her so, with appropriate affect. Other analysts have reported comparable experiences. Was that an unnecessary, anti-analytic addition to the treatment, a mistake, an indulgence powered by counter transference alone? Was the opening up of the analysis that resulted an artifact, a transference phenomenon, a flight into health, a seduction of the patient, a permanent deflection of treatment from its proper course, more of a closing down than an opening up, a sure sign that this was not an analysis? I am not being rhetorical; no one knows the answers to those questions" (p. 206).

In agreement with Winnicott, Stoller advocated the creation of an analytic space akin to a holding environment. Such a space provides a framework for both physiological and psychological investigation in an atmosphere of maternal safety and nurturance. The analytic situation must recapture the mother's creation and recreation of an ambiance of security through a serene and focused embrace of the infant, that is, a relatively non anxious and attuned stance whereby the holding is established. Analysts, Stoller astutely points out, are also held by their patients. If the holding environment is "essential" for the analysis to establish and for the patient to discover, he paradoxically urges analysts to ignore the metaphor of holding. He justifies this in the name of analyzing the transference, arguing that transference can best take root, be made visible, and then dominate the treatment situation only in a context of frustration and abstinence. Too much holding results in a supportive kindness and provision, thus diminishing the potential for a fuller investigation and working through all aspects of the transference. Analysts have to be on guard against the seductions of the holding environment, which might dilute or even nullify the healing potential of the analytic experience. Maternal nurturance and optimal provision must be rejected by the analysts because it results in the illusion of a cure through love, as well as the dangers of gratifying and reassuring the patient. "If either analyst or patient tries too hard to manifest this kindness, games of love are played and real gratifications pulse through the analysis, jeopardizing the delicate ambience that then allows the past to be present" (p. 117).

My strongest disagreement with Stoller on technique turns on this point. It is contradictory to assert that both analysts and patients need the holding environment, but then to suggest that we ignore this basic piece of loving care, this creation of a therapeutic space, which informs the entire framework. Does ignore mean repress, suppress, or disavow? How does this ignoring build mutual self-awareness and self-reflection? Psychoanalysis in my mind consists in reliving and exploring precisely these love games. In my clinical experience, the establishment of a kind, safe, sensitive, and trusting framework allows for the transference to emerge more distinctly, enabling the analysts to gather more pertinent data, permitting a high measure of working through, including reflection on and making use of the countertransference. And the past is always present, no matter what technique or theory is employed.

In his conclusion, Stoller admits that he was fortunate to have had Belle as his patient. She also served as his supervisor and teacher. One important meaning of the Erotic Daydream was to instruct the dirty old man, a symbolic condensation of her mother, her father, her stepfather, and Stoller, about her sexual arousal. This had to be stimulating to Stoller in the writing of the case, in which excitement figures so prominently in the title, themes, and subtexts of the book. Sexuality, after all, was the core of her being. Yet he claims that with Belle erotic themes were indivisible from the analysis, that the idea of writing the book was an after-effect of the analytic experience. "My interest in analyzing her excitement was always in the analysis, years before I imagined writing on the subject" (p. 86 n). Writing a case history always misrepresents the analytic process because the author employs impressionistic language, because writing fails to convey the feeling, tone, and inflections of how patients and analysts really talk to one another; we must remember that written report can never entirely recapture what unfolded orally and that was part of an oral interpretation (Michels, 1998). Further, if he wants to be understood, an author must shape and edit the material to make it coherent to readers, thereby distorting the messy way it emerged in the process (p. 96 n).

Despite his adherence to a conservative, classical form of analytic technique, Stoller describes contemporary ways of working and thinking about the process with Belle. He refers to communication operating on a body-to-body level, from her preconscious to his preconscious; indeed, messages were at times conveyed from her unconscious to his unconscious. Though he adopted a rigorous analytic stance of abstinence, distance, non-self-disclosure, a refusal to answer questions, and a method of precise and repetitive application of interpretation, Stoller also operated on a bodily level with Belle, "speaking so that Belle knows that I now have that understanding also within my guts" (p. 106). In short, Stoller's method blended tradition and spontaneity, analytic tact and restraint oscillated with emotional and bodily responsiveness to his patient.

In the context of a detailed inquiry into her anal eroticism, Stoller mentions how she allowed him to move into her body, despite the presence of some resistance; her bowels literally opened up to him (p. 109). During a session focused on inspection and abandonment, Stoller addressed the mutuality of bodily attunement as a legitimate vehicle of analytic understanding: "It is clear to her, as the hour moves on, that I finally know, have it in my body that I know, and she lets me in because she knows I know, and that I know because she lets me in" (p. 105). He appears to be describing a clinical process in which penetration and being penetrated become a reciprocal capacity, a capacity that tolerates, even encourages, role reversal, perhaps reaching its highest expression in mutuality. Analysts, Stoller proposes, are like optimal musical instruments, increasingly attuned to and pulsating, able to play with and be played by their analytic patients, in order to receive their subliminal messages, overcoming all kinds of barriers, including the tendency of the analyst to intellectualize: "We must vibrate as sensitively as a musical instrument, or we will not know except intellectually, what the patient is experiencing and what the patient does to provoke responses in others" (p. 277, note 1).

Stoller includes some discussion of his sexual arousal in the countertransference. If we remember that the book appeared in the late 1970s, while the analysis occurred considerably earlier, most probably in the 1960s, then we might understand that Stoller is both candid and evasive in these passages. There were limits to what analysts could express about their subjectivity, given their anxiety about exhibitionism or stimulating voyeurism in the analysand; or fear that one's writing might engender indifference that it might be ignored (Scharff, 2000). Given these conscious and unconscious barriers, and remembering what was possible at that time, we ought not to expect Stoller to reveal the naked truth about himself. We have gone further in these areas of expression in the past 30 years; some analysts have explored their erotic excitement in work with analytic patients in a constructive, illuminating way and have been supported by the analytic community; this is now a relatively acceptable method and discourse (Lichtenberg, 2008; Mann, 1999).

Stoller is unable to go this far. He tells us that Belle knew he was never turned on by seeing her bottom on the couch. Had he been aroused, she would not have trusted him and been so disclosing and self-observing with him. At a particularly dramatic moment, Stoller interprets the deeper meaning of her exhibitionism, to clarify it for both Belle's sake and his own. "But let me word it even more clearly, because perhaps there is even a sexual quality to it – about being bare-ass naked." She then reveals that she has been coming to sessions without panties. More significantly, the interpretation, though direct and brutally honest, allowed Belle to mobilize the previously unknown part of her and to bring it into the treatment; she began to realize that her exhibitionistic and masochistic self precluded the emergence of a more genuine self.

Stoller explicitly disavows, though this is relegated to the endnote, any sexual excitement in the years of work with Belle, no matter how naive this may seem to his reader. Invoking the authority of Freud, recalling the ethical stance of the therapist and physician he wishes to do no harm to his patients, he intended to understand Belle's personality dynamics, stating unequivocally that sexual excitement was missing in him in the analytic setting. It was lacking not because it was forbidden, or because its presence might tilt in the direction of boundary violations, or because he had repressed it with a high degree of frustration. Rather, the erotically excited analyst was being inappropriate, interfering with his desire to analyze, to conduct his clinical inquiry. Such a countertransference eruption would have contaminated the investigation with the analyst's desires. Consistent with his theory, since he had no conscious hostility toward Belle, the desire to harm her never produced sexual arousal in him. Yet Stoller admits that it was necessary to vibrate sensitively to her unconscious messages in order to grasp her experience and comprehend what she provoked in others. Here he decenters himself from the process, attempting to empathize with how other men in our culture might respond to Belle's sexual display and provocations. Stoller ultimately was not enticed by Belle because he sublimated his response into analytic investigation, transforming his erotic desire away from sexual enactments and into a wish to transmit analytic knowledge. "When Belle tried to buy me off with a bit of thigh, I have to know – empathically, not just theoretically – what other men in our culture also know about flashing thighs. But my response is minimal, a signal; it has behind it no pressure toward action" (p. 257, note 1).

Stoller's sublimated desire must be understood in the framework of late 1970s analytic writing, that is, in a context in which analysts rarely disclose what actually happened in the analytic process, rarely revealed their bodily or emotional states, particularly when it touched on sexual arousal. Stoller may have had in mind his analytic readers, possibly fearing that he would be regarded as conducting wild analysis; he remained prudent about any perception that he might be enacting intense erotic countertransference wishes with a vulnerable patient. He might have been concerned about rejection from respected analytic clinicians, despite his enjoyment of his maverick status and his relative independence as a researcher and writer (Person, 1997). He may have heard that too much exposure might have shifted the delicate balance of his case study, manifesting too much investment in himself rather than the exploration of the patient's dynamics. Nor could Stoller count on much understanding or validation from the medical school where the UCLA Department of Psychiatry had already turned against psychoanalysis toward biobehavioral and psychopharmacological approaches. Within psychoanalysis, he risked having his work marginalized or dismissed as sexology, where his analytic work might be perceived as overly titillating, misrecognized as largely about teasing his female patients and gratifying his own latent desires.

Every analyst has transference to senior colleagues (which may easily be displaced onto the American Psychoanalytic Association), anticipating disapproval or misunderstanding, perhaps even isolation or banishment. In his blurb on the book's jacket, Ralph Greenson, Stoller's mentor and friend in Los Angeles, wrote tellingly, "With all our knowledge about the vicissitudes of erotic behavior, however, there has been a huge *gap* in our understanding of the essential ingredients of sexual excitement. Dr. Robert Stoller fills in that *gap*. His breakthrough in *Sexual Excitement* renders all of us who are seriously interested in human behavior a tremendous service. At last, we have a book which makes all the components of eroticism come alive" (emphasis added). It is significant that Greenson did not mention that one feature of that gap was the erotic excitement of the analyst in his work with patients who experience intense erotic transferences; the double mention of a "gap" may also indicate some unconscious erotic innuendo on the part of Greenson, possibly some awareness of what was being omitted by Stoller and him, as if discussing female genitalia was a dangerous area of analytic investigation, triggering intense anxieties, inhibition, and a necessary disavowal of countertransference desire.

In this brief section "An Addendum to the Treatment," Stoller reports having Belle read, correct, and approve every word in every draft of his case history. He also invited her to resume analysis for an undesignated period to investigate her reactions to the various experiences of reading the book, written many years after her termination. He refers to this vaguely as "a piece of analysis" (p. 218). Stoller's conscious motivation here was his passion to conduct accurate scientific research, to check his impressions for interpretive correctness, and to reinvestigate the transference dynamics that were rekindled, especially around Belle's sexual themes. An additional factor, certainly not the least, was his ethical concern about the possibility of Belle's submitting to his wishes out of a desire to accommodate him, or, more deeply, his fear that Belle might return to a masochistic position around the Director's Fantasy: "For surely it is unethical to get her permission if she is unduly influenced by a persisting, powerful transference effect .... Only when we both felt this was worked through, when we knew it was depleted of erotic charge, were we at ease that I could proceed" (p. 218).

Stoller adds that he found the results of the brief reanalysis "amusing and sobering," while recommending his method to colleagues in a similar situation, particularly those invested in publishing their clinical findings. With a bow to epistemological relativism, he modestly concludes: "not all of my truths, we discovered, were Belle's truths" (p. 218).

This switching of positions after the completion of the analysis and the writing of the text requires further exploration. Here the voyeuristic, passively receptive analyst radically exchanges positions with his patient, moving into a displaying and active role, offering penetrating interpretations and a compelling narrative about her life history and how the analysis unfolded. For her part, Belle functions to read, gaze, and interpret his impressively written and formidable performance. Requesting a former patient to read a case report is always an intrusive request to some degree; inviting her to resume the analysis further suggests a degree of impingement. Yet intrusion ought to be differentiated from invasiveness. Perhaps Stoller was unconsciously playing out the Director's Fantasy, becoming sadistic and exhibitionistic himself, requiring that Belle submit to his powerful, comprehensive account of her inner world and erotic desires, to yield to his master narrative of how the analysis unfolded and how her desires became transformed into something more adaptive. Or perhaps Stoller was reenacting in the countertransference the Underground Fantasy, that is, adopting a calmer, less threatening, non-phallic male role. Such a role might help her restore her true self, as if Stoller assumed the stance of a fireman helping extinguish some of her passionate masochistic fire, enabling her to relate to him as a good father with no desire to dominate, tease, or abandon her.

It is difficult to decide which role Stoller adopted without having access to Belle – material not integrated explicitly into his account. Stoller, in short, might have added a chapter, or at least a section – "Who is Robert Stoller?" – to complete his account and to complement the chapter "Who Is Belle?" Lastly, the anxiety and potential traumatic enactments of working with such an exciting, young, seductive, exhibitionistic female patient might have required him to write about the case subsequently, an after-effect as it were, enabling him to work through his own desire and anxiety about the sexual excitement catalyzed in the treatment situation.

Stoller hoped his readers would attempt to grasp his basic ideas and argument; he assumed that each reader would experience the book differently, each coming from his or her subjective point of view. Yet he wrote the book to enliven psychoanalytic discourse, to return psychoanalysis to its original interest in sexuality and the unconscious roots of erotic excitement. He hoped the book would demonstrate that sustained analytic clinical work would generate new ideas and data that could be imaginatively interpreted, serving to stimulate new research and new modes of creative, rigorous, and audacious thinking. If he modestly confessed the limitations of his study, admitting that he did not achieve his goals, he also insisted that it was a "start" – the beginning of serious thinking that would generate new hypotheses and eventually better results (pp. 218–219; see also Stoller, 1988).

Stoller's case history of Belle is one of the richest, most complex, and most revealing cases in the psychoanalytic clinical literature. It is particularly well crafted, operates on multiple levels simultaneously, and was written with the self-awareness of an author about the ability of language to obscure as well as clarify psychological issues.

A case history is never transparent. As we celebrate the 30th anniversary of the publication of this case, it needs to be studied, to be interpreted, to be analyzed, and ultimately to be seen as a whole. Beautifully written, it approaches the status of a classic. We can perform a rigorous exegesis of case history texts, moving in an obsessional direction, or can decipher a text by reading it dialectically and entering into an extended conversation with it. I prefer the latter form of interrogation, that of living dialogue.

We all recognize that the case history is a major vehicle for transmission of psychoanalytic knowledge. A case history must describe a two-person interaction, that is, must encompass the dynamics of both transference and countertransference, or, if you prefer contemporary terminology, the patient's subjectivity and the analyst's subjectivity. The case history must describe the overcoming of resistance, the patient's and the analyst's, in the conducting of the analysis. A truly literate case study makes references, implicitly or explicitly, to other case histories in the canon, particularly to Freud's case histories (Forrester, 2007).

A case history must demonstrate its clinical method, specifically here, Stoller's insistence on the primacy a fantasy and on the need to understand primal sexual and masturbatory fantasies, and to decipher them all in their beauty, bizarreness, and complexity. In demonstrating its clinical method, a case study must address the challenges and regressive pulls on the analyst, including in the Belle case the aspects of erotic countertransference. For highly gifted writers of case histories who are versed in theory (as Stoller certainly was), a case permits the elaboration of various levels of theorizing about the person being studied, the themes in the process, and issues of conceptual importance to the author. In particular, in this case, these would include Stoller's concept of primary femininity and his argument about the critical importance of hostility in generating sexual excitement.

In opposition to Freud and classical psychoanalytic formulations, Stoller theorized that primary femininity should be differentiated from passivity, masochism, penis envy, disappointment in the mother, renunciation of pleasure, and weak superego functioning; in short, it should be distinguished from defenses against castration. He posited that it existed in a preoedipal, non-traumatic, nonconflictual stage, where a little girl experiences "a fundamental fixed state of being rightfully a female" (p. 39). This primary, unquestioned sense of femaleness means that women are not inferior to men but simply different; Stoller clearly states that the individual's sense of core gender identity, that is, of maleness in males and femaleness in females, is a psychological and not a biological construct, that it is culturally determined and probably not universal, and that it results in automatized behavior, based on convictions, attitudes, fantasies, and daydreams. Lastly, primary femininity manifests itself in style, inflections, carriage, reveries, play, games, choice of clothing, and even in language. This early uncomplicated phase of primary femininity occurs before later disappointments set in at the oedipal stage and later; this richly textured and complex femininity implies an early identification with feminine women (pp. 39, 40, 45, 53, 55).

Stoller's "Patient's Responses to Their Own Case Reports" (Stoller, 1988) elaborates on the clinical methodology in the case history of Belle. Taking a radical, far-reaching position for his time, he argued that analysts must receive explicit written permission from their patients to publish clinical reports. Not one of his patients had refused Stoller permission to use records, take notes, dictate process material, or publish clinically grounded case studies. Stoller insisted that receiving patient permission is both an ethical and a scientific position. While respecting patients' privacy and confidentiality, taking precautions by employing necessary disguises, he held that it was also advisable to check the written version with the patient's view of what occurred in the analysis. This would work against the "defensively authoritarian tone" of analytic writing, a style of writing that assumes the analyst's version of this story is the only one to be credited. It would inject a healthy skepticism about the sureness of our "own beliefs" and relativism into the mix, reminding us that the patient's view of the process adds a necessary component of the experience that is mostly discounted in traditional narratives.

Patients, as well as readers, will have transferences to the text; that, too, becomes part of the dialogue, and experienced analysts will have to account for the role of transferences in transmitting their "truth." Stoller calls for a new rhetoric of writing case histories, one in which the patient's feelings, thoughts, and fantasies are visible. Including these vital experiences will make the report more rigorous, accurate, and accessible to readers and less dependent on analytic jargon or theory. "Even more complex: for each of us – patients or doctor – there is no *one* version" (Stoller, 1988, p. 388). Emphasizing that the ethics of case histories is situational, Stoller affirms the critical importance of context, of capturing contradiction in the accounts, including the role of uncertainty and confusion on the part of the analyst in various stages of the clinical process. He assumes there is a continuum of partial conclusions and paradox in the case report that reaches into levels of the unknown and unknowable, possibly moving "into unconsciousness." Lastly, he acknowledges in a footnote the enormous importance of monitoring and using the analyst's countertransference and making case studies alive and vibrant: "More and more, these notes are filled with what went on in me. Otherwise, besides leaving out a crucial element, they risk turning dead cold if I review them years later" (Stoller, 1988, p. 372, note 2). Stoller regrettably omitted publishing any precise record of Belle's reaction to his case study of her.

As we all understand, there are inevitable distortions in all case histories. The author needs to edit, select, condense, omit, synthesize, and add emphasis to the material. Few authors have the literary ability to evoke a complex character, or the prose style to describe the intricacy of the clinical process, including the chaos and messiness of a long-term character analysis. Clinicians must be able to tolerate long periods of uncertainty and not knowing. They must be suspicious about their interpretations, about what they apparently know for sure, not just skeptical about the utterances and self-deceptions of their patients. There are limits to what is knowable about any human being.

Even the most subtle and penetrating analyst must be aware of tendencies toward arrogance and omniscience and must not embrace the false security of thinking that he or she really knows.

Stoller himself seemed to be updating Montaigne's potent form of questioning, always posing the problem "What do I know?" In applying methodical doubt to the clinical investigation and to writing of the clinical report, Stoller applied suspiciousness both to the patient's associations and to his own confidence that he had achieved reliable, replicable, and transmittable knowledge, a knowledge based on the scientific method. Stoller loved to ask, how do you know what you know? How do you differentiate fact from theory, metaphor from reality, and the analyst's report of what went on in the analysis from a rhetoric that accurately describes the patient's position?

In reading *Sexual Excitement*, in learning about the various dimensions of Belle and Robert Stoller depicted in the text, we grasp that the case history method is endless, that there is no finite conclusion in the levels of meaning to be assigned, affective experiences to be explored, associations to be traced, and interpretations to be offered and relinquished. Stoller's case reveals the beauty, evocativeness, ambiguity, and caring possibilities of analytic work. The result calls up in readers multiple responses, reinterpretations, and the recreation of his presence as a psychoanalytic researcher and writer, theorist and caretaker, artist and scientist, and philosopher and clinician.

On the occasion of introducing Joyce McDougall (private communication, 2007) to an audience of mental health professionals in Los Angeles, Stoller improvised, providing us a further clue to his understanding of sexual excitement. I view these remarks as an eloquent epilogue to the case history of Belle: "I hereby appoint myself Aesthetician. And thereby – as self-assured as an art critic – pronounce as truth my conviction that the construction of erotic excitement is every bit as subtle, complex, inspired, profound, tidal, fascinating, awesome, problematic, unconscious soaked, and genius-haunted as the creation of dreams or art" (Stoller, quoted in McDougall, 1995, p. 171).

Stoller is explicitly telling us that the psychoanalyst needs an aesthetic attitude in approaching analytic theory, method, and clinical process, especially if studying erotic arousal. The aesthetician needs the appropriate level of distance and closeness to the object of study. Just as the analyst would investigate the dream or an elusive work of art, he begins his inquiry into erotics with an orientation that privileges emotion and sensation over intellectuality. He studies sexually exciting states of mind and affects in relation to his sense of what is beautiful, ugly, sublime, tragic, and comic – the whole spectrum of experience in arriving at valid critical judgments. We honor Stoller, then, by appointing ourselves psychoanalytic aestheticians. We update and thereby revive his subversive and destabilizing approach to erotics as we study case by case this construction of individual desire.

Previously published in *The Journal of the American Psychoanalytic Association*, Vol. 58, No. 1, February 2010, pp. 147–168.

References

Fisher, D. J. (1996). Remembering Robert J. Stoller (1924–1991). *Psychoanalytic Review*, 83, 1–9.

Forrester, J. (2007). The Psychoanalytic Case: Voyeurism, Ethics, and Epistemology in Robert Stoller's Sexual Excitement. In A. Creager, E. Lumbeck, & M. N. Wise (Eds.), *Science without Laws: Model Systems, Cases, Exemplary Narratives*. Durham: Duke University Press, 189–211.

Hughes, J. M. (1999). Artificial Selection: Robert J. Stoller and Nancy Chodorow. In *Freudian Analysts/Feminist Issues*. New Haven, CT: Yale University Press, 87–124.

Kernberg, O. F. (1995). *Love Relations: Normality and Pathology*. New Haven, CT: Yale University Press.

Lichtenberg, J. D. (2008). *Sensuality and Sexuality across the Divide of Shame*. New York: Analytic Press.

Mann, D. (1999). *Erotic Transference and Countertransference: Clinical Practice in Psychotherapy*. London: Routledge.

McDougall, J. (1995). *The Many Faces of Eros: A Psychoanalytic Exploration of Human Sexuality*. New York: W. W. Norton.

Michels, R. (1998). The Case History. *Journal of the American Psychoanalytic Association*, 48, 357–375.

Person, E. S. (1997). Foreword. In Robert Stoller, *Splitting: A Case of Female Masculinity*. New Haven, CT: Yale University Press, vii–xii.

Scharff, J. S. (2000). On Writing from Clinical Experience. *Journal of the American Psychoanalytic Association*, 48, 421–447.

Stoller, R. J. (1974). *Splitting: A Case of Female Masculinity*. London: Hogarth Press.

Stoller, R. J. (1979). *Sexual Excitement: Dynamics of Erotic Life*. New York: Pantheon Books.

Stoller, R. J. (1985). *Observing the Erotic Imagination*. New Haven, CT: Yale University Press.

Stoller, R. J. (1988). Patients' Responses to Their Own Case Reports. *Journal of the American Psychoanalytic Association*, 36, 371–391.

Chapter 2

Transitional Objects and Generativity

Ekstein's Blending of Erikson and Winnicott

Occasionally, an essay appears that is designed to enchant, to strike an emotional chord, to stimulate thinking, to make surprising linkages, while simultaneously serving as an exercise in self-analysis. This late essay by Rudolf Ekstein (1912–2005) does all this and more. As the title suggests, this essay juxtaposes two strong, analytic thinkers, Erikson and Winnicott, who emerged from different analytic schools and cultures, and who are rarely associated together in the analytic literature.

Ekstein packs his imaginative and emotionally resonant piece with telling vignettes, personal disclosures, and autobiographical fragments while drawing on his rich clinical experience and his ability to handle conceptual ideas precisely without being pedantic. Like an orchestra maestro, readers witness a master conductor teaching a master class with the lightest of touch. This is a teacher we want to learn from, one with whom we wish to open up a dialogue. He offers an elusively simple, but profound argument, namely, that individuals depend on transitional objects throughout the life cycle and that the concept is operative beyond the psychological storms and stresses of the infant's separation from the mother's breast and oral dependency needs. Throughout the life history of the personality, from infancy to adolescence, to early adulthood, to maturity, to old age, individuals employ transitional objects, which perform different functions and condense different meanings.

Winnicott perceptively described the infant's need to construct an intermediate space through the use of a blanket, teddy bear, or toy to tolerate the excruciatingly painful feelings of separation in the absence of his mother. The transitional object allows the fragile infant something palpable and external to himself to hold onto, a "not-me object"; this permits him to endure the terrors of abandonment, loneliness, and isolation of loss; it also enables him to cope with the miseries of extreme dependence, helplessness, longing for love, and the anxiety inflected desire for mutual recognition. Closely faithful to the spirit of Winnicott's writing, Ekstein holds that the transitional object is useful not only to describe normal as well as pathological phenomena but is also helpful in understanding the creative and adaptive strategies of traumatized individuals in many phases of life experience.

To illustrate, Ekstein poignantly describes how three cohorts and he suffered massive dislocation and the violent rupture of their lives as a result of Nazi Germany's annexation of Austria in 1938. Transitional objects helped these vulnerable individuals to survive and reconstruct their lives, despite living in a highly precarious and uncertain environment. Opening up an in-between space allows the individual to forge a creative response and partial solution to existential anxieties being faced in extreme situations in life, including significant, dangerous moments of rites of passage. Leaving Europe at this chaotic moment was a new diaspora for these three men. Distinct transitional objects and transitional phenomena helped to mediate moments of crisis and potential fragmentation.

Late in his life, Ekstein was a bridge builder; he looked for linkages in the different schools of psychoanalysis, emphasizing areas of agreement in the various theories that often postured against one another. He viewed many disagreements in the history of psychoanalysis as sectarian and petty, as polemics often hiding personal and narcissistic agendas, privileging power interests over genuine scientific disagreements – or most importantly, oblivious to what was in the best interests of the patient. When I was a candidate in the 1980s, he was one of the few training analysts who belonged to both medically dominated institutes in Los Angeles; he also joined several non-medical institutes as a Training Analyst. As a lay analyst who was both an insider and an outsider, Ekstein's membership in several institutes went with a refusal to invest himself in sterile doctrinal struggles or ideological disputes that were no longer relevant to the generation of sound clinical practice in the present.

In this paper, Ekstein constructs a transitional space between Erikson's ego psychology, that is, the school of psychoanalysis that he was educated in during his training in Vienna in the 1930s, and the clinical insights embedded in the tradition of the Independent British Object Relations School. He was also identified with Winnicott's style of personal playfulness, warmth, independence, spontaneity, and willingness to be himself and to be real in all situations, including with children and patients, even with colleagues. He admired Erikson's attempt to integrate the social and historical with the psychoanalytic, identified with his artistic sensibility, and not least embraced the concept of the life cycle. For Erikson and Ekstein, the life cycle implied that the individual's search for identity, meaning, and dignity was a life-long quest, something unending, conflictual, unreachable, and fraught with the potential for failure and inadequacy, potentially rich in new areas of self-awareness and growth.

Erikson's concepts of identity and the life cycle brilliantly advanced the earlier psychoanalytic emphasis on early psychosexual development and the determinate aspects of early childhood. In positing eight stages of the life span, an epigenetic principle, which accounted for growth and regression over time and in a larger social community, Erikson widened the scope of the analytic comprehension of the individual personality. For him, interpersonal interactions and relationships were vitally important in whether a person achieved individual growth, or whether he remained emotionally isolated, lonely, and depressed. Erikson argued that successful development turned on striking a balance between two conflicting sides in each stage of the life cycle. Successful resolution of the conflict might bring about a strengthened sense of self, built on competence, ego strength, mastery, and autonomy. Failure to achieve competency and loving relationships might result in inadequacy and a compromised sense of self.

When I was in analysis with Ekstein, I observed a woodcut from Erik Erikson, above the couch, adjacent to a photo of Freud. It was a beautiful image of the Madonna and child. It was personally inscribed, "To Rudy, Best wishes, Erik." From this art object, Ekstein communed with Erikson and perhaps his lost mother. It was also a transitional object keeping alive an intense relationship, mediating between fantasy and reality, the inner world and the external world, possibly between Christian and Jew, ego psychological and relational psychoanalytic perspectives, between Vienna and London, culminating in this essay.

Transitional objects allow the individual the time and space to separate and differentiate, to let go of significant but not always primitive, introjected objects. They allow the vulnerable individual to construct an imaginary space for play, spontaneity, personal affirmation, self-soothing, cultural pursuits, and ultimately the expression of courage. Courage refers to the capacity to endure pain and loss, to verbalize and master massive trauma rather than endlessly repeat trauma. At the highest level, it encourages the individual to function responsibly in the world and in one's own environment.

In the vignettes presented here, Ekstein speaks of his adolescent son's wish to let go of feeling like a child, his desire to be grown up, symbolized by the wish to have age-appropriate transitional objects. All of this exists in a dynamic continuum where the adolescent, caught between the regressive pulls of childhood and the uncertainties of adulthood, desires to be free and self-reliant while continuing to be dependent on early objects and early sources of holding and security. The adolescent wish stems from a desire to be less supervised and monitored by parents and teachers, less burdened by the parents' desire for the child to follow their own desires, and less circumscribed by parents who are not always attuned to the adolescent's aspirations and emerging ideals. The conflict between identity and confusion about one's sense of self can escalate into a crisis, one which places the adolescent in severe difficulty.

For the elderly the transitional object works to establish affective experiences of memory and linkages to the past; it also embodies a desire to transmit a powerful legacy to the younger generation, to pass on insights and strategies to permit survival in an increasingly dangerous world. Looking toward the future, transitional space may generate some hope that the next generation might find valid forms of commitment to justify their existence. Ekstein loved the quote from Goethe about the younger generation's readiness to inherit and earn the legacy from the parents. "What you have inherited from your fathers, acquire it, to make it your own." Inheritance is of course an ambivalent venture. Partly, it meant holding on to the traditions and values of the elders that still made sense and still resonated emotionally for the next generation. It also required the younger generation to negate, preserve, and recreate that inheritance to make it meaningful to the present and future. Successful development meant striking a mature balance between two opposing sides at any given stage of the life span.

A good-enough analyst is also a transitional object when he establishes an adequate form of holding environment, when there is an ambiance of understanding, safety, confidentiality, provision, and emotional attunement to correct deficits in family relationships or self-organization. These new and corrective emotional experiences, often moving and life transforming, are condensed in the person of the analyst. Like a transitional object, the analyst functions to be of use to the analysand, to assist in the process of healing and repairing. But he too is someone who can be dropped at an appropriate time, just as the child discards the teddy bear.

This elegant, evocative essay has a special importance to me. In writing this piece to introduce and comment on it, I realized how it served as a transitional object for me – and on several levels. I had just concluded a ten-year training analysis with Rudy Ekstein in the spring of 1989. This was our first post-analytic encounter and collaboration. His essay was written for and published in an in-house organ of the Los Angeles Psychoanalytic Institute that I would eventually edit. In that same number, I wrote an essay on Bettelheim, about whom I would subsequently write a book. Bettelheim and Ekstein were close friends, so there is a bridging function going on here, as well as the creation of an analytic third. The publication of my Bettelheim piece in the same issue as Ekstein's transitional object piece allowed me to continue the painful work of grief at the end of the analysis. In addition, it encouraged me to let go of him purely as a transference figure as my analyst, gradually evolving into a real relationship as colleague and associate. This assisted me to become an active society member, joining the faculty and developing into a respected contributor to the literature. Now I am trying to link past, present, and future by keeping Ekstein's memory alive through the publishing of his essay, hoping it will reach a larger and contemporaneous public reading audience.

Lastly, my analysis concluded before I began my own family in 1991. Like Ekstein, I have a son and a daughter. When his essay first appeared, I lacked the lived experience of being a parent, not able to appreciate his developmental clarity and psychological astuteness about parenting. Rereading it now, I realize that he still speaks to me about the pleasures and poignant losses of parenthood, the ups and downs of watching our children grow up, and of their need to separate and differentiate from us. Parents also observe the sometimes painful process of our children getting into struggles in life, sometimes being stuck, and their own often messy journey of establishing a professional and personal identity, as well as a cohesive sense of self. Ekstein, blending Erikson and Winnicott, understood how parents needed to promote the child's differentiation from the parents in order to find their own distinct voices and specific meaning in their own lives; it is a worthwhile quest, even if it is confusing and chaotic.

This is a truly beautiful paper. It was written in his late seventies. It is clearly a reflection on life, conducted without regret, bitterness, or despair. It looks toward the future and the end of life with a sense of hope and inner tranquility. Perhaps most beautiful of all is Ekstein's loving and tender depiction of his daughter Jean and how she encountered the teddy bear Winnicott, perhaps seeing him as an ideal father. Her brief encounter with the British analyst provoked her father's associations with Erikson, facilitating his ingenious insights into the life cycle of transitional objects and transitional space. This moment became part of her father's self-reflection and ultimately part of the wisdom literature of psychoanalysis.

Previously published in *Internationalpsychoanalysis.net*, April 21, 2014.

Chapter 3

Concerning the Life Cycle of the Transitional Object (by Rudolf Ekstein)

Many years have passed since Winnicott (1951) introduced us to the concept of "transitional objects," a concept that has become more and more alive for us as we learned to appreciate Winnicott's contributions. They are themselves a transitional link between different psychoanalytic schools that have developed in central Europe, England, the United States, and other parts of the world. I have in my possession a number of communications between Winnicott and myself: exchanges of reprints and the sharing of our work with children and adolescents and of our personal lives. It was back in 1965, a few months after one of the international psychoanalytic conferences, that he sent me "Miss Ekstein's Glossary of Epithets" that he had collected while chairing a panel that, so he said, bored him. He compared the adjectives and adverbs of my then adolescent daughter (who would one day become a teacher) with expressions of young British people. While all of us at the party of Dr. DeMonchy tried to meet the analysts of different countries, he sat somewhere in a corner with the adolescent girl and they talked, while he was trying to form a link in his own mind between American and British youngsters. More than 20 years later, our daughter still speaks about her meeting with Winnicott, her transitional object of the time, away from the parental home and moving toward the profession of teaching. And of course, I felt a little jealous of the attention my daughter got from him, since he is, for those of us who remember him, an eternal transitional object. Except that transitional objects have a life cycle of their own, and this brings me to my considerations, stimulated as they are by Donald W. Winnicott.

The last letter that Winnicott sent me was to thank me for my support of the statue of Freud to be erected in Hampstead. This statue, to be sure, is a transitional object, but really an eternal one and is to secure the way back to Freud. Perhaps I can make my thoughts about Winnicott's concept more alive if I tell about their origin, a kind of autobiographical comment, and have the reader accompany me for a few minutes into my very private world.

One night I did not sleep well, a rare occasion for me. I found myself occupied with the trip that was to bring me back once more to Vienna, my native town where I would be guest professor once again in a medical school. My thoughts were concerned with the question as to what I would want to buy myself in Vienna, what I would bring home, moving as I would be from the home of origin to the home of choice, from Austria to America. Will it be a porcelain figure, such as *Der Rosenkavalier* or Mozart or Strauss? Will I bring home some old German novels of the 19th century? What will it be? Why should all that disturb my sleep? And suddenly, I thought of Winnicott's transitional objects. Are these mementos transitional objects like my teddy once was? And it struck me that the teddy bears of little children, their blankets or old toys they could not let go of, have a different function than the mementos related to visiting other countries and other cities. But what is really the difference? Who has ever forgotten his old teddy bear? I did not forget mine. The last time I remember having seen him as a little boy, he had already lost one leg and one arm, and I once played with the idea that even after these many, many years, I might find him somewhere, such as the furniture, the photographs, the paintings, the old clock in our home, all that had been taken from us after the invasion.

The teddy bear of the little boy was to help him, having now "the first possession," as Winnicott puts it. That teddy would now be the infant's object, recognized as "not – me," and would help him to transit, to move away from the original oral eroticism and thus move to true object relationships. For example, the transitional phenomena, the little songs and tunes which the infant sings, that help him to move toward a higher state of development away from autistic and symbiotic dilemmas to more mature object relationships. What then is the difference between these first possessions and the possessions that I want to acquire as I travel back to the original fatherland and to the original mother tongue?

The original transitional objects lead me forward. The new objects that I want to acquire – may I also call them transitional objects? – are leading me back to the past. I want to come home again to the States where I have lived now for almost 50 years, but I want to have in my home objects and memories that lead back to the past.

If one were to go to the homes of one's friends, friends of different generations, one would learn a great deal about them, their character and their personal history. One needs only to study what they collect, what they have brought back from different situations, and what they have inherited and have thrown away. One could well, without ever talking to them, get a good psychological picture of them. True enough, much of what they may have collected and how exhibit may simply be a mask, a pretense of what they want to appear to be their friends, to the other people who try to assess them. But behind the mask, the collected treasures, a partial picture of their past, a true picture, would be the truer self. We could observe the struggle between the original and the acquired, and we could then think of them as of actors of the past in the classical Greek or Roman theaters who wore masks and could not be themselves.

I say then that the objects we bring from our trips serve a similar purpose. But usually as we get older, they lead not forward but back into the past. What we find in the home of our parents and treasure is the tradition, and what we hold onto as our first possessions, the transitional objects of early childhood, which serve adaptation.

I suggest then that all through life transitional objects will change as they either serve us in moving toward the future, toward adaptation, and toward liberation, or they serve to return to the past, to holding on to the tradition.

It seems to me an interesting task to think of transitional objects in terms of representing the ever-changing life cycle.

In the beginning of life, transitional objects are offered to the child and they are merely passive acquisitions. But later in life, childhood, adolescence, early adulthood, mature adulthood, and old age, the transitional objects are now active acquisitions. And they have a different meaning in the process of development, of maturation, and the process of aging, of letting go.

Perhaps I can illustrate this if I describe the changing toys and acquisitions of one of my children. For years, as a little boy, my son went out for Halloween. He would go with friends or with his parents from door to door to acquire candy and apples and little gifts in the recurring ritual of "tricks or treats." One day when he was about 13 years old, friends of his had not come and he did not want to go out. I was willing to accompany him. He went to one or two doors, got some candy, and came to me crying and said, "it's no fun any longer." For years he enjoyed all these candies and this time he wanted to go home. I realized that for him childhood was over. As we went back into our house, he went to his room where he had all kinds of little cars displayed on a bookcase, all kinds of memorabilia acquired on some of our trips. He started to take them from the shelves and put them into a big box. He put everything away that he had proudly displayed in years gone by. I wondered how he could destroy this beautiful collection and he got angry with me. He told me that he was not a little boy any longer and all his friends laughed about all these objects. Also, toys are transitional objects that permit the child to weave fantasies around them which lead to growth, to the solution of conflicts, to that moment when he puts them all into a big box out of sight from his comrades. But he left a few posters that he had acquired, colorful posters of music stars and movie stars of the kind that adolescents collect and exhibit. Of course, they were also transitional objects, but they were the transitional objects of adolescence, not the objects that lead away from the mother as did the teddy bear. The objects had changed.

As I look at the home of the young man, now in his thirties, I find none of these old posters. The taste and expectations have changed and much of what was once important, he has given away or keeps somewhere in a dark closet. There are now some objects that we have given him, small pieces of art that make his home start to look a little bit like the home of his parents. He moves back to the family tradition.

I have often listened to people who are on the move, who give up an apartment, a home, move elsewhere, and who then have to make the decisions as to what they want to take along and what they want to give up. It is not only their moving day but also the moving day of transitional objects. I think of old people who have to give up their homes, moving to a smaller apartment, or moving to an old age home, and having perhaps but one room left. I see how they must struggle with what they must choose to give up, what they can leave behind, sell, destroy, give away, and what they want to keep. What keeps them together? Usually, transitional objects allow them to maintain continuity. What will people save first of their possessions as they escape the inferno of a burning home? Will it be the pictures of the family, the documents, the money, and what loss will be most painful for them that they can never replace?

May I recall an unforgettable experience? It was the time when, as a refugee in 1938, I sailed on a ship from England to America. There were four of us, four young men who did not know each other. We were together deep in the hold of the ship in a small cabin, having attained tickets from a refugee organization. Each of us had something among his meager possessions that he would not let go. I recall that having otherwise no more than one suit, I had taken along two suitcases with German books: novels, philosophy, psychology, and psychoanalysis. One of the young men had a Mezuzah from the Old Testament, which he carried around his neck. The third one showed us how he had some money that he brought to the new world and had it also around his neck so that he would not lose it and no one could take it from him. And the fourth young man had a little booklet around his neck filled with addresses of friends and acquaintances all over the world so that in case he might have to leave the States, another upheaval expected, he could use these contacts. I often wondered why each of us had selected completely different objects in the transit from Europe to America. Each of us trusted something different that would help him to move into the future. Each had another teddy bear. If only I could find these other men. I am sure that the selection of transitional objects is a very personal one and has deep meaning in the forming of personalities, in the formation of goals and finding a meaning for one's life.

Each of these four young men took his own transitional objects in giving up Europe and moving toward America. Each had a way of his own, his belief in books, religious commitment, the protection through money, or the protection of human contacts. What will their transitional objects be when they become old? And what will finally happen to the objects they collected later in life and will occupy their minds when they move toward old age and must think of the end of the life cycle? What kind of monument, what kind of memory would they want their children, the survivors, to maintain? What do they want to stand for? In other words, what kind of monument will they want for themselves as transit moves toward the exit? What is it that they once inherited from their own parents, from the past, and what would they want to be the inheritance of those who will survive them? Each of them, I suppose, if these young men turned out the way I imagined they would, will want their values to be written into their testament. What can they do to maintain tradition? Thus I am occasionally occupied now, when I don't sleep well, with my books.

Of course, I do not think just of their physical existence, but whether they will play a role in the minds of those whom I love.

Goethe's words, "What thou has inherited from your fathers, acquire it, and make it thine and thee," is the demand for those of us who are young and transit toward the future. The demand of the older people, the inheritance that they leave to their successors, an appeal to conscience, to self and to desire, are concerned with the question as to whether they have done enough to make the younger world capable of using this inheritance. This is the eternal question of education and – if education fails – of the psychotherapeutic, the psychoanalytic process.

This process, a play between identification and counter identification, between transference and countertransference, and between regression and adaptation, is reflected in the fate of transitional objects during the psychotherapeutic process.

These transitional objects, be it now the love for the teddy bear or the love for a psychotherapist, need further discussion.

Winnicott hints at this when he says:

> Following this, we can allow the transitional object to be potentially a maternal phallus but originally the breast, that is to say, the thing created by the infant and at the same time provided from the environment. In this way I think that a study of the infant's use of the transitional object and of transitional phenomena in general may throw light on the origin of the fetish object and fetishism. There is something to be lost, however, in working backwards from the psychopathology of fetishism to the transitional phenomena which belong to the beginnings of experience and which are inherent in healthy emotional development (p. 241–242).

The patient, child, adolescent, or adult, whether play, acting out, or free association, creates then a transference to the therapist, provided from the environment, a transitional object that he is, and that allows us to transmit toward healthy emotional development.

I hope my daughter, one of the other teachers in my family, will forgive me if I quote her. She told me after she met Winnicott when she was a young adolescent that he's lovable, that he is a teddy bear. Little did she know then that it was Winnicott who wrote about the transitional object, or perhaps, indeed, she did know.

For me he is an eternal object of great admiration that gave me the strength to travel forward to new experience and discovery. I was able to move forward to America, to new ways of thinking, and also back to my homeland, to Vienna, back to Freud. And with new strength and possessions, I was ready to maintain the dialectic struggle between yesterday and tomorrow, mirrored in the private life cycle and the coming and going of generations.

Previously published in *Los Angeles Psychoanalytic Bulletin*, Summer, 1989, pp. 36–41. [Published with the permission of Jean Ekstein-Tiano.]

Reference

Winnicott, D. W. (1951). Transitional Objects and Transitional Phenomena. In *Collected Papers – Through Pediatrics to Psycho-analysis*. New York: Basic Books, 230, 241–242.

Chapter 4

A Conversation with Adam Phillips

It's my privilege to introduce Adam Phillips as NCP's first Master Clinician in Residence. This program is designed for our institute to interact with someone who has produced a significant body of psychoanalytic writing. Phillip's books and essays are grounded dialectically in clinical knowledge and subtle understanding of the therapeutic process. His visit will present him with an opportunity to be immersed in the life of our institute, exchanging ideas with our candidates, members, and faculty.

What more can I say about Adam Phillips? To begin with, he doesn't have e-mail. [Laughter] I am of two minds about this. On the one hand, I find it charming and on the other hand, a pain in the neck. Perhaps it is a critique of technology, a protest against the age of social media, of overtly rapid e-mailing and texting, and of facile forms of non-relating. More significantly, Phillips is adept at communicating and non-communicating. He has a special quality of relating intimately, of listening and being attuned; he then can courteously withdraw, retreating into a much cherished solitude.

Mark Twain once quipped that England and America were two countries separated by the same language. Phillips represents much of the best in British intellectual and psychoanalytic life. Our own tradition, blending classical and contemporary psychoanalysis, will hopefully form an intermediate and transitional space between our different psychoanalytic languages, attitudes, and methods.

Adam Phillips is a distinguished and productive writer. He has written 21 books and edited eight others. He's the general editor of the new *Penguin Modern Classic Freud* translations. There are seventeen volumes of them, published in inexpensive and lovely paperbacks. He is the author of intellectual biographies of Winnicott and Freud: *Winnicott* (1988) and *Becoming Freud: The Making of a Psychoanalyst* (2014). He is a psychoanalyst and essayist whose writings have appeared in important mass circulation journals and reviews including the *London Review of Books*, *Raritan*, *The Observer*, and *The New York Times Book Review*. Among his varied publications, I will mention my favorites: *On Kissing, Tickling and Being Bored*

DOI: 10.4324/9781003488439-5

(1993); *Monogamy* (1996); *On Kindness* (2009); *Unforbidden Pleasures* (2015); and the recently published and provocative volume, *In Writing* (2017). As one of the most versatile of contemporary psychoanalytic writers, he is a rare example of the psychoanalytic public intellectual, someone who has a unique capacity to appeal to clinical specialists and an educated lay public.

There are those among us who have a will to power and others who have a will to knowledge. Phillips has a ruthless and relentless will to write. He has put into practice my favorite quote from Henry Miller: "And wanting to write, he wrote."

Roland Barthes wrote a famous book called *The Pleasures of the Text*. Phillips clearly has made reading and writing a pleasure. He writes fluently, playfully, and spontaneously. He is often eloquent. He has a love of paradox, a well-developed visual eye, expressing himself in a strong voice. He is rarely polemical in his writings, seemingly indifferent to or outside the warring ideological infighting that has diminished psychoanalysis from its birth. His writing is never definitive, but open to multiple interpretations. He is rarely cheerless or disillusioned, a tendency that plagues much psychoanalytic writing, perhaps emanating from our work with primitively organized and traumatized individuals, daily encounters with resistance and severely depressed patients, and repeated encounters with intractable and rigid psychopathology.

Nor is he a facile and sentimental optimist. If he is not a scholar, a theorist, or a researcher, Phillips draws expertly on scholarship, handles theory with finesse and subtlety, while being vibrantly aware of contemporary developments in research on psychoanalytic themes. As a quintessential writer of essays, he continues the finest traditions of British, American, and Continental essayists, including Walter Pater, Matthew Arnold, Oscar Wilde, Emerson, and Nietzsche, as well as authors from the analytic literature (I think here of classic texts by Freud and Winnicott). He spices his writing with cogent insights from Lacan, Ferenczi, Bion, and others. As an essayist, he writes in an associational manner, embracing the creative aspects of skepticism, including a healthy skepticism regarding psychoanalysis itself. Yet Phillips is a skeptic who is open to experiment.

He believes the contemporary crisis of psychoanalysis is more an opportunity than a tragedy. If psychoanalysis survives, it will have to transform itself, finding a new audience and legitimizing many of its rich discoveries and subversive methods.

Phillips is not wedded to one core theory of psychoanalysis or to one method, though he clearly esteems the tradition of playfulness, critique, and creative thinking of the British independent school. From the Middle School, he has inherited and updated a fascination with free thinking and intellectual independence, with the exploration of regressive processes in psychotherapy, and the rich cultural possibilities of spontaneity, potential space, and the transformational aspects of intimate relating and empathic forms of interpretation and of redescription.

He also demonstrates an abundant interest in the unconscious and sexuality, in relational modes emanating from the analytic dyad, and in developmental perspectives derived from work with children and adolescents. He illustrates how the project of self-understanding emerges from the relationship of self and others in a creative and ultimately endless dialogue.

As an essayist, Phillips writes like a *flaneur*, leisurely strolling through his themes with no definitive goal or destination. He is clearly suspicious of analytic positions grounded in dogma, jargon, or cult-like organizations. He rejects the posturings of analysts who speak with great certainty but only to members of their coterie. He is vehemently anti-authoritarian and anti-essentialist. If he strongly advocates, he also practices the application of cross-disciplinary fertilization between analysts and specialists from other disciplines. He argues that literature, history, and philosophy have as much to teach us about the human condition and human personality as psychoanalysis has.

In summary, I am optimistic that Phillip's visit here as our first Master Clinician in Residence will generate good conversation and good company, robust debate, and lively interactions. It will be an opportunity for us to show a mutual capacity to be together as vulnerable and real people. Let us give a warm welcome to Adam Phillips. [Applause]

David James Fisher: I have twenty-eight questions.
Adam Phillips: Fine.
David James Fisher: You proudly call yourself a psychoanalyst and yet you did not attend or graduate from the British Psychoanalytical Society. Can you tell us about your analytic background and your immersion in psychoanalytic and psychotherapeutic supervision in London?
Adam Phillips: I don't think of the word "psychoanalyst" as an honorific, just as a description of a kind of work. I trained – I would have to go back a bit just to make sense of this. I studied literature at university. Before I went to university, I read Winnicott's *Playing and Reality*. Having read that, I knew exactly what I then wanted to do. So when I qualified – that is, when I got my undergraduate degree – there were three places in London you could train. There was what was then called the Hampstead Clinic, which was "Anna Freudian." There was the Tavistock Clinic and there was a place called the ICP, the Institute of Child Psychology. The ICP was nominally eclectic and what that meant was there were Jungians as well as Anna Freudians and Freudians and so on. I then applied for the ICP because I thought it was obviously the worst place and partly because it was eclectic. Within six months of my starting there, it folded. We were then taken over by an overarching body called the Association of Child Psychotherapists, and what it meant was that in practice I was trained at the Tavistock Clinic

and the Anna Freud Centre. So entirely by luck, I had in a way the best possible training I could have had. In the middle of that, I also had a middle group analysis and a trainee post in the Middlesex Hospital, the Department of Child Psychiatry. Then, for the next seventeen years or so, I worked in the National Health Service as a child psychotherapist, and that was working in child guidance clinics, child psychiatry departments in hospitals, children's homes, etc. A whole range of things.

The wonderful thing about that then as opposed to now was actually two things. First of all, there was a National Health Service, anybody could walk in and have psychotherapy free. And also, the completely mental health profession was much less professionalized, so there was less differential diagnosis. And what that meant was that I saw a huge range of people that I wouldn't otherwise, whom I wouldn't see now, for example. I saw many people who were– not a lot – I saw *some* children who were autistic, adults who were, I think probably would be diagnosed schizophrenic, a large range of people. Then, after 18 years of that, the Health Service began to fall apart. This was a terrible thing. When I started as a child psychotherapist, I could see children for as long as it took. By the time I got to the end, they were saying, "We'll pay for two sessions." And it's familiar to everybody. It was basically the rise of neoliberalism and we were managed by people who had no interest in what we did. Several of my friends and I and colleagues left the National Health Service very, very dismayed about this, but there was nowhere else to go, and went into private practice against my wishes, but I wanted to go on doing it. Since then and so for the last, whatever it is, 18 years, I've been in private practice. And in private practice, I see adults for psychoanalysis. By psychoanalysis, I mean psychoanalytic psychotherapy. I see people once, twice, very occasionally three times a week, and quite a lot of people come when they want to. And once I qualified, I had no particular involvement with psychoanalytic groups because that wasn't my idea of fun. What I was really interested in was doing the work and at that time I also started writing. I didn't want to be a writer, I wanted to be a reader. But the writing started – it started and then it continued.

Is that the beginning of an answer to your first question?

David James Fisher: Excellent: Thank you. You were analyzed by Masud Khan. Without impinging on the privacy and integrity of that relationship, can you share the experience of being on Khan's couch?

Adam Phillips: [Laughs] Yes, I can. But again, I'll have to tell you all a bit of a story about it. I'd read books. I'd never met an analyst. It wasn't in my world. So I didn't, obviously, know who anybody was. I didn't know how the whole thing worked. I was also twenty-three, so I was really young. When I got into the training, I was given a list of analysts. One of the people on the list was Masud Khan. I can remember going to an exhibition with my then-girlfriend and there used to be phone boxes in London. Of course, there aren't anymore. Going to a phone box and ringing up this man, Masud Khan, and he answered the phone, which I was surprised by. Anyway, he answered the phone and I explained I was in training to be a child psychotherapist and that I wanted training analysis. He said, "I need to let you know that I can't do anything under fifty pounds a session." I said, "How about five?" He said, "Come see me on Monday at two." [Laughter]

I went to see him on Monday and it was kind of love at first sight I think, for both of us. And I felt I could talk to this man forever and he was a combination of very sweet, very funny, and very, very interesting. And so I went into analysis with him. The notoriety that some people in the room may know about, I of course didn't know about then. I could talk a lot about this and I don't particularly want to, but I can just give you two clues. I arrived at the first session, I lay down on the couch, and I started doing what I thought of as free associating, twittering away. After about twenty minutes of this, Khan said to me (he was very, very courteous), he said, "Mr. Phillips, could I interrupt you?" So I said, "Sure." He said, "You haven't come here to talk about your childhood, to tell me your dreams, to talk about your sex life. You've come to say something significant. If you've got nothing significant to say, please don't talk." [Laughter] And I just loved that. I just thought it was very funny and very, very interesting. [Laughter]

Secondarily, when – in those days I had long hair – he would think of me resisting, he would sometimes pull my hair from behind the couch. [Laughter] And he would say to me, "Stop resisting and listen to what I'm saying." Or, "stop resisting, I haven't been selling potatoes for the past 30 years." I didn't realize then because I was young, but I realized it retrospectively that he was extremely mindful of how young I was. He really took me on in the sense of he taught me psychoanalysis. He both gave me an analysis and gave me books, and he introduced me to people. He made it his business to teach me psychoanalysis. And because psychoanalysis was and is for me a romance, he really played his part in that because he too believed in the romance of psychoanalysis and he was very, very obviously interested and engaged by it and loved it. Just as a footnote to this, there was only one occasion when he was ever anything remotely anti-Semitic to me. As a child, I knew my grandparents knew people who'd got out of Germany, some of them had been in concentration camps. As a child, I had the experience of meeting older German people who had numbers on their wrists. I can remember talking about this to Khan. At one point he said it was the end of the session; he said, "I'll leave you to your Wailing Wall." And I said to him, "Is that an anti-Semitic remark?" There was a silence and he said, "Yes, I'm very, very sorry about that." I never, ever felt there was anything anti-Semitic to me about him, even though I don't doubt a lot of the things that have been said and written about him. A lot of it sounds very plausible to me.

David James Fisher: You anticipate the next question.

Adam Phillips: Which is?

David James Fisher: Khan himself has been the subject of significant controversy in his analytic career. No one disputes his brilliance as a thinker and his versatility as a writer. He is the subject of Linda Hopkins' biography, *False Self: The Life and Work of Masud Khan* (Hopkins, 2008). Were you disturbed by learning of the loose boundaries between Winnicott and Khan during and after Khan's analysis? How did you feel about learning of his sexual relations with several female analysands, his expulsion from the British Psychoanalytical Society, and his anti-Semitic outbursts late in life?

Adam Phillips: I think anything I say about this is going to be provocative, but actually, it made no difference to me at all, any of that stuff. I believe a lot of it was true. It wasn't that I was in a state of denial. But I suppose it becomes a question, or there are two questions here. One is how complicated you can allow people to be. It's also a question about love, really, and my relationship with him was completely trustworthy. And I had no reason to doubt his integrity in relation to me, and that was what counted. And I also knew that I could ask him about anything that was said about him, which I sometimes did. And he was not defensive about these things. It didn't have much effect on me and it hasn't subsequently. Not that I thereby endorse some of the things that he may or may not have done. But it hasn't altered my view of him.

David James Fisher: What was the frequency of your analysis?

Adam Phillips: It was four times a week for four years.

David James Fisher: How important and how trivial is analytic genealogy? You were analyzed by Khan, who was analyzed by Winnicott, who was analyzed by Strachey, who was analyzed by Freud. That's a distinguished line of analytic ego ideals.

Adam Phillips: I like the idea of it – in some ways. I think there's also something fanciful about it in that I don't think there's a source that one can get closer to in psychoanalysis. I do think that that is an interesting genealogy that I happened to enter upon, but of course anybody who goes for any kind of therapy is entering into a huge, unknown history. They're entering into their analyst's own childhood and history; they're entering into their analyst's transgenerational history; they're entering into a huge set of assumptions about what a person is, what a person might be, what a person could be, and so on. So it seems to me that there's a version of this going on in any relationship. I don't feel beglamoured of it. When you recited it then I thought, that is interesting, and of course it must have its effect. For me, it's fantastical in the sense of I can't tell myself an interesting story about those facts. I was told stories from within that tradition in my analysis. For instance, just very briefly, because this I think is a good one or a very bad one. You'll have to see what you think. [Laughter]

And you may know the story. Winnicott went to analysis with James Strachey. He went five times a week, and for the first six months Strachey never said anything. After six months of this, Winnicott got up from the couch one day and said to Strachey, "I've been coming for six months and you haven't said anything." And Strachey said, "But you haven't either." [Laughter]

Now that's either a great story or a terrible story, but it is an interesting story.

David James Fisher: It was a question of mine, and you said you are haunted by this story. I'm curious about why it haunts you, and do you see this vignette, if it's true, as an example of the young Winnicott's compliance, or as an example of Strachey's analytic rigor about how to listen to a patient?

Adam Phillips: I see it as part of Winnicott's compliance, but I don't see it as rigor. I see it as straightforward authoritarianism because, obviously, nobody else can decide what is significant beforehand. I don't like the idea of there being people who can claim to know when other people are really speaking or, from a psychoanalytic point of view, what is it to really speak? I think those are interesting questions.

David James Fisher: Can one ever work through the analytic transference, especially if one works in the field, particularly if it is a training analysis?

Adam Phillips: I think Laplanche is right about this. You can't resolve a transference. You can only displace it. I think it is absurd and unrealistic to be too ambitious about "resolving" transferences. Transference is one of the mediums of sociability; it's not only the way the past preempts the present and the future. It's also the way it transforms and enlivens them. There is really no such thing as a training analysis, who has had one. Training analyses only exist because there are

David James Fisher: so-called trainings, and people who believe psychoanalysts are trained. You can no more train someone to be an analyst than you can train someone to be a poet, or a friend, or a parent. The only question the student of psychoanalysis needs to ask herself is, who do I really enjoy talking with about psychoanalysis? And it could be anyone.

David James Fisher: Your interest in psychoanalysis began at the age of seventeen. It came through reading Jung's *Memories, Dreams, Reflections* and Winnicott's *Playing and Reality.* What specifically resonated for you in that reading experience? Why after developing an affinity for Winnicott's book did you decide you wanted to be a child psychotherapist? What was the inner connection?

Adam Phillips: I read *Memories, Dreams, Reflections* when I was sixteen and I'd just started reading books. I wasn't a child who read or wrote or any of that stuff. But I had a teacher at school who taught me English literature in a very powerful and passionate way. Anyway, I came across Jung's autobiography. When I was sixteen, I was interested in what I then thought of as the depths. I read Jung's autobiography, and I thought this was an amazingly exciting life. I imagined that Jung was in the depths or knew about the depths, and I thought it was absolutely an extraordinary account of somebody's own myth, mythmaking. But it was the first remotely psychoanalytic book I'd ever read.

    Then I read Winnicott's *Playing and Reality* when it came out in 1971, and when I read this book, I had an experience that I think lots of people have in adolescence, but they have sometimes have it with music or books. Well, I read this book and I knew that I knew exactly what this book was about and I really thought not that I could have written it, because obviously that's absurd, but I really thought this book was as much mine as his. Now I can't imagine what I was then thinking at seventeen, obviously. It must be partly wishful but not only wishful because there was a real affinity that was detected there. And when I read that book, I knew exactly what I wanted to do, which was to become a child psychotherapist. How it worked I don't really know, except that I've had similar experiences not quite of that intensity with certain other writers, where I read them and felt it's not quite what I could have written it, nor is it quite it was written for me or to me. I felt a profound sense of affinity, as though in reading the book or hearing this voice, something in me that must have been latent came to life. There was something very fundamentally enhancing about it and it was like the book came to collect me. I knew exactly then what I was going to do. But it wasn't as though before then I was baffled. It was as though in a sense I'd always known this, but then I *knew* it. That's how it worked.

And then the Khan thing was a coincidence in that I didn't make the connection. I didn't know about the connection when I went to see him.

David James Fisher: It's going to be interesting because on Saturday we're going to be having a conference almost exclusively devoted to *Playing and Reality*, so this is going to be a homecoming for you.

Adam Phillips: Well, it was of course very interesting, as it always has been, rereading the book, because the book gets more and more interesting to me and more and more difficult to understand. But it seems to me a very remarkable book, out of which a lot of future psychoanalysis could come.

David James Fisher: Your first experience of reading Freud was also very powerful. His description of Jewish family life was familiar to you. What specifically do you recall about it that made it seem uncanny? What text or texts by Freud influenced you?

Adam Phillips: I think in the first instance what amazed me about Freud was how accessible he was, that it was entirely readable. I can remember reading *Civilization and Its Discontents* and *Beyond the Pleasure Principle* and thinking these were, as they are, extraordinary books, essays. I think there was something about Freud's sensibility. I wouldn't have called it this then, but there was something very familiar to me about his preoccupations. Freud talked about things that my family talked about. They didn't talk about them psychoanalytically, but it was all there. So when I read Winnicott, Winnicott's very, very English, and my family – well, I am very English but certainly my family were not, so having read Winnicott first and then Freud, Freud felt much more familiar to me. It wasn't quite uncanny so much as very, very compelling. There was something about the voice that was very familiar to me and also there was something very hospitable about it. I thought Freud wanted us to read his books. I thought he wanted us to be interested in what he was interested in, and I loved that. It seemed to be really genial. In my fantasy, I thought of him as a very, very ordinary Jewish man who also did something rather extraordinary, but that he was really ordinary in the best sense. And it's a very interesting life story.

David James Fisher: Winnicott, you say, is quintessentially English and Freud essentially a godless European Jew with close psychological connections to your family. Would you agree that a consistent thread runs through your writings, namely,

Adam Phillips: a dialogue between Winnicott and Freud, reflecting the two dominant parts of your origins and education, two strong components of your sense of self?
I think that must be true although, you know, I'd be the last to know and the first to find out, in the sense that I think other people might have a clearer sense of that than I do. I think it must be of some significance that these are two preoccupations, but of course they're not my only preoccupations, and I'm much more interested in William James than I am in either of those two people or in Wallace Stevens, or I could go on.

David James Fisher: Go on.

Adam Phillips: Well, I don't want to go on too much, but for me these people are writers among many other writers I'm interested in. I don't think of any of their works as being the "supreme fiction," I'm not suggesting you're suggesting that either. But they are part of what I take to be a cultural conversation about certain preoccupations and they're compelling versions of this. I don't think Freud's better than Henry James, so to speak, and I don't think we need to rate them. There is an elaborate cultural conversation going on in which there are clearly discernible themes and preoccupations.

David James Fisher: Phillips is an anglicized name. It was changed from Pinchas-Levy when your grandparents emigrated from Russian Poland to Cardiff, Wales. We analysts know proper names are significant in the formation of the self. Are you predominantly Phillips or Pinchas-Levy?

Adam Phillips: Yes. [Laughter] The Pinchas-Levy thing I only knew about when I was considerably older. The story in the family was, and it sounds true, is that they arrived in Swansea, which is in Wales. They said Pinchas-Levy and were called Phillips because Phillips is a very common Welsh name. And that seems entirely plausible. Phillips seems to be anonymous to me. Pinchas-Levy seems excessively middle European. I'm struck, though, by the fact that my partner and my children want to change our name to Pinchas-Levy, but I don't. [Laughter]

David James Fisher: Why was your family so committed to being assimilated?

Adam Phillips: A lot of the British Jews of their generation really wanted to be British. It wasn't that they were denying being Jews, because certainly nobody I knew denied they were Jewish. They had tremendously powerful aspirations toward what in shorthand we call the Bloomsbury Group, let's say, a fantasy of cultured English upper-middle-classness.

	My father was also in the war and in the war he met a lot of very, very posh ruling-class people whom he clearly liked and I imagine aspired to be like. And there was a very, very powerful wish. It was a combination of not to stand out, not to stand out as vulgar – in other words an internalized anti-Semitism – but also a feeling in a family romance way that there was something wonderful about British culture. Now of course this was not a consideration of the Empire, racism, etc. It was a fantastically pastoral myth of England as a wonderfully civilized country, which of course actually colonized most of the world in the most appalling way. But of course, there was and is a myth about England as immensely civilized, which in some ways you could say it was, or could have been. But it very much appealed, partly because it felt like a real option. Jews who went to other countries didn't feel this in quite the same way. I don't know if this is true, but it seems to me to be true. Whereas in some ways it wasn't that there was no anti-Semitism in Britain, but it wasn't as virulent as say it was in France or Italy, so there was a kind of hospitableness in English culture. My parents, certainly, and the parents of my friends really responded to that.
David James Fisher:	Did you notice you used the word posh? I learned that word when I was in London. Did you hear him say the word *posh*?
Adam Phillips:	Do you use that word here?
David James Fisher:	No. It's a great word, though.
Adam Phillips:	It is a good word.
David James Fisher:	You have said your parents were left-wing and that politics were much discussed in your family. What specifically were their politics?
Adam Phillips:	My parents were socialists, anti-Tory, anti-royalist, and so people troubled by privilege, especially by the privilege they aspired to. If you lived in Wales in the time I was growing up, the news was dominated by the fate of miners and the trade unions. I was given Michael Foot's biography of Aneurin Bevan for my bar mitzvah; that more or less answers the question, at least for those who know who Bevan was. If you don't, and you are interested, you should look him up.
David James Fisher:	In the elegant book you wrote with Barbara Taylor, *On Kindness*, you explicitly link kindness and fellow feeling to the politics of social democracy. How politically engaged are you? Should analysts be more public about their

Adam Phillips: subjective, progressive political positions (or reactionary ones for that matter)? Is socialism as a form of government and social structure a logical and inevitable expectation of those immersed in the British independent group, a humane extension of the relational point of view?

Adam Phillips: I think psychoanalysis doesn't make sense as a refuge from politics. There are no refuges from the political, or from group life. We are always involved – in Crick's definition of politics – in "the conciliation of rival claims," both internally and externally. Psychoanalysis is a way of working at a more truthful sociability. If analysts are asked about their political positions, there is no reason they shouldn't disclose them, but they don't have to, and they don't have to only do that. The question is never "Am I doing psychoanalysis properly?" The question is "What kind of person do I want to be?" I do think you are right, though. The often tacit, or implicit, politics of the British independent group psychoanalysis is, literally and metaphorically, anti-imperialist, anti-colonial, that is, somewhere between socialism and a communism akin to the seventeenth-century anti-royalists like Winstanley. In order to understand the independent group, you need to know about the [English] Civil War, and you have to understand the word "commonwealth," which means understanding its history and its contemporary distortions.

David James Fisher: Has anti-Semitism been a factor in your personal or professional life?

Adam Phillips: No, not really. It's hard to tell in some way because I think part of the wish to assimilate is the wish not to experience anti-Semitism. I can remember having dinner with Harold Bloom and he said, "I couldn't bear being in London because the English are so anti-Semitic." I was amazed by that. And I believed him; it wasn't that I thought he was obviously wrong, but it hadn't been my experience. It had been the experience of people of my parents' generation much more than that of my generation. But I haven't experienced it in my life.

David James Fisher: Your family were secular Jews who did not deny their Jewish identity. You were bar mitzvahed. Being Jewish for you involves an awareness of the Jewish past and a shared sensibility or collective psychology with fellow Jews. Do you see yourself as a "non-Jewish Jew"? As described by Isaac Deutscher (1968), Leon Trotsky's biographer, non-Jewish Jews are committed to the betterment of the common good,

	to social justice, to thinking radical and revolutionary thoughts, and to critical thinking. Freud was a non-Jewish Jew. Are you?
Adam Phillips:	Probably, yeah, I think so. The thing for me is every so often I think being Jewish is the most interesting thing about myself for about ten minutes. [Laughter] And so I have patches when I read lots of Jewish history or I begin to think this is immensely important, but I have long swatches of time where it is of no interest to me at all. And so of course, like everybody else, I'm impressed by what we think we know about history. You know, we don't meet Hittites in Barcelona now, but we do meet Jews, but of course I admire lots of people who aren't Jews. So I, in a familiar Jewish way, I'm baffled by it, but I certainly feel much more Jewish than I do British, incomparably more, whatever that means.
David James Fisher:	You've written that you were inspired by the writings of Jewish American novelists, particularly Bellow, Mailer, and Roth. Besides the energy and vitality emanating from their writings, what else did their works evoke for you?
Adam Phillips:	I'm not sure there was a "besides." What I didn't like about them was the scale of the misogyny, and that is a strange, complicated thing here. I assume that psychoanalysis was invented to address everybody's terror of their own misogyny, and what strikes me about those writers is they're not terrified enough or *ostensibly* they're not terrified enough. But what I did like about them as an adolescent was the vigor and strength of the prejudicial intelligence and the willingness to be brash, gauche, pretentious, all that stuff. There is no British-Jewish culture. There's no great British-Jewish novel, for example. As an English Jew brought up with English literature, reading American literature was startling to me and it felt very, very much what I wished I'd grown up with, but of course it's a fantasy.
David James Fisher:	The music of Bob Dylan, Neil Young, and Joni Mitchell has been critically important in your life and to other members of your generation. You say their music helped you to imagine yourself. How did that happen? Was it the beginning of a self-analysis?
Adam Phillips:	Oh, no, no, no, I think the best thing that happened in my life culturally was the music that was parallel to my adolescence and then the poetry. It was a learning experience in which you weren't taught anything. But it was powerfully evocative in indiscernible ways such that when you heard

David James Fisher: those voices and heard that music, you really had a sense of possibility. And it wasn't defined possibilities. I didn't want to be one of those people nor do I think how fabulous it would be to be so rich and famous. It was much more to do with the way in which the music communicated something that was not analytic, that was not even thought of particularly, but it had a powerful sense of freedom about it, and of sexual energy and possibility.

David James Fisher: And emotionally?

Adam Phillips: And emotionally, yeah, all those things. But it was in the tones of voice.

David James Fisher: Kohut recommended that analysts listen to chamber music to sharpen their listening capacities. Are you into classical music?

Adam Phillips: I like classical music as well, yes. But I think the best way to learn how to listen is to read.

David James Fisher: In "Against Self-Criticism" (2015), you advocate forms of overinterpretation in understanding dreams, neurotic symptoms, jokes, lapses, and literature. You take positions also against the violence of interpretations that are simplistic, reductive, and authoritarian. Is your view of overinterpretation consistent with Freud's and Winnicott's approach to interpretation?

Adam Phillips: I think it is. In the sense that one of Freud's most interesting ideas is the idea of overdetermination and one of Winnicott's most interesting ideas is that the aim of the analysis is to facilitate a capacity for surprise. And both of these ideas are linked to the sense in which analysis, at least to me, is about being able to redescribe the patient's material from many aspects. The assumption being it has many aspects, that there couldn't possibly be a single authoritative interpretation, but there could be a multiplicity or a configuration or a kaleidoscope. There are lots of possible analogies of this. In other words, you're not looking to get it right. The other very interesting idea of Winnicott argued that it's not what the analyst says that matters. It's whether and how the patient can use it. Now this is a very, very different view of authority, as is indeed Freud's view of dreamwork. These are very different pictures of the human exchange, of sociability. And for me, the trouble with the word *overinterpretation* is it suggests too much interpretation, whereas what it means really is that you can't afford to allow yourself to be the emperor of one idea, to allow one interpretation that things have to be looked at from a multiplicity of points of view; otherwise they are impoverished.

David James Fisher: In his late paper "The Use of an Object," Winnicott argues that he interprets only to let patients know the limits of his understanding. Many analysts interpret to experience the narcissistic gratification of being clever or self-satisfied. Winnicott states that only the patient has answers and that analysts ought not to deprive the patient of the pleasures of creativity and the joys of self-understanding. Do you agree with Winnicott on this? If so, is this consistent with the strategy of overinterpretation, or is this another Phillips paradox we need to play with, not collapse into black-or-white categories, either/or thinking?

Adam Phillips: I think it's misleading to say that only the patient has the answers: (a) because it's not all about questions and answers and (b) because it seems to me anybody could have the answers. That is to say, either the patient or the analyst could say the useful thing. So I think there's a huge overstating of definitive interpretations. I can see what it is reactive to. It's reactive to authoritative Kleinian interpretation. But I still think that it doesn't matter. In the conversation that is psychoanalysis, ideally, either person can say a useful thing. It doesn't matter who it is. But of course, it would be very anti-Winnicottian to think that only the analyst could or would. That would be an absurdity. There's a kind of disingenuousness in Winnicott, an English version of Protestant modesty, which is to say, "I don't know anything. I'm very naïve. I'm curious. I'm sort of innocent," etc. Now some of it is wonderful, but some of it is ghastly, as in it's really arch and it's stagey. Winnicott very often wants to tell us how little talent he has, but that he's got one very big talent, which is a talent to elicit the talent of the patient. For me, I'm not saying this is true for Winnicott, but there's sometimes a disingenuous modesty problem in Winnicott's theorizing because the theorizing is actually extremely bold in many ways very, very ruthless and aggressive. It's almost as though Winnicott was sometimes frightened of his own aggression in the theorizing. He then backtracks.

David James Fisher: When I began analytic training in 1980, there was a consensus about three desired outcomes of a successful analysis. Namely, that the analysand would emerge with a firm capacity to be heterosexual, genital, and monogamous.

That consensus has faded considerably, except for monogamy, regarded by most analysts as a capacity reflecting a highly evolved, responsible, and above all mature personality. You call into question that sacred cow in your intriguing book *Monogamy* (1996). What does it mean to be an agnostic on monogamy? If one is agnostic about monogamy, does it mean that everything may be permitted in the erotic register?

Adam Phillips: No, what it means is you can't talk on other people's behalf, so there couldn't be a position on monogamy. People would have to decide for themselves and in their particular relationship. The book *Monogamy*, as I read it (and I'm obviously only one reader among many), is neither pro-nor anti-monogamy. The idea of the book is that people can think about it because it is a problem. Now there must be a reason why it's a problem. The analytic presumption that one could know beforehand the nature of the necessary or the good or the valuable relationship is the problem, not the solution.

David James Fisher: You're advocating not knowing, not knowing in advance.

Adam Phillips: Not knowing but also experimenting. There are experiments in living. You find out how you want to live with other people. Your life could be an experiment in sociability. There are plenty of people who will tell you how you should live, of course. Plenty of people will tell you that monogamy is wonderful, and plenty of people will tell you it's terrible. Well, you have to find your way through this. But it would be a shame to assume that anybody could know beforehand.

David James Fisher: Including analysts in the analytic community.

Adam Phillips: Especially analysts. [Laughter]

David James Fisher: In a series of aphorisms about the dialectic of masturbation and monogamy, you link the two to monotonous, repetitive, and uninventive stories. For you, how important is the role of storytelling, actually fantasizing, in the sexual life of an adolescent or adult?

Adam Phillips: I don't, in the book or outside the book, think of monogamy as linked essentially to masturbation. I think both can be inventive, so to speak. I think there is no sex without fantasy, and possibly no fantasy without sex. I value psychoanalysis because it is alert to just how defensive narrative is; there is a reason people love, or think they love, storytelling. Psychoanalysis frees us not to be overimpressed by coherence. Or by plausibility. Just as, in Khan and Stoller's formulation, "Pornography is the stealer of dreams," so I think psychoanalysis is useful because it shows us how much of sexual fantasy preempts, or kidnaps, or exploits sexuality. Fantasy is the formulation of unconscious desire, but with emphasis on "unconscious," not as yet known.

David James Fisher: In the beginning of life, the infant and mother form a monogamous relationship, at least from the point of view of the child. When the infant confronts separation and mourning from the mother, he experiences it as a mutilation. Then you add, "Growing up means becoming a phantom limb. Falling in love means acquiring one." Is dismemberment an illusion all that is possible with regard to the romantic couple?

Adam Phillips: I don't understand that quote from *Monogamy*, really.

David James Fisher: That's your quote.

Adam Phillips: I know. [Laughter] The point is that no one is going to get around the agonies of sexual jealousy, so no one should be minimizing the suffering involved in this, but also no one should minimize the difficulties of relationships. There are many ways in which the mother-child relationship is not the best model for all other relationships. Or maybe we have to find out whether it is. Because I think it's sleight of hand for me to say we begin monogamous, because we don't begin monogamous. We begin very dependent on our mother, or the person who looks after us. That isn't monogamy. We don't use the word as babies, nor do our mothers tend to talk to us as babies about our being monogamous. Things are being conflated here that don't go well together.

David James Fisher: You write in your preface to the reissued volume on Winnicott (Phillips, 2007) that he was one of the great psychoanalytic thinkers about the experience of sexuality. This is contrary to your own earlier views, and contrary to Robert Rodman's biographical view in *Winnicott: Life and Work* (2003), that sexuality and the role of the father are largely missing from Winnicott's perspective. What is your textual or contextual evidence for your claim of his "radical redescription of erotic possibility"?

Adam Phillips: Winnicott's theory of sexuality is coded in his theory of use of the object. This is a story about how people become sexually alive to each other. It's useful when reading Winnicott, any couple he talks about, to be able to see it as both as it often is, mother and child, but also as a heterosexual or homosexual adult couple. In other words, Winnicott is talking about lots of ways in which children relate, obviously,

	exchanging things with their mothers and vice versa. The risk is of desexualizing the theory, and by that I mean colluding with his desexualizing the theory.
David James Fisher:	Because the essay really is about destructiveness.
Adam Phillips:	Well ...
David James Fisher:	It's about the capacity of the mother and then the analyst to survive destructiveness, not retaliate, and not abandon the child.
Adam Phillips:	Yeah.
David James Fisher:	I don't see this as erotic.
Adam Phillips:	You may not, but my description of this would be that Winnicott is describing what it is for two people to, as passionately as they are able, engage with each other to test whether the other person can survive one's love and hate. This is, among other things, a story about erotic life, which is what kind of intensity can you bring into the relationship and what's the inhibition on the intensity.
David James Fisher:	You insist that Winnicott be currently perceived as a countercultural voice, not just a maverick psychoanalyst, in the small and isolated world of psychoanalysis. Why should we regard Winnicott as a writer who went beyond psychoanalysis and pediatrics? Does this description also apply to your own work?
Adam Phillips:	You can see this in terms of Winnicott's own theorizing because when Winnicott talks about the use of an object, he's talking about something being defined by the ways in which it can be experienced and in the best sense used. It's a clue also about how we should read Winnicott's writing. It should be read. Because the definition of a traumatic experience is that it's something beyond transformation. Well, any theory that you're unable to transform is akin to a trauma. It's something you can either comply with or not. Whereas the point of all the psychoanalytic stuff is that we make something of our own of it. We don't use it to abide by. We don't use it as a blueprint about what to say and when. We actually use it as something we can use, that is, transform. Transform means redescribe, reinterpret. So then everybody should, if they're interested in Winnicott, have their own Winnicott. But it shouldn't be about learning what Winnicott thinks and then as it were adhering to this clinically, because that is to miss the point. That's to comply.

I think good analysis always goes beyond psychoanalysis. After all, psychoanalysis is "about" what all the cultural artifacts we love and hate are "about."

So it has been a lot of work for psychoanalysts to make psychoanalytic writing quite so boring, quite so in-house. And we should wonder a little more about why they have been so keen to do this work. Psychoanalytic writing can be of value only if it is at least potentially of interest to people outside the profession. I assume this is why I have really only wanted to write for people outside the profession. I don't mind, of course, if psychoanalysts are interested in my work, but I do not think of it as addressed to them. It is addressed to anyone who may be interested, for whatever reason. I like it when psychoanalysis is used for something that is not psychoanalysis.

David James Fisher: As general editor of the new Penguin translations of Freud, you belong to the *chutzpah* school of publishing, given that you are not fluent in German, not a linguist or a Germanist. You state that you supervised the translations looking for readability, hoping to find different voices in Freud's writings, multiplying the Freuds available to us with an alternative to Strachey's *Standard Edition*. Why do you think we need these competing English translations of Freud?

Adam Phillips: I don't think we need them at all, but we might want them. When the topic of the new Freud translations came up, I was consulted, and I said all of the things I thought should be done and then they asked me to do it. One of the things I said – two of the things I said were, first of all, the translators should not be analysts. Preferably, people who have never read Freud, but people who have translated literary texts, so they'd bring something else to it. The other thing had to do with the idea that it was to find out who might be interested because it's an absurdity to have something called the *Standard Edition* any more than there could be a sort of standard interpretation. So Strachey and others had really egged it by calling it the *Standard Edition*. I thought it was useful to bear in mind that actually Freud was translated. And if you have a translation, you could have another translation. Does it sound different? Now the beauty of my not knowing German, from my point of view, was that I could read these texts comparatively, but not compare them with the original, and that's what I was interested in. When we did an event when these translations came out to the ICA in London, a woman got up, who was obviously German, and said, "You're so lucky because if you're German, you've only got one Freud." [Laughter] And that seemed to me a really interesting remark. We did these translations not with a view to replacing the *Standard Edition* or implicitly as a critique of it, but just simply to

	ask does it sound different? Is it different? Some of these translators found that Strachey was wrong in places. Well, that's kind of interesting. Strachey's really good, but there could be variety, and so anybody who's interested and curious can find out.
David James Fisher:	There's a brilliant essay on translating Freud that you included in the recent *In Writing* (2017), which I recommend that all of you read. It's an outstanding essay. Did Winnicott suffer from therapeutic zeal, from the fervor to cure? Was he grandiose about his ability to handle any case no matter how primitive the regression, no matter how pervasive the psychopathology, and how distressing and early the trauma?
Adam Phillips:	Jack Tizard, a pediatrician who worked with Winnicott, said in his obituary of Winnicott that it wasn't that he understood children but that the children understood him. I bet that was right. It sounds right from reading him. I think one of the things that's wonderful about Winnicott is he's very, very ambitious, and of course it's going to be called grandiose when it fails and wonderful when it succeeds. That's the risk you take. I like Winnicott's willingness to believe in people's potential for growth and change. And the Winnicott that writes, anyway, is doing his best to work out what it is realistic to think that somebody is capable of. Of course, no one could assess that, but you can make a more or less informed guess. He may have erred on the side of therapeutic zeal, but I think it's a better side of the line to err on. I didn't know him, but it sounds like he really had the capacity to allow people to be, and that in and of itself is an extraordinary thing.
David James Fisher:	Do you feel strongly about confidentiality between therapist and patient?
Adam Phillips:	I don't think people should speak of clinical work in public except in individual supervision.
David James Fisher:	Final question. There's a journal entry by Masud Khan written on December 21, 1968, after Winnicott had suffered a heart attack: "How wise DWW is, and yet how blind about himself. He cannot accept that anyone else can treat a case. This is a malignant bias of most analysts, an incapacity to believe he can be *blind, treat, damaged* by others. Hence his incapacity for gratitude! And yet his is the truest and most profound devotion to his patient and his self-questioning vis-á-vis them most incisive and austere. But as a man, he had not questioned his malice, envy, and

hate" (Rodman, 2003, p. 342). Do you agree with Khan's harsh and generous assessment of Winnicott the man and his approach to the therapeutic process?

Adam Phillips: Well, unlike Khan, of course, I didn't know Winnicott. It does strike me as rather harsh in many ways and rather, indeed, malicious and envious. But clearly there was something that lots of people picked up on Winnicott. Khan isn't the only person. Kleinian people had much more vicious accounts along those lines. We have got a lot from Winnicott's ambition. In other words, he experimented, he tried things out, and he left us this incredible body of work which if it happens to work for you is very, very inspiring. He was a very remarkable analyst and there aren't that many of them. I'd also just like to add that people don't know much about themselves. The idea that people are going to go around saying somebody doesn't know much about himself is absurd. We don't know very much about ourselves. It's not about self-knowledge; it's about something else, and I think it's a low blow on Khan's part.

David James Fisher: What's the something else?

Adam Phillips: I don't know. I could phrase it for you, but it's actually about unconscious communication. John Ashbery said, "The worse your art is, the easier it is to talk about." The better your psychoanalysis is, the harder it is to talk about. The scale of the authority of these people talking about psychoanalysis is astounding when you think what psychoanalysis is about. How could you know that much? [Laughter] How could anybody be an expert on the unconscious? It's absurd. So the idea there could be authoritative analysts is preposterous. Where did anyone get this belief from? The beauty of the thing is it undoes that. [Applause] You can only ever be a student of psychoanalysis and that's one of the great things about it.

Previously published in *The Journal of the American Psychoanalytic* Association, Vol. 66, no. 5, October 2018, pp, 913–940.

References

Deutscher, I. (1968). The Non-Jewish Jew. In T. Deutscher (Ed.), *The Non-Jewish Jew and Other Essays* (pp. 24–41). New York: Verso.
Hopkins, L. (2008). *False Self: The Life of Masud Khan.* New York: Other Press.
Phillips, A. (2007). *Winnicott.* London: Penguin.
Rodman, F. R. (2003). *Winnicott: Life and Work.* Cambridge, MA: Da Capo Press.

Chapter 5

Comments on James S. Grotstein's Dreambook

James S. Grotstein died in 2015 in Los Angeles at the age of 89. He was a leading psychoanalytic figure for decades, celebrated for his intellectual verve and versatility, wit, love of puns, theoretical reach, personal kindness toward his students, and generosity toward his colleagues. He was most recognized for his transmission and explication of the works of Klein and Bion. Although I was not in his intimate circle, we had friendly relations for 35 years. When I applied for analytic training at the Los Angeles Psychoanalytic Society and Institute in the late 1970s, he was a member of the Admissions Committee. When he introduced himself to me at the institute, he said "hi, I'm Jim Grotstein. I'm a Kleinian/Bionian." As a candidate, I attended his seminar on primitive mental states, focusing on the psychoanalytic treatment of borderline and psychotic patients, where we studied many of his writings on the subject. After graduation, I was personally supervised by him for several years, wanting to learn the cutting edge of Kleinian/Bionian technique he practiced.

After the publication of *Who Is the Dreamer Who Dreams the Dream? A Study of Psychic Presences* (Grotstein, 2000), I received a copy of the book in the mail with a personal inscription: "To Jimmy, With my eternal gratitude for your encouragement. Jim." When the Institute organized a Meet the Author evening to honor the publication of the book, he requested that I be the discussant. What follows is the unpublished discussion from that event, "Comments on James S. Grotstein's Dream Book." It can now serve as a memorial to Jim Grotstein.

Grotstein's orientation arguably reflects postmodernism's modest intellectual ambitions in its commitment to particularism and difference and in its opposition to totalizing concepts. He is postmodern in his appreciation of the limitations of understanding in the face of irreducible complexity, chaos, and the attempt to penetrate the realms of the unknown – those realms that are unthinkable and beyond the grasp of words. Regarding the elusive notion of unity, I think Grotstein straddles the pre-modernist, modernist, and postmodernist camps. He appears to believe that unity of the self is possible, at least for moments, but he is quite aware of the self's tendency to fragment, regress, and experience gaps.

Grotstein's version of postmodernism does not necessarily move in the direction of social constructivism or the extremes of a relativist position, despite his reliance on the authority of thinkers from mystical, theological, metaphysical, linguistic, and philosophical traditions. He is one of the exceptionally few medically trained analysts who have read deeply in the fields of phenomenological philosophy and critical theory and who maintains a living dialogue with the works of Bakhtin, Rene Girard, Heidegger, Kristeva, and Nietzsche. He is firmly immersed in the analytic discourse of the Kleinian and object relations school, where we meet many of the usual suspects, such as Klein, Fairbairn, Bion, Meltzer, and Winnicott, as well as a number of unusual suspects, such as Jung and Lacan. To Kleinian clarity, verging on dogma, he counterposes Bion, who introduces confusion, ambiguity, and the bizarre, reminding analysts never to be smug or complacent in thinking they really get things – they will be unprepared for surprise, for uncertainty, for shifts, for eruptions and disruptions; they will practice static psychoanalysis.

If he is a modernist/postmodernist he is grandly ambitious. He hopes to sketch a psychoanalytic theory that enters zones of the "beyond," that moves into the ineffable nature of subjectivity, beyond the realm of the natural into the domain where the analyst becomes attuned to infinity, mystery, and the transcendental. Ineffability is hard to hold on to conceptually, that dimension of human experience that is critically important but can't be expressed, described, or defined. Readers of the book will be required to approach these texts with a supplement of imagination that will be both taxing and rewarding. Actually, an alternative title for this book might be "The Psychoanalytic Imagination," reflecting Grotstein's poetic versatility and his theoretical dexterity, but also provoking the audience to tap into their own supplies of intellectual curiosity and emotional vitality, in order to enter his universe of discourse.

The key to the book is the specimen dream of the first chapter:

> The setting is a bleak piece of moorland in the Scottish Highlands, engulfed in a dense fog. A small portion of the fog slowly clears, and an angel appears surrealistically, asking, "Where is James Grotstein?" The voice is solemn and awesome, almost eerie. The fog slowly reenvelopes her form, as if she had never existed or spoken. Then, as if part of a prearranged pageant, the fog clears again; but now some distance away, on a higher promontory where a rocky crag appears from the cloud bank, another angel is revealed, who in response to the angel's question, answers: "He is aloft, contemplating the dosage of sorrow upon the Earth."

The volume may be read as Grotstein's continuous and discontinuous associations with this dream. If there is a royal road to the understanding of his writings, it is embedded in the lived experience of the dream. The reader must enter a state of reverie in reading this text, a state derived from patience, tolerance of uncertainty, and a willingness to be immersed in dread, confusion, fog, suffering, and darkness. Disorientation spatially and temporally will gradually yield orientation, a narrative solution, as well as new and fresh access to the unconscious. The unconscious can only be approximated after long and laborious labor and multiple plunges into the obscure.

If I were interpreting this evocative dream, I would investigate the narcissistic, reparative, and rescue fantasies that seem particularly transparent in the dream's manifest content. I would wonder how to connect suffering, grief, and deep pain to Grotstein's search for abundance, aliveness, and awakened imagination. I would wonder about the meanings of the predominance of female images in the dream, two angels and the fog twice referred to in the feminine. I would inquire into the associative meanings of "eerie," "awesome," "surreal," and "pageant." I would be curious about the underlying emotional vulnerability and helplessness of the situation. And finally, I would probe the meanings of why James Grotstein locates himself aloft (what distance or closeness is that precisely?) And finally, I would be puzzled about why he cannot find his own authentic voice, why his voice is displaced onto angels.

Grotstein's psychoanalytic methodology radically contrasts with Freud's approach to dreams, with its emphasis on wish and defense; nor does the former appear to be specifically interested in investigating the transference components of dreams, the various puzzles of self and others that frequently occur in the primary process. Nor does he think that various aspects of his self appear in the various objects presented in the dream. Grotstein asserts that his specimen dream is about the act of dreaming itself, including the components of beauty, spirituality, and otherworldliness – a dream ultimately about the mystery of the genesis of dreams. To decipher Grotstein's book, the reader must enter into the structure or the architecture of the dream. In order to find the self, there must be a necessary loss of self, and a temporary suspension of time, place, and causality.

There are several beautiful sentences in Freud's Dream Book that evoke the problematic in Grotstein's researches. Freud wrote:

> There is often a passage in even the most thoroughly interpreted dream which has to be left obscure; this is because we become aware during the work of interpretation that at that point there is a tangle of dream-thoughts, which cannot be unraveled and which moreover adds nothing to our knowledge of the content of the dream. This is the dream's navel, the spot where it reaches down into the unknown.
>
> (Freud, 1900, SE, p. 5)

Grotstein's explorations, in effect, begin where Freud's ends. His project promises a sustained and metaphoric contemplation of the navel, the region of the mind that is a tangle, that is obscure, contradictory, and that may exist beyond the contours of language and symbolization.

To be sure, there are dangers and risks in moving in this direction. Investigating the part of the soul that is mysterious, hidden, concealed, foreclosed, that is shrouded in darkness and terror, may result in an epistemology that is itself obscurantist. It may also lead to a prose style that is overly condensed, deliberately vague, or abstruse, which may risk alienating or discouraging Grostein's readers. At other times reading his prose can be exasperating. One wishes he would leave the angelic realm and come back down to earth. Some of his terms and special vocabulary seem ill chosen or downright pretentious. The term "autochthony" (self-creation) is not particularly felicitous, or particularly generative of emotional echoes or preconscious resonance. Simplicity of expression is not necessarily simple-mindedness. Let us follow Grotstein's tactical advice about approaching Bion: to decode Grotstein, we ought not to take him literally, thus allowing his paradoxes to reverberate. The ideal reader would open up his mind and heart to Grotstein's suggestive ideas, rather than press for concepts that are definitive, razor tight, or conclusive. He had been reanalyzed by Bion; he adopted some of Bion's oracular style of speech and writing, attempting to be as evocative and astonishing as possible, opening up the dialogue and relationship with the patient and the reader, and bracketing out the analyst's "memory and desire" to enter into the communicative realm only possible in the intimacy of the analytic dyad. The project was to keep the conversation fresh, open to surprise, orienting the analysand through its disorienting and perturbing method.

I do not believe that Grotstein's work ought to be categorized with those of occult writings or esoteric traditions, even though he cites approvingly many heretical sources, including those coming from mystical and religious authorities. He is not an advocate for religion or spiritual ideologies. The dual-track method makes him fully acceptable to the atheists and secularists in our ranks. In declaring himself a mystic and in urging the psychoanalyst to practice as a mystic, Grotstein opens himself up to the critique that his writings are incoherent and incomprehensible – a mystification, as it were.

For his part, Grotstein self-consciously states that he is searching for "something more." For him, mystical traditions embody spiritual quests to see clearly, to seek after truth, and to learn without disguise and deception, including self-deception. I think that he is extending the parameters of rationality without quite embracing the irrational. And his audience must remember the difficulty, if not impossibility, of writing about the unknown and perhaps unknowable. We must also be aware of the limits of science and of reliable, clinical knowledge in entering these realms.

It is arguable that much of the opposition to Grotstein's theoretical efforts derives from analysts whose thinking is linear, Cartesian, and prosaic; they tend to dismiss unscientific language as esoteric, idiosyncratic, and not capable of validation or falsification. To those positivistic fetishizers of data, Grotstein's book will never rise to the top of their best seller list. But it would be a mistake to dismiss Grotstein in this way. Most chapters contain clinical material, often highly condensed. Many analytic readers who read attentively will discover a clinical rigor in these passages, as well as a sensitivity to the analytic process. In a recently published tour de force, "Bion and Binocular Vision," in *The International Journal of Psychoanalysis* (October 2000), Albert Mason recalls Bion replying to audiences who were perplexed by his style of thinking: "They said that I am psychotic. Well, that may be so, but I am not insane!" The same could also be said of Grotstein's writing.

Theodore Adorno once remarked that "nothing is true in psychoanalysis except the exaggerations." Grotstein might refine that aphorism of excess by stating that "nothing is true in psychoanalysis except the paradoxes." Paradoxes are tenets that work contrary to received opinion. A paradox is a statement that is seemingly contradictory or opposed to common sense and yet it is often true. Paradoxes ought not to be collapsed into binary divisions. Grotstein's reliance on paradox does not stem exclusively from cleverness, irreverence, quickness of mind, or self-display. He has a love of contradictions and self-contradictory statements because he believes they most closely approximate the concept of the unconscious. Most significantly, Grostein's paradoxes are mental constructs that do not move toward resolution – they exist in a state of flux, dynamic tension, and conflict between opposites. His love of punning may also be linked to his devotion to paradox, to the ways that opposites are linked in the unconscious.

Love of paradox is linked to Grotstein's proposal of a dual-track method of thinking in terms of infant development; namely, that a differentiated infantile self exists as well as an undifferentiated self; that the infant is both separate and not separate from the mother and early internal objects. Dual-track thinking enables him to evade the dead ends of embracing either a one-person or two-person psychology. Grotstein insists that we need both. Similarly, he draws on the insights of those analysts working intra-psychically and those working intersubjectively as if both were part of a complementary series. Grotstein's openness to paradox also makes him receptive to the psychoanalytic Hegelians (Lacan, Ogden, Winnicott, and the intersubjective school), who posit a dialectical tension between the subject and the object, and who illuminate the infinite variations of Hegel's insights into the master/slave relationship, including the realm of transference/countertransference matrices, facilitating our grasp of unconscious shifts, reversals, and transformations.

Scattered throughout these essays are Grotstein's views of the unconscious, which are closely linked to his assignment of the goals of psychoanalysis. The unconscious, following Freud, is the unknown. After he developed the structural model, Freud referred to the id as a seething cauldron. For Grotstein, the unconscious is simultaneously part of the human, personal self and also part of the impersonal self, the "it." The unconscious can also be conceived as a computer, accounting, for instance, for the beauty, creativity, and architectural forms of dreams. Opposites exist in the unconscious without contradiction. The unconscious is timeless. Resorting to paradox, Grotstein posits that the unconscious is absolutely everything and absolutely nothing.

If the unconscious is a labyrinth, it is also a place where monsters, demons, and Satan reside – it is where the Minotaur is located. Relying on Kleinian concepts of the paranoid-schizoid position and its dialectic with the depressive position, Grotstein evokes the dread, terror, and enormous terrifying anxieties generated by persecutory retaliation and primitive guilt. He makes us aware of the punishing role of the superego – describing it vividly at one point as the "harassing, taunting, denigrating superego."

Grotstein analogizes the psychoanalytic process to a guided journey into the labyrinth of the unconscious. He has a pre-modernist view of this process as a heroic journey, a movement from passivity to activity, an exploration that requires risk, courage, and competence from both analysand and analyst. Both must demonstrate the will to think; both must dare to claim and reclaim their own thoughts and mind; both must tap into their reservoir of curiosity, emotional availability, and instincts toward knowledge and mastery.

Just as the infant is engaged in a mythical, titanic struggle between exercising his vigorous, enthusiastic, exploratory, and self-expressive activities, so too is the analysand in the analytic setting. Both infant and analysand will encounter massive opposition in the form of persecutory anxiety and depressive dread in striving to accomplish these heroic tasks; namely, to be courageous, to be competent, to be active as one's own agent, to face the world and themselves, to mourn and to seek reparative relationships, to move from envious resentments to gratitude and love, and to do battle with and overcome these internal demons.

The goals of psychoanalysis are not to make the unconscious conscious, not fortification of the ego, but rather to allow the individual to be in emotional touch with, to resonate with, his or her own sense of inner authenticity, what Grotstein calls "subjective I-ness." The analyst's curative function consists in taking the analysand into his preconscious where the pain is contained and where the massive anxiety is simultaneously disciplined through the use of sense, myth, passion, intuition, and knowledge, where it can be transformed into "learning from experience." Containing, following Bion, derives from the analyst's capacity to be sensitive, to employ reverie, intuition, and awareness in a healing manner; it requires a capacity to absorb projections, aggression, and hatred without falling apart and without retaliation.

Psychoanalysis is ultimately about a process of unconcealment – or revelation – of the true self. The task of analysis is to decode alienated subjectivities, to name exiled and fragmented parts of the self, and to repair a stunted subjectivity. Undergoing the therapeutic process of unconcealing, the true self will promote analysands to self-reflection and to make intimate, emotional contact with the authentic nature of their own beings. This process can be liberating for the individual.

Here Grotstein introduces his most original and fascinating concept, the idea of a transcendent position. Extending Bion's concept of O, the realm of serenity, of pure unaltered Being, the place in the soul where the absolute and the infinite intersect, O is yet another unknowable and indefinable register which can be radiant, dark, terrifying, chaotic, and unconcealed. O also relates to the areas of mental experience where the individual encounters brute reality, raw necessity, massive trauma, death, and other extreme phenomena that cannot be rendered into language. The transcendent position is a state of being at one with O. Without citing these sources, Grotstein's writing on the transcendent position reminded me of Freud's sense of the "oceanic feeling," which he described as eternal, limitless, and unbounded. It is similar to Romain Rolland's description of the oceanic as a feeling of contact, a vital and regenerative force, beyond the power of words, and constituting the deep structure of all religious feeling. It is somewhat reminiscent of Erikson's writings on basic trust between infant and mother. It also recalls Lacan's concept of The Real, a terrifying register of the mind unable to be transformed into language or symbolic forms.

The individual arrives at the transcendent position when he embraces without fear or hesitation the infinite creative possibilities of the id, the lofty, versatile, profound, and brilliant possibilities of the unconscious. For these moments, Grotstein sees the individual as overcoming his own defensive armor, his arsenal of trivial concerns, his guilt, shame, narcissism, and his obsessive need for certainty and closure. The transcendent position speaks to the possibilities of achieving aliveness, realness, and humanness in everyday life, not just in lofty or exceptional situations. Being in the transcendent position, finally, allows the individual to become emotionally connected to his inner world in a palpable, vivid state of abundance, of presence within oneself. It requires the work of unconcealment, the steady overcoming of masks and self-deceptions. The genuineness of the transcendent position fosters the vitalistic contemplation of the exquisiteness of life and the mystery and unknowability of certain moments. This concept may also illuminate Grotstein's specimen dream, where he is aloft and where angels speak to him.

The Kleinian-Bionian version of psychoanalysis has tended to emphasize the individual's primitive states, with its attention to the self's primitive defenses against greed, envy, hatred, destructiveness, and self-destructiveness. While Grotstein carries his own dosage of sorrow, grief, and traumatic loss, he reverberates to the despair and pain of others in the world. Grotstein engages in his scholarly projects as a fluent speaker of the various dialects of psychoanalysis. At his best, he is a proponent of synthesis and bridge building, not of polemic, exclusion, or vilification. At his worst, probably generated by his own anxieties and his desire to impress, intellectually and clinically, he can be dismissive and debunking of other analytic approaches. His volume is ultimately an act of love, a loving invitation to resonate with his ideas, as he demonstrates to us how to deepen our thoughts on the unknown and ineffable aspects of subjectivity and unconscious process. Grotstein presents himself as someone akin to a psychoanalytic Blake or William Butler Yeats. Not everyone will desire to enter into his esoteric vocabulary or baroque inner world. But even if his writings irritate, they will also inspire. Even if they violate some of the standard rules of analytic scholarship, Grotstein's work will certainly disrupt our preconceived notions, shatter our intellectual and clinical complacency, and unleash a desire in the reader to know more and to reach beyond. Entering into a dialogue with Grotstein may yield epiphany while hastening the internal process of revealing the inner worlds of our patients and ourselves.

Previously published in *Internationalpsychoanalysis.net*, March 2016.

References

Freud, S. (1900). *The Interpretation of Dreams. Standard Edition*. Vol. 5. London: Hogarth Press.
Grotstein, J. S. (2000). *Who Is the Dreamer Who Dreams the Dream? A Study of Psychic Presences*. Hillsdale, New Jersey: The Analytic Press.

Part II

The History of Psychoanalysis

Chapter 6

Sartre's Freud

Dimensions of Intersubjectivity in *The Freud Scenario*

Jean-Paul Sartre, the philosopher of freedom, was an unrepentant moviegoer, a lifelong enthusiast of the cinema. He went to the movies often, for the pure sensual enjoyment of viewing. Sartre experienced emotional freedom there, allowing his imagination to soar. From the time he was a boy in Paris, he and his mother were accomplices in escaping the oppressive, patriarchal tutelage of Sartre's grandfather, Charles Schweitzer, by going to see silent thrillers together. Movies entered Sartre's arsenal in struggling against the rigidities and pretensions of high culture. His charming autobiographical account of his visits in 1912 to the Panthéon Cinema on the rue Sufflot blends phenomenological descriptions of the sights, smells, and sensations of the movie theater with a democratic assertion of Sartre's parallel history with the cinema: "This new art was mine, just as it was everyone else's. We had the same mental age: I was seven and knew how to read; it was twelve and it did not know how to talk. People said that it was in its early stages, that it had to progress to make; I thought that we would grow up together. I have not forgotten our common childhood…." (Sartre, 1963).

Sartre and psychoanalysis

I view *The Freud Scenario* (Sartre, 1985) as Sartre's most important, most highly elaborated, and best realized text on psychoanalysis. It has been neglected for at least five reasons:

1 It was written as a screenplay and screenplays do not command the same level of serious attention as do philosophical treatises, essays, novels, biographies, plays, and cultural criticism.
2 The text was unfinished (as were a number of Sartre's most significant writings).
3 It has been unfairly and inaccurately equated with John Huston's film, *Freud*.
4 Sartre himself repudiated the work in his lifetime, as did Simone de Beauvoir after his death.

Major commentators on Sartre's relationship to psychoanalysis have failed to consider this work (Izenberg, 1976) or have minimized its significance, including one of Sartre's foremost English translators and critics (Barnes, 1989). The author of a recent book, *Sartre and Psychoanalysis*, provides no sustained analysis of the text, arguing that Sartre remained opposed to Freudian metapsychology before, during, and after his writing of *The Freud Scenario* (Cannon, 1991). Several scholars have perceived the text's brilliance as a piece of dramatic writing, but have failed to provide a detailed interpretation of its thematic structure (Koch, 1991; Collins, 1980).

Sartre first encountered psychoanalytic theory as a schoolboy in a French lycée in the 1920s. His fascination with it persisted until the 1970s, as can be seen in his final work, the multiple volumes of his biography of Gustave Flaubert, *The Family Idiot*. During this 50-year period, Sartre's ambivalence toward psychoanalysis was marked. Initially, he was attracted to the phenomenological possibilities of the psychoanalytic method, its capacity to describe and illuminate aspects of an individual's fantasy and emotional life. Later, in 1957, he spoke of psychoanalysis as "the one privileged mediation" in elucidating children's lives and family relationships inside a given society (Hayman, 1987). Yet a number of issues distanced him from psychoanalytic theory and technique, first and foremost Sigmund Freud's conception of the unconscious. The idea that consciousness was split through the psychical mechanisms of repression and censorship was unacceptable to Sartre. He believed that the Freudian unconscious served to rationalize and create alibis for bad faith, one of the central tenets of his own philosophy as developed in *Being and Nothingness* (1943) (Sartre, 1963).

Sartre thought that Freud mistakenly biologized meaning by accounting for it ultimately in neurophysiological and evolutionary terms, whereas for Sartre meaning was an expansive social project involving the creation of value and significance in the individual's life. He also objected to Freud's attempt to reduce human behavior to environmental and biological determinism, that is, to psychosexual urges and unconscious striving. Such a view, Sartre contended, violated the possibilities for freedom, choice, intentionality, responsibility, and good faith, despite the limitations of each individual's historical situation. Along the same lines, Sartre refused psychoanalytic nosology. Instead of categorizing personalities into diagnostic clusters and thereby reifying them, Sartre emphasized the individual's choice, which, according to his existential philosophy, was the fundamental project of being and becoming.

Sartre also strongly opposed the authoritarian techniques that he associated with classical psychoanalysis where the analyst became the privileged subject while the analysand was relegated to the position of the object. Sartre worked toward a more reciprocal, egalitarian model for what he called existential psychoanalysis. Finally, Sartre objected to psychoanalytic methodology. He viewed Freudian psychoanalysis as regressive and thought that there was something infantilizing about the analytic situation itself. Sartre wished analysis to be progressive as well as regressive, to have a synthetic as well as an analytic function, and to reach out to the future as much as it delved into the past (Sartre, (1956); Hanly, (1979); Soll, (1981); Walker & Waldman, (1990).

At the very least, Sartre's drafts of his script for Huston's film, written between 1958 and 1960, revised his earlier repudiation of Freud (since the 1940s) and orthodox psychoanalysis, a critique that had been grounded in superficial readings of selected writings and was excessively violent because of Sartre's hyperbolic need to polemicize against competing theories. Sartre demonstrated that he understood and embraced the concept of the dynamic unconscious, specifically its power and efficacy in the analysis of defensive operations, transferential and countertransference distortions, and the exploitation of subjective meanings in the emotional life of the individual, including the analyst. Likewise, he no longer rejected Freud's theory of psychic determinism because he now saw how it could be incorporated into a framework in which freedom and necessity were also operative concepts. He even revised his opposition to Freud's language, no longer dismissing it as the antiquated residue of nineteenth-century biology and psychiatry. Sartre came to appreciate how Freud had broken with these discourses, inventing a new language for psychology and a new discipline of systematic inquiry at the interface of the mind and body as well as between two subjectivities.

As Sartre immersed himself in research on Freud's topographical model, in which the key conflict is between the unconscious and the conscious, he reversed his dismissal of psychoanalytic metapsychology. The way in which Freud discovered and practiced his theory neither depersonalized nor reified his patients, and Freud did not assume the doctor's social, moral, psychological, or intellectual superiority over the patient. The Freud that Sartre depicts in his screenplay changes as he grows older; the mature Freud does not impose his values or theories on his patients. He does not regard his patients as passive objects to be classified, observed, disciplined, and cured, nor does he practice his craft according to strict scientific rules in an atmosphere of abstinence and silence but rather as a joint, open-ended undertaking in which both analyst and analysand have clear responsibilities and commitments.

In short, Sartre's *The Freud Scenario* (Sartre, 1985) was the decisive moment in his fifty-year history of ambivalence toward psychoanalysis. For a brief conjuncture, and in brilliantly executed fictional form (although paradoxically in a failed text that Sartre would later discard), the otherness of psychoanalysis became less alien, less remote, and less an object of contempt. It was a moment in which the existential-Marxist Sartre gave way to a Freudian Sartre, a Sartre who temporarily became the intellectual and affective son of Freud. Sartre was notorious for thinking outside the boundaries of conventional wisdom and searching the limits of language. In his best writings, he had an empathic ability to comprehend others who had a different ethnic, sexual, intellectual, and vocational formation from his own. He wrote on the Jewish question as a non-Jew (Sartre, 1948), on homosexuality as a non-homosexual (Sartre, 1963), and on psychoanalysis as neither an analyst nor analysand – a typical pattern, then, of Sartre's capacity to think against himself about subjects beyond his lived cultural or emotional experience.

In composing a fictional biography of Freud, I believe that Sartre was pursuing his own self-analysis and writing part of his own autobiography. Perhaps his great sense of affinity with Freud derived from their joint capacity to fight intellectual and moral battles and oppose consensus thinking while promoting an honest, self-reflexive discourse. The existential Sartre had placed bad faith at the center of his project of demystification; the individual was enjoined to be suspicious of what others showed of themselves, to be aware of the tricks of consciousness and the human capacity for duplicity. The Freudian Sartre became acutely aware of the deceptions as well as self-deceptions derived from unconscious conflicts, the multiple distortions of superego and ego ideal pathology which resulted in massive unconscious guilt and shame for the individual. These distortions disrupted what we now call the intersubjective bond, often resulting in violence to one or both individuals involved.

Sartre and Huston

Sartre's screenplay was commissioned by John Huston for $25,000 in 1957. Huston asked for a script about the heroic period of Freud's seminal discoveries, which Sartre wrote in three installments between 1958 and 1960. It was to be an "intellectual suspense story," in Huston's words (Huston, 1980); he admired Sartre's theatrical skills: in fact, he had produced No *Exit* on Broadway in 1946. According to de Beauvoir, Sartre accepted the assignment strictly for money, and she dismissed the results as insignificant (Barnes, "Sartre's Scenario for Freud"). In an interview in 1969 with the editors of *New Left Review*, Sartre historicized his "repugnance for psychoanalysis," while describing that he broke with Huston over the project "precisely because Huston did not understand what the unconscious was. That was the whole problem. He wanted to suppress it, to replace it with the pre-conscious. He did not want the unconscious at any price." Sartre held that his immersion in the French Cartesian tradition had formerly led him to be "deeply shocked by the idea of the unconscious." Though still reproaching psychoanalysis for being a "soft" theory with a syncretistic rather than a dialectical logic, though still opposed to the mechanistic, biological, and deterministic features of analytic thought, Sartre found himself "completely in agreement with the *facts* of disguise and repression, as facts." He also claimed to be intellectually astonished by Freud's mind: in reading *The Psychopathology of Everyday Life* "your breath is simply taken away" (Sartre, 1969).

In 1975 Sartre disavowed his work on *The Freud Scenario* in the following terms: "There was already something comical about the project, which was that I was being asked to write about Freud, the great master of the unconscious, after I had spent my whole life saying that the unconscious does not exist" (Sartre, 1977). In a second interview that year, Sartre repeated his opposition to the theory of the unconscious and voiced his bitterness toward Huston: "Around 1958, John Huston sounded me out on doing a film about Freud. He picked the wrong person, because one shouldn't choose someone who doesn't believe in the unconscious to do a film to the glory of Freud .... I wrote a complete script. In order to do it, I not only re-read Freud's books, but also consulted commentaries, criticism, and so forth. At that point, I had acquired an average, satisfactory knowledge of Freud. But the film was never shot according to my script, and I broke off with Huston" (Schilpp, 1981).

Sartre needed the money but, beyond that, he was intellectually and emotionally intrigued by the project. He accepted the invitation, plunging into a serious reading of early texts by Freud, including *Studies on Hysteria*, the case history of Dora, and *The Interpretation of Dreams* (Pontalis, 1985). He studied the French translation of the first volume of Ernest Jones's biography of Freud and commissioned a translation of the two subsequent volumes. He had access to Freud's relationship with Wilhelm Fleiss through *The Origins of Psychoanalysis* (Roudinesco, 1990; Schilpp, 1981), a collection of letters between the two men that detailed the process of Freud's discovery of early childhood psychosexual development and bisexuality, his self-analysis, and his insights into the universal aspects of her Oedipus complex. He also read critical commentary on Freud and the psychoanalytic movement.

Sartre explained his intentions as a screenwriter in an interview with Kenneth Tynan in 1961:

> What we tried to do – and this was what interested Huston especially – was to show Freud, not when his theories had made him famous, but at a time, around the age of thirty, when he was utterly wrong; when his ideas had led him into hopeless error .... That, for me is the most enthralling time in the life of a great discoverer – when he seems muddled and lost, but has the genius to collect himself and put everything in order. Of course it is difficult to explain this development to an audience ignorant of Freud. In order to arrive at the right ideas, one must start by explaining the wrong ones, and that is a long process: hence the seven hour scenario.

The other problem was that Freud, like the majority of scientists, was a good husband and father who seems to never have deceived his wife, and even to have been a virgin before he was married .... In short, his private life was not very cinematic. We therefore had to blend the internal and external elements of Freud's drama: to show how he learned from his patients about himself (Sartre, 1976).

Three versions of the project were written, which were later published as *The Freud Scenario* (Sartre, 1985): a 95-page typewritten synopsis (1958), a long first draft (1959) which could easily have resulted in a film over five hours long, and an even lengthier second version (1959–1960) that came to some 800 typed pages. Between the first and second drafts, Huston and Sartre agreed to work at Huston's home in St. Clerans, Ireland. Together for ten days, the two strong-willed, intransigent men developed a fierce mutual hostility. Everything collided: culture, sensibility, and character. Sartre saw Huston as a controlling Hollywood director, affluent, narcissistic, shallow, anti-intellectual, and self-deceived, while to Huston, Sartre was a bohemian Parisian intellectual, megalomaniacal, a writing and speaking machine, seemingly blind to external beauty, and oblivious to the practical necessities of the medium of film. This was a creative collaboration that was doomed to failure.

Here is Sartre to de Beauvoir on Huston: "The man has emigrated. I don't know where. He's not even sad: he's *empty*, except in moments of childish vanity, when he puts on a red dinner jacket or rides a horse (not very well) or counts his paintings or tells his workmen what to do. Impossible to hold his attention for five minutes: he can no longer work, he runs away from thinking" (Sartre, 1993). In return, here is Huston on Sartre: "a little barrel of a man and as ugly as a human can be. His face was both bloated and pitted, his teeth were yellowed and he was wall-eyed" (Huston, 1980). Sartre reported again to de Beauvoir about his "boss": "Speaking of his 'unconscious,' concerning Freud, [Huston says], 'In mine, there is nothing.' And the tone indicates the sense, *no longer* anything, even the old unavowed desires. A gross lacuna" (Sartre, 1993). And again, listen to Huston on the impossibility of working in collaboration with Sartre: "I've never worked with anyone so obstinate and categorical. Impossible to have a conversation with him. Impossible to interrupt him. You'd wait for him to catch his breath but he wouldn't. The words came out in an absolute torrent" (Huston, 1980).

Finally, Huston decided to remove Sartre from the project by bringing in another writer, justifying his decision based on pragmatic considerations. Years later, Sartre's memory still evoked repugnance in him:

> A filmmaker takes a risk when he decides to use someone like Sartre in the sense that filmmakers are still looked upon as being despoilers of intellectual works. You decide to get, possibly, the man who is best suited to do the work. He then proves unsuitable because he really had no idea of what the film medium actually requires. You have to then either use someone else, or cut down what that person has done for you, and then you run the risk of being criticized for having ruined what was originally given to you. I thought Sartre would be ideal for it. There's a little smell of Sulphur about everything Sartre does...
> (Pratley, 1977)

The only area of agreement between the two involved an inspired casting decision. Sartre wanted to have Marilyn Monroe play the lead role of Cecily Kortner, a woman who suffers from hysterical symptoms (Huston, 1980) (Cecily was a composite character drawn from Josef Breuer and Freud's *Studies on Hysteria* and Freud's case history of Dora). This was a potentially brilliant device to exploit and comment critically on the Hollywood star system in view of Monroe's status as a celebrity actress and patient. But Monroe did not play the part. In all probability, it was psychoanalytic politics that prevented her from doing so. Anna Freud, in London, let it be known that she strongly objected to the idea of a Hollywood film about her father's life and work, arguing that it would trivialize his ideas and his cause. She evidently used her influence on Monroe's psychoanalyst in Los Angeles, Ralph Greenson, to dissuade Monroe from accepting the role (Huston, 1980; Farber and Green, 1993).

With the personal rift between director and writer deepening as the length of the script increased, Huston made known his wishes to replace Sartre as the principal writer. Wolfgang Reinhardt, Huston's producer and the son of Max Reinhardt, greatly admired Sartre's philosophy and thought his original treatment was good;

he sided with Sartre against Huston (Huston, 1980). In the end, it was Sartre who decided to leave Huston. As a final gesture of his contempt for the director, Sartre removed his name from the script and stipulated that it should not appear in the credits when the movie was released. In fact, Sartre thought Huston lacked intellectual and artistic integrity: "It was not because of the cuts that I removed my signature – I knew perfectly well that cuts would have to be made – but because of the way in which they were made. It's an honest piece of work. Very honest. But it's not worthwhile for an intellectual to take responsibility for questionable ideas" (Sartre, 1976).

Although the final screenplay was a hybrid creation (Huston and Reinhardt, 1962; Freud, Typescript) – Charles Kaufman and Wolfgang Reinhardt collaborated with Huston – Huston claimed that "much of what Sartre had done was in our version – in fact, it was the backbone of it. In some scenes his dialogue was left intact" (Huston, 1980). Huston's *Freud* starring Montgomery Clift in the title role and Susannah York as Cecily was released in 1962. While it was critically acclaimed, it was a commercial flop. *The Freud Scenario* was published four years after Sartre's death by Gallimard in 1984 as part of French psychoanalyst J.-B. Pontalis's prestigious series "Knowledge of the Unconscious." It contained Sartre's synopsis, both versions of his screenplay, and an introduction by Pontalis. An English translation appeared in Sartre, 1985.

In my view, Sartre's Freud scenario is a major event in French intellectual history as well as in the evolution of Sartre's thought, marking one master thinker's encounter with another. I shall not focus on Sartre's theory of the cinema (Polan, 1987) and his other writings on movie making or psychoanalytic issues related to Huston's film (Gabbard and Gabbard, 1987; Walker & Waldman, 1990). Rather, I will speak to three overlapping themes: (1) Sartre's depiction of the dialectic of anti-Semite and Jew in turn-of-the-century Vienna; (2) Sartre's dramatization of how Freud's clinical work with patients coincided with and provoked his self-analysis, which yielded significant personal transformations; and (3) Sartre's understanding of how Freud's struggles with father surrogates became linked to his intersubjective grasp of the father–son conflict.

The dialectic of anti-Semite and Jews in turn-of-the-century Vienna

When interviewed about his script on Freud, Sartre claimed he had introduced a social and political dimension into it by emphasizing the prevalence of anti-Jewish opinions in Central Europe at the turn of the century: "There is one great problem that the analysts tend to sidetrack: Viennese anti-Semitism. It seems to me that Freud was profoundly aggressive, and that his aggressions were determined by the anti-Semitism from which his family suffered. He was a child who felt things very deeply, and probably immediately" (Sartre, 1976).

Viennese anti-Semitism saturates the three versions of Sartre's screenplay. It was not a theme emphasized in Jones's biography nor in the psychoanalytic literature on Freud through the late 1950s (Jones, 1953, 1959; Kris 1954), and it was dropped from Huston's movie. In a scene that takes place in August 1886, Freud, then thirty years old, is walking with his fiancée, Martha, on the Ringstrasse. They pass a street vendor hawking anti-Semitic tracts and reciting anti-Jewish slogans to a crowd of passersby. Freud reacts spontaneously to this blatant display: seizing one of the pamphlets and tearing it to shreds, he utters a single word: "Imbecile!" (Sartre, *The Freud Scenario* (Sartre, 1985) [Hereafter *FS*]).

Later, in a scene before the Vienna Medical Society in October 1886, Freud encounters the anti-Semitism of the "respectable" middle classes, represented by this group of physicians. Freud makes a speech summarizing Jean-Martin Charcot's research on hysteria, including male hysteria and the possibility of hypnotism as a mode of treatment, which he had learned during his recent five-month stay in Paris. Professor Theodor Meynert takes the lead in condemning Freud's lecture sarcastically, without rational argument. When Freud leaves the amphitheater, several doctors in the audience allege that Freud's arrogance before his elders seems like a Jewish trait and that his studies in Paris with Charcot, who had been scientifically discredited, reflect Freud's Jewish cosmopolitanism and his lack of national roots in Austria. A dejected Freud is convinced that the theories he presented have been resisted because he is Jewish.

In another address before the same medical society ten years later, after the pathbreaking publication of *Studies on Hysteria* with Breuer, Freud presents his theoretical paper on the sexual origin of neuroses, a paper summarizing his views on the traumatic effects of the seduction of children by adults. Breuer is in the audience but refuses to endorse Freud's positions in public. He urges his younger colleague to be cautious, reminding him that these conservative male doctors will object violently to the insinuation that fathers have sexually molested their daughters. Freud delivers his address in a dignified fashion. His audience reacts with howls, shouts, whistles, and stamping feet. Sartre indicates that no one in the audience is below forty years of age. In such a context, dialogue is impossible. Freud is somber, hard, and disillusioned. He states ironically: "I thank my colleagues for their kind attention: not for one moment have they failed to show the calm and objectivity appropriate to true men of science" (*FS*, p. 320). As Freud exits from the meeting hall, the doctors shout: "Dirty Jew! Dirty Jew! Filthy Yid! Back to the ghetto! Back to the ghetto!" (*FS*, p. 321).

In a telling scene with Cecily Kortner, Sartre's Freud confronts the subtle yet insidious anti-Semitism of the wealthy middle classes, a Christian anti-Semitism which hypocritically distinguishes between "good" and "bad" Jews. The "good" ones have attempted to assimilate. They have money, manners, and patriotic opinions; in other words, they appear to be bourgeois. As a young doctor attempting to escape poverty and driven by personal ambition, Freud is shown to be intensely self-conscious about his impoverished social status. He even reproaches himself about his "worn and slightly outmoded" clothing (*FS*, p. 394). Freud's consciousness of himself as a poor Jew in this context transforms him into a social reformer.

"By force of circumstance," as Sartre puts it, he becomes "a spokesman for all poor people" (*FS*, p. 395).

In the scenario, Freud articulates his despair about his intellectual and moral isolation because of Viennese anti-Semitism, a racism that merges with parochialism, ignorance, and a pervasive mean-spiritedness. His inability to leave the city means that he will have to conduct his research alone, in radical opposition to the cultural mainstream, which, in his eyes, is morally reprehensible and scientifically bankrupt. "Do you like Vienna?" Freud says: "I hate it. Petty People! Petty lives! Petty riffraff! And if you count the tourists, more anti-Semites than there are inhabitants" (*FS*, p. 232). In the second version of Sartre's scenario, Freud voices his opposition to Viennese anti-Semitism with "an expression of passionate fury." He not only hates the anti-Semites who hate him, but he has arrived at a pragmatic, unsentimental assessment of the dangers of such racial degradation: "In the old days, they drove our family out of Germany. During my childhood, they drove us out of Moravia. Tomorrow, they may drive us out of Vienna" (*FS*, p. 399).

Sartre's Freud has a penetrating gaze devoid of self-deception. He accepts his Jewishness in the face of the Viennese contempt for the Jewish minority, which resulted in "quarantining" Jews, giving them the status of lepers, even at the university. This reality wounded the young Freud, who had academic ambitions. Freud's good faith solution, to use Sartre's term, pivots on cultural insight and self-understanding: he will confront his situation as a despised other by neither retreating nor assimilating (Sartre depicts Breuer opting for assimilation).

Instead, Freud rejects the domination of the gentile majority, refusing to be objectified and stigmatized as a Jew. With anger, he tells Breuer: "I won't be a good Jew, and honorary *goy*" (*FS*, p. 401). Neither submissive nor passive, Freud will rechannel his aggression; he will take revenge on the gentile world by developing his intellectual and emotional faculties to their fullest. He chooses to pursue his scientific research alone and to push his theoretical hypotheses to their limits. Being Jewish in an anti-Semitic context fuels his passion for originality, nonconformity, and boldness of thought; "To be like everybody else: sometimes that's my dream. Ruled out! Everybody else – that means the *goyim*. If we aren't the best at everything, they'll always say we're the worst. Do you know that a Jew is condemned to genius? Seeing that I'm damned, I'll make them afraid. I'll avenge myself, I'll avenge all our people. My ancestors have bequeathed to me all the passion they used to put into defending their Temple" (*FS*, p. 401).

The post-Holocaust Sartre had lectured to his Parisian audience in 1945 that man was existentially condemned to be free (Sartre, 1947). The psychoanalytic Sartre of *The Freud Scenario* postulated that the secular, atheistic, Jewish Freud was condemned to be extraordinary, a genius in the midst of a reifying and potentially murderous anti-Semitic population. Freud's ambition to be the "best" was catalyzed in part by his personal need to counter and transcend the anti-Semitic stereotypes and racial practices that pervaded turn-of-the-century Vienna, including the attitudes of many Jews toward themselves. Sartre's Freud will learn how to defend himself with a powerful and increasingly disciplined rage. He will struggle and take responsibility for himself as a Jew, physician, father, and theorist, and he will forge his own destiny with the invention of psychoanalysis (Sartre 1947).

Freud and his patients

The Freud Scenario depicts how Freud's interactions with patients progressed toward a reversal of the authoritarian practices of nineteenth-century European medicine as well as the reifying concepts of positivistic science. This movement, nothing less than a paradigm shift, required a bond of reciprocity between Freud and his patients, grounded in the analyst's fundamental respect for their suffering and aspirations. Freud came to believe that his patients' internal psychological conflicts would not be overcome unless he was simultaneously engaged in a parallel self-analysis. We see Freud gradually rejecting the notion of the doctor's superiority over patients; rather, he learns how to heal without depersonalizing or objectifying them, no matter how severe their symptomatology is. Rather than regard them as pathological others who were to be observed, classified, manipulated, and cured, Freud learned to approach patients without condescension in an environment of mutual collaboration, trust, and dialogue. Just as analysts should not view patients as clinical specimens, they should also avoid imposing their own narratives (as we would say today), values, or research projects onto their therapeutic work. The psychoanalyst was explicitly enjoined to interact with the patient in a compassionate, humane, and attentive mode designed to maximize introspective dialogue.

Sartre came to realize that the psychoanalytic method was intrinsically intersubjective; it was predicated on a voluntary and joint understanding by two free subjects, each speaking to the other in an unfettered, increasingly authentic (according to Sartre's existentialist terminology) dialogue, each with mutual responsibilities. "The subject of the scenario is really: a man sets about knowing others because he sees this as the only way of getting to know himself; he realizes he must carry out his research upon others and upon himself simultaneously. We know ourselves through others, we know others through ourselves" (*FS*, p. 505).

According to the first version of Sartre's scenario, the film begins in a Viennese hospital ward in September 1885. Freud's teacher, Dr. Meynert, in the course of his rounds, stops at the bed of a blind female patient and lectures coldly and dogmatically to his younger colleagues, treating the patient in an accusatory, perfunctory manner. Meynert calls hysteria "a supposed illness." He describes hysterics as liars, actresses, and, most egregiously of all, patients who waste doctors' valuable time (*FS*, pp. 5, 7, 9, 11). Our first view of Freud at age twenty-nine reveals a conflicted individual; he believes in the efficacy of empirical science and reason, yet he is baffled by "forces within us" which cannot be explained by physiological factors. He feels compelled to solve these riddles by throwing light on the hidden forces in himself (*FS*, pp. 18, 20, 21). As depicted by Sartre, Freud's earliest view of psychopathology blurs the line between himself and his patients, between the apparently normal and the pathological. Studying sickness also illuminates the behavior and internal forces at work in normal men and women; sickness only "underlines and intensifies" certain characteristics of the healthy (*FS*, p. 509).

As he intuited the possibilities of constructing a depth psychology, Sartre's Freud developed the concepts of transference and resistance which became central to the emerging psychoanalytic clinical method. Freud at first resisted his own observations about the doctor/patient dyad. He was uneasy when he saw that Dr. Breuer's female patients found Breuer exceedingly attractive. But after one of Freud's own female patients embraced him, he began to hypothesize that psychical conflict caused by sexual desires might be at the root of neurotic personality disorders (*FS*, p. 520). Through his exploration of his transference toward his patients and their transference toward him, Freud began his investigations into the dynamics of amorous attachments, concentrating on "forbidden and impossible feelings being entertained for someone else" (*FS*, p. 524).

As a clinician, Sartre's Freud maintains the stance of an intrepid researcher and committed philosopher who wants to find out the darkest, unembellished truth. To this end, he repudiates hypnotism and embraces the method of free association. The talking cure emerges as Freud gradually subdues his anxieties and zeal in order to gain his patients' trust, as he learns to listen and immerses himself in his patients' words, their manner of speaking, and the inner world they reveal. After repeated mistakes, he realizes that working with patients is as much an affective process as it is an intellectual one. It is Freud's intellectual curiosity and his desire to express the subjective dimensions of truth that impel him to contest the authority of Meynert, thereby calling into question the prevailing medical and scientific practices of his day (*FS*, p. 85).

In scenes portraying Freud's work with Karl von Schroeh, a fictionalized forty-year-old obsessional neurotic with phobic symptomatology, we glimpse the pre-psychoanalytic Freud struggling with himself to develop a viable way of interacting with and learning from his patients. Sartre depicts a deeply conflicted Freud. When he feels at ease, he projects a natural authority, kindness, and sensitivity in the rapport he builds with his patients. He replies to their concerns with sincere empathy for their pain and distress. He is able to listen to them and communicate with them effectively.

However, when Freud does not understand what he hears – for example, when themes of parricide and the fear of castration surface in the analysis of a young man – he becomes anxious and sometimes repulsed. The patient's terror becomes his own. Freud's resistance is manifested in defensiveness or evasiveness; he is tempted to flee from his patient or to respond aggressively. Disoriented by his own unanalyzed anxieties and guilt feelings, Freud commands his patient not to think such thoughts. He abruptly calls off a session. He becomes hostile when he looks at his patient and becomes distressed, almost "demented," by the "idiotic and disgusting things" he has been told (*FS*, pp. 91, 97, 98, 100, 105). With another patient, the adolescent hysteric Dora, Sartre portrays an intrusive and judgmental Freud, reacting harshly and counter therapeutically when Dora tells him she is reading Flaubert's *Madame Bovary*. A frowning, interdictory Freud asserts that this novel is "disgusting" (*FS*, p. 110).

Sartre shows that in devising a coherent method to arrive at deep truths about his patients, Freud has to discipline himself in order to respond to their words, fantasies, and emotions. Otherwise, his patients will not confide in him (*FS*, p. 131). Freud observes that the physician–patient relationship is like that of a romantic couple, marked by shifts in power relations and saturated with desire, anxieties, guilt, and fantasies, including the analyst's. Sartre's Freud learns to respect the various dimensions of the transference only when he moves toward accepting and mastering his own powerful and sometimes primitive transference to his patients, "the strange and profound bond between them [Breuer and Cecily], the intimacy between them" (*FS*, p. 147).

The analyst's responsibility, then, is to work with the transference rather than abuse transferential relationships with patients or retreat from them, which would be irresponsible and constitute a fundamental violation of what Freud would later define as analytic method (*FS*, p. 161). Sartre's Freud discovers that the psychoanalytic method involves understanding and undoing defensive processes to allow the truth to unfold, no matter where it may lead. Interpreting resistance permits the patient a way of comprehending and resolving his or her internal struggles, particularly those that involve transference (*FS*, p. 167).

In an important scene depicting Freud's deepening rapport with Karl, Sartre suggests the psychic misery that links patients and doctors. Freud grasps the possibility of overcoming his scientific detachment. He renounces posturing as a cunning detective searching for clues from an unwitting suspect. On the contrary, he learns to work compassionately and collaborate in a shared maturity. "But what distinguished [Freud] from a policeman is his neutral air, devoid of mistrust, almost benevolent: he is not dealing with a rival or enemy but with a patient, and we sense that he is determined to give him of his best. For the first time, we must sense the *couple* relationship between patient and doctor" (*FS*, p. 421).

Later in the same scene, Sartre shows Freud overreacting to Karl's parricidal fantasies, his regressive episodes, and his desperate longing to be helped. Because Freud is disturbed by the disintegrating content of what Karl experiences, he himself becomes anxious, regressing to the authoritarian mode of the late nineteenth-century medical scientist. He becomes sardonic, objective, stern and, most crucially, betrays a desire to dominate the patient. Freud behaves sadomasochistically as if he were the domineering parent and Karl were a surrendering child, a variation on the master/slave dialectic. Freud has not learned to tolerate his own uncertainties and blind spots, nor the regressive pull of the analytic relationship on the analyst, including its erotic dimensions. Sartre explains the intersubjective drama of the scene with lucidity: "From their exchange of looks, this time we gain a radical insight into the bond between patient and psychiatrist (and into the genesis of transference and counter-transference). This image must be powerful enough – and, in a certain way, disturbing and disagreeable enough – for us to recall it when

Freud, much later, broaches the problem of transference. And the unpleasant thing about the couple which has just formed is precisely the very faintly homosexual appearance of domination and submission" (*FS*, p. 423).

Under the influence of hypnotism, Karl relives vivid scenes of castration between him and his father, including fantasies of rape and homosexual incest. Freud is nauseated by these reenactments and he resumes his scornful voice, demanding that Karl forget what he has just recounted. Instead of working toward restoring his patient's memory despite his own powerful resistance, Freud contradicts Karl's words and repeats clichés about filial piety (*FS*, p. 430). The session with Karl also begins to impinge on the doctor's unconscious desires. In a nightmare following this session, Freud calls his patient "a filthy swine" (*FS*, p. 433).

It is only after a brutally honest self-analysis that Sartre's Freud will be able to master his intense puritanical anxieties and guilt, and his need to reassure and be reassured. His self-analysis allows him to work through the disruptive dynamics of domination and submission in his work with his patients. By the end of the scenario, Freud will have achieved an internal calm. He will possess radical insight into himself, at least while he is analyzing his patients. Only after this self-analysis will Freud escape from his paralyzing self-doubt, enabling him to resolve the chronic mood swings and aggressivity that had prevented him from being genuinely receptive to his patients. He achieves inner tranquility, and because of this, a receptive, sensitive demeanor that projects his caring respect for the patient. "The man we see today is (at least in his relations with his patients and their relatives) rid of the doubts, passions, and the shyness which we associate with him (and which he will recover – though less intensively – when he is personally involved). On the contrary, he displays a calm, deep-rooted authority (which derives from his work and his knowledge) ..." (*FS*, p. 443).

The mature Freud realizes that an analyst who is annoyed with patients, who brags about himself and forces issues, employing techniques that demand compliance or exploit suggestibility, quickly leads to therapeutic impasses, if not outright failures in treatment. He also realizes that the cathartic method of analysis does not relieve patients of their symptoms permanently. Aware of the dynamic interplay between analyst and patients, aware of the unconscious lures of his patients and his own susceptibility to being tricked, he begins to learn to avoid these traps. And, according to Sartre, "It is Freud's strength to admit to his mistakes calmly" (*FS*, p. 450). Sartre emphasizes that the analyst is able to use recurring feelings of anger and malevolence at patients and their families in a constructive fashion. Sartre's Freud begins to succeed in freeing himself from his own "tyrannical violence and despotism" (*FS*, p. 453).

Freud is able to do this because he undertakes a penetrating, long-term self-analysis, including his own dreams, using the method of free association and gradually incorporating his reflections on the multiple manifestations of transference in his life. In his notes, Sartre urges Huston to focus on Freud's face, which should illustrate the wish for self-understanding as well as the torments and pleasures of self-reflection: "To read a forceful resolve to peer into himself and decipher his own riddles" (FS, p. 466). Self-analysis, then, becomes a form of self-acceptance and self-interrogation, a method to gain perspective on one's deepest contradictions, particularly the internal conflict between arousal and hatred, hostility, and guilt.

In contrast to Freud, Breuer has backed away from investigations that probe too deeply because they may intrude upon or violate the patient's soul. Breuer is equally distrustful of Freud's theories about how the mind is structured. But Freud has left Breuer behind. He will advocate "healing through knowledge," while Breuer will avoid that form of investigation as dangerous and forbidden (FS, p. 467).

According to Sartre, Freud, the analyst, masters his clinical art when he replaces scientific weightiness with playfulness and spontaneity, albeit within a framework of benign neutrality, that is, within the context of the analytic situation that is formal, tactful, and courteous. The analyst is enjoined to engage his analysand; the attention and accessibility of the analyst to the patient reciprocate the injunction to the patient to say what comes to mind without censorship or delay. "[Freud] has retained his air of passionate, slightly crazy gaiety. Even in his voice there is something frivolous and wild. He is very sincere (through exploiting his sincerity): he means that an adventurer of science is everything but 'serious'" (FS, p. 482).

Freud creates an impasse with his patients when he violates his newly discovered method, engages in power struggles or verbal duels, or asserts his authority and insists on the patient's compliance. All of these things provoke rebelliousness and create distance in the analytic situation because his patients try to protect themselves from being judged and dissected (FS, p. 488). When Sartre's Freud relinquishes the posture of the pitiless hunter or avid researcher and perceives the patient's call for help, the battle ends. He can be moved and his remarks become gentle (FS, p. 496). As we watch Freud integrating the analytic process, both the patient's inner resistance and his own internal resistance to the material begin to dissolve. When Cecily asks him not to disturb her chain of associations (FS, p. 497), he can respond with receptive silence. On the other hand, when Freud experiences shame, as when Cecily imagines herself as a prostitute, Freud derails the intersubjective analytic process by making premature, incorrect interpretations (FS, p. 500).

The method Freud develops encourages the analyst to listen and attend to the vicissitudes of free association without knowing in advance what he may encounter. As the analyst begins to tolerate uncertainty, he learns to accept his and his patient's own capacity for surprise. Surprise generates insight and vitality in the analytic dialogue, opening up significant pathways for further psychic exploration. "She stops, taken aback. Freud is looking at her in astonishment: he realizes simultaneously that he has made a mistake and that he has just discovered a more important trail" (FS, p. 501).

The climactic doctor/patient scene in Sartre's Freud scenario captures the mutual anguish and liberating potential of psychoanalytic therapy for both members of the dyad. This potential is fully intersubjective in that it is co-created and reciprocal. The episode pivots on Freud's willingness to disclose conflicted aspects of his own mental life to Cecily. These disclosures include secret details about Freud's family history which he has previously associated with powerful feelings of shame and guilt. Sartre clearly had strong convictions about this scene because he included a version of it in the original synopsis he wrote for Huston in 1958, in which Freud responds to a shattered Anna O. by revealing a screen memory in a flashback, voicing his erotic desire for his mother, and his conflicted feelings of love, reproach, and murderous intent toward his father (*FS*, p. 537). Cecily herself is racked by wildly fluctuating wishes toward both of her parents, an ambivalence with roots in an early childhood trauma that becomes attached to painful, disintegrating memories or converted into physical symptoms and feelings of humiliation and self-loathing.

Scene in Cecily's room

Cecily: What are you thinking about?
Freud: My past.
Cecily: Did I try to kill my mother?
Freud: Yes. Or rather, it wasn't you who tried to do that; it was the child Cecily who came back from the dead and thought Magda was being sent away
Cecily (disgustedly): The child Cecily was a little monster.
Freud: No, she was a child. That's all. I've won Cecily. Thanks to you. I think I understand both of us. And that I can cure us. (*A pause.*) Do you know the story of Oedipus?
Cecily: He killed his father, married his mother, and put his own eyes out, so he wouldn't be able to see what he'd done anymore.
Freud: Oedipus is everybody. (*A pause.*) I must talk to you a bit about myself. In neuroses, I've viewed the parents as guilty and the children as innocent. That was because I hated my father. It's necessary to reverse the terms.
Cecily: It's the children who are guilty!
Freud (*smiling*): Nobody's guilty. But it's the children who ... (*Flashback to the primal scene between Jakob and Frau Freud and two-year-old Sigmund.*)
Freud: I loved my mother in every way: she fed me, she cradled me, she took me into her bed and I was warm. (*Flashback to Freud's mother slipping between sheets of the bed next to the child.*)
Freud: I loved her in the flesh. Sexually.
Cecily: You mean I was in love with my father?
Freud: (*He speaks as if to himself. He seems to be almost asleep.*) I was jealous of mine because he possessed my mother. I loved him and hated him at the same time (*FS*, pp. 370–371).

Sartre, here, is not advocating the practice of mutual analysis, in the manner of Sándor Ferenczi's experiments. He is not criticizing psychoanalytic techniques from the perspective of antipsychiatry or existential psychoanalysis. Rather, through a dramatic, even a melodramatic, version of psychological discovery, Sartre invents a dream-like sequence that leads to a joint epiphany. Sartre is making a philosophical statement about depth psychology, namely, that the decisive moment of illumination in the history of psychoanalysis and in Freud's personal history involved a lived mutual relationship between two individuals, each of whom arrived at insight when they simultaneously learned to speak, decipher, and hear. Such understanding could only occur within the light of a passionate, intimate, two-party relationship. Sartre condenses this intersubjective process into one sentence: "Cecily listens to him, but translates as she does so: it is her own story she hears" (*FS*, p. 371).

Sartre penned an important letter on November 9, 1963, to serve as the forward to R.D. Laing and David Cooper's book, *Reason and Violence*. In praising their effort to construct "a truly human psychiatry," Sartre summarized his own thinking regarding the proper study of the family and how best to conceptualize mental illness. We can also view it as a critical commentary on his intentions in his scenario for Huston's *Freud*: "Like you, I believe that one cannot understand psychological disturbances *from the outside*, on the basis of a positivistic determinism, or reconstruct them with a combination of concepts that remain outside the illness as a lived experience. I also believe that one cannot study, let alone cure, a neurosis without a fundamental respect for the person of the patient, without a constant effort to grasp the basic situation and to relive it, without an attempt to rediscover the response of the person to that situation – and like you, I think, I regard mental illness as the way out that the free organism, in its total unity, invents in order to be able to live through an intolerable situation" (Laing and Cooper, 1964). Sartre's scenario shows Freud and his patients within that lived intersubjective experience and able to reflect on it as part of a psychoanalytic dialogue. We witness Sartre's Freud as he gains respect for the patient's individuality, working systemically from the inside, jettisoning the remnants of nineteenth-century positivism and medical detachment, while he carries out the affective and subjective experience of his own self-analysis.

The bonds of paternity: A portrait of Freud

In a celebrated passage of his autobiography, *The Words* (1963), Sartre attributed his lifelong theory and practice of freedom to the death of his father, Jean-Baptiste Sartre, which occurred when he was fifteen months old. The paragraph concludes with a psychoanalytic reference, which can also be read as a provocation:

> The death of Jean-Baptiste was the big event of my life; it sent my mother back to her chains and gave me freedom.

> There is no good father, that's the rule. Don't lay blame on men but on the bond of paternity, which is rotten. To beget children, nothing better; to *have them*, what iniquity! Had my father lived, he would have lain on me at full length and would have crushed me. As luck had it, he died young .... I move from shore to shore, alone, and hating these invisible begetters who bestraddle their sons

all their life long. I left behind me a young man who did not have time to be my father and who could now be my son. Was it a good thing or a bad? I don't know. But I readily subscribe to the verdict of an eminent psychoanalyst: I have no Superego.

(Sartre, 1963)

Instead of dismissing this passage as bravado or evidence of Sartre's psychological naiveté, I would like to propose that we read Sartre ironically – that the death of his father was an event of monumental significance in his life and that Sartre, as a result of writing this work on Freud, was conscious of it. Writing Freud's fictional biography allowed Sartre to undertake some of the work of paternal mourning. In describing how Freud navigates the bonds of paternity with his various father surrogates and finally his own father, we can observe Sartre coming to terms with the psychological burden of being fatherless.

The Freud of Sartre's scenario is not the usual Hollywood protagonist. He has depth, texture, and inner divisions, and he does not particularly like himself. He resembles the mental patients he treats. Sartre's Freud is burdened by multiple psychical symptoms which are probably manifested as physical problems, including arrhythmia, breathlessness, and burning around the heart (*FS*, p. 528). Moreover, he is phobic about traveling in trains, which is a displacement of his deep-seated fear of death, and he is addicted to cigars (*FS*, p. 510).

Emotionally, Sartre's Freud possesses many traits common to a depressive personality: he is frequently gloomy, tense, ascetic, secretive, preoccupied with himself, and uncertain of his ability to escape his own madness (*FS*, p. 87). He is melancholic, has difficulties regulating his self-esteem, and is torn apart by destructive impulses and a powerful desire for independence which is constantly thwarted. He is ashamed of his poverty and has great difficulty building a private practice that can support his large family. For Sartre, Freud's material poverty is linked to being Jewish in an anti-Semitic context. It becomes a persistent source of anger and resentment that drives his sadism, self-loathing, and contempt for others (*FS*, p. 395).

One of the chief tensions of the script evolves around Freud's capacity to work through his aggressivity: will he turn his gaze against himself in the form of self-disgust and self-sabotage? Will he turn it against his patients, thereby returning to the stance of the cold physician who dominates his patients? (*FS*, p. 210). Or, will he be able to follow Charcot and move toward self-clarification and the caring alleviation of his patient's misery? (*FS*, p. 250).

Sartre's Freud, then, is astonishingly vulnerable: he is persistently depressed and lost; he is often furious and dismayed; and he experiences himself in the world as if he were a monster and his affective state as if he were someone vile (*FS*, p. 276). The face of this young man reflects his tortured inner world (*FS*, pp. 394–399).

I do not want to suggest that Sartre's portrait of Freud is one-sided, static, or excessively pathologizing. As he was carrying out his research for the project, he delightedly said to his colleague, the psychoanalyst J.B. Pontalis (both were on the editorial board of *Les Temps Modernes*), "That Freud of yours, I must say, he was neurotic through and through" (Pontalis, 1985). Coming from Sartre, this was a compliment of the highest order. The neurotic Freud also has healthy and admirable traits, especially an indomitable quest for knowledge, a boundless curiosity. Sartre's Freud moves from someone who does not know, but wants to know, to one who creates an innovative method for investigating and uncovering psychic reality. As a man with a rigorous background in science, Freud was devoted to rational thinking and empirical experimentation, even when his subject became irrational (*FS*, p. 20).

Freud's empathetic understanding of the other is thematized in the screenplay through a dramatization of the vicissitudes of his self-analysis. In the absence of viable options and because of a logic internal to the structure of his own character, Freud turns to teachers, colleagues, and mentors, in short, to father surrogates, to find his way. Three main father surrogates receive extensive and, at times, riveting attention in Sartre's scenario: Freud's teacher, the neurologist and psychiatrist Theodor Meynert; Freud's friend and older colleague, the psychiatrist Josef Breuer; and the Berlin nose and throat specialist, the slightly younger Wilhelm Fleiss.

Meynert plays a disappointing and destructive role throughout the script. In a splendidly rendered scene at his deathbed, lifted from Freud's *The Interpretation of Dreams* (Freud, 1953), Freud receives some belated recognition from this scientific father. Meynert confesses that he has been a (male) hysteric his entire life. His pompous academic bearing disguised this shameful secret: his hypocritical scientific rhetoric served to deny his symptoms: "I've kept the secret ... all my life – even from myself; I've refused to know myself" (*FS*, p. 135). The scene concludes with the dying Meynert urging Freud to resume his courageous research into the unconscious roots of neurosis, even if it means scrutinizing Freud's own darkest and most painful secrets: "A disciple of knowledge must *know*, mustn't he? I don't know who I am. It's not I who has lived my life: it's an Other. Break the silence. Betray us. Find the secret. Expose it to the light of day, even if it means revealing his own. It's necessary to dig, deep down. Into the mud" (*FS*, p. 136).

Freud's relations with Breuer are even more complicated than with Meynert. Breuer becomes an intimate friend, co-worker, and supporter of Freud, and there is genuine warmth between their two families. Though both Freud and Breuer are secular Jews, Freud is militantly atheistic and irreverent in his attitudes while Breuer is assimilationist. Freud accepts money and patient referrals from Breuer with ambivalent feelings because he wants to be independent and he is acutely wary of his vulnerability to financial dependence. (Breuer is well established in Viennese medical circles and has built up a wealthy clientele.)

In Sartre's script, Breuer establishes an easy rapport with Cecily, a young, attractive, intelligent, and remarkably sensitive hysterical patient. The "strange and profound bond" between them develops into an erotic transference (*FS*, p. 146). When Breuer is confronted with the fact that Cecily has fallen in love with him, immense difficulties arise because he remains oblivious to his own erotic feelings for her (*FS*, pp. 523–524). Sartre shows that Breuer cannot organize these disorienting urges because he has no theory or technique to calm his anxieties: he has rejected Freud's theory of the sexual etiology of neuroses as repugnant.

Sartre dramatizes the situation further by indicating Mathilde Breuer's concern about the amorous bond between her husband and Cecily, followed by her jealousy and rage. She pressures Breuer to take her on a second honeymoon to Venice to remove him from Cecily. Breuer declares prematurely that Cecily is cured, but the day he leaves, Cecily manifests the symptoms of hysterical childbirth – she imagines she is pregnant with Breuer's child. Freud is called to help Cecily through this emergency, but her mother wonders if her daughter's illness was not iatrogenic, that is, precipitated by Breuer's mismanagement of the case.

Just as Cecily was abandoned by her physician because of unresolved and barely acknowledged erotic transferences to her, so too was Freud abandoned by Breuer. In advancing his more radical theories concerning the sexual origins of neuroses and the ways in which repression becomes the motive force of intrapsychic conflict, motivating defensiveness, compromise formations, guilt, and disturbances of memory, if not amnesias, Freud would be forced to go it alone. Sartre's Freud reacts strongly to Breuer's abandonment. He feels betrayed and temporarily depleted of strength, which leads to a crisis in self-confidence and self-assurance. Freud needs to take stock of himself from falling under the sway of a beloved authority figure.

According to Sartre's scenario, Freud regains his composure when he begins to formulate the psychoanalytic theory of transference, which helps him comprehend his own and Breuer's therapeutic failures and also enables him to grasp the structural motive for Cecily's feelings and fantasies toward Breuer (which are displaced onto him when he begins to treat her). An intersubjective analysis of transference provides Freud with a way to understand the meaning of Breuer's betrayal of him, his weakness. Only through confronting the intense affective bond between physician and patient, only through acceptance of the inevitability of transference as a revised edition of older and more primitive relationships, will Freud be able to see his way clear. These new editions of some earlier persons are aroused and displaced onto the person of the physician. The work of analysis is to bring these facsimiles into focus, to extrapolate the latent meanings in them.

Freud's resolution of his transferential relationship with Fleiss will yield the concept of the transference neurosis, a cornerstone of Freud's analytic therapy. Fleiss presented Sartre's Freud with a new challenge, namely, pursuing his research as a visionary and building a theory as a prophet (*FS*, p. 172). Fleiss exhorted Freud to be great and to believe unconditionally in his greatness. They were twins according to Fleiss, scientific geniuses of the same mold. If Freud was awed by Fleiss's Prussian demeanor and by his mathematical intellect, he was equally fascinated by Fleiss's concept of constitutional bisexuality and by his theories of sexual rhythms and periodicity.

As Sartre's plot unfolds, Fleiss reveals himself to be another omnipotent doctor, only this time without the modesty of the scientific researcher or the caretaking vocation of the clinical healer. In breaking with Fleiss, Freud deepens his introspective abilities; he discovers his unconscious desire for a master (*FS*, p. 317) and learns that an intense attraction to friends often conceals the opposite need, namely, to hate the person he loves (*FS*, p. 273). Breaking with Fleiss enables him to pursue his own project autonomously, without being under anyone's orders or conceptual umbrella. Freud's next task is to understand and work through his unconscious hostility to his own father (*FS*, pp. 376–377). The break with Fleiss, then, becomes truly emancipatory in a Freudian sense. It leaves a man of forty who knows, despite his fears, that he must relinquish what is infantile in himself, including an array of self-deceptions and psychological ignorance, in order to approach maturity (*FS*, p. 273).

Sartre's scripts contain a number of riveting scenes with members of Freud's family. Freud's father, Jakob, is described as something of a babbler, a bit senile, but with a natural capacity for tenderness. He is seventy but appears much older. Freud realizes he harbors a vast unregulated supply of anger and guilt, remorse and embarrassment toward his enfeebled father. He is unable to look at him. Freud associates Jakob's financial troubles with an even more profound sense of disillusionment. As a boy, Freud had idealized his father, seeing him as an incarnation of Moses: strong, hard, and implacable. In reality, Jakob was a flawed and frightened human being, intimidated by superior forces in society, unable to summon up courage. Sartre narrates a scene that took place in 1862 when Sigmund, then six years old, and Jakob, then forty-five, are confronted by a heavyset, well-dressed anti-Semite who forced them onto the street: "Not on the sidewalk, Jew!" The man is haughty and menacing, knocking Jakob's cap into the gutter, exclaiming, "Pick up your cap and stay in the roadway" (*FS*, pp. 284–285). Jakob's obsequiousness as he stoops to pick up his cap in this humiliating situation enraged his son. It also demolished Freud's intense idealization of his father.

Later that evening, in view of his father's apparent cowardice and weakness, Freud draws a lesson from Roman history: "Hamilcar makes his son Hannibal swear to avenge the Carthaginians." Freud is identified with Hannibal the avenger, insisting that his father is Hamilcar. The child then savagely intones, "I mean to avenge my father, the hero Hamilcar and all the humiliated Jews. I shall be the best of all, I shall beat everybody, and I shall never retreat." Sartre adds that this episode will weigh on "his son's entire life," the struggle to eradicate being ashamed of his father (*FS*, pp. 286–287).

The day after Jakob's funeral in 1896, Sartre's Freud remains tormented about his dead father, telling Fleiss, "His death is driving me mad." Freud needs to come to terms with this matter; "the event that counts most in a man's life is his father's death" (*FS*, p. 536). This is a paraphrase of the celebrated passage in the preface to the second edition of *The Interpretation of Dreams,* in which Freud announces the subjective intention of his text, namely, "my reaction to my father's death – that is to say, to the most important event, the most poignant loss of a man's life."

To come to terms with his surges of monstrous hatred from his father, somewhat incomprehensible because of a faint but persistent love for him, Freud decided to conduct a self-analysis. It begins when he admits: "What makes you think I'm not repressing, in the depths of my unconscious, some childhood memory that is … vile? I ought to apply my own method to myself. If only I could squeeze myself like a lemon …" Echoing a phrase from Cecily, it is again the patient and the analytic setting, that is, the intersubjective context, that shows Freud the way toward authentic self-awareness (*FS*, p. 342).

One aspect of his self-analysis allows Freud to accept the intersubjective sources of his own jealousy and hostility toward his father without blaming either his father or himself for weakness. He begins to understand his father's situation more realistically and historically: "And out of jealousy I accused him of being incapable of raising or even feeding his family. But it wasn't true: it was anti-Semitism that ruined him" (*FS*, p. 371).

In the final scene in the screenplay, we find Freud in front of Jakob's grave in the Jewish cemetery in Vienna. Freud encounters Breuer there and begins to realize the strength and durability of his psychological change. With his father dead, he can now admit, "A part of myself is buried there." Freud resolves to pursue his self-analysis, applying the method of free association and dream interpretation to himself so that he can liberate himself from the paralyzing ambivalence and infantilism of his thralldom to the other father figures in his life. Despite his father's tender love for him, Freud was both jealous and aggressive in return. The combination terrified him. Moreover, he realized that he was unable to accept the presence of unheroic weakness in Meynert, Breuer, or Fleiss because it aroused the memory of Jakob Freud's cowardice, the traumatic event of de-idealization before the anti-Semite (*FS*, pp. 380–381).

Freud, in effect, will no longer be torn apart by his chronic aggression toward his father figures and no longer be obsessed with finding strong fathers to love and protect him. He can exploit his own abundant vitality that was depleted in perpetual struggles against himself. Having examined the deep sources of his hatred, he will be able to love again. Having buried his father and transcended his need for father surrogates, Freud has earned the right to be autonomous, to work alone, to be the sole witness and evaluator of his work, but more crucially to be a loving father to his own children and to his "adopted sons – men who'll believe in my words – if any such can be found. I'm the father now" (*FS*, p. 383).

Sartre's original synopsis opens with Freud's voice-over, at age sixty, surrounded by his most trusted disciples. He reminisces: "Everything began with my father's death" (*FS*, p. 503). In working with patients who have suffered the traumatic loss of parents, Sartre's Freud clarified the central importance of the psychic role of the father: "The Father! Always the Father! I felt acutely anxious: I don't know why. But I wanted to get to the bottom of it and I knew I'd go to the very end this time" (*FS*, p. 530). In 1901, where the script ends, Freud is described as "free, absolutely free" (*FS*, p. 538). Freedom means no longer needing a guardian, no longer being under somebody's influence or criticism, being relieved of internal criticism, no longer depressed or anxious, capable of choice, reflection, and imagination. The renewed Freud is calm and can stand upright. He has just broken with Fleiss.

A young physician arrives, someone who has been attending Freud's lectures at the university and who is familiar with his writings. The disciple senses the groundbreaking direction that Freud's work will take as well as its potential clinical benefit for mankind. He is full of enthusiasm and wishes to question his master. Freud, for his part, accepts him slightly ironically, but with courtesy and dignity, adding in voice-over narration: "I was forty-one. It was my turn to play the role of father" (*FS*, p. 539).

J.-B. Pontalis has questioned the view that Sartre was advancing either a "personal or original 'interpretation'" of Freud in *The Freud Scenario*. I should like to disagree with his assertion by suggesting five original contributions.

First, Sartre's dialectical mind and his sensitivity to various forms of racism combine with a growing historical consciousness to transform his Freud scenario into an extension of his earlier reflections on the Jewish question. Sartre privileges Freud's social dilemmas as a secular Jew in Vienna, a point of view that is de-emphasized in the analytic literature and in Jones's biography, as well as in the Huston film.

Second, most accounts of the early Freud focus on his writings on the psychology of the unconscious via his elucidation of psychosexuality in human thought, fantasy, and behavior. Sartre's portrait ingeniously displaces sexuality toward aggression. Perhaps because of the French writer's own vicissitudes of aggression. Perhaps because of his own violence and preoccupation with violence (Cohen-Solal, 1987; Hayman, 1987), Sartre zeroes in on the vicissitudes of aggression in Freud's greatest decade of imaginative and theoretical fecundity. It is possible that Sartre's extremely negative transference to Huston which arose while he composed the script alerted him to Freud's unconscious struggles with transference figures and with his own hostile urges. Sartre's focus on aggression and its vicissitudes explains the gloominess of the portrait, but also the exuberant aspects of Freud's liberation from his internal oppression. Sartre's fictional biography shows Freud gradually coming to terms with his vengeful resentment, the sadistic aspects of his guilt, the masochistic aspects of his shame, and resolving both his superego and his ego ideal pathology.

Third, Sartre, dramatizes the subversive aspects of the analytic method – the dialectic of free association and meticulous analysis of transference – through powerful scenes in which two characters interact. As Freud learns to respect his patients, he is able to work analytically from the inside, not from the safe distance of pseudo-scientific objectivity. By stressing the intersubjective aspects of the analytic dyad, Sartre makes an early compelling case for the constructivist point of view of psychoanalysis, namely, that the analytic situation pivots around one subject interacting with another subject, establishing reciprocal attachments, mutual responsibilities, co-created meaning, and a shared process of growth, change, and self-discovery.

Fourth, Sartre avoids trivializing Freud's discovery of the Oedipus complex. He breathes new light into the concept by showing the Oedipal configuration from multiple points of view and from different perspectives of gender, generation, and psychosexual development. Sartre emphasizes Freud's realization and working through his ego ideal and superego pathology.

Fifth, Sartre powerfully dramatizes three relationships that are deeply conflicted in different ways: between anti-Semite and Jew, on the one hand, and that between physician and patient, father and son, on the other. From Sartre's perspective, all of these relationships are necessarily alienating. He shows how, in the context of Freud's lived history, these conflicts could dehumanize an entire group of men and women, reducing individuals to the condition of subhuman objects. Sartre's Freud is tormented by these converging predicaments, but struggles to overcome alienation and isolation, including the distortions of the self and the incoherence of thought and behavior that result from reification (the process of transforming a person into a thing). The resulting analytic process is shown to have striking effects on the perception and treatment of the mentally ill as well as on the difficulties of being a son in a patriarchal society.

The way out of reification in this text, the way of recapturing the authenticity of the other (as Jew, patient, son) turns simultaneously on practical and theoretical work. As he blurs the boundaries between mental illness and health, Freud will learn to see these relationships as dialectical ones that require a rigorous intersubjective approach. Freud's triumphant solution in the script occurs when he develops a discipline explicitly designed to help the analysand become conscious of the genuine sources of this alienation as well as his authentic needs and desires. That solution is optimistically offered to Sartre's audience through this vehicle of psychoanalytic intersubjectivity.

The author wishes to thank the following readers for their incisive critiques of this chapter: Janet Bergstrom, German Brée, Peter Gay, James Grotstein, Peter Loewenberg, George L. Mosse, Joseph Natterson, Robert Nye, and Robert Stolorow.

Previously published in *Endless Night: Cinema and Psychoanalysis, Parallel Histories* (University of California Press, 1999), ed. Janet Bergstrom, pp. 126–152.

References

Barnes, H. E. (1989). Sartre's Scenario for Freud. *L'Esprit Créateur*, 29(4), 52–64.
Brown, L. and Hausman, A. (1981). Mechanism, Intentionality, and the Unconscious: A Comparison of Sartre and Freud. In P. A. Schilpp (Ed.), *The Philosophy of Jean-Paul Sartre*. Open Court: La Salle, 539–581.
Cannon, B. (1991). *Sartre and Psychoanalysis: An Existential Challenge to Clinical Metatheory*. Lawrence, KS: University Press of Kansas, 7–8.
Cohen-Solal, A. (1987). *Sartre*. (A. Cancogni, Trans.). New York: Pantheon Books, 44, 46, 63, 66, 72, 83, 153, 163, 181–182, 328, 509.
Collins, D. (1980). *Sartre as Biographer*. Cambridge, MA: Harvard University Press, 89–91.
Farber, S. and Green, M. (1993). *Hollywood on the Couch*. New York: Morrow, 157–159.
Freud (typescript). (1980). In University Research Library, Arts Special Collections. University of California, Los Angeles.
Freud, S. (1953). *The Interpretation of Dreams*. The Standard Edition of the Complete Psychological Works of Sigmund Freud. (J. Strachey, Trans.). London: Hogarth Press, vol. 5.
Gabbard, K. and Gabbard, O. (1987). *Psychiatry and the Cinema*. Chicago: University of Chicago Press, 106–110.
Koch, G. "Sartre's Screen Projection of Freud." *October 57* (summer 1991), 3–17.
Hanly, C. (1979). *Existentialism and Psychoanalysis*. New York: International Universities Press.
Hayman, R. (1987). *Sartre: A Life*. New York: Simon & Schuster.
Huston, J. (1980). *An Open Book.* New York: Knopf
Huson, J and Reinhardt, W. (1962) *Freud. Typescript, Arts-Special Collection, UCLA Research Library*.
Izenberg, G. N. (1976). *The Existentialist Critique of Freud*. Princeton: Princeton University Press.

Jones, E. (1953). *The Life and Work of Sigmund Freud*, vol. 1. New York: Basic Books, 292–293, 339.
Jones, E. (1959). *Free Associations: Memories of a Psychoanalyst*. New Brunswick, NJ: Transaction Publishers, 199–205.
Kris, E. (1954). Introduction in The Origins of Psycho-Analysis; Letters to Wilhelm Fleiss, Drafts and Notes: 1887-1902. S. Freud, M. Bonaparte, A. Freud and E. Kris (Eds.) (E. Mosbacher and J. Strachey, Trans.). New York: Basic Books, 3–47.
Laing, R. D. and Cooper, D. G. (1964). *Reason and Violence: A Decade of Sartre's Philosophy 1950-1960*. Foreword by Jean-Paul Sartre. New York: Pantheon.
Polan, D. (1987). Sartre and Cinema. *Post-Script*, 7(1), 66–88.
Pontalis, J.-B. (Ed.). (1985). Preface. In Sartre, J.-P., *The Freud Scenario*. (Q. Hoare, Trans.). Chicago: University of Chicago Press.
Pratley, G. (1977). *The Cinema of John Huston*. New York: A.S. Barnes.
Roudinesco, E. (1990). *Jacques Lacan & Co.: A History of Psychoanalysis in France, 1925-1985*. (J. Mehlman Trans.). Chicago: University of Chicago Press, 1990.
Roudinesco, E. (1990). *Sartre lecteur de Freud*. Les Temps Modernes, (46), 531–533, 589–613.
Sartre, J.-P. (1947). *Existentialism*. (B. Frechtman, Trans). New York: Philosophical Library.
Sartre, J.-P. (1948). *Anti-Semite and Jew*. (G. J. Becker, Trans.). New York: Schocken.
Sartre, J.-P. (1956). *Being and Nothingness*. (H.E. Barnes, Trans.). New York: Philosophical Library.
Sartre, J.-P. (1963). *Saint Genet: Actor and Martyr*. (B. Frechtman, Trans.). New York: Braziller.
Sartre, J.-P. (1963). *Search for a Method*. (H. E. Barnes, Trans.). New York: Vintage.
Sartre, J.-P. (1963). *The Words*. (B. Frechtman, Translator). New York: Braziller.
Sartre, J.-P. (1969). Itinerary of a Thought: Interview with Jean-Paul Sartre. *New Left Review*, I (58), 45–47.
Sartre, J.-P. (1976). *Sartre on Theater*. (M. Contat and M. Rybalka, Eds.) (F. Jellinek, Trans.). New York: Pantheon.
Sartre, J.-P. (1977). Self Portrait at Seventy. In P. Auster and L. Davis (Eds. and Trans.), *Life/Situations: Essays Written and Spoken*. New York: Pantheon.
Sartre, J.-P. (1985). *The Freud Scenario [FS]*. J.-B. Pontalis (Ed.) (Q. Hoare, Trans.). Chicago: University of Chicago Press.
Sartre, J.-P. (1993). *Quiet Moments in a War: The Letters of Jean-Paul Sartre to Simone de Beauvoir*. New York: Scribners.
Schilpp, P. A. (1981). An Interview with Jean-Paul Sartre. In P. Schilpp (Ed.), *Philosophy of Jean-Paul Sartre*. La Salle, IL: Open Court Publishing.
Soll, I. (1981). Sartre's Rejection of the Freudian Unconscious. In P.A. Schilpp (Ed.), *The Philosophy of Jean-Paul Sartre*. La Salle, IL: Open Court Publishing, pp. 582–604.
Walker, J. and Waldman, D. (1990). John Huston's Freud and Textual Repression: A Psychoanalytic Feminist Reading. In P. Lehman (Ed.), *Close Viewings*. Tallahassee, FL: Florida State University Press, 282–300.

Chapter 7

Reflections on the Psychoanalytic Free Clinics

Elizabeth Ann Danto's *Freud's Free Clinics: Psychoanalysis and Social Justice, 1918-1938* (Danto, 2005) is a timely book, reopening the debate around the radical political core and the degree of social commitment to be found in classical psychoanalysis, particularly as it emerged in Vienna, Berlin, and Budapest in the period between the two world wars. Danto's thesis is both stimulating and inspiring. Self-reflective disciplines such as psychoanalysis ought to be aware of their own history. Danto builds her history with a superb use of archival material, personal interviews, and interview transcripts, as well as a fine ability to analyze texts. Her narrative is important and not precisely known; she weaves her ensemble of stories and character portraits by always returning to the theme of the free clinics. She contextualizes her material, recording shifts and changes over time and place. A problem with her strategy of dividing her chapters into linear descriptions of what happened year by year is that a more thematic approach would have permitted a more sustained storyline and critical appraisal. Unlike many other historians of psychoanalysis, she avoids gossip, eschews a prurient interest in her intriguing cast of characters, and seems uninterested in idealizing or pathologizing the various personalities that appear in her narrative. She neither avoids charged issues nor backs off from controversial critical analysis.

The history of psychoanalysis is incredibly exciting if practiced by an imaginative and audacious historian, one directed to preserving memory but, more significantly, committed to reviving the idealism, vitality, and subversiveness of these pioneering generations. Through Danto, we encounter some amazing figures who made this history, figures such as Max Eitingon, Ernst Simmel, Otto Fenichel, Eduard Hitschmann, Erich Fromm, and Siegfried Bernfeld who were open to improvisation and innovation in determining how to understand and care for their patients. Simultaneously, they engaged in various forms of introspection and experiments in personal growth. These narratives also illuminate struggle, professional and political, to challenge worn-out traditions, to rebel against received ideas, to take risks, and to participate in projects that did not revolve around personal and financial security or petty questions of personal power and prestige in local institutes, or national or international organizations. Living oneself into these narratives, then, is a vital way of understanding the passionate choices and analytic minds and attitudes of our forerunners. It will inevitably inform us in the present as we face the dilemmas of preserving and revitalizing psychoanalysis in urban, multicultural settings in the twenty-first century, where problems of poverty, social and class inequalities, inadequate health care, horrific public education, racism, and xenophobia still exist and still divide us in our own environments, often in our own hearts.

Prior to Danto, other scholars approached the left Freudians from different angles, often breaking new ground. Paul A. Robinson's *The Freudian Left*, written in 1969, draws its energy from the sexual revolution and cultural upheavals of the 1960s. His heroes, Wilhelm Reich, Geza Roheim, and Herbert Marcuse, each explored the implications of Freud's research into psychosexuality, each imaginatively elaborating the concept that politics and sexuality were intimately bound together (Robinson, 1969).

In two significant books, Russel Jacoby, first in *Social Amnesia* (1975) and, even more influentially, in *The Repression of Psychoanalysis: Otto Fenichel and the Political Freudians* (1983), writes from the subversive theoretical and political perspective of the Frankfurt School, that is, a form of cultural criticism that polemically opposes non psychoanalytic and alternative psychologies as conformist; Jacoby's scholarship combines a transparent commitment both to psychoanalytic and Marxist humanism. He bases his research on the 119 letters from the *Rundbriefe*, the circular letters, largely composed by Fenichel from 1934 to 1945, until 1998 unpublished. Originally discovered on Ralph (Romi) Greenson's washing machine in Los Angeles, and turned over to Jacoby by Randi Markowitz, Jacoby unearthed a treasure trove of archival material, allowing him to reconstruct a secret and lost history of psychoanalytic radicalism, which was repressed after World War II. The letters were sent to a core group that included Edith Jacobson, Annie Reich, Kate Friedlander, Barbara Lantos, Edith Gyomroi, and George Gero, and included Erich Fromm, Martin Grotjahn, and Berta Bornstein on the periphery. This suppression and conservative turn, Jacoby argued, were to be explained by the triple convergence of medicalization, professionalization, and Americanization that not only blunted the radical edge of the psychoanalytic left-wing intellectuals but also forced them underground. Though Jacoby privileges the maintenance of an activist theoretical psychoanalysis, he insists that the Fenichel group was a significant, well-respected minority within the psychoanalytic mainstream, all of whom wished to avoid Wilhelm Reich's expulsion from the Psychoanalytic International in 1934. They would remain a loyal opposition, not breaking with organizational psychoanalysis, nor distancing themselves from Freud, while cherishing his metapsychology, his clinical methodology, and his basic humanity (Jacoby, 1975, 1983).

Although Danto lists Robinson's book in her bibliography and cites Jacoby's Fenichel book in a small number of footnotes, she might have been more generous to her predecessors. More significantly, she missed an opportunity to enter into a discussion with these scholars' pathbreaking and influential arguments, indicating a continuity in the historiography regarding a politically subversive version of psychoanalysis. In writing her history, Danto appears to be taking the stance of standing alone, of discovering a field of inquiry that has not had distinguished precursors. That impression would be inaccurate.

The story of the rise and decline of the free clinics in the period from 1918 to 1938 captures the heart and soul of the international psychoanalytic movement from Vienna, Berlin, Budapest, to Zagreb, Moscow, Frankfurt, Trieste, and Paris. The free clinic movement did not represent a minority on the left, or left opposition within psychoanalysis, but rather the majority social democratic mainstream. Even liberals and apolitical figures in the analytic movement gravitated to the social democratic theories, ideals, and aspirations in the period between the wars. For Danto, in short, the free clinics demonstrate the strong progressive impulses at the core of European psychoanalysis in this era.

A narrative within a narrative, the history of the free clinics is largely a story of a broader attempt to democratize medicine and society. Accepting a definition of human beings as social creatures, this second generation of analysts, born around 1900, explicitly designed the free clinics to provide mental health services to those poor and indigent individuals who were excluded from access to psychoanalytic treatment. In effect, this meant treating sectors of the population of the city that one would not ordinarily see in private practice. Hence, the free clinics were formed and sustained by an ethic of the social responsibility of psychoanalysis to the wider community. Very much in line with Austro-Marxist assumptions and the Social Democratic ideology of the interwar period, the free clinics embodied this social service idealism.

Analysts in Central Europe were politically left, politicized by World War I, radicalized by the outbreak of social revolutions for a brief moment in 1919 in Hungary, Munich, and Berlin, by the interest generated by the communal experiments of the Kibbutz in Socialist-Zionist circles and, above all, by the impetus for social and sexual experimentation catalyzed by the Russian Revolution. Many embraced an egalitarian communitarian spirit.

Psychoanalysis fits beautifully into this model because of its emphasis on sexuality and its attempts therapeutically to free up neurotic individuals from unnecessary sexual misery, to liberate them from chronic psychological unhappiness and suffering. The Viennese Social Democrats viewed healthy sexuality as good for the community and as good for workers. Healthy sexuality is generally fused with its pro-family orientation. Part of this outlook moved toward gender equality; women were to be as emancipated sexually as were men. Furthermore, children had to be protected within the family framework, the child's right to a safe environment being one of the more revolutionary positions articulated by Julius Tandler and Austrian Social Democracy. One of their slogans beautifully captures the ethic: "He who builds palaces for children tears down the walls of prisons."

In terms of the actual operation of the free clinics, Danto emphasizes that they were flexible, experimental, and less hierarchical and bureaucratic than our contemporary analytic institutes, contradicting the image of the classical institute as fundamentally formal and rigid, even a paranoid structure. My own view, in agreement with Jacoby, is that a rupture occurred after emigration and World War II, that is, that the émigrés from Central Europe found themselves in significantly different cultural and political contexts in England and America. Furthermore, the post-World War II framework, culturally and clinically, brought them into contact with a divergent political atmosphere from the one they had experienced in Central Europe in the period between the wars. Besides the dominance of medical orthodoxy, at least in America, there was severe opposition to lay analysis, in addition to a conservative climate of Cold War thinking, with McCarthy-like paranoia about almost any left-wing position. This meant that, in practice, it might be considered un-American to combine a radical social work perspective, a committed European sensibility, and provision for the mental health of poor people, individuals, and groups who were priced out of access to psychoanalytic treatment.

At the free clinics, the atmosphere was relaxed and non-hierarchical, demonstrable warmth existed between analyst and analysand; reading rooms filled with analytic literature were open to both. Because candidates were offering free or low fee treatment, often receiving free supervision and referrals from their supervisors and training analysts, an excellent *esprit de corps* existed. In creating a climate of mutual collaboration, of participation in an unusual adventure, psychoanalysts united around a common social and therapeutic cause. Privately, bickering and rivalries of course developed, particularly around transference themes, for example, of vying for the admiration of Freud and other senior members of the Society.

At the free clinics, psychoanalysis was practiced not just by unseasoned clinicians and candidates, but by experienced clinicians as well. The free clinics cannot be dismissed as a utopian dream. As a movement, they linked creativity and experimentation with practicality. They had strong popular appeal as well as intellectual flair. Patients in trouble flocked to those clinics seeking help. The local press wrote favorably about them in its newspapers. Artists and intellectuals were more impressed by their outreach. Not surprisingly, lay analysis was encouraged, though it ran into considerable opposition from the conservative psychiatric associations, who periodically attempted to shut down the clinics. Psychiatry in Central Europe in the interwar years tended to be reactionary in politics, nationalist, Catholic, anti-Semitic, and profoundly opposed to the penetration and diffusion of analytic ideas and practice. Many of its own practices were transparently brutal, including the treatment of patients with electric shock to the point of death or suicide, the placing of patients in isolation cells, the use of straight-jackets, and the use of disciplinary measures. Many of its policies were grounded in greed and naked self-interest.

Clinical experimentation was broadly supported at the free clinics, including child observation and child analysis. Melanie Klein extended her first child analyses, beginning with her own children, while still residing in Budapest prior to 1920, at the Berlin free clinic. There were efforts to develop forms of marriage and couples counseling and crisis intervention, using analytic principles. The free clinics promoted psychoanalytic research based on the gathering and organizing of clinical data. Some of the first outcome studies came out of this research, where hypotheses could be tested empirically, sometimes statistically, and verified. The free clinics buttressed the rigorous psychoanalytic training of their candidates and the scientific growth of the clinical discipline by their promotion of such research, often leading to publications.

At the free clinics, psychoanalytic technique was safeguarded and preserved, including the reaffirmation of patient privacy and confidentiality; analytic tact was really a code word for compassion and sensitivity to the patients. Trust between analysts and analysand was emphasized, as was establishing rapport with one's patients. Candidates were asked to work at the free clinics for two years without remuneration. In return for their sacrifice, they received broad exposure to the varieties of psychopathology, receiving opportunities for analytic supervision from experienced analysts, often free of charge. In Vienna, they learned developmental perspectives from Anna Freud, August Aichhorn, Willi Hoffer, Siegfried Bernfeld, and other analysts who were pioneering methods of both supportive and play therapy and working analytically with children. The ethos was to respect their clinic patients and to practice with the highest forms of empathy, professionalism, and seriousness toward them, just as they would treat their higher paying patients in private practice. Critics of psychoanalysis have often commented upon the apparent elitism and exclusionary class biases of analytic practice. The history of the free clinics documented a vast social experiment attempting to universalize analytic treatment, opening it up to all who were in need of its service and expertise. Analysis and analytic therapy were not to be confined to the middle and upper middle classes, and to those privileged members of the liberal professions who could afford individual fees. It was designed to extend downward vertically to include the poor, the unemployed, the artistic, and those deserving but underserved members of society.

One of the best aspects of Danto's book is to rehabilitate the life and work of Wilhelm Reich, a figure who had been demonized and pathologized in certain official histories; Reich has sometimes been deleted in recent historical accounts (Breger, 2000; Gay, 1988; Sulloway, 1979), a prime example of what Foucault has called "counter-history." Psychologizing critics tend to trivialize his politics and dismiss his fertile ideas, underestimating his seminal contributions to the early psychoanalytic movement (Stolorow & Atwood, 1979). He is the key figure in Danto's story. One of Reich's more marvelous innovations was to create continuous case conferences at the free clinic. Reich was highly respected in Vienna in the 1920s by other clinicians and theorists. He conducted some of the earliest investigations into the defensive maneuvers of the ego, developing his own form of ego psychology. He was considered a crackerjack clinician with an uncanny feel for unconscious dynamics. His students regarded him as a terrific teacher. Reich hoped that case presentations would engender heated clinical debate. He also had the courage to discuss treatment failures and to present his own clinical work, not fearing the vulnerability that often accompanies such presentations; Reich assumed analysts could learn more about the analytic process by studying errors and blind spots than by exploring successful case histories. The clinical case presentation still persists as an essential part of the teaching methodology at contemporary analytic institutes. Candidates often think of these seminars as unique opportunities to have a dialogue about the confusing, complex aspects of analytic clinical work. Clearly for this to function effectively, a safe and trusting situation needed to be optimally created, to enable students to get inside of the elusive clinical process. Reich designed the clinical case conference to explore difficult or intractable patients, which might include investigations into the analysts' countertransference and analyst discouragement and disappointment (Sharaf, 1983).

The free clinics sponsored the treatment of primitive mental disorders, including borderline and psychotic illness, despite the cautionary stance diagnostically about analyzability. In exposing their candidates to a wide variety of psychopathology, psychoanalysis was clearly broadening its scope and practice beyond neurotic disorders. In Berlin, Vienna, and Budapest, debates were held about attempts to standardize techniques which might rationalize the curriculum of analytic institutes, but which risked the imposition of dogma and rigidity. Other experimental figures like Ferenczi urged analysts to be spontaneous, warm, alive, and engaged with their patients, to operate in a relaxed and elastic manner based on a case-by-case assessment of specific patient needs. Serious questions were raised not only about the length of an analytic treatment but also about the appropriate length of the analytic hour. Collegial exchanges occurred over controversial clinical material, exchanges that required that analytic colleagues of different generations and sensibilities, also with different degrees of analytic experience, operate with reciprocal trust, confidentiality, and commitment to the integrity of the patients and the dignity of the psychoanalytic cause. Solidarity around this cause was widely shared.

At the Frankfurt clinic, analysts established a potent connection to the Institute for Social Research, thus initiating dialogue between clinical and theoretical psychoanalysis and the brilliant critical theorists at the Frankfurt school. Despite lasting only several years in Europe, subsequently relocated to Columbia University, this alliance proved to be generative in terms of the quality and quantity of work generated by this exceptional coterie of intellectuals. If we think of the writings of Erich Fromm, Theodor Adorno, Max Horkheimer, Walter Benjamin, and Herbert Marcuse, we will recall the imaginative and intellectual power unleashed in this initiating effort to bridge psychoanalysis and the university, to link clinical psychoanalysis with high-powered theorists. Figures like Simmel, Fenichel, and Fromm understood the possibilities of cross-fertilization of many disciplines in the human and social sciences that might result if this alliance could be forged.

To maintain this position of advocacy for the patient, the analysts at the free clinics constructed a patient-centered approach. To implement this, psychoanalysts made adjustments to their fee structures. They made personal sacrifices in terms of time and income. Thus, an integral part of the free clinic movement was both the volunteerism of the analysts and candidates and the willingness of analysts to provide financial support to these clinics. Freud himself actively supported this ethic both in word and deed. He contrasted it to bourgeois moral uplift and charity, the former which he believed was hypocritical and self-righteous and the latter condescending toward less fortunate human beings. One of the most brutalizing aspects of being poor in contemporary, urban society was to be systemically denied access to quality health care, including care of the self and psychological health. Lacking money and lacking the necessities of life meant being deprived of a basic social right: the right to receive necessary mental health care.

From Freud's 1918 speech and his commitment throughout the interwar era, psychoanalysts consistently promoted the concept that individuals be granted access to health care. Access to the best of mental health care meant psychoanalysis or analytic forms of therapy, depending on the diagnosis and the individual's degree of psychopathology. At the speech before the Fifth International Psychoanalytic Congress in Budapest, Freud hoped to initiate a broad program of free clinics. Here was how he plainly and eloquently put it: "institutions or out-patient clinics ... where treatment shall be free. The poor man should have as much right to assistance for his mind as he now has to the life-saving help offered by surgery ... It may be a long time before the State comes to see these duties as urgent. Probably these institutions will be started by private charity" (Freud, 1918, p. 167). Danto rightly describes this passage as progressive and inclusive in spirit and in practice. The profoundly liberal Freud here embraced a Social Democratic ethic, consistently holding on to this position throughout the period between the wars.

Marx had famously condensed the core humanism of his philosophy into one sentence: "From each according to his capacities, to each according to his needs" (Marx, *Critique of the Gotha Program*, 1875). The free clinic movement updated that doctrine by advocating help for the poor, indigent, underprivileged, unemployed, under-employed, and marginalized by stating that specific diagnosis and the particular needs of the individual mattered most, not the individual's ability to pay for the services. This shifted the model, formerly based on the principles of an individual medical entrepreneur, to one based on service and responsibility to the community. Eitingon had proposed that patient payment was not an important influence on the outcome of an analysis – and, even more provocatively, that payment was always a more significant issue for the analyst than for the patient. Payment, in short, had to be analyzed in terms of countertransference dynamics, possibly in terms of the analyst's own resistance to what was best for his patient.

The Reich that emerges in Danto's narrative is endlessly fascinating, mercurial, and ultimately tragic. Charismatic, a gifted orator, with a deep sense of humanity, Reich had a powerful and imaginative intellect; his major project was to build a conceptual and practical bridge between Freud and Marx, attempting to link the practices and theories of both. During the 1920s, he saw sexual freedom as an issue that was both political and personal. As he developed his own brand of socially revolutionary psychoanalysis, he began to challenge existing political, medical, and academic traditions. He also developed a critique of psychoanalysis from within the movement. The author of *Character Analysis* (1933) and *The Function of the Orgasm* (1927) (Reich, 1933a, 1927), Reich functioned as an articulate, at times angry and abrasive, advocate of the sexual revolution. He equated health with untrammeled sexual expression, endorsing genitality, orgasmic potency, and free consensual sexual expression, so long as it did no harm to others. Reich posed trenchant questions about monogamy, about the dulling and routinized aspects of married life, and about the process of desexualization that he heard about from his patients and informants.

Reich rapidly moved left in the 1920s, first as part of the left opposition within Austrian Social Democracy, subsequently moving to Berlin in 1930 and joining the German Communist Party. This outraged and frightened many psychoanalysts. After insisting that repressed sexuality was the cause of neurosis, he began to tie repression to the political apathy of the masses, their tendency to accommodate to the status quo. Reich expressed an early, penetrating understanding of the irrational roots underlying the mass appeal and dangers of Hitlerian fascism. He would synthesize these perspectives in his book, *The Mass Psychology of Fascism* (1933), a book of astonishing insights into the collective psychological power of international fascism and virulent anti-Semitism (Reich, 1933b).

Reich's Sex-Pol engagement, both in Vienna and Berlin, could easily be dismissed as a hotchpotch of agitprop activity. He advocated the rights of children and mothers, supporting legalized abortions, contraception, adolescent sexuality, and a woman's right to choose. Yet Sex-Pol constituted consciousness raising at a rather high level, clearly moving toward prevention rather than individual treatment modalities. Reich blended forms of counseling, radical social work perspectives, propaganda, and sexual education. Sexual suppression made the masses passive and uncritical. Reich also understood the economic dependence of women as feeding the multiple aspects of misery on the everyday level, sexual, social, educational, and vocational (Reich, 1972).

Reich's assertions about sexual expressiveness for all, including the young, the unmarried, and women, upset both his constituencies: the organized political left and institutional psychoanalysis. Many analysts, after all, remained tied to Victorian attitudes and bourgeois lifestyles. Reich stirred up a hornet's nest in his searching critique of sexual monogamy and his perspective on lasting, romantic love. This triple assault on bourgeois respectability, the sanctity of the family, and conventional sexual morality demystified much of the prevailing hypocrisy and sentimentality about human sexuality. As a spokesman for the subversive edge of psychoanalysis and Marxism in this period, Reich raised the specter of both social and sexual revolution. He became too much for everyone: expelled from the Communist International in 1933 for being too Freudian and from the International Psychoanalytic Association in 1934 for being too Marxist. His marriage to Anne Reich failed. And he ruptured relations with his best friend, Otto Fenichel (Corrington, 2003).

Before reading Danto, I was under the impression that most analysts in the psychoanalytic tradition, following Freud, operated with a sliding fee scale, usually seeing one or two patients in their clinical roster for low or moderate fees. I had no idea that analysts worked for free. I assumed wrongly that such practices were based loosely on an unspoken agreement widely current in the analytic community. Danto corrects this view. Beginning with Freud, she asserts that every analyst saw two candidates for free as part of his or her own practice, in addition to seeing clinic patients for free or low fees; or, if too busy, they would contribute to the clinic through vouchers. Freud donated money collected for his seventieth birthday in 1926 and at other times to the free clinics. In Berlin, analysts affiliated with the Society were expected to contribute four percent of their total income to support the clinic. Wealthy individuals like von Freund, Eitingon, and Marie Bonaparte could not manage to subsidize these expensive ventures without assistance from analytic colleagues.

We know for certain that Freud treated patients for free, including Marianne Kris, Eva Rosenfeld, the Wolf-Man, and Bruno Goetz. I cannot imagine that he charged his daughter, Anna Freud, when she was in analysis with him, though not much is known of that experience. This set a tone for the entire analytic movement. It is often polemically alleged that Freud did not care about his patients, that he opposed therapeutic zeal because he disliked or was bored by his patients, that he preferred theory building to actual contact with suffering individuals, and that he became misanthropic and bitter about human beings as he aged. But contrary evidence exists that he also gave money to patients in need, like the Wolf-Man, his compassion going well beyond the limits he recommended in the papers on technique.

Freud, it should be said, was no saint. Nor was he particularly sentimental about his fees. From the 1890s on, he treated wealthy patients and charged high fees when he could. During the interwar period, when Central Europe was hit first by high inflation, then by the depression, Freud took foreigners into treatment, including Americans, who paid high fees. He apparently operated with a Robin Hood model: taking from the rich and giving to the poor. Freud gave money to people in need, and whether or not they were or had been patients was not a particular concern to him in this respect; his financial generosity and decency were legendary and consistent over several decades; he also pointed out in his self-analysis that his generosity had its roots in the poverty of his early childhood.

Freud had carefully outlined his position on the analyst's fees in "On Beginning the Treatment" of 1913. There he advised analysts to be candid and unashamed about their fee for services. He urged them not to retreat into prudishness, inconsistency, or hypocrisy regarding payment. Just as he counseled them to be a matter of fact in analyzing powerful sexual factors that emerged in treatment situations, so he argued that money had to be dealt with in the same spirit of honesty. Analysts needed money for their self-preservation. Psychoanalysis was not a philanthropic activity. Patients, Freud said, did not always find that treatment was enhanced if a low fee was asked for and granted. Analysts were urged to value their time, to bill on a consistent monthly basis, and to function in their own specialty as if they were surgeons, rendering a unique and highly skilled service. Furthermore, if analysts were to agree to work for free or for low fees, it would be a tremendous sacrifice on their part, possibly constituting one-seventh or one-eighth of their weekly time and income. Freud anticipated that analysts accepting low fees would resent their patients, possibly feeling exploited by them. Psychoanalysts ought to recognize from the beginning of their training that they would not earn as much as other medical specialties. By implication, greed or the wish to amass wealth ought not to be a motivating factor in choosing analysis as a profession.

In his own experiments with treating patients for free, Freud discovered that gratuitous treatment increased a patient's resistances, that it exacerbated oedipal dynamics, and intensified ambivalence about seeking and receiving help. Moreover, eliminating the fee might remove the relationship too far from the real world, where a patient might lack incentives to terminate the treatment. Yet even Freud in his 1913 paper qualified his opposition to free treatment by saying that he had achieved "excellent results" with certain deserving people and that free treatment had been no obstacle to the desired outcome of restored health, efficiency, and improved earning capacity (Freud 1913).

In turning to Freud's politics, Danto makes the case that Freud was essentially a progressive, a social democrat, that he was identified with a younger generation of social democrats in the 1920s, and that there was a complementarity between Freud's liberalism and democratic socialist ideals and practices. Within the context of Red Vienna, Freud politically positioned himself to the left of the Christian Socialist Party because of that party's reactionary policies and its anti-Semitic orientation. There was a small and politically irrelevant liberal Party in Austria. The university was hostile to psychoanalysis, and psychiatry was very much opposed to its theory and technique. In some ways, Austrian Social Democracy was the only option available to him.

Contrary to Danto's thesis, Freud thought of himself as a liberal of the old school. He had translated John Stuart Mill and admired English parliamentary forms of government, remaining a lifelong Anglophile. Freud's long public career manifested a deep commitment to social reform, sexual enlightenment, and medical and scientific progress, positions derived from the Enlightenment and from classical European liberalism. Austrian and Catholic anti-Semitism alerted him to the pernicious effects of racism and prejudice, which he countered by praising the virtues of tolerance, secularism, atheism, and critical thinking. There were also many instances of conservatism in Freud's basic attitudes, perhaps most egregiously expressed in some disparaging passages about women.

Danto does not consider the seminal essay, *Civilization and Its Discontents* (1930), as Freud's polemical reply to Reich and to the psychoanalytic left in this period, though she rightly detects ambivalence and a combative attitude from Freud toward Reich. Danto implicitly reads this morally resonant essay by Freud as a Social Democratic document, contextually influenced by Freud's relationship to Red Vienna and by his social commitments to the community, as evidenced by his support of the free clinics. I interpret both the text and context differently, beginning with its polemic against Romain Rolland's oceanic feeling and Freud's wish to deconstruct theoretically mystical forms of knowledge, all forms of religious and utopian liberation (Fisher, 1991). I view the text as emerging out of a historical framework where Freud became aware of the rise of fascist mass movements, including those of a particularly virulent anti-Semitic variety. Informed by the massacres and mass horrors of World War One, Freud wrote eloquently of the lethal potentialities of modern science and technology, even raising the possibility of world destruction, revealing his increasing pessimism about the inherent aggressiveness of human beings.

In *Civilization and Its Discontents,* Freud took sharp issue with all utopian viewpoints, offering a searing attack on sexual and social revolution, in short, on Reich and the Freudian left. Reich considered the text a frontal attack on him. (Higgins, M & Raphael, 1967). In arguing that civilization made individuals miserable, Freud conceived of no possibility of overcoming the frustrations and restrictions of modern civilization other than through sublimation, that is, the rechanneling of powerful instinctual urges into cultural, scientific, and artistic activities. Deeply pessimistic about the individual's conflict with society, Freud posited that sexuality would be severely impaired and happiness diminished by modern civilization. Freud first suggested this tension between the individual and civilization as early as 1908 in "'Civilized' Sexual Morality and Modern Nervous Illness," suggesting an important social and cultural continuity in his work over many decades (Freud 1908).

As for Communism, Freud disagreed with the assumption that private ownership of property was at the root of what corrupted man's nature. He asserted that human aggression existed before capitalist economic systems were formed and that violence and hostility were built into human nature, embedded in our own psyches, emerging out of early childhood psychosexual conflict and development. Modern civilization's task, he proposed, was to contain the outbreak of cruelty and aggressiveness. Socialist conceptions of human nature were built on a basic misconception, namely, a naïve belief in the essential goodness of man. Psychoanalysis, for Freud, was not compatible with Marxism; he was skeptical about the possible mediations between the two clashing worldviews and explanatory models.

Moreover, Freud had deep reservations about aligning psychoanalysis either to a political party or to a political philosophy. Freud wished to preserve psychoanalysis as an autonomous scientific association, preventing it from being either absorbed by a political party or co-opted by an ideology on the left. To safeguard its legitimacy and credibility as a scientific method with therapeutic concerns, Freud insisted that psychoanalysis remain suspicious of totalizing worldviews.

Lastly, Freud's main thrust in the period between the wars turned on the politics of the psychoanalytic movement, with particular emphasis on the primacy of its therapeutic concern. Even in his training analyses in this period, Freud prioritized the cause of the psychoanalytic movement over clinical or therapeutic outcomes. In short, his political efforts went toward popularizing psychoanalytic ideas and practices to the world. After the victory of the Nazis in Central Europe, Freud hoped to preserve psychoanalysis as a viable entity in exile.

The history of the free clinics was not an uninterrupted story of glory and successful experimentation. In Berlin after the Nazi takeover in early 1933, Ernst Simmel, both a Jew and a prominent Socialist, was arrested and forced to flee for his life in Switzerland. Martin Grotjahn's own four-month analysis with Simmel came to a harrowing conclusion in 1933 when during a session a friend alerted Simmel by telephone that the Gestapo would be sweeping his neighborhood, arresting psychoanalysts. Grotjahn had to assist his analyst to escape by pushing him out a window, allowing him to exit through a backyard route. Other left-wing analysts were threatened, harassed, and jailed by the authoritarian and racist policies of the National Socialist government, including Edith Jacobson, who was imprisoned for hosting anti-fascist meetings in her home. The Berlin Poliklinik became rapidly Aryanized where Jews, homosexuals, and Marxists were expelled. As the process of Nazification accelerated from 1933 to 1935, the Nazi slogan for psychoanalysis as "Jewish-Marxist filth" became transformed into institutional practice. Filth had to be cleansed. Renamed the Göring Institute, the Nazis purged the Berlin Society of all Jewish practitioners of psychoanalysis, leaving the institute under the direction of Felix Boehm and Carl Müller-Braunschweig, both of whom subscribed to the fascist ideology, both of whom would sign their letters with "Heil Hitler!" Freud's books were prohibited and subsequently burned. Carl Gustav Jung lent the prestige of his name, in addition to furnishing a spiritual-ideological framework, to the Göring Institute in his role as director of the German Medical Society for Psychotherapy in these years.

Similarly, the Nazi takeover of Austria in March 1938, the Vienna Society of Psychoanalysis expelled 100 Jewish members, excluded for being "non-Aryan members," leaving behind two gentiles from its original coterie. Müller-Braunschweig presided over the dismantling and ultimate Aryanization of psychoanalysis in Vienna. His actions effectively destroyed the Vienna Ambulatorium, abruptly concluding its history of free clinics at the same time. As a symbolic gesture, the Nazis draped a swastika over the door to Freud's home and office on 19 Berggasse.

In terms of the export of free clinics to England and America, this historical legacy was considerably limited. Only Chicago and Topeka in America, both enclaves of progressivism, established free outpatient clinics. Clearly the existing traditions of medical hegemony, conservatism, and individual, professional, and entrepreneurial activity would trump, or co-opt the left-wing practices and spirit of the free clinics.

Let me share a vignette told to me by Bruno Bettelheim about Wilhelm Reich. The time of the episode was Vienna in the late 1920s, that is, at the height of Reich's Sex-Pol activities, a phase of militancy, of heightened Freudo-Marxist intellectual and political work. Reich had just met a recently graduated physician, who requested an analysis with him. Finding him a person of quality, well-motivated, analyzable, with serious issues that required analytic attention, Reich hesitated about taking him into analysis. The prospective analysand was poor and could only pay a low fee. Accepting him into treatment at four or five times a week would have meant a long-term commitment on Reich's part, specifically an expenditure of time and a serious loss of income. Bettelheim described Reich's intense and anxious reflection on his situation, how Reich paced the room, agonizing over what to do. The vignette ended on a note of indecisiveness. Bettelheim never indicated to me what Reich opted for. Now Bettelheim was a tricky storyteller, a lover of fairy tales. What will we do when confronted with Reich's decision? What will we choose?

In conclusion, the story of the free clinics was a story of hope, of outreach, of prevention, and of the self-confidence of the psychoanalytic movement, despite the presence in the period between the wars of serious opposition and political impediments. In studying this movement, we help ourselves in the present by imagining ways to strengthen and vitalize psychoanalysis in contemporary urban centers, where many of the same problems persist, and where analysts sometimes fail to engender any strategies for progressive solutions to social, political, racial, gender, and personal ills.

Previously published in *Psychoanalysis and History, Vol. 9, No. 2, 2007,* pp. 237–250.

References

Breger, L. (2000). *Freud: Darkness in the Midst of Vision*. New York: John Wiley & Sons.
Corrington, R. S. (2003). *Wilhelm Reich: Psychoanalyst and Radial Naturalist*. New York: Farrar, Straus & Giroux.
Danto, E. (2005). *Freud's Free Clinics: Psychoanalysis and Social Justice, 1918-1938*. New York: Columbia University Press.
Fisher, D. J. (1991). Reading Freud's *Civilization and Its Discontents*. In *Cultural Theory and Psychoanalytic Tradition*. New Brunswick, NJ: Transaction Publishers.
Freud, S. (1908). 'Civilized' Sexual Morality and Modern Nervous Illness. In *SE*, vol. 9 London: Hogarth Press, pp. 181–204.
Freud, S. (1913). On Beginning the Treatment. In *SE*, vol. 12, London: Hogarth Press. Pp. 131–134.
Freud, S. (1918). Lines in Advance in Psychoanalytic Psychotherapy. In *SE*, vol. 17, London: Hogarth Press, pp. 157–168.
Gay, P. (1988). *Freud: A Life for Our Time*. New York: Norton.
Higgins, M. and Raphael, C. M. (Eds.). (1967). *Reich Speaks of Freud*. New York: Farrar, Straus & Giroux.
Jacoby, R. (1975). *Social Amnesia: A Critique of Contemporary Psychology from Adler to Laing*. Boston, MA: Beacon.
Jacoby, R. (1983). *The Repression of Psychoanalysis: Otto Fenichel and the Political Freudians*. New York: Basic Books.
Reich, W. (1933a). *Character Analysis*. New York: Simon & Schuster, 1972.
Reich, W. (1933b). *The Mass Psychology of Fascism*. New York: Farrar, Straus & Giroux.
Reich, W. (1972). The Imposition of Sexual Morality and The Imposition of Sexual Morality. In *Sex-Pol Essays, 1929-1934*. L. Baxandall (Ed.). New York: Vintage, pp. 1–74, 91–249.
Robinson, P. A. (1969). *The Freudian Left*. New York: Harper & Row.
Sharaf, M. (1983). *Fury on Earth: A Biography of Wilhelm Reich*. New York: St Martin's Press.
Stolorow, R. D. and Atwood, G. E. (1979). *Faces in a Cloud, Subjectivity in Personality Theory*. New York: Jason Aronson.
Sulloway, F. (1979). *Freud: Biologist of the Mind*. New York: Basic Books.

Chapter 8

A Power Structure Analysis of Psychoanalytic Institutes (Followed by an Interview with Douglas Kirsner)

Recent scholarship in the history of psychoanalysis has concentrated on the reception of Freud's theories in various national frameworks. Researchers tend to be divided between those who see the history of psychoanalysis as a relatively autonomous field and those who see it more broadly as part of either intellectual history or the disciplinary apparatus of cultural studies. In meticulous detail, Nathan Hale (Hale, 1971, 1995) a professional historian, has employed a chronological framework to narrate in two volumes the diffusion of Freudian ideas in America from 1917 to 1985. Writing from a comparative sociological perspective, Edith Kurzweil (1989) has studied the resistance to and assimilation of Freudian psychoanalysis in five national contexts – the United States, England, Germany, Austria, and France. Sherry Turkle (1978), drawing her methodology from sociology, furnishes a shrewd understanding of the rise and collapse of Lacan in the Parisian milieu. Even more encyclopedically, Elisabeth Roudinesco (1982, 1986) offers a two-volume history of psychoanalysis in France, following its trajectory from Freud's visit to Charcot in 1885 to battles over Lacan's legacy in the 1980s. Subtitled "the one-hundred-year battle," Roudinesco's book is written by a Lacanian insider who has mastered a vast armamentarium of French philosophical and poststructuralist perspectives; she has also had access to the personal archives of seminal individuals in the French analytic movement and conducted interviews with them. She capped her investigations with a perceptive and disturbing biography of (Roudinesco, 1997), which in its French version is subtitled "Sketch of Life, History of a System of Thought."

An Australian philosopher and critical theorist, Douglas Kirsner is an outsider who writes as neither a historian, nor a sociologist, nor a psychoanalyst. (Kirsner, 2000) He casts his well-informed narrative as a series of detailed microhistories. These offer a picture of the "inside" operations of the governing bodies of four analytic institutes in the United States. The key question for Kirsner is who had the power, and who opposed it.

Kirsner deploys a very strong argument, even if the reader can find details and nuances to quibble with. In his view, psychoanalytic institutes "everywhere and always" (p. 3) have been troubled, undemocratic associations. They have operated like elite organizations, perhaps most closely analogous to an exclusive gentlemen's club. Within the club, there prevails a clear hierarchy, an authoritarian ideology, a dogmatic conception of truth, and contempt for the opposition as incompetent and "nonanalytic." Typically, power resides with either the Director or the Dean of Education of a given institute.

This mode of governance has engendered deep mistrust and resentment on the part of the membership. The educational climate is sectarian and paranoid, more like what one would expect in a religious cult than in a scientific organization. Intellectual independence is rarely rewarded, causing creative individuals to feel estranged from their analytic "families." Because most analytic institutes lack affiliation with a university, they tend not to keep up with changes in allied disciplines. In short, institutional psychoanalysis in the United States has become shut off from the outside world and obsessively preoccupied with safeguarding the rituals of clinical practice (use of the couch, length of the hour, frequency of sessions, and so forth).

Inherently unfortunate, this development led to disaster when psychoanalysis faced severe economic decline and talking cures were threatened by the rise of managed care and the turn of psychiatry toward behaviorism and pharmacology. Candidates trained in such hostile environments imbibed a form of secularized religion, rather than cultivating psychoanalysis as a radical mode of investigating subjectivity, demystifying knowledge, analyzing familial dynamics, and unraveling the intricate knots of character structure. Kirsner discovered that most analytic institutes have been governed by oligarchies, which tended to be self-replicating political elites. Professional advancement in analytic institutes followed a careerist logic. Candidates incorporated a body of received truths (often under the rubric of "standard technique"), handed down by a group of clinicians who operated as wise elders. These "anointed" figures claimed to possess a corpus of scientific knowledge that was impervious to challenge; Kirsner found that the leaders of analytic cliques were often not particularly eminent. They rarely presented their own clinical work; many had few or no publications. The truly distinguished thinkers in various institutes – such as Heinz Kohut in Chicago or Heinz Hartmann, Rudolph Loewenstein, and Ernst Kris at the New York Psychoanalytic Institute – were not at the centers of power, possibly because they justifiably felt that its pursuit would deflect them from their theoretical projects.

Thus, as Kirsner sums up his thesis in an inspired title, analytic institutions are "unfree associations" because they stifle the unfettered use of skeptical intelligence and the radical self-reflection of the psychoanalytic method. They have required analysts to bend to hegemonic forces to secure advancement. What is more, psychoanalytic institutes have been more oppressive and alienating regardless of the dominant theory or technique, the size of their membership, or whether they were largely medical or lay. This dynamic appears to be true even if the institute is mainstream and conservative, or alternative and more putatively democratic.

Kirsner gained "inside" access to analytic institutes by conducting about 150 personal interviews with key players in the four sites he studied. He also received 35 personal communications that allowed him to check conflicting information. Some of these date back to 1981. He was, however, denied access to many documents, sometimes for legitimate reasons of confidentiality, but more often simply because of a desire to preserve secrecy. Perhaps a fear of lawsuits was lurking in the decision of analytic institutes to refuse to open their archives to a researcher who had no obvious axe to grind. Kirsner also supplements his documentation by citing published accounts whenever possible. He tells four distinct stories in his book, specifically, the institutional histories of the New York Psychoanalytic Institute, the Boston Psychoanalytic Institute, the Chicago Psychoanalytic Institute, and the Los Angeles Psychoanalytic Society and Institute (LAPSI), thereby allowing for differences in region, climate, culture, and theoretical and technical bias. He focuses on the methods of governance within each institute, studying how power was deployed, consolidated, and transmitted from generation to generation. In short, it is a power structure analysis, to borrow a phrase popularized by C.Wright Mills.

Kirsner's history of the New York Psychoanalytic Institute is a riveting, demythologizing account of the "anointed." To outsiders, the New York Institute possessed a mystique, as if it were the Harvard of American analysis. Its members behaved as though they were the defenders of high standards and all others were out to alloy the pure gold of psychoanalysis. The power structure tended to be controlled by the European-trained analysts who arrived in New York City in the 1920s and 1930s. These analysts disdained the Americans who supposedly lacked the culture and sophistication of those who had been close to Freud. Many of the immigrants had been analyzed by someone who had been analyzed by Freud, if not by Freud himself, conferring upon them a superior pedigree and the status of keepers of the flame. From the late 1930s through the 1960s, loyalty to Freud was displaced onto his daughter; many analysts at the New York Institute had strong ties to Anna Freud and helped her in her political and doctrinal battles in London with the Kleinians.

During the so-called "golden age" of psychoanalysis, which lasted through the 1950s, many of the luminaries who dominated the New York Psychoanalytic Institute were also leading theorists of ego psychology. Hartmann, Kris, and Lowenstein formulated a clinical, theoretical, and aesthetic doctrine that modified classical Freudian id psychology and functioned as an updated form of orthodoxy within not only the New York Institute but also the American Psychoanalytic Association. Yet, as I have noted, none of the triumvirate seemed particularly interested in exercising power; neither did such distinguished European colleagues as Annie Reich, Margaret Mahler, or Marianne Kris, all of whom remained marginal to the political intrigues of the Institute.

Power resided chiefly in the hands of Otto Isakower, a relatively unknown analyst outside of the New York Institute who worked behind the scenes. Despite publishing only four papers, Isakower controlled the Education Committee and was supported by twenty other émigré analysts, including Kurt and Ruth Eissler and Anne-Marie and Fred Weil. Kirsner described Isakower as both a guru and a dictator, someone who had an aura but also a contempt for participatory democracy. He postured as a repository of psychoanalytic truth as if it magically resided in him. He could intimidate colleagues and candidates with caustic sarcasm. He fostered an educational climate in which teachers and supervisors were to be mimicked, not challenged or criticized. To be trusted within the New York Psychoanalytic Institute, one had to be a protégé, a loyal believer both in Freudian orthodoxy and above all in those who ran the institute. This oligarchic structure meant that a climate of paranoia and distrust pervaded the institute for almost three decades after the Second World War.

Aspirants picked to ruse in the hierarchy were convoyed, that is, tapped for teaching assignments and guided along the track to become training analysts. Even small variations in technique were mercilessly criticized; theories from other analytic schools were either not placed on the curriculum or were branded as "deviations." Eissler (1953) elaborated his concept of "parameters" as a way of forestalling anyone who sought to depart from the accepted posture of surgical detachment and the primary of analytic interpretation. Reverence for Freud – annotating his texts as if one were attending a Yeshiva – replaced an unprejudiced engagement with the clinical data. Those who questioned the leaders of the institute were accused of vulgarizing or contaminating psychoanalysis – a code for Americanizing it – and had difficulty in making their careers.

At the New York Psychoanalytic Institute, as elsewhere, issues of power came to a head around the appointment of training analysts. Inevitably, there was nepotism and cronyism. Being a training analyst conferred great prestige within the organization, as well as referrals, economic security, and the mystique of authority. Competence did not seem to weigh heavily with the self-perpetuating oligarchy that tyrannized over the institute. For more than twenty years beginning in the 1970s, Jacob Arlow and Charles Brenner battled unsuccessfully against its consolidation of autocratic power. For those who view Arlow and Brenner as psychoanalytic conservatives, Kirsner's account of their role as reformers will be a welcome counterweight. Brenner's democratizing amendment twice failed to receive a two-thirds majority in an atmosphere marked by name-calling and acrimony. Although the American Psychoanalytic Association paid several site visits to the New York Institute, it produced reports that evaded the substantive issues of governance.

All in all, the history of the New York Psychoanalytic Institute reflects a style of governing based on secrecy and charisma. As Kirsner rightly notes, attempts to inculcate a uniform technique during training are likely to foster a guild system of masters and apprentices, not collegial dialogue. Furthermore, excessive concentration on technique tends to efface the centrality of the analyst's subjectivity and its curative role in the treatment. Against the backdrop of such authoritarianism and dogmatism, it is not surprising that the reputation of the New York Psychoanalytic Institute has in recent decades undergone a decline. It appears intellectually stale and clinically retrograde, locked into an antiquated metapsychology. Candidates in New York City have increasingly preferred to take their training at institutes where the climate is less haughty and authoritarian and more respectful of their autonomy and creativity as clinicians and human beings.

The centerpiece and longest chapter of the book aptly called "Fear and Loathing in Los Angeles" focuses on the Los Angeles Psychoanalytic Society and Institute. In order to grasp the internal power dynamics of LAPSI, Kirsner needed a dose of Kierkegaard's existentialism and the gonzo flair of Hunter Thompson. He had a "Rashomon"-like experience when analysts gave divergent but internally consistent and "truthful" accounts of its tumultuous history. In the interests of disclosure, I should say that I was trained at LAPSI from 1980 to 1988, that is, in a relatively tranquil phase largely after the events described in this account. I continue to serve on its faculty and I have written a personal account (Fisher 1991, of my training there. This chapter of Kirsner's book is thus naturally the one that holds the greatest interest for me.

Even more than that of most institutes, LAPSI's history is one of splits and near splits, threatened and actual lawsuits, and impasses between charismatic and narcissistic leaders. In addition, the institute experienced two major challenges to psychoanalytic orthodoxy – first by analysts influenced by non-Kleinian British object relations theory and subsequently by those hoping to introduce Melanie Klein's perspectives in the curriculum.

Over the years, LAPSI developed a rigorous training program that generated a culture of high seriousness around issues of what did and did not constitute a psychoanalytic process, a pride in affiliation, and a sense that those trained in other institutes (especially in Los Angeles) were second rate. Those who graduated felt a comradeship that was at times a negative solidarity. But beneath a forbidding façade, there existed. an undercurrent of sustained excitement about psychoanalysis: Members appeared really to care about their discipline.

LAPSI could also point to a distinguished history of leaders, beginning with its European founders – Ernst Simmel, Freud's doctor and the author of an important paper on war battle induced trauma, (Simmel, 1918) and the erudite and dynamic Otto Fenichel, the author of a major work of theoretical synthesis (Fenichel, 1945) and an evocative book on technique (Fenichel, 1941). The institute also had on its faculty several excellent scholars who contributed to the literature, as well as flamboyant individuals who could speak extemporaneously with passion and flair. Public criticism of others became part of LAPSI's culture; being supportive, or even tolerant, of those under attack was deemed soft and sentimental. For many who graduated in the 1960s and after, this climate could be exceptionally intimidating; many never dared to speak at meetings, let alone publish.

Bright and dedicated individuals were drawn to the institute, often out of a desire to be analyzed, supervised, or taught by one of LAPSI's notables. Teaching was normally at a high level, explicitly aimed at integrating theory and practice. Until the mid-1960s, there tended to be a unified body of theory and technique, grounded in Freud and mainstream ego psychology, perhaps codified in Greenson's volume on analytic technique. (Greenson, 1967).

In 1950, after being in existence for only four years, LAPSI split. This led to the creation of the Society for Psychoanalytic Medicine of Southern California. The schism turned on issues of lay analysis versus medical orthodoxy as well as the tension between American-trained physicians and European-trained lay analysts. While LAPSI's curriculum rested on the cornerstones of Freud's thinking, it had lay analysts; what became the Southern California Psychoanalytic Institute had a medical orientation but perceived itself as more innovative, embracing the ideas of Franz Alexander, who moved from Chicago to Los Angeles in the mid-1950s.

Alexander argued that one could do analysis at a frequency of three sessions a week; he asserted that psychoanalysis was efficacious as a cure because of its educational value, famously referring to psychic change as a "corrective emotional experience" (Alexander and French, 1946).

During LAPSI's golden years from 1950 to 1964, when the theory was unified, referrals were abundant, and candidates flocked to training, the institute experienced pervasive internal strife, primarily centered on a personality conflict between its two most visible and brilliant leaders, Ralph (Romi) Greenson and Leo Rangell. Despite both having been influenced by Fenichel and being of a similar intellectual cast, the two developed an intense antagonism that had disastrous results. Greenson is best known as the author of the textbook (Greenson, 1967) on psychoanalysis, as the creator of the concept of the working alliance (Greenson, 1965), the concept of the real relationship between analyst and analysand, and as the analyst of Marilyn Monroe. By his detractors, Greenson is described as self-aggrandizing, historionic, lax with boundaries, derivative as a thinker, and prone to anger. To his many admirers, Greenson was someone of vision who could be generous, inspiring, an electrifying public speaker, and a man with an unquenchable thirst for knowledge. His followers likewise praised his attunement to the unconscious process, his complex understanding of motivation, and his commitment to psychoanalytic research.

Rangell, for his part, published prolifically and was gifted at synthesizing others' ideas. He wrote a popular book on Watergate (Rangell, 1980). There is much ambivalence about Rangell locally. His supporters speak glowingly of his acute intelligence, his ethics, and his interest in promoting a unified theory of psychoanalysis that remains rooted in the early pioneers. To his critics, Rangell appears resistant to new ideas and consumed by ambition, chronically complaining of a lack of appreciation despite having received many honors. He was twice elected President of the American Psychoanalytic Association and subsequently became twice President of the International Psychoanalytic Association. The Greenson-Rangell quarrel split LAPSI's Education Committee into two factions. Kirsner describes the atmosphere as malicious and backbiting. No new training analysts were appointed, and candidates were expected to side with their analysts.

The struggle reached a climax during the so-called "Wexler Affair" in 1964–1965, an ugly episode that had terrible consequences for the Institute. Wexler was a New York-born lawyer who then trained as a clinical psychologist and he spent time at the Menninger Clinic in Topeka, Kansas; he made important contributions to the analytic treatment of schizophrenics. He was politically and personally close to Greenson. In 1964, Wexler was alleged to have physically attacked one of his patients. The Wexler affair exacerbated the hostilities between Greenson and Rangell. Besides indicating how politics and innuendo could dominate ethical considerations, it demonstrated how poorly the Institute was functioning. Wexler, it should be noted, was never convicted of any wrongdoing, nor did he receive much in terms of due process; in the aftermath, however, he withdrew his energy and creativity from LAPSI. Rangell himself pulled back from the institute in the late 1960s in protest against the uncivil tone of those years.

In turning to the Kleinian controversy that rocked LAPSI in the early 1970s, it is important to underscore that most institutes affiliated with the American Psychoanalytic Association considered Kleinianism a derogatory epithet and Melanie Klein herself a crazed woman. Kleinian theory and practice were never included in curricula or discussed at scientific meetings. Ivan McGuire, an independent-minded training analyst at LAPSI, recommended to his supervisees that they read the writings of Fairbairn, Guntrip, and Winnicott. McGuire often supervised or reanalyzed younger graduates of the Institute, many of whom found classical theory lacking in clinical efficacy, experienced distant, and who gravitated to relational forms of thinking. McGuire also suggested that his protégés read Klein, although he later turned violently against both Klein and Bion.

LAPSI analyst Bernard Brandchaft initiated contact with leading Kleinian thinkers in London such as Herbert Rosenfeld, Hanna Segal, and Wilfrid Bion and organized meetings where they were brought to Los Angeles to lecture and supervise. Because of the 1950 split and the Greenson-Rangell rift, the introduction of Kleinian perspectives did not occur in an atmosphere of dispassionate reflection. By the mid-1960s, the Kleinian approach was widely considered to be incompatible with the dominant Freudian ethos of the Institute. The debate took on a religious tonality; accusations were met by counteraccusations, recriminations by counterrecriminations. It became violent and acrimonious.

Meanwhile, interest surged among candidates and recent graduates in Kleinian psychoanalysis, so much so that the ruling cliques feared a takeover. Greenson did all he could do to thwart the growth of Kleinianism at LAPSI. Rangell, for his part, had no use for Kleinian theory, but he voiced his objections in a "gentlemanly" manner. The Kleinian analysts faced a threat to their livelihoods and reputations, which they regarded as a witch hunt, and many countered with inflated rhetoric and an angry sense of martyrdom. In 1968, Bion moved to Los Angeles, remaining there until shortly before his death in 1980. An original and powerful thinker, Bion reformulated Kleinian theory in his own language. He re-analyzed and supervised many members of the LAPSI community, but never formally affiliated with the Institute or played an active part in its political strife.

Problems escalated when a leading Kleinian training analyst, Bernard Bail, was suspended from teaching seminars in 1974. Bail aggressively threatened a lawsuit and organized a written protest to the International Psychoanalytic Association to document LAPSI's discrimination against the Kleinians. Local Kleinians issued inflammatory statements and claimed to be sole possessors of the truth, becoming more inflexible and dogmatic than their counterparts in London. Seminars pitted militant Kleinians against militant Freudians, both of whom caricatured authentic Kleinian teachings, causing many instructors to conclude that they could no longer continue their pedagogical activities. The institute became polarized and there was a discernible loss of civility.

The site visit of the American Psychoanalytic Association in 1973 made matters worse, as the national body dreaded a Kleinian infection in one of their constituent societies. At a certain point, the American requested that LAPSI "get rid of the

Kleinians." In 1976, an elite group of sixteen analysts prepared to secede from LAPSI and form a new institute, so disgusted were they about the waste of their energies and the unbridgeable rifts. Within a few days, the "impulsive and hasty" decision to form a new institute was abandoned. Under the leadership of a number of conciliatory LAPSI members, who excelled at mediation, aided by Joan Fleming of the American, LAPSI by the mid-1970s entered into a period of de-escalation. The years of ideological warfare had exhausted everyone and a calm gradually returned to the Institute. Over the next decade, much of the suspicion and distrust began to abate. Ultimately, the American proposed a policy of nondiscrimination against the Kleinians. Currently, Kleinian psychoanalysis forms an integral part of the Institute's curriculum, as do relational, self-psychological, and intersubjective perspectives, along with a thorough grounding in Freud's theory and practice.

In his conclusion, Kirsner reiterates many of his earlier observations, particularly about the authoritarianism and cultism of analytic institutes. He calls for the abolition of mandatory training analyses, which he believes perpetuate a system built on hierarchy, patronage, and anointment. It is notoriously difficult to assess psychoanalytic proficiency; those who profess to be guardians of high standards are actually engaging in a language game based on mythical notions of analytic knowledge. Many analysts teach psychoanalysis as if it were irrefutable, scientific truth. This impedes genuine learning by promoting delusions of expertise, defensive idealization, denigration of outsiders, and dismissal of alternative theories. Although Kirsner thinks that it is too late to affiliate free-standing institutes with universities, he prescribes academic culture as an antidote to the insularity of establishment psychoanalysis, with its often grandiose claims to knowledge. He ends pessimistically observing that many psychoanalysts aspire to function as secular priests. The codification and bureaucratization of psychoanalysis have produced "unfree" and "narcissistic" institutions, which have hindered psychoanalysis from taking its rightful place as a humanistic discipline, a powerful and effective therapy for certain emotional illnesses, and a branch of the human sciences open to skeptical inquiry, revision, research, expansion, and scrutiny by the external world.

While there is much to praise in Kirsner's book, there are also grounds for a critique. One of the pitfalls faced by Kirsner is his reliance on gossip, often about events that are difficult to corroborate. He reportedly comes up against, but provides no clear solution to, the problem of bias. In recounting partisan battles, combatants and their allies are inclined to furnish prejudiced and self-serving versions of events. Within psychoanalysis, there has been a nasty tendency toward *ad hominem* arguments. Instead of dealing with an opponent's idea in a rational manner and a civil tone, a personal attack, often tinged with a psychoanalytic vocabulary, becomes the rule. People's ideas get dismissed because they are supposedly "unanalytic."

Oral testimony always has to be weighed carefully, placed in its political and cultural contexts, and evaluated against written sources. In his chapter on LAPSI, I was not convinced of the reliability of Kirsner's informants; he might have been more alert to their biases, rather than simply accepting their versions of how the history unfolded. Kirsner does not take into account the precariousness of memory and the proclivity of storytellers to fabricate or present archetypal narrative structures. When I asked him in a recent interview about the methodological problems inherent in oral history, Kirsner replied honestly but somewhat evasively: "I tried to get whatever information I could get from whatever source I could. I needed source material from interviews for lack of other material ... Of course, interviews require a good deal of judgment of what is valid, true, and reliable evidence, so I checked evidence from a variety of sources where possible, including any available documentary evidence. The Rashomon phenomenon in particular created problems. Which narrative was I to believe? ... I circulated drafts to a wide range of analysts for comment. Mercifully, I think the feedback helped me get through many bottlenecks" (Fisher, 2000, p. 7). Kirsner does not spell out how he assessed the accuracy of his informants; often, one senses, the sheer verbal power of the account carried great weight. As in the clinical process or in teaching, however, a dialectical complexity and important points of view often emerge from witnesses who may lack full coherence.

Kirsner does not adequately acknowledge his transferential ties to his informants, nor did he always have access to those who come off badly in his account. He does not, for example, appear to have secured an interview with George Pollock, who was the czar of the Chicago Psychoanalytic Institute. In researching the history of the Greenson-Rangell struggles, he does not offset Rangel's testimony with those of articulate Greensonians, even though he attempted to interview Wexler, who declined to speak to him. I also felt that his account of the controversies at LAPSI was tilted in the direction of his Kleinian informants like Albert Mason and Jim Grotstein.

A conspicuous omission of Kirsner's book is any discussion of economics, of how referrals can generate loyalty and solidify political alliances. Private practitioners are often anxious and insecure individuals who depend greatly on the referrals of more popular and influential colleagues. The 1960s dictum that sometimes Marx trumps Freud remains true. Most analysts refer patients to those who refer others back to them; usually, they share the same theory and technical orientation, but not always. It does not hurt to be good looking, a ready talker, and to be perceived as likeable or decent. It is often impossible to know how a given analyst works behind closed doors or to what degree he or she is attuned to countertransferential resonances and the unconscious dynamics in patients. This may depend upon how close the analyst remains to his or her own experience on the couch and on whether the analyst has an innate capacity for empathy to subjective processes as they unfold in clinical work.

There are purists in every institute who do not refer patients to their own analysands or supervisees. This can create resentment and exacerbate generational conflicts. Conversely, there are analysts who do give such referrals, thereby fostering unanalyzed idealizations and dependence, transference gratifications, and a deep-rooted sense of specialness among those who receive the referrals. These issues are rarely discussed at analytic institutes and even more rarely do they receive attention in the literature. A book on the politics and psychology of referrals still needs to be written.

Prestige in analytic institutions has traditionally resided with the training analysts. In democratized institutes where every graduate is eligible to become a training analyst, prestige gets displaced onto who treats the most candidates and has the most supervisees. Often, one becomes recognized by teaching seminars, above all, those on technique or other required courses. Visibility in these seminars generates referrals, which in turn bestows the aura of power. In my experience, alternative institutes with new theoretical paradigms often replicate the hierarchical structures and toxic ambiance of the more conventional institutes, often with a loss of clinical and conceptual rigor. The targets of demonizing may change, but uncritical thinking, ideological posturing, and religious fervor are nearly impossible to eradicate.

In the long run, I suspect, psychoanalysis will cease to be an impossible profession only when historians, cultural critics, and practicing analysts come to grips with the unconscious tendency toward discipleship that is built into any educational structure. Discipleship is endemic to analytic training because of the regressive aspects of a personal training analysis and how one learns from another to identify and use one's own subjectivity in clinical work. Blinded by unanalyzed narcissistic countertransferences, many training analysts insist that their analysands agree with them on issues of ethics and practice, extending even to political allegiances. But when we finally understand the pervasiveness of the unconscious transferences that underlie discipleship, we may have less need for masters and a discourse that purports to be all-explanatory. In most analytic institutes today, there is still little reward for thinking critically and imaginatively or for taking on the establishment, even if it happens to be an anti-establishment.

Previously published in *American Image,* Vol. 59, No. 2, Summer 2002, pp. 209–223.

References

Alexander, F. and French, T. M. (1946). *Psychoanalytic Therapy: Principles and Applications*. New York: Ronald Press.
Eissler, K. (1953). The Effect of the Structure of the Ego on Psychoanalytic Technique. *Journal of the American Psychoanalytic Association*, 1, 104–143.
Fenichel, O. (1941). *Problems of Psychoanalytic Technique*. Albany: Psychoanalytic Quarterly.
Fenichel, O. (1945). *The Psychoanalytic Theory of Neurosis*. New York: Norton.
Fisher, D. J. (1991). "Introduction" in *Cultural Theory and Psychoanalytic Tradition*. New Brunswick: Transaction, pp. xx–xxxi.
Fisher, D. J. (2000). Interview with Douglas Kirsner. *The Free Associator: The Free Associator: LAPSI Quarterly Newsletter*, 4(3), 6–9.
Greenson, R. R. (1965). The Working Alliance and the Transference Neurosis. *Psychoanalytic Quarterly*, 34, 155–181.
Greenson, R. R. (1967). *The Technique and Practice of Psychoanalysis*. New York: International Universities Press.

Hale, N. G. Jr (1971). *Freud and the Americans: The Beginnings of Psychoanalysis in the United States*. New York: Oxford University Press.

Hale, N. G. Jr (1995). *The Rise and Crisis of Psychoanalysis in the United States: Freud and the Americans 1917-1985*. New York: Oxford University Press.

Kirsner, D. (2000). *Unfree Associations: Inside Psychoanalytic Institutes*. London: Process Press.

Kurzweill, E. (1989). *The Freudians: A Comparative Perspective*. New Haven: Yale University Press.

Rangell, L. (1980). *The Mind of Watergate: An Exploration of the Compromise of Integrity*. New York: Norton.

Roudinesco, E. (1982). *La bataille de cent ans* [One Hundred Year Battle]. Paris: Editions Ramsay.

Roudinesco. (1986). *Histoire de la psychanalyse en France, 1925-1985* [History of Psychoanalysis in France, 1925-1985]. Paris: Seuil.

Roudinesco. (1997). *Jacques Lacan*. (B. Bray, Trans.). New York: Columbia University Press.

Simmel, E. (1918). War Neuroses and Psychic Trama, in Karl Abrahma, Ernst Simmel, and Ernest Jones, *Psychoanalysis and the War Neuroses* (J. Strachey, Trans.). London: International Psychoanalytic Press.

Turkle, S. (1978). *Psychoanalytic Politics: Freud's French Revolution*. New York: Basic Books.

An Interview with Douglas Kirsner

DJF: *You have technical training as a philosopher. What motivated your turn in interest from philosophy to psychoanalysis?*

DK: I see psychoanalysis as inherently philosophical. Psychoanalysis seemed to me a very cogent stab at the big questions about the nature of the self, relationships, and human nature, applied in a detailed way to our human experience. I was always interested in the related area of history of ideas, of how concepts don't arise in a vacuum but have a career in a social context. So investigating the interrelations of psychoanalysis and its socio-historical context seemed an excellent idea. I ran the Deakin University Freud Conference for twenty years in Melbourne and teach psychoanalytic studies at Master and Ph.D. levels at Deakin University.

DJF: *How did your immersion in, and knowledge of, Australian culture provide a perspective on events at LAPSI? What is your inner connection to Los Angeles and to LAPSI?*

DK: I don't think Australian culture ever prepared me for LA or for LAPSI. Since I first came to LA in 1977, I have always found LA and Angelinos endlessly fascinating. In particular, the analysts I met in the early 1980s in LA filled me in on the then relatively recent dramatic events with the Kleinians and the American. I vividly remember standing in Albert Mason's kitchen in 1981 saying, "I hear there were some troubles with Bion, the Kleinians and the Institute." "Trouble!" Albert exclaimed and regaled me with a story I had to pursue. I made many friends among the analysts I interviewed in subsequent years, and, I hope, no enemies. I was most struck with how perfectly decent analysts had quite different takes on "the same" events, what I called the "Rashomon" phenomenon. I thought this was such a puzzling and important story that I wanted to be able to account for the whole elephant rather than just seeing it from partial perspectives.

DJF: *How would you characterize the political culture of LAPSI in the period from the middle 1950s through the later 1970s?*

DK: Until the Reorganization, I think that the culture stymied creativity and the normal career expectations of the vast number of analysts. The right political ladder had to be played by the relatively rare person who was promoted to training analyst. I think that Greenson's influence was scarcely an unalloyed benefit and that many sensed there was something wrong with the establishment. They often sought other approaches not only because new ideas were exciting but also because the setting was rife for them, as the scent of corruption was never far off. I believe that the Wexler Affair was symptomatic of many of the real flaws that LAPSI suffered at the time. The Reorganization clearly brought a breath of fresh air, but the American was not prepared to tolerate it. The American was very critical of LA in the 1973 site visit and wanted to shut the Institute down later. Just why they were critical is a mix of reasons, some good and some bad. There is no doubt that they wanted to get rid of the Kleinians. On the other hand, there were enduring problems within LAPSI that contributed to the problems that the American was concerned about. I think that the Committee for the Unification of the Institute led by Mel Mandel and Leonard Rosengarten together with the educative endeavors of the Fleming Committee contributed to an important healing process within LAPSI. Yet LAPSI's subsequent history with the creation of new institutes and the relative lack of enthusiasm within what was sometimes a shell may bear some relation to some unresolved historical problems.

DJF: *You draw heavily on interviews as source material. What are some of the methodological problems in your reliance on the interview technique?*

DK: I tried to get whatever information I could from whatever source I could. I needed source materials from interviews for lack of other material (with the notable exception of the dossier that Bernard Bail, Albert Mason, and others submitted to the IPA). Of course, interviews require a good deal of judgment as to what is valid, true, and reliable evidence, so I checked the evidence from a variety of sources where possible, including any available documentary evidence. The Rashomon phenomenon is particular created problems. Which narrative was I to believe? Trying to work out which if any of conflicting narratives were true was most difficult. I did something quite unusual to try to resolve this problem – I circulated drafts to a wide range of analysts for comment. Mercifully, I think the feedback helped me get through many bottlenecks. Also, going back to the creation of the Institute and the time of the 1950 split helped me situate the later troubles within a long-term historical context. I am particularly grateful to Leo Rangell for helping me along this historical path.

DJF: *In understanding the conflict between Greenson and Rangell, it is clear that they were very close in matters of psychoanalytic theory and technique. How, then, do you account for the persistence of their animosity? How destructive was this conflict within the institute?*

DK: Their conflict was not theoretical, although it is also true Greenson more and more took on the ideas of Wexler about closeness to patients despite his textbook. They obviously had completely different personalities. It's so hard to know. Was Greenson envious of Rangell's achievements? Probably, but this wouldn't explain why there was so much animosity well before Rangell started to achieve national and international positions. As was demonstrated in the discussion after my presentation at LAPSI, many, including Rangell, felt that Greenson did not use his power well within LAPSI and violated many protocols. As Jim Grotstein said, Greenson "dealt the cards" and there were no rewards for anyone opposing him. Rangell led the fight against the negative side of Greenson's considerable influence over a long period and the unfortunate results of the Wexler Affair put an end to Rangell's struggle within LAPSI against Greenson. Greenson's influence did not abate for some time after that. It's a sorry story.

DJF: *Without having interviewed him, you tend to approach Greenson in an* ad hominem *manner, seeing him as self-aggrandizing, power hungry, loose with boundaries with his patients, derivative as a thinker, and a polarizing presence within the organization. Others have focused on Greenson's generosity, inspirational qualities, attunement to unconscious process, his humor, theatricality, and deep-seated commitment to psychoanalytic research and practice. Is your portrait overly negative?*

DK: I often asked myself similar questions. It would have been great to be able to meet him but of course he died before I began this project. Clearly, he inspired many people and had great enthusiasm for psychoanalysis in all its aspects. I think Greenson was a very complex character with many virtues as well as vices. He was both more creative and more destructive than most, creative in his ideas and in lecturing but destructive in psychoanalytic policies. On many reports, he often was carried away by grandiosity despite his charisma. His entertaining qualities stood in the way of a more measured, rational approach. Even his friends told me of many negative qualities. Boundaries were a major problem for him even if you take the published accounts of his behavior with Marilyn Monroe with many grains of salt. He gossiped about patients a lot, etc. I relied on testimonies not only from his enemies but also from neutrals and friends. I circulated drafts of my chapter and requested feedback from a variety of LAPSI members, then amended my drafts accordingly. And then there were documented matters such as his fund for Psychoanalytic Research detailed in Young-Bruehl's book on Anna Freud where she didn't even interview Leo Rangell. Many of the accounts given in the discussion of my LAPSI presentation further confirmed my views.

I really don't have an axe to grind in relation to Greenson but I haven't heard anything that makes me want to change my view that, despite his contributions and the qualities you mention, he was a very difficult person who had many negative influences in the development of LAPSI. Would the same thing have happened if he were in another institute, especially away from Tinseltown? I don't know, but

I guess the focus has to be on the climate at LAPSI in which this took place, the soil rather than just the individual personality, even where that personality was especially strong and charismatic as Greenson's was.

DJF: How did the introduction of Object Relations theory and Klein's thought shake the very foundation of LAPSI? Was this a major confrontation between two master discourses where one had to predominate? Did Kleinian thought represent an epistemological break with Freud and "mainstream psychoanalysis"? Was the debate less about scientific and clinical issues and more about hegemonic influences at the Institute?

DK: I think the debate was far less about the scientific issues and had a major affective component. I am not saying that the scientific issues were irrelevant. I am sure that the popularity was not only affective, given that there was also excitement about new ideas. But in analytic disputes, trainees normally follow their training analyst's orientation – or sometimes rebel against it. I agree with Leo Rangell who argued in "Transference to Theory" that many of the wrongs analysts experienced in their analysis and in their training are transferred over to the wrongs of the theories that were being propounded. The soil for the changes was prepared in the disturbed history that preceded the Kleinian development. In a way, it was an "opportunistic infection." Don't get me wrong. I think Klein and the Object Relations theorists made significant contributions to psychoanalytic theory and therapy. The question is why this happened then. LA was the only institute in the United States where Kleinian ideas were propounded and became popular. The complex mix of answers that involves the politics and the institutional systems as well as the theories is part of what I try to develop in the book.

DJF: With LAPSI's Kleinian controversies as a backdrop, how can innovative ideas and clinical approaches be introduced into analytic institutes without being so disruptive to the educational, healing, and governing functions of the institute?

DK: I think that Kernberg's idea of a university culture within institutes is on the right track. An emphasis on public protocols and function is important. Clear criteria for decisions need to be on the table, particularly around the training analysis and training analyst status. I have the impression that the concept of training analyst as a status to be attained through the anointment has lost much of its allure in many institutes, obviously led by LAPSI's experiment in the Reorganization. If training analysts are a higher breed, this needs to be demonstrable in each case. Justice must not only be done, but seen to be done. Otherwise it becomes political, destructive of confidence and trust, and productive of acute paranoia. The institutions need to produce trust and confidence and keep paranoia as far away as possible. So there are structural problems, and some of these can be addressed politically. The other, harder issue is the scientific or conceptual one of trying to get analysts to use the same definitions for the terms they are using.

Otherwise analysis becomes a confusion of tongues where little development can take place because nobody uses fundamental concepts in the same way, even within the same schools.

DJF: *What changes need to take place in LAPSI's current political and educational culture to permit more healing of past traumas? How can the current administration avoid repeating some of the errors, rigidities, and insensitivities of the past?*

DK: Obviously analysts need to do institutionally what they do in their offices. Something like the South African "Truth and Reconciliation" Commission would be going too far, but there's a point there institutionally. As every analyst knows, we are doomed to repeat what we don't understand, what we are unable to say. So it is an error to avoid the history that shapes an institution if that institution is far from optimal. I would like to compliment LAPSI on having a fine start in airing some of the dirty clothing at an official occasion. I gather that the reaction to the evening has been a positive one primarily because such issues have begun to be talked about openly.

I would think that more discussion of such issues in a variety of settings including smaller groups could be useful as a way of working toward an effective future. What does this history show us about the nature of LAPSI, psychoanalytic institutions, and people? How far has LAPSI contributed to its own problems, and how far have other factors such as the American been responsible? I don't think it's just a question of the people who no doubt played their part in the problems. A focus on systemic, structural issues that are at play, together with the conceptual and theoretical ones, would be helpful.

DJF: *How is it possible for LAPSI to be organized so as to promote and foster creativity and enthusiasm about ideas and practice which are so interrelated?*

DK: LAPSI has demonstrated enthusiasm for new ideas in the past with the introduction of Kleinian, Object Relations, and Self-Psychological theories, but this was mitigated by the political and historical context responsible for many of the affective reasons for seeking and adopting these new ideas. I think such issues need to be addressed together with issues around training such as those discussed in Kernberg's latest article in the *International Journal of Psychoanalysis* this year, issues connected with LAPSI's relationship with the American as well as ways of exploring theoretical and conceptual problems.

Previously published in *The Free Associator, The LAPSI Quarterly Newsletter*, No. 3, 2000, pp. 6–9.

Chapter 9

On the History of Lacanian Psychoanalysis in France

In July of 1975, I was completing my second year of post-doctoral studies at the Sixieme Section of the Ecole Pratique des Hautes Etudes in Paris. Summertime in Paris features late sunsets and a blue-black evening sky, well-rendered in Van Gogh's late paintings. Gorgeous light and mild weather transform an enchanting city into one of romance and adventure. I had become a Parisian *flaneur:* strolling leisurely along the boulevards of the Left Bank, with no destination, landing in a lovely outdoor café on the rue Jacob with a spectacular view of the Saint-Germain Church. I did not know it then, but this café was adjacent to a bookstore specializing in psychoanalytic literature. A couple arrived at the next table. They were quintessentially Parisian: young, hip, voluble, and exceedingly attractive. Their conversation was animated, and they soon included me. They carried with them two paperbacks with elusively simple titles, *Ecrits I* and *Ecrits II* (Lacan, 1966). These former leftists of the late 1960s claimed, quite hyperbolically, that the insurrectionary mood of the sixties had been replaced by the new revolutionary outlook condensed in these two volumes. The author of the *Writings* was Jacques Lacan. His texts, they asserted vehemently, merited the rigorous study and exegesis of social and political philosophers and critical theorists. Lacan was a brilliant genius, at the intersection of the linguistic and the subjective. They waved the volumes like Chinese students gesticulated before Mao's Little Red Book. I was amused and slightly irritated by them; they seemed histrionic and rhetorically excessive in a recognizably French manner. But something about the episode remained with me. The anecdote takes on meaning if placed in the context of the history of French psychoanalysis; this trendy and appealing Parisian couple represented the victory of Lacanian psychoanalysis in France, an implantation (some say glorious, others horrid) that had reached its zenith in the middle 1970s, where he ranks just beneath Freud.

   Lacan was original, innovative in technique, charismatic, profoundly and wrenchingly modern in his approach to the mind. He re-imagined psychoanalytic discourse, making it relevant to contemporary audiences. Reading him is never easy, always stimulating, at times maddening. Whether one thinks of him as a genius or a master thinker, Lacan reinvented psychoanalysis; along the way, he offered a new language, created a major new school of analytic thinking, and significant departures in analytic theory and practice. His presence in Paris was an extraordinary spectacle with powerful reverberations throughout France and the world.

Elizabeth Roudinesco is the historian of this somewhat bizarre and somewhat baroque history. She and her family lived some of its history; she chronicles it with verve, intelligence, wit, passion, and a global if polemical view. She has also written an intellectual biography of Lacan (Roudinesco, 1997) and important essays on psychoanalytic cultural criticism (Roudinesco, 2014). She is an accomplished and versatile writer with a trenchant point of view.

The century-long story of French psychoanalysis from 1885 to 1985, the 100-year battle, as Roudinesco subtitles her study in the original French, emerged from and was enmeshed in the cultural and political history of France during this age (Roudinesco, 1990). In effect, it is a story of how French psychoanalysis found its authentically French, that is, Lacanian identity. French psychoanalysis was influenced by the rejection of so-called "Jewish" psychoanalysts in the 1940s because of the racial policies connected to the Nazi occupation of France and the anti-Semitic policies of the Vichy government; this profound loss meant that French psychoanalysis moved more toward theory and textual analysis rather than in a more practical, clinical direction. Roudinesco argues that only a truly French thinker, rooted in the language, mores, and Catholic culture of France, but atheist and modernist in sensibility, could have been the agent of such an implantation. Freudian psychoanalysis penetrated into France slowly, tortuously, and after encountering powerful, entrenched forces of opposition.

By the 1890s, the French already had established a tradition of psychology, well-articulated by its writers and moralists. The French possessed their own competing discipline and profession of psychiatry, imagining that they had no need for other perspectives. French xenophobia and cultural nationalism made the French suspicious of, if not hostile to, a German science like psychoanalysis. Finally, French ethnocentrism merged with a conservative variety of anti-Semitism, particularly strident after the Dreyfus Affair, to obstruct the rapid diffusion of psychoanalytic methods and insights. It was easy to dismiss Freud's ideas as Jewish; to isolate his disciples as another disreputable clan of Jewish subversives, bohemians, and undesirables.

Roudinesco's book is part novel, part intellectual history, part journalism, part gossip, part cultural commentary, part polemic, part biography, part autobiography, and part institutional history. It reads well and is accessible, though it deals with difficult ideas (Roudinesco, 1990). It is fluently translated by Jeffrey Mehlman, who himself helped to disseminate Lacan's thought in America by translating the latter's "Seminar on 'The Purloined Letter'" in 1972 (Lacan, 1972). Roudinesco belongs to the fourth generation of French psychoanalysis. Her mother, Jenny Aubry, nee Weiss, was a physician who worked to introduce psychoanalysis into the French hospital world. Described by Roudinesco as rebellious, activist, and feminist, Aubry practiced what she preached; she joined a Communist branch of the Resistance in the struggle against the Nazis. In the early 1950s, she became affiliated with Lacan. This half-Jewish, half-Protestant woman maintained a lifelong passion against authoritarianism. Roudinesco tellingly writes, "In the Weiss family, women did not conceal their frequently extreme opinions" (p. 240). Nor does Roudinesco. She is an erudite and incisive intellectual with a facile command of the French structuralist and poststructuralist arsenal. She is an authoritarian anti-authoritarian. She writes as a partisan insider with distinct ideological allegiances; her biases are transparent and she makes no attempt to be balanced or fair. Discussing intellectual encounters over the sixty years, Roudinesco decides who wins debates, whose mind is most subtle, and who wields the nastier and more corrosive pen. Her criteria are not always self-evident. She refers to Lacan as his majesty and our hero. She can become omnipotent, telling us without evidence precisely what was on Lacan's mind. As part of the generation that came into consciousness in the 1960s, Roudinesco, born in 1944, carries with her a 1960s sensibility; her volume is loaded ideologically, and her ideology is Lacanian. Like many of her generation in France, some of her extreme left Marxist militancy appears to have been displaced onto a Lacanian intellectual and clinical framework. This is a subtext of Lacanian discourse: self-assured, self-righteous rhetoric about saving the world that masquerades under different labels. She engages in intellectual duels with aggressivity and phallic narcissism of the pen. Because she is a practicing analyst, I was troubled by her judgments of people, finding them to be summary, lacking empathy or compassion, sometimes lacking soundness or plausibility. She is consistently cruel and dismissive, for example, in her remarks about Rudolph Loewenstein, Lacan's analyst, and Marie Bonaparte, Lacan's rival and an analysand of Freud. In Lacanian fashion, she privileges theory and metaphor, especially favoring those gifted in flamboyant and self-reflexive commentary, over rigorous scholarship, clear prose style, and comprehensive documentation.

The book's documentation is flagrantly uneven. She cites French sources primarily and parochially, a representative practice of thinkers such as Foucault, Lacan, Althusser, and those immersed in the Parisian cultural context. She rarely cites non-French contributors to her narrative or analytic sections, even when these writers have been translated into French and deal directly with her themes. Emulating Lacan, she is dogmatically anti-American and postures against the International Psychoanalytic Association (IPA) the way Leninists once railed against international imperialism. The first is a glaring, sectarian feature of the entire Lacanian enterprise, though reminiscent of de Gaulle's attitudes toward America; and the second is an illustration of the pitfalls of thinking monolithically. When she turns to events and factual details about the personalities within the Lacanian movement, however, Roudinesco is exceptionally well informed, many of her sources for the period from 1969 to 1980 derive from her own personal archives. She knows and has interviewed most of the leading figures around Lacan.

As an intellectual historian of the non-Lacanian sector of French psychoanalysis, Roudinesco is dazzling, putatively encyclopedic, but superficial. Her treatment of thinkers and cultural movements is almost always inadequate, decontextualized, and without mastery of the existing scholarly literature. She is misleading and erroneous about Andre Breton and the history of Surrealism, of Romain Rolland and his idealism and debates with Freud, of Andre Gide and the cultural politics of *La Nouvelle Revue Française*, and of the importance of Pierre-Jean Jouve and his use of analytic themes in his poetry and writings. Yet her knowledge of the crosscurrents of twentieth-century French psychiatry and of the convergence of Marxism and Hegelianism with psychoanalytic thinkers is pertinent and excellently rendered. Her insights into the personalities in the Lacanian movement and in the Parisian university system, many of whom were fellow travelers of Lacan, are also superb, if marred by caustic irony and excessive familiarity.

Roudinesco captures the history of French psychoanalysis, its passionate, politicized, schismatic events, and above all its intellectual vibrancy. In detail, scope, and breadth, her book far exceeds the previous scholarship in the field (Barande & Barande, 1975; Mijolla, 1982). Some recent scholarship is excellent and historically sophisticated, especially about the French non-Lacanians (Mijolla, 2010). She describes the major splits in the French analytic movement in 1953, 1963, 1969, and the final dissolution of Lacan's Freudian School of Paris in 1980. This last event constituted a rupture of the Lacanian Empire by Lacan himself and his designated heir apparent, his son-in-law Jacques-Alain Miller. She astutely demonstrates the ruthlessness and maniacal spirit of French psychoanalysis, including that exhibited by partisans for and against Lacan. This sectarian spirit became exacerbated and intensified after the death of Lacan in 1981, when his movement fragmented into a number of competing groups and associations, all claiming his name, language, and legitimacy (Turkle, 1992).

The destruction and self-destruction of the Lacanian movement in the 1980s may indicate the French followers' inability to grieve the death of a founding father; it surely underscores how sharp the contradictions were while Lacan was alive. French psychoanalysis thrived with the promotion of competing chapels, groups, journals, and gurus. The subculture generated a great deal of camaraderie and self-importance, as well as a heightened sense of dissension, including a paranoid flavor of suspicion and persecution. Bridge builders were suspect and few, if any, peacemakers were tolerated. Psychoanalytic education and practice seemed closer to the reflective disciplines of philosophy, critical theory, and structural linguistics, rather than those thinkers who valued introspection and who were indebted to psychological forms of investigation. In Paris, during the last 30 years, theory building became linked to empire building, which in turn unleashed massive rhetorical warfare and great institutional strife.

The Lacan of *Jacques Lacan & Co.* is a fabulous mix of the mythical and the problematic. From his youth to his maturity, he adopted a nonconformist, grandiose, regal posture. As a member of the Parisian Catholic bourgeoisie, he grew up despising the middle classes and was enamored of twentieth-century modernism, including Dadaism, Surrealism, Freudianism, and experimental literature and painting. Depicted by Roudinesco as princely, the young Lacan sought out celebrity and was eager to acquire wealth and social status. He collected rare books and art objects. He enjoyed driving expensive cars fast. Charismatic, good-looking, and capable of being charming and seductive when he chose to be, this Regency aristocrat developed into a dandified ladies' man with a succession of mistresses. At other times, he could be difficult, angry, inaccessible, arrogant, and unpredictably rebellious.

Though he had a relatively ordinary medical career and received neuropsychiatric training in Paris from 1926 to 1930, he took the extraordinary step of immersing himself in philosophical studies and the writings of Spinoza. Moving easily into the world of the Parisian Surrealists, he became knowledgeable about the psychodynamics of crime, including the various psychotic features of criminals, while refusing to dehumanize the criminal. His brother, Marc-Francois, became a Benedictine priest. Lacan abandoned all belief in a Christian God and Christian practice. One wonders if they shared many personality qualities. The young Lacan attended meetings of the royalist, chauvinist, and proto-fascist Action Française, where he admired the reactionary Charles Maurras while rejecting the principles of anti-Semitism which this organization of the extreme Right espoused.

Lacan's 1932 medical thesis, a lengthy case study of a paranoid personality, synthesized his training in French psychiatry under Gaetan de Clerambault (the theorist of erotomania), the insights of the Surrealists on automatic writing and mad love, and his earliest comprehension of Freud's writings on the psychodynamics of paranoia and homosexuality. Roudinesco regards the 1932 thesis, the case history of Aimee, as a seminal text in the French psychoanalytic movement. Lacan demonstrates that paranoia was a coherent method of knowledge, arguing for the primacy of the unconscious in clinical understanding. His thesis exemplified his genius in synthesizing apparently disparate forms of knowledge. The young Lacan wrote beautifully and excessively. The mature Lacan's writings (particularly from the 1950s through 1964) created intentional difficulties for his readers; here he wrote obscurely, as if he were inventing a new language, re-imagining the entire psychoanalytic enterprise. Roudinesco compares his early prose to Flaubert's *Madame Bovary*.

Lacan attended Alexander Kojeve's classes at the Ecole Pratique des Hautes Etudes in the 1930s. Kojeve pitted Hegel against the prevailing idealism in French philosophy and against Cartesian logic and rationality. His version of Hegel stemmed from a precise and elaborate reading of Hegel's *The Phenomenology of the Spirit*. Here Lacan encountered the master-slave dialectic, a view of history as one of the triumphs of tyranny, and first learned of the Hegelian concepts of desire, alienation, and recognition. Desire, Kojeve taught, is the desire to be recognized, not by an object but rather by another's desire. What one desires, then, is the other's desire. Lacan would reformulate these notions in terms of his own grasp of the analyst-analysand relationship and in developing a theory of unconscious psychic structure.

Kojeve became Lacan's intellectual and professorial ego ideal. Provocative and enigmatic, he interpreted elusive texts subversively and imaginatively, maintaining a distaste for publication (publication being synonymous with poubellication, a French pun suggesting placement into the garbage can). Kojeve was both marginal and well respected within the Parisian university system. He defiantly claimed that his exegesis of Hegel in the 1930s was fundamentally Marxist; he always referred to himself as a strict Stalinist. Lacan would subsequently refer to himself as a Freudian. His philosophical commentaries on Freud's texts were designed to disseminate and reinvigorate Freudian studies in France. They succeeded admirably. By 1936 Lacan became the bearer of his own personal theory, with the first draft of his article "The Mirror Stage." There is a parallel in the history of Hegelianism and of Freudianism in France; Lacan is the key figure in both histories. If intellectual France was Hegelian by the 1960s, those cultural sectors influenced by psychoanalysis were Lacanian by the end of the same decade. Lacan situated his reading of Freud between Surrealism and Hegelianism. His theory emphasized the desire of the other, through the mediation of speech and language. After the Second World War and in the 1950s, Lacan concluded the most creative aspect of his theoretical project by rethinking, in terms of structural linguistics, the Freudian concept of the unconscious, sexual desire, and the idea of the decentered subject, that is, the concept of primary and irreconcilable splits in the constitution of the psyche.

Sometime in 1932 Lacan entered analysis with Rudolph Loewenstein, who was himself trained in Berlin. Though only three years older than his analysand, Loewenstein arrived in Paris supported by Marie Bonaparte and quickly became a leading analyst of the French SPP, the *Societe Psychanalytique de Paris*, affiliated with the IPA. Lacan's analysis with Loewenstein lasted six years and ended sometime in 1938. Roudinesco considers it a failure despite Loewenstein's clinical finesse and personal decency. She claims that the analysis reached an impasse, that Loewenstein employed techniques then current in the IPA for attending to specific psychological symptoms and working through character resistances. Lacan could not abide by the length of the sessions nor the duration of the treatment; he seems to have agreed to undertake the training analysis out of arrivisme, or plain opportunism, doing it to get the credential. Lacan, she asserts, was far less interested in the clinical dimensions of psychoanalysis than in its philosophical contours. He saw it as a theoretical journey, an intellectual mode of understanding the mind, a critical and self-reflexive contribution to cultural life, resulting in a contribution to the symbolic. His version of psychoanalysis had little to do with the expression or exploration of affects, of working through defensive self-deceptions, traumas, or losses, or with the direct understanding of transference dynamics. Rivalry and envy, Roudinesco asserts, separated Loewenstein and Lacan, as well as major differences on key issues such as the death instinct (which Lacan defended and Loewenstein rejected).

Pre-World War II French psychoanalysis was notoriously ingrown and incestuous. The young Loewenstein was inevitably influenced, Roudinesco alleges, by the negative perceptions and anxiety about Lacan of Marie Bonaparte, who was then Loewenstein's lover. Roudinesco concludes that Lacan learned nothing in his training analysis. She rather preposterously proposes that Lacan had no transferential relations with any senior members of the Paris Society. The ideological dispute over psychoanalytic technique that erupted in the 1950s may have been born in Lacan's incomplete or failed analysis with Loewenstein in the 1930s.

This would include Lacan's experiments with the short session and his fierce opposition to various tenets of ego psychology, including the concept of adaptation.

Loewenstein was disappointed with Lacan, who had evidently promised to continue his analysis after he was accepted for full affiliation with the Paris Psychoanalytic Society, but who abruptly terminated his analysis. In a letter to Marie Bonaparte dated February 22, 1953, Loewenstein made harsh and punitive statements about Lacan's character, clearly upset by the abrupt ending of his analysis; this judgmental letter violates analytic boundaries, breaches the confidentiality of the analytic situation, and privileges politics over the ethical responsibilities of the clinical relationship: "What you tell me of Lacan is depressing. He always constituted for me a source of conflict: on the one hand, his lack of character, on the other, his intellectual value, which I prize highly, though not without violent disagreement. But the problem is that even though we had agreed he would continue his analysis after his election [into the Society], he did not come back. One does not cheat on so important a point without dire consequences (let this remain between us). I hope that his trainees who have been analyzed in a rush, that is, not analyzed at all, will not be accepted" (Roudinesco, 1990, p. 122).

Lacan's true analyst, Roudinesco states, was Aimee, his paranoid patient. She argues that Lacan's clinical experience with Aimee paralleled that of Freud's with Fliess; it was a spontaneous self-analysis. As for a direct relationship with Freud, there barely was one. Freud sent Lacan a polite postcard acknowledging receipt (but not necessarily the reading) of Lacan's 1932 medical thesis. When Freud went into exile, passing through Paris in 1938 on his way to London, Lacan declined an invitation to meet him. Yet he developed a permanent transference to Freud's writings; his own mission would be to found a kingdom in France receptive to the forms of knowledge and methods of inquiry to be discovered in Freud's texts. The key transferential tie was not personal, but an intellectual transference between author and reader, ultimately a method of reading texts psychoanalytically, informed by an understanding of transference and countertransference reactions to texts and by an incisive grasp of the structure of Freud's language and conceptual apparatus. This became his celebrated "Return to Freud."

Roudinesco describes the mature Lacan of *Jacques Lacan & Co.* as neither a dictator nor paranoid, but as a "constitutional monarch," a relatively benign autocrat. As his lectures in Paris became famous, as his followers multiplied, a movement developed where it became fashionable to hear the master speak, to parody his language, and to decode his increasingly obscure message. The late Lacan appeared to parody himself. Lacan's idiosyncrasies intensified. He needed to be loved or served; he gave way to capricious whims; he surrounded himself by sycophants and courtiers. After the publication of the *Écrits* in 1966, Lacan became well recognized in the French intellectual world outside of psychoanalysis and psychiatry. He appeared on television. He saw himself grandiosely as the founding father of French psychoanalysis, but he operated as director, master thinker, legislator, and analyst of all concerned.

Other scholars have pointed out the characterological and ideological affinities between Lacan and Breton (Fisher 1991). By experimenting with a shorter analytic hour, Lacan became the principal analyst of an entire generation. Lacan legitimized his experiment with the short session by emphasizing the intensity, lack of routine, and the pressure and pleasure it placed on the analysand to embrace the analytic process. Since he rejected analyzing a patient's defenses, and since the temporal dimension of the unconscious works non-chronologically and in a non-linear fashion, Lacan justified the use of the short sessions analytically. For him, the real focus of the analysis was to understand the analysts' resistances through their spoken language, pauses, and accidental eruptions of desire, pain, or repetitive utterances. Patients were expected to reveal hidden aspects of themselves in the process of free associating; saying what came to mind was their job and a given in the analytic setting. Rather than focus on meaning or analytic understanding of content, rejecting the idea of insight, analysts were enjoined to attend carefully to their patient's speech patterns and punctuation. The analyst's task was to listen as if working on a crossword puzzle, that is, based on a ruthless, consistent desire to analyze slips of the tongue, puns, pauses, the intensity of speech, and various contradictions in the patient's words, as the process gradually flowed from empty to full speech, from the imaginary to the symbolic. If the analyst was unaware of his own countertransference resistances, the patient's transference would be heightened. This ultimately interfered with the unleashing of free speech, the rich flow of associations, and with allowing the unconscious to speak. It was for this reason that an analyst needed to be psychoanalyzed.

Roudinesco, generous in her discussion of his technique, says it cannot be transmitted. Lacan did not adopt a standard model of technique to be used with all analysands: he varied his approach widely and was iconoclastic; he trained a diversity of analysts each with little similarity to one another; he had no fixed appointment time and no determined length of a session; he was always in a rush; he could not refuse a case; he charged exorbitant fees yet practiced with a sliding scale; he treated many incurable and non-analyzable cases, including those suffering from addictions, delinquency, and chronic suicidality.

Roudinesco argues that Lacan personally prevented many militants and extremely disturbed personalities from descending into terrorism, death, or madness. She quotes lengthy testimonials from his former analysands during these years. In a curious omission, she fails to comment on those testimonials, even though they are widely divergent as documents. Here, she apologizes for rather than explains or critiques Lacan. She holds that he had the courage to accept suicidal cases for treatment, which other clinicians had refused. The alarming number of suicides (no statistics or evidence is provided) raises serious questions about Lacan's own unorthodox practice of psychoanalysis and suggests that his scandalous and libertine methods may have bordered on the unethical, even the harmful.

The story of Lacan's decline is sad. As the structuralists and poststructuralists aged, their anti-humanism seemed to lapse into irrationality or massive self-sabotage. The elderly Lacan was greatly diminished, a fading shadow of his former self. Much of the Lacanian discourse in the period of the late 1960s and 1970s became lame, an imperialistic doctrine, reflecting the atrophy of creativity and intelligence in this sector of the Parisian intellectual world. To paraphrase Braque on the late Picasso, Lacan used to be a great thinker, now all he was a genius. Lacan's words, even if misunderstood, or inexplicable, were justified in the name of his genius. Roudinesco believes that Lacanism became reduced to "puns and cryptic language" (p. 634), a language suitable only to the converted, to fanatical devotees. Prior to his death, Lacan alternated between lucidity and affability, descending into dissociation and silence.

With both weariness and dramatic intensity, Roudinesco recounts the episode of the dissolution and reestablishment of Lacan's school. An intense power struggle was unleashed to inherit Lacan's kingdom, including the right to issue and edit his unpublished texts. Here, French psychoanalysis displayed its ugliest and most primitive side. One analysand was publicly denounced by his analyst as a forger and swindler; factions accused each other of fraud and falsification of documents; insults, rumor, and violent vituperation accompanied an administrative rule by arbitrary whim and lack of accountability. Democratizing factions clashed with those advocating hierarchy. Roudinesco understates this civil war, referring to "the conflictual, remarkable, odious reality of the French psychoanalytic scene" (p. 657). Counterattacks were mounted in the press and intellectual world, where the Lacanians were depicted as shallow, uncaring practitioners, and charlatans. Lacan came under intense scrutiny for being a false prophet, deeply invested in creating disciples. Hagiographers have replied (Schneiderman, 1983).

Perhaps a more accurate historical rendering would stress how the post-Lacanian world reflected many of the ambiguities of the Lacanian world. Without the presence of this unusual master, fusing leadership styles of Spinoza, de Gaulle, and Mao Tse-tung (along with a dash of Breton and Salvador Dali), nothing could have held together this rebellious, ambitious, and anarchic association; this meant an association that was opposed to bureaucratization and standardization, that remained committed to scandalous utterances and outrageous actions, and to the advancement of libertarian principles, ones that subverted loyalty to tradition and uncritical worship of authority. Roudinesco reports that at least 1,600 Lacanian analysts remained in France in 1985; Lacanism has firmly implanted itself in the Parisian publishing world and in the university. But its immediate legacy has been splits, splintering, intense bickering, and a tearing apart of the school. Roudinesco concludes with cautious optimism about Lacanism's ability to conquer the world, that is, pose a serious challenge to the theoretical and administrative apparatus of the IPA.

I returned to Paris on May Day, 1987. I was entertained by a psychoanalytic couple who were active in a splinter group of the Lacanian movement. They were high-powered and deeply committed, but they reminded me of the Parisian couple I encountered at Saint-Germain in the summer of 1975. The woman was currently a candidate at a Lacanian institute, after specializing in a psychoanalytic reading of Joyce's novels. Her partner, Marcel Czermac, was a psychiatrist and psychoanalyst, who had assisted Lacan in his clinical presentation at the Sainte-Anne Hospital Center and also had been analyzed by Lacan. He judiciously refused to speak of that experience. But clearly Lacan remained his "master." He specialized in the

Lacanian treatment of psychoses (Czermac, 1986). He invited me to attend the group's meetings, to observe seminars and clinics, urging me to return to Paris to learn in depth Lacanian technique. I was both flattered and offended by their proselytizing zeal reminding them that I was a proud faculty member at a psychoanalytic institute in Los Angeles, as well as a member of the American Psychoanalytic Association and the IPA. With slight malice, I offered a Lacanian interpretation of the analysand's interminable idealization of his analyst, as a way to temper his messianic enthusiasm, to mute the glorification of the dead master. I objected to this idealization as a form of infantile dependence, as a defense against thinking one's own thoughts. I quoted Lacan's aphorism about transference: the analysand views the analyst as the subject who is supposed to know. Without hesitation, Czermac replied to me with yet another epistemological proposition: What happens if your analyst *truly* knows? Lacan, he implied, was such a knower. Those who worshipped him and his theory could not accept a critique or non-alliance; those who deified his language were impervious to others speaking an alternative language, or wishing to speak in their own voice.

Previously published in *Psychoanalytic Books*, Vol. 5, No. 3, 1994, pp. 365–378.

References

Barande, I. and Barande, R. (1975). *Histoire de la psychanalyse en France*. Toulouse, Privat Collection: Regard.
Czermac, M. (1986). *Passions de l'objet: etudes pssychanalytiques des psychoses*. Paris: Joseph Clims.
Fisher, D. J. (1991). Lacan's Ambiguous Impact on French Psychoanalysis. In *Cultural Theory and Psychoanalytic Tradition*. New Brunswick, NJ: Transaction, pp. 3–26.
Lacan, J. (1966), *Ecrits I and Ecrits II*. Paris: Le Seuil.
Lacan, J. (1972). Seminar on the Purloined Letter. In *Yale French Studies*, 48, pp. 39–72.
Mijolla, A. (1982). La psychanalyse en France. In R. Jaccard (Ed.), *Histoire de la psychanalyse*. Paris: Hachette, pp. 9–105.
Mijolla, A. (2010). *Freud and La France, 1885–1945*. Paris: PUF.
Roudinesco, E. (1990). *Jacques Lacan & Co: A History of Psychoanalysis in France, 1925-1985*. Trans. Jeffrey Melhman. Chicago: University of Chicago Press.
Roudinesco, E. (1997). *Jacques Lacan: An Outline of a Life and History of a System of Thought*. Trans. Barbara Bray. New York: Columbia University Press.
Roudinesco, E. (2014). *Lacan: In Spite of Everything*. Trans. George Elliott. London: Verso.
Schneiderman, S. (1983). *Jacques Lacan: The Death of an Intellectual Hero*. Cambridge, MA: Harvard University Press.
Turkle, S. (1992). *Psychoanalytic Politics: Freud's French Revolution* (2nd ed.). New York: Guilford.

Chapter 10

What Was Revolutionary about the Psychoanalytic Revolution in Mind?

What is the revolution that *Revolution in Mind* Makari addresses (Makari, 2008)? Essentially, it is a psychological revolution, including a major conceptual breakthrough about the structure of the mind, a new form of therapeutic practice in working with emotionally disturbed patients, and a theory of culture that contains innovative and radical ethics. According to Makari, Freud synthesized three disparate intellectual disciplines: first the findings of nineteenth-century French academic psychology, specifically the works of Theodule Ribot, Pierre Janet, and Jean-Martin Charcot, centered on the study of psychopathology; second, the tradition of German psychophysics, especially the work of Gustav Fechner, with its emphasis on outer and inner experience and the postulation of a threshold between unconscious and conscious phenomena; and third, the perspectives of Viennese and English sexology, particularly the writings of Richard von Kraft-Ebbing on perversions and Havelock Ellis on autoerotism. These discussions are the clearest and best summaries I have read on the subject matter in English.

It should also be noted that Makari neglects or underplays how the philosophical elements in Freud's formation helped him to construct his synthesis. He includes neither the integration of a phenomenological neo-Kantianism from Freud's studies with Franz Brentano at the University of Vienna, nor his proficiency in dialectical modes of thinking that derive from Hegel and other dialectical thinkers. He misses Freud's deep reading of ancient and contemporary literature, including the Greeks and Romans, Shakespeare, Goethe, Lessing, the nineteenth-century Russian novelists, and Nietzsche. Freud learned a great deal from psychologically minded authors of past and present, including subversive strategies of interpretation, of reading texts imaginatively and with attunement to emotional latencies in them. These humanistic, cultural influences are deemphasized by Makari in terms of building his argument around professionalization; it represents a bias, perhaps indicating his own debts to a medical psychoanalytic tradition and a legacy of Anglo-Saxon scientific empiricism emerging from his own training and transferential affinities. While downplaying the hermeneutic nature of psychoanalytic methodology, a key component of extrapolating understanding and insight from the complex patient association, he omits or gives short shift to the array of fascinating,

DOI: 10.4324/9781003488439-12

talented, brilliant, idiosyncratic, and contentious women and men who provided the center and periphery of the history of psychoanalysis in this era.

Freud's synthesis belonged to a larger intellectual inquiry on the place of reason originating in the Enlightenment, an investigation still relevant. Foucault argued that the Enlightenment's perception of and policies toward the mad were neither enlightened nor reasonable. Freud's synthesis represented both continuity and rupture with the post-Enlightenment history of unreason, a history that privileges the role of critical thinking and a fundamental respect for those suffering from serious mental disorders. Carl Schorske once called for a project studying how psychoanalytic theory and practice ought to be situated in the controversies over the nature and significance of reason. That integration remains to be written.

Makari posits that Freud's discovery of intrapsychic conflict and of psychosexuality marked his revolutionary synthesis. Psychosexuality became the link between reason and passion; mind and body; the individual and the species; and the human and the animal. Libido was a critical and determining source of unconscious wishing in dream life and fantasies.

Yet Makari leaves out of Freud's synthesis his early and consistent understanding of the social, of how the social impinges on the intrapsychic and relational realms. From the 1907 article "Civilized Sexual Morality and Modern Nervousness" to his inspired 1930s essay, *Civilization, and Its Discontents*, he realized that there were persistent tensions between the individual and society, not just anxiety created by repression. These conflicts between the human subject and culture are illustrated by the ways in which restrictions and interdictions are externally imposed on the child; they derive from child rearing, family systems, and educational, religious, and ethical imperatives. Freud underscored that the social nature of shame and guilt, as well as intrapsychic sources, could impose limits, laws, regulations, and prohibitions often resulting in misery for the individual. Civilization, Freud grasped, also contributed to modern nervousness and to mankind's uneasiness. Makari understates the role of social theory in Freud's paradigm, the ways in which early psychoanalysis was attentive to social and cultural pressures on the individual, influencing his psychic makeup and his choices.

Freud, Makari argues, solved Compte's paradoxical thesis that there could be no objective and scientific exploration of psychology if that investigation included inner experience. This became a cardinal principle of positivist thought. Freud's approach to the science of subjectivity permitted the observer to maintain the boundaries of observer and observed, despite the subjectivity of both members of this dyad. We now know from the contemporary analytic perspectives on intersubjectivity and the relational school just how elusive this boundary is, how shifting and unstable the interaction is between analyst and analysand. In addition, we know that the observer changes the outcome of what is observed, that there are limits to objectivity. We also realize that the observer in the analytic situation is also observed. As a scientific venture, Freud grasped the destabilizing aspects of the unconscious, comprehending the levels of uncertainty in his clinical and theoretical projects.

Today, psychosexuality no longer shocks. Psychoanalysis no longer can claim its revolutionary status by this standard. Or can it? If psychoanalysis has been transformed into a discounted ideology, its very success may have undermined its continuing efficacy and its radical questioning stance. Professionalization, the central subject of Makari's work, may have paradoxically contributed to the taming of disturbing, unconscious truths about our inner world first articulated by Freud and his early analytic cohort. Institutionalization in many ways resulted in the medicalization of psychoanalysis, where lay analysts were marginalized or excluded from training, practice, and positions of prestige. The history of lay analysis, right down to the lawsuit against the American Psychoanalytic Association, seriously weakened the dissemination of psychoanalysis into society, limited its creativity, narrowing the rigorous thinking and innovative approaches to be found in non-medical disciplines. Furthermore, the prejudice against lay analysis delayed the acceptance of women in the field, curtailed research on children, and the creation of open-ended, brainstorming cross-disciplinary dialogue, a conversation that was often imaginative and subversive.

Medicalization also went with bureaucratization, with its inherently conservative turn, blunting the revolutionary edge of analysis's destabilizing truths, often co-opting the non-conforming methods and collapsing the paradoxical findings of psychoanalysis. As psychoanalysis penetrated throughout Central and Western Europe and to America, it became softened, diluted, and prettified – making the dark and disturbing truths about our inner world easy to assimilate. Linear thinking replaced the dialectical complexity of Freud's style of discourse. Mechanistic and reductionistic formulations hardened into dogma, supplanted the early metaphorical, earthy, personal, and self-reflexive modes of thinking epitomized by Freud's theorizing.

Standardization of analytic theory and technique became a problem for perpetuating the revolutionary nature of analysis. Gradually, conformism and adherence to an authoritarian formula replaced the need for freedom, dissent, creativity, and genuine independence, where a clinician was urged to think through a clinical problem for himself. Following received ways of working with primitively disordered and traumatized patients, generations of analysts were not encouraged to be elastic and relaxed in their approach to patients, not to privilege flexibility, imagination, caring, and emotional attunement. Discipleship rose and many of Freud's followers proudly echoed Freud's positions, promoting an uncritical loyalty to the founder, including an internalization of a mythical and heroic history of Freud.

Over time this tendency limited the free flow of ideas and the cross-fertilization of analysis with allied fields. This pattern of discipleship was repeated with endless variations as followers gathered around seminal psychoanalytic schools, Kleinian, Bionian, Anna Freudian, Lacanian, Mahlerian, and in recent years around Kohut, Kernberg, and the various luminaries of the relational and intersubjective schools, such as Winnicott and Fairbairn. These diverse schools have repeated the pattern of bickering, of distinguishing themselves from their fathers by unknowingly returning to their grandfathers and by setting up straw men arguments. These battles generated splits, acrimony, and difficulty in conducting clinical or intellectual exchange.

Makari astutely delineates clinical, theoretical, and even ethnic differences in studying different schools in psychoanalysis. He is convincing on the early collaboration and tensions between Vienna and Zurich until 1912; Vienna versus Berlin in the 1920s; Budapest under Ferenczi's influence vs. Vienna; and London versus New York City. As psychoanalysis became diffused, distinct theoretical languages emerged in these capitals. These reflected divergent assumptions about the structure of the mind, the developmental sequence and significance of early childhood, disparate emphases on the environment and innate influences, and, above all, contrasting transferences to theory and to a theory of technique. Ultimately, these debates reflected differing attitudes of closeness or distance from Freud's authority and paradigm. Not every analyst embraced his methodology or his key metapsychological, humanist, and modernist principles. It became unclear how to define a psychoanalyst, or what constituted an analytic identity. Some defined it as unconditional loyalty to Freud's postulation of psychosexuality, the primacy of the Oedipus complex, and adherence to the structural model of the mind. Others argued that psychoanalysts adhered to scientific methodology and technique, with its privileging of free association and analysis of the transference. Still others suggested that it was surprise and mutual collaboration that epitomized the therapeutic dialogue, generating curiosity and growth. Still others argued that it was the consolidation of the sense of self and the development of adequate forms of self-esteem regulation that constituted structural change.

Resistance to the diffusion of psychoanalysis came from many sources and corners. Makari is quite good about tracking this opposition to core analytic principles. Conservative physicians in Central Europe rejected analytic ideas because of their explicitness about sexuality, their privileging of unconscious dynamics, and their racial bias against the Jewish founders of the discipline. In his discussion of the French scene, he mentions the French resentment of Freud for appropriating many of their significant findings in psychopathology. He neglects the role of French anti-Semitism in obstructing a more dispassionate discussion and receptivity to Freud, especially after the Dreyfus Affair. Likewise, he minimizes the role of French cultural nationalism; many Frenchmen dismissed Freud as a "German" thinker simply because he wrote in German. Makari also misrecognizes what was distinctly Viennese in Freud's cultural context and development, a point of view beautifully illuminated in the sparkling essays of Carl Schorske and Bruno Bettelheim, and in the scholarship of Allan Janik and Stephen Toulmin, Jacques Le Rider, Peter Loewenberg, and William M. Johnston. He does not appear to be sensitive to the multiple meanings, difficulties, and dangers of being a secular Jew in an anti-Semitic city.

The history of psychoanalysis can be thought of as the study of Freud's intellectual history, the formation and revision of his ideas. Yet Freud's authoritarian style interfered with the transmission of psychoanalytic approaches to the mind. Always the medical professor, the patriarchal founder of the discipline, Freud did not tolerate challenges to his authority. He legitimized his authority as a master clinician, a trenchant empirical observer, and if not a systematic thinker, a breathtaking theorist – brimming with speculations, insights, and *apercus*. Many of

Freud's early disciples depended on him for referrals and prestige, for approval and the regulation of their self-esteem as analytic practitioners. In return, they provided loyalty. Freud used *ad hominem* arguments, polemical and rhetorical strategies, to discipline his unruly followers and to create order out of messy and anarchic associations. Analysts in other cities emulated this authoritarian style, including the stance of being omniscient. In practice, this authoritarianism meant that new ideas could not always be debated and critiqued openly; scientific or clinical differences became transformed into personal ones. Intellectual exchange focused on substantial differences in ideas, clinical data, and treatment options collapsed into political, personal, and uncivil exchanges, often designed to discipline or pathologize one's opponents. At times, this would lead to expulsion from the psychoanalytic movement, or being denigrated as a rebel or deviant.

Intellectual disagreement, rather than being welcomed and embraced, was seen as a sign of emotional resistance, of immaturity, and of infantile rebellion. This attitude injured the analytic community, despite Freud's own somewhat idiosyncratic tolerating of skeptics, dissenters, oddballs, mavericks, and radicals in the movement. Freud, Makari aptly points out, would characteristically rebuff criticism and challenges to his theory and then quietly internalize certain valid ideas which would enlarge his model of the mind. He did not always acknowledge his debt to others, failing to provide documentation of shifts in his point of view. This is particularly evident in Freud's introduction of the death drive in his 1919 essay, *Beyond the Pleasure Principle*, where previous authors, many of whom were followers or former followers, received no attribution in his references, most notably Sabina Spielrein. Perhaps all great creative thinkers have the license to not cite their precursors, as if ideas immediately sprang full blown from their minds. This tone of correctness, arrogance, capriciousness, and omniscience has impeded the dissemination of psychoanalysis, continuing to this day. We are all too familiar with the condescending tone of: "That is not psychoanalysis"; "Colleague X does not understand the unconscious"; and "Colleague Y does supportive psychotherapy." These dismissive expressions do not promote serious and intelligent exchanges.

One antidote to the bureaucratization and medicalization of psychoanalysis was the presence of lay analysts in the movement. This assortment of humanists, scholars, social workers, analytic psychologists, cultural and political radicals, including some sexual revolutionaries, anarchists, bohemians, socialists, and those inspired by the Russian Revolution often functioned as non-conforming, critical thinking alternatives to the emerging mainstream. These freethinkers demonstrated a willingness to speak truth to power, contesting the hegemony of charismatic leaders locally and nationally. Yet lay analysts did not always overcome their own tonality of arrogance and authoritarianism, of narcissistic self-inflation and political posturing against their intolerant and condescending opponents. Freud was somewhat receptive to these original and imaginative thinkers, willing to contemplate some of their brilliant suggestions and offbeat ideas. Lay analysts opened up the study of cultural formations from the point of view of how dreams, fantasies, and emotions functioned in works of art, literature, anthropology, philosophy, and history. They also provided a bridge between the natural sciences and the cultural sciences, a strong resistance to the conservative, exclusive, and elitist trend of a medicalized psychoanalysis, including an alternative to strictly empirical investigation.

What is revolutionary about psychoanalysis now? Perhaps not much. If psychoanalysis represented a psychological revolution in its earliest history, it was above all a hybrid cultural revolution. In short, it revolutionized our ideas about sexuality, aggression, insatiable desire, and the role of the unconscious in mental life. Makari's Freud is less a revolutionary thinker than one who tweaked and promoted already existing progressive trends in psychopathology, sexology, and psychophysics. Certainly, Freud helped to erase the distinction between the normal and the pathological. He clearly functioned as a social and sexual reformer in the early decades of the twentieth-century. As an initiator of discourse, his language has penetrated into every possible sphere of everyday life, into myriad aspects of high and popular culture. Perhaps the triumph of Freud's synthesis can be seen in the ways our thinking and speaking about the individual is indebted to his writings. For several generations, Freud decisively transformed the self-image of the Western mind. What remains of that self-image and legacy is an open question.

George Makari has written an engaging and erudite book on the creation of psychoanalysis. His lucid historical study of this cultural movement provides an understanding after the conclusion of the events. Our own society and psychotherapeutic practices have moved to a stage beyond which early psychoanalysis was concerned. Minerva's owl flies out at dusk. Knowing the history of psychoanalysis in the current context, then, encourages us to reaffirm the practical significance of theory. We need to remember that theoretical elements are productive of insight and deep self-reflection while being key intellectual tools to calm anxieties about uncertainty, complexity, and not knowing. Revisiting the revolutionary core of psychoanalytic theory and practice can engender a mood of mourning about the loss of a now dead paradigm for human emancipation. Or, more positively, it can provide hope that psychoanalysis can rediscover its subversive vitality. Such a reinvention might allow psychoanalysis to flourish again in our sick, depressed, polarized, and narcissistic society that desperately needs its healing perspective and liberating methods.

Reference

Makari, G. (2008). *Revolution in Mind: The Creation of Psychoanalysis*. New York: Harper Collins.

Previously published in *Internationalpsychoanalysis.net*, February 21, 2012, pp. 1–11.

Chapter 11
Discovering Wounded Healers in *A Dangerous Method*

The 2011 release of the film *A Dangerous Method* has generated controversy and intense debates about the founders of depth psychology, Freud and Jung, both among clinicians and a curious public. The movie depicts the beginnings, flowering, and ultimate demise of their collaboration. The film has first-rate acting with Viggo Mortensen as Freud, Michael Fassbender as Jung, the incomparable Vincent Cassel as Otto Gross, and the courageous Keira Knightley as the film's true heroine, Sabrina Spielrein. In addition, there is a compelling script by Christopher Hampton, based largely on a book by John Kerr with the title *A Most Dangerous Method* (Kerr, 1993) and a previous play by Hampton (Hampton, 2002). The characters come alive on the screen with a combination of nuanced acting, the accurate rendering of the times through the period costume designs, interiors, and shots of Switzerland and Vienna from 1904 to 1913. Director David Cronenberg expertly draws on photographs of Freud and Jung to create uncanny likenesses and to render historically the ambience and personalities of his protagonists, including the accurate reproduction of the interior of their offices and consultation rooms. Outer appearances and inner worlds mutually reflect on one another.

A Dangerous Method is an excellent film not just because of its beautiful images and complex and psychologically well drawn characters, but also because it raises issues touching on a key moment in the history of psychoanalysis – issues which have much contemporary relevance. The narrative reveals the triangular relationship between Freud, Jung, and Spielrein, at first based on clinical concerns, specifically the treatment of a sick young patient, Spielrein. The humane treatment of Spielrein by Jung, employing Freud's methods, at the Burgholzli Psychiatric Clinic in Zurich evolves into a complicated nexus where professional, political, and personal issues intersect and ultimately clash.

What focuses the film is Spielrein's story, a previously forgotten, fabulous figure in the history of psychoanalysis. Spielrein was an exceptionally gifted Russian Jewish woman, who first entered this history as a patient of the Burgholzli Hospital in Zurich, suffering from severe hysteria. Spielrein is the real discovery of the film. She is nothing less than extraordinary: flawed, ill, traumatized as a child, suffering from dissociation, conversion symptoms, and sexualization. The grotesque jutting of her mouth is an excellent metaphor and filmic device to emphasize that these distortions of her speech will not be resolved until she works through her conflicts. By undergoing the talking cure, she finds her voice, internally discovering her sense of self.

We first meet Spielrein as she is carried into the Burgholzli in a horse-drawn carriage with violent symptoms, bodily contortions, yelling and screaming, laughing and crying histrionically, and actively resisting treatment. The film documents her gradual recovery. It then shows her transformation into a physician as she develops an astute comprehension of psychological process. She demonstrates proficiency with word and image association as developed by Jung and, not least, an uncanny access to the unconscious. The film alludes to her subsequent emergence as a respected psychoanalyst, who made pathbreaking contributions to the literature on the understanding of schizophrenia and the dialectic of sexuality and destructiveness. Spielrein would also become interested in the psychology of language in the unconscious, the importance of early bonds with the mother, and ways in which object relations structure aspects of the personality. Her writings anticipate later elaborations of Melanie Klein, Jacques Lacan, and relational theorists. She would later integrate some of the perspectives of Jean Piaget on cognitive development in children, whom she analyzed in the early 1920s (Civington, C. and Wharton, B. (2003)).

The film is explicit about the issue of sexuality, brutally honest; some critics of the film would say the sexuality portrayed was prurient, an unnecessary Hollywood need to scandalize the audience; admirers of the film would say it was authentic. The movie frames its exploration of key relationships by setting up a dialectic between love and destructiveness, erotic desire, and self-sabotage, all themes in Spielrein's writings. Spielrein and Jung move beyond the bounds and limits of the analytic relationship, engaging in a passionate love affair. The love affair is consummated sexually. There are vivid scenes of Spielrein losing her virginity to Jung; we are shown her blood spilling onto her white dress. We watch them having sado-masochistic sexual foreplay with Jung standing up, Spielrein leaning over a bed, while he forcefully, sadistically, spanks her backside, first with his hand and secondly with a strap. She is aroused to a frenzy by these sexual encounters, experiencing pleasure in her pain.

Spielrein, we learn, had been beaten by her father, an early trauma which terrified, shamed, and excited her. She is exposed to embarrassing and degrading feelings and is easily humiliated, as are all patients who suffer from traumatic abuse. She has a history of compulsive masturbation, of sudden eruptions of anger, and a massive problem with feelings of unworthiness. As a defensive strategy and attempt to master these early experiments of abuse and traumatic shock, Spielrein expresses an omnipotent sense of her own importance with a grandiose sense of her destiny in history. In the film, she is cured; this is largely due to the care, attention, consideration, and sustained listening and tender approach of Jung. There are lovely scenes which condense how the treatment unfolded, beginning with Jung sitting behind her on a chair and inviting her to free associate without looking at her analyst. Other scenes show Spielrein's associations to images, moving into words, calling up painful, affectively tinged reminiscences. With a pictorial imagination, Jung functions like an artist with unusual access to the primary process connected to the visual;

thing representations appear to matter more than words. He and she are eventually able to translate the pictorial into the secondary process of speech and language.

Jung clearly treats his patient with compassion and sensitivity. With Jung's assistance, Spielrein overcomes horrendous memories through the retrieval of horrific events in her childhood. The film shows that early psychoanalysis was attentive to trauma and the need for affective expression of emotions. Jung employs the cathartic therapy developed by Freud and Breuer in their early *Studies on Hysteria*. She becomes his research assistant and collaborator, learning his methods, rapidly assimilating his understanding of the unconscious process. Jung and Eugen Bleuler, Director of the Burgholzli Clinic, encourage her to return to her formal studies, facilitating her attendance at the University of Zurich Medical School.

The film suggests that a critical component of the curative process of early psychoanalysis was the analyst's complex love for his patient. Part of this love consisted of deep respect for the inner world of the patient. Freud once wrote to Jung that psychoanalysis was essentially a cure through love. Jung optimally responded to under-developed, constricted, but beautiful aspects of her personality; he understood empathically the pervasive cultural and familial modes of repression during this era, which deprived women of educational, research, cultural, and scientific opportunities. There would be no cure without the lifting of these repressions. The healing process would turn on a corrective emotional experience with the analyst.

If Jung was aware of the dynamics of transference during his clinical experimentation, he seemed unaware of, even oblivious to, countertransference, which would ultimately create enormous difficulties for Spielrein, Freud, and him. Jung's inability to reflect upon and use therapeutically his erotic excitement resulted in an acting out of the countertransference. This ultimately unleashed a scandal, requiring him, he believed, to break off relations with his former patient. Hurt, bewildered, and enraged by Jung's betrayal and rationalizations, and above all the cover-up of the affair, Spielrein violently attacked Jung in his office with a knife. She cut him on his face, leaving him scarred. The audience gasped at this scene as it unfolded on the screen. Reconciled once again, they resumed their love affair, only to have Jung break it off again in a state of agitated shame and guilt. Jung permitted formal but distant relations with Spielrein after the rupture of their relationship, but without the mutuality of their previous bond. Spielrein turned to Freud, traveling to Vienna for an analysis with her master and hoping for acceptance into the Viennese Psychoanalytic Society.

Unlike his other patients at the Burgholzli Hospital at this moment, Spielrein was intelligent, cultivated, well-educated, cosmopolitan, and well-traveled. She was fluent in German, French, and English and knew classical languages and a great deal about ancient mythology and the history of religion; in addition, she was musical, particularly enamored of Wagner's operas. Throughout the film, exquisite music from Wagner's "Siegfried Idyll" plays in the background. It captures the love duet between Jung and Spielrein. In her approach to people, she revealed a consistently compassionate attitude, one exquisitely attuned to the suffering of others in her environment. The film shows a scene of an early experiment with Emma, Jung's young and wealthy wife. Based on a reading of Emma's responses, Spielrein resonated with the latter's anxieties about pleasing Jung and producing a male son.

She intuited that Emma recognized her husband's shallow investment in preserving his emotional relationship with her. Spielrein also correctly intuited that the lady undergoing the experiment was Jung's wife.

Intellectually, the Spielrein of the film emerged as an original thinker, with a distinctively idealistic, romantic, and mystical orientation. These qualities were linked to her being Russian. Unlike either Freud or Jung, she leaned toward the synthetic in her thinking, blending opposites, seeking unity and complementarity as the theories of her two mentors radically diverged. She hoped that somehow a dialectic could emerge which might integrate the ideas of these two master thinkers. She felt personally hurt by their dispute, imagining it would damage the subsequent history of the psychoanalytic movement. Capable of bold forms of theorizing, Spielrein in the film fashioned modes of thinking far ahead of her male contemporaries, including Freud and Jung, who were begrudging in their acknowledgment of her groundbreaking studies. A significant female figure in the early history of psychoanalysis, Spielrein would be forgotten, relegated to footnotes or vague bibliographical citations because of the scandal with Jung, her precarious position between Freud and Jung, and because she was a woman. While adhering to Freud's version of the psychoanalytic technique, believing in the clinical efficacy of his honest and penetrating grasp of sexuality and its unruly discontents, she continued to value Jung's research and writing. Spielrein saw greatness in his emerging theory, significance in his cosmic speculations. The film shows her transformation from naïve to sophisticated, from sick to healer, and her suffering from illusions to a more adult, realistic view of herself and the world.

The film uses the device of mutual analysis to dramatize and focus the audience's attention on various couples that become central to its themes. At the same time that Jung was treating Spielrein, he also began the analytic treatment of Otto Gross, a trained psychoanalyst, physician, and one of two figures in the early analytic movement that Freud thought a genius. Yet Gross was a mad genius, capable of repeated destructive actions and sado-masochistic dynamics. Gross was institutionalized at the Burgholzli Clinic against his wishes by his powerful father, the criminologist, Hans Gross. Besides being a brilliant, handsome, seductive, and flamboyant figure, Otto Gross expressed a powerful libertarian critique of patriarchal society and the authoritarianism of the modern family. He advocated polygamy, the sexual rights of women, while attacking monogamy and myriad forms of bourgeois respectability. He had incisive insights into hypocritical sexual attitudes and practices, which functioned to make society sick and individuals defensively organized, leaving them tortured and tormented. Modern urban civilization, he prophesized, would remain neurotic and oppressive unless individuals freed themselves sexually, liberating their desires, imagination, and capacity for freely chosen relationships. Gross would ultimately self-destruct because of his addiction to morphine and cocaine. He is depicted throughout the film as filching substances to sustain his addiction. He appears to be in denial or to lie about his compulsion to using these habit-forming medicines.

Gross switched positions with Jung in the film, refusing to surrender to the privileged power and scientific knowledge of his male physician analyst. He cannot bear the asymmetry and implicit hierarchy of the analytic relationship, which, for him, recapitulated his disturbed and sadistic relationship with his father. Engaging in an experimental form of mutual analysis with Jung, Jung disclosed much intimate detail about his inner world, fantasies, and difficulties in his marriage. Stimulated by these exchanges, he felt immensely understood and helped by Gross. At the same time, he was naively enthusiastic about Gross' progress in the treatment, until Gross rather summarily bolted from the Burgholzli. When he discussed the case with Freud on a walk, Freud mentioned his disillusionment with Gross, stating that analysis did not work with addicts. Freud added that figures like Gross would damage the diffusion of the psychoanalytic movement, making the public mistake psychoanalysis as a disreputable form of pansexualism, as if it functioned to unleash the instincts.

Gross is the one figure in the movie who is caricatured historically and badly served; his visionary thinking about sexuality would see further elaboration by Wilhelm Reich in the 1920s and 1930s and would be taken up by cultural radicals in the 1960s. He is shown in the film always wearing a black turtleneck, an anachronism consistent with his depiction as an intrusive, reckless, drug popping crackpot, a wild bohemian anarchist. In point of fact, Gross articulated a rigorous critique of society and an emancipatory view of the individual. For a corrective, the reader is advised to consult a new collection of essays on Gross's broad influence (Heuer, 2011).

Under the influence of Gross, Jung established a mutual analysis with Spielrein. As analysts know from their own clinical work, mutual analysis opens up profoundly moving, pleasurable, and intimate encounters, potentials for insights, as well as possibilities for twinships, mirroring, and idealizing self-object transferences. It also contains risks, possibilities for the blurring of boundaries, confusions, merger fantasies, and enactments. Reciprocal mirroring can be seductive and difficult to resist, particularly if the members of the analytic couple have deep emotional affinities. There is also the danger of exploiting the patient. Mutual analysis can justify the acting out of incestuous and other forbidden sexual and aggressive fantasies. Yet Spielrein recovered under the care of Jung. The treatment gradually slides into collaboration, intense sharing of ideas, and charged intellectual and clinical exchanges. No longer asymmetrical, therapy got blurred as friendship, sliding into passionate embraces, romantic outings, and a sensual love affair. This was first initiated by Spielrein in an active masculine manner and not resisted by the passively receptive, feminine Jung. Though there is no definitive evidence that the love affair was sexually consummated, the film assumes that they were lovers. There are papers in the literature that hold that their relationship did not include sexual intercourse (Lothane, 2000). Jung's biographer also sees the evidence as ambiguous (Bair, 2003). I am unconvinced by their arguments.

The consummation of the love affair in the film may provoke moral outrage by opponents of psychoanalysis and denunciation from our more self-righteous and legalistic colleagues, particularly of those who are present-centered and ignorant of psychoanalytic history. It is easy to judge and condemn, after all. The protagonists of this film are developing psychoanalysis in a different era, an era of massive sexual repression, without our contemporary knowledge of boundary violations and present-centered ethical considerations. They are pioneers, experimental, literally exploring the uncharted terrain of the world of unconscious dynamics. We need to remember the level of temptation involved in practicing our dangerous method, not just of symbolic interpretations, but more essentially of building and sustaining the most intimate of exchanges between two vulnerable human beings left in a room alone for two years. This is one reason that analysts are required to be analyzed. The intersecting of two subjectivities in mutual analysis can be endlessly fascinating and transformational to both participants, particularly if the two share common interests, aptitudes, sensibilities, and emotional constellations, and especially if there is a potent unconscious to the unconscious mode of receptivity and communication. The closeness that is constructed and the sharing of deep affective experiences may not be replicable outside of this unique framework of the talking cure.

Rather than condemn or apologize for Jung's behavior with Spielrein, the film attempts to contextualize the love affair, to understand without blame, and to empathize with all involved. These intrepid practitioners of psychoanalysis neither fully grasped the destructive potential of certain enactments, nor the ways in which mutual analysis might distort the exploration of transference-countertransference dynamics. Love relations may have hidden the underlying power relations. Jung and Spielrein participate in this experiment in the name of freedom and the authentic search for truth, including the understanding of romantic love. Freud coined the phrase countertransference in addressing Jung's difficulties dealing with erotic transference as it emerged in his treatment of Spielrein. He spoke of it as a persistent problem, as a clinical phenomenon requiring careful monitoring. Freud held that young male analysts were particularly susceptible to these enactments, while we now know that these boundary violations transcend gender and can occur through the life cycle of the analyst.

The film condenses Spielrein's ambiguous Siegfried complex. Based on dreams, reveries, associations, and emotional connections, Spielrein's Siegfried fantasy derived from Wagner's Ring cycle. There is a scene where Spielrein and Jung observed mental patients while they were listening to a recording of Wagner's music. Siegfried was both the great figure of Teutonic mythology and the son of a hero destined to perform great deeds. For Spielrein the unconscious meanings of the prophetic Siegfried dreams involved self-sacrifice, perhaps even a tragic death, in fulfilling her wish to bear a blond Aryan son to her hero Siegfried. Within the context of the therapy with Jung, it is plain to see the erotic transference contained in this fantasy. Spielrein, however, believed her dreams to be prophetic, thinking of herself as a clairvoyant, similar to Jung. Jung also alleged that his dreams were premonitory.

Presenting Jung with a son would be a manifestation of their love union, conclusive evidence of Spielrein's conviction that she would accomplish something great in life. This achievement would entail enormous misery and suffering on her part. Contemporary analysts will see various narcissistic-masochistic character traits embedded in this fantasy. During the merger stage of their relationship, Jung shared Spielrein's fantasies about the symbolic meanings of the Siegfried complex. We could interpret her wish to bear Jung a deeply desired son, view Jung as

Siegfried, with Spielrein functioning as the good-enough, protective, and altruistic mother, Brunhilde. Freud, of course, deconstructed Spielrein's Siegfried complex, seeing her infatuation with her "Germanic hero," as nothing more than a failure to mourn her relationship with Jung, an inability to sever her infantile dependence on her mythical savior and rescuer, and a denial of her Jewishness, a basic repudiation of her sense of self. He was skeptical about trusting the Aryans.

Jung was never formally analyzed. He shared this peculiarity with Freud. Some might consider this absence a conspicuous deficit. Like Freud, he continued to do self-analysis for most of his mature life. Some of his self-analysis would yield trenchant discoveries; at other times, it threatened to obscure his comprehension, overwhelming his ability to recognize his own blind spots. It is elusive, perhaps impossible, to analyze the countertransference while doing a self-analysis. Narcissistic issues may go beneath the radar and field of vision in self-analysis; similarly, it may be tricky to grasp how we are perceived by others. While treating Spielrein, Jung met and corresponded with Freud, seeking out his advice, tactical counsel, and supervision. As the gossip and innuendo in Zurich circulated about his love affair with Spielrein, Jung realized the high stakes if the love affair becomes more widely public. Rumors of the romance spread to Vienna, orchestrated by Emma Jung, who hoped to preserve her marriage. Disclosure of the love affair would cause major damage to his reputation, harm his anointment as successor to Freud. It would potentially stifle his vast ambitions to make a name for himself as a world class psychologist; it might jeopardize his marriage. Things blew up when Emma Jung wrote Spielrein's mother about the love affair. Spielrein appealed to Freud to intercede. Freud behaved badly at first. He initially supported Jung, placing psychoanalytic politics and personal loyalty to his chosen, Christian successor. Fraternal psychoanalytic fidelity trumped the interests – and ultimately the truth – of this specific patient appealing to him in a state of great pain and anguish.

Over time, Jung's involvement with Spielrein influenced Freud's view of Jung's suitability to succeed him. His disappointment with Jung over the Spielrein affair, along with significant differences in his sexual theories, exploded leading to their break in 1913. Even though he claimed to be open-minded, Freud found Jung's interest in the collective unconscious, archetypes, Aryan psychology, mysticism, and the occult far too distant from the clinical process, far too unscientific, and non-verifiable by clinical experience. Though a latent theme in the film, he increasingly discovered in Jung an uncomfortable level of anti-Semitism, including a condescending view of Freud and his largely Viennese Jewish followers, whom Jung dismissed as second-rate "bohemian artists and degenerates."

In the film, Freud and Jung participated in their own form of mutual analysis. As they first became acquainted, there are scenes where they met and talked for a thirteen-hour interlude – I am tempted to call it an extended analytic session. Time disappeared and the two have much to dialogue about. They engaged in a passionate correspondence. They exchanged photographs. Freud visited Jung in his grand home on Lake Zurich. Jung took him for an expedition in his newly purchased sailboat. Both the mansion and red sailboat were extravagant gifts from Emma Jung. Jung was shown to be the dominant captain, Freud the diminished and ill at ease passenger. We see Freud crouching down in the sailboat with his walking cane, uncomfortably small and vulnerable. The sailboat is a recurring symbol in the film, standing for research and exploration of the depths; it also serves as an image of Jung's oceanic connection to the vast and eternal possibilities of human existence.

Freud invited the Jungs to visit his flat at the Berggasse 19, where there is a telling scene at the dinner table. Sitting next to Freud, Jung is offered a platter of meat and vegetables. Oblivious to the rest of the table, he piled an enormous helping of food onto his plate, while the Freud children watch (as do the viewers of the film) with astonishment. Freud stated ironically that there are no restrictions at his table. The greedy, oral, self-involved Jung had no idea about how he comes across to others; he was accustomed to be cared for, fed, and babied by Emma. The narcissistic Jung has no idea how he is perceived by others.

In another scene, we observe Jung sitting in Freud's study, finding himself perturbed by sounds coming from Freud's bookcase. Disorganized, he tells Freud that this was a premonition of something important, that he knew the disruption would be repeated, and that he can feel the vibrations in his body. Jung referred to the incident as a "catalytic exteriorization phenomenon." Freud, for his part, was put off by this display of Jung's mystical leanings, his immersion in the occult and esoteric psychology. The episode deepened his skepticism about Jung's allegiance to basic Freudian scientific procedures and clinical methods. Other scenes addressed the dissolution of their mutual analysis, diluting the regard between the two seminal thinkers. On the ship traveling to America in 1909, Jung shared his dreams with Freud; Freud finds them hostile toward him, suggesting the death wishes of the son toward the powerful father. Feeling threatened, Freud refused to share his associations with one of his own dreams, very much to Jung's chagrin and disapproval. When asked why, Freud stated that it would risk eroding his authority.

Freud refused to participate in further mutual analysis, preferring to maintain his distance, privacy, and prestige as the founder of the psychoanalytic movement. Though the movie is not explicit about prior disappointments, he will not repeat his prior relationships with Breuer and Fliess in terms of personal revelations. Assuming the stance of analytic distance, he treated his disciple as he might approach a patient. This engendered great resentment on the part of Jung, who disliked being infantilized and pathologized. Freud did not relate to Jung as his equal. Lastly, at one of his congresses, Jung and Freud had another encounter, where Jung's self-disclosure injured Freud's sense of safety and trust around him. Jung, once again, revealed his aggression toward Freud. Freud fainted. As Jung picked him up, Freud ambiguously stated, "How sweet it would be to die." This utterance foreshadowed the death of their relationship, a split that continues to this day in the analytic movement. Jung would eventually refuse to be Freud's disciple, his son, someone less than Freud. Freud's suspicious interactions with him, the breakdown of the mutual analysis, injured Jung's narcissistic sense of his originality, his ambition to expand psychology toward the exploration of cosmic and mystical realms of the unconscious. The deeply wounded Jung understood that Freud would never treat him in a reciprocal manner.

The Jung of "A Dangerous Method" is rather primitively organized. He is a fragile character. Over the course of the film, he is drawn as serious, intense, brooding, ambitious, and vital. Revealing a powerful desire for recognition, he is dissatisfied with a secondary position in the movement. He rejected the universality of Freud's libido theory, even though his psychological and emotional constitution seemed to fit the theory precisely. Incapable of monogamy, Jung repetitively got involved with women and former patients such as Toni Wolff, who is mentioned in the epilogue of the film. He could be self-serving, insensitive, and cruel, particularly in defense of his cover-up and callous break with Spielrein. He lacked irony and a sense of humor. He clearly belonged to a different social class from Freud and his followers; there was a telling scene on the ocean liner traveling to America where Jung separated from his comrades to stay in the stateroom cabins. There are knowing looks in the eyes of Freud and Ferenczi as they move on to their second class accommodations; their gaze captured a sense of Jung's wealth, cold and detached bearing, haughtiness, his sense of entitlement, and his considerable socio-economic differences from them. Economic wealth contributed to his arrogance. After the break with Freud, Jung experienced a nervous breakdown, perhaps a psychotic break. He was flooded with dreams about a world historical catastrophe threatening civilization; his dreams contained an apocalyptic vision about the rise of barbarism, and the coming of a tidal wave that would engulf Europe, ending in mass bloodshed; this dream was possibly a premonition of the mass violence of World War I and the barbarous unleashing of the Second World War.

Like Jung, the Freud of Cronenberg's film had distinct flaws and weaknesses. Like Jung, Freud, too, was oral. In every scene in the movie, Freud was seen with a cigar in his hand or his mouth. In terms of anal organization, he demonstrated a fierce, relentless insistence on the correctness of his libido theory, stubbornly refusing to relinquish or modify it to include other perspectives. On the phallic and Oedipal level, he was a confident, virile, and well defended father preoccupied with the rebelliousness and opposition of his sons, worried about secession, and the preservation of his cause and movement. We view his character rigidity, specifically his fixed and obsessional ideas about the correctness of his theory of instinctual drives. He was unforgiving toward past and present figures who have disappointed or broken with him. We are shown him to be angry, hold grudges, and be fiercely proud, pompous, and polemical toward those who opposed his core ideas. He appeared more concerned about aging and finding a reliable successor than in continuing to develop a clinical method that overcame obstacles to understanding and resistance to healing. Shown to be a secular, godless Jew, emotionally disconnected and alienated from metaphysical concerns, Freud's perspective was linked to a rational and compassionate wish to help suffering individuals understand themselves as they are. Above all, this required a fundamental self-acceptance, based on self-knowledge and the exploration of unconscious dynamics.

Freudian therapy, then, becomes oriented to people as they are actually constituted, not as they might become, linking them to their own defensive and adaptive tendencies. In the film, Freud insisted on making the distinction between fantasy and reality, advocating sober analysis of illusions and self-deceptions. He worked with a hermeneutic of suspicion toward imaginative leaps into the unknowable, speculations about the unknown. Though a cultivated European intellectual, surrounded by art, antiquities, and books, the Freud of this film was materialistic, desiring his technique to focus on the individual's psychological states at the frontier of the body, mediated by individual biology, and the mind, viewing body and mind as part of a continuum. Freud urged therapists to reject the role of prophet or priest since therapy was not about offering spiritual advice or transcendent solutions. In his debates and final break with Jung, we hear Freud rejecting mysticism, intuition, and spiritual strivings as dead ends, as forms of knowledge that cannot be scientifically validated.

In the film, Jung rejected Freud's theory as too narrow, deterministic, materialistic, far too preoccupied with sexual motives, and cut off from higher, quasi-religious strivings of the individual.

Ultimately, Jung saw Freud's theory as "too Jewish." As Jung turned toward the study of religion, myth, and cosmology, he moved from psychological typologies toward the positing of a collective unconscious. He wished to provide sick individuals something transcendent to believe in, some form of wisdom to mediate between their lives on earth and those realms beyond the individual – past and present. For Freud and for director Cronenberg, Jung's orientation lacked the specificity and rigor of Freudian psychoanalysis. It was a reductionism upwards, as it were.

There are different transferences to the theories and personalities of the two protagonists in the film. This provides the film with more dramatic intensity and complexity. The story on the screen can be interpreted on multiple levels and from many perspectives, depending on the viewer's transferences. In the epilogue of the film, we are told that Jung recovered from his breakdown, becoming the "world's leading psychologist" after 1939. This is a somewhat dubious statement. Freudian psychoanalysis held significantly more influence than its Jungian rival, penetrating and diffusing itself in Europe and America. It also glosses over Jung's complicity with the Nazi regime in the period 1933–1934 and some of the affinities of his thought with National Socialist ideology.

One of the most significant triumphs of this excellent, artistic film is the way in which it captures the analytic method, transforming it from the screen to the audience. Viewers engage in the analytic process itself, wondering about the various meanings of the utterances, picking up on contradictions and gaps in the accounts, on the defensive maneuvers of the characters, and on deciphering the unconscious meanings of what is being said and shown. The historical film about the founders of the analytic discipline establishes an intriguing drama about these pioneering psychologists on one another and upon Spielrein. More significantly, it illustrates how the unconscious operates in intimate personal relationships and various institutional and doctrinal conflicts, many of which are still not settled. This is a remarkable achievement by Cronenberg, unusual to see in a popular Hollywood film.

At the end of the film, we saw Jung seriously ill, unable to work, dysfunctional, not seeing patients, and not writing. In short, he was fragmented. Although there is no historical evidence of this encounter, it serves as a beautiful epilogue to the film. It restores artistically a symmetry where the former, now recovered patient is asked to treat the former doctor, now suffering as a vulnerable patient. Emma Jung invited a recently married and pregnant Spielrein to a visit at their Zurich mansion. Emma asked Spielrein if she would be sad about not having a son. Spielrein replied no, that she is wishing for a daughter; a daughter would further release her from her ties to Jung and her Siegfried fantasy. Emma has struggled with several pregnancies to present Jung with a son, an heir apparent, always trying to satisfy her insatiable husband whom she indulged as a child. She said that Jung admired Spielrein's clinical acumen and insight, asking her to stay in Zurich in order to take her husband into analysis with her. Spielrein declined, saying that she has transitioned into clinical work studying the psychology of children.

Emma asked her to speak to Jung. Sitting next to Jung on a bench overlooking Lake Zurich, but facing in opposite directions, Spielrein reversed positions once again with her former therapist. She was the well analyzed one, centered and mature, the adult capable of holding onto a realistic view of the world and of people, of continuing with her projects, and breaking her bonds to those (especially to her family and to Jung) who traumatized her. She now functioned as a therapist to the sick Jung. Freud had told Spielrein that they were Jews and that as Jews they would be misunderstood and misrecognized by gentiles. In this film, this is a bit softened; in their letters, Freud wrote: "We are and remain Jews. The others will only exploit us and will never understand or appreciate us" (Carotenuoto, 1982; Fisher, 2009).

Spielrein correctly intuited that Jung has a new love, Toni Wolff, not coincidentally a former patient, an analyst in training, and a Jewess. This is the one historical error I could discover in the film. Jung's biographer, after doing archival and genealogical research, can discover no Jewish family ties in the Wolff family tree (Bair, 2003). Spielrein knew that Toni reminded Jung of her. After initially denying it, he reluctantly admitted it. Jung asks about her husband. Spielrein replied that he was a Russian Jewish physician. Jung inquired what she liked about him. She answered with one word: "kind." Spielrein was returning to her Russian Jewish roots. Once again, she appeared to be separating and individuating from Jung, by emphasizing the Jewishness of her husband and his fundamental decency – contrasting implicitly with Jung. Jung gazed at her pregnant stomach, saying that it ought to be their baby. With tremulous emotion, Spielrein agreed. This was the final return of the Siegfried fantasy; its appearance and disappearance would permit her to terminate their relationship. We view a crying Spielrein leaving the Jung estate in a car. The film has not gone full circle. Knowing that Jung and she have definitively broken, she must grieve the loss once again, integrate the experience, leave Zurich permanently, and attempt to lead a constructive and loving life as a physician, mother, and creative practitioner and contributor to psychological knowledge.

In the epilogue of the film, we are told that Spielrein and her two daughters perished at the hands of the Nazis who invaded Rostov-on-Don in 1942, tragically massacring them in a synagogue.

A Dangerous Method is a relatively short film that illustrates a significant moment in the history of psychoanalysis, Freud's break with Jung. It will provoke much reflection. It does much good in restoring the memory of the magnificent and forgotten Sabina Spielrein. The film is really her story, recounting her recovery first through the psychoanalytic method, then through the force of her personality, and her own creative and reparative way of building a life after much trauma and destructiveness. Keira Knight's performance captures Spielrein's recovery after being disillusioned with idealized authority figures, without losing a cohesive sense of herself, still able to affirm her own idealistic world vision. The film simultaneously humanizes Freud and Jung, showing their strengths, courage, and revolutionary insights, while not glossing over their flaws, limitations, and at moments their indecent and self-serving behavior. Instead of romanticizing this history and exalting the forerunners of psychoanalysis, the film beautifully and successfully shows all of the early psychoanalysts as wounded healers.

Returning to the poignant late scene between Spielrein and Jung, sitting on the bench overlooking Lake Zurich, Jung referred to the two of them as "wounded physicians." He says, "Only the wounded physician can hope to heal." This metaphor refers to the intense vulnerability of the analytic therapist, his or her difficulties in handling the regressive tendencies of his patients, and his subjective reactions to these regressions, to the projections into the analyst, to the process of not knowing, to the ways in which the therapist is himself a recovering patient, fully capable of suffering pain, confusion, dissociation, and anguish. This thoughtful movie helps us to contemplate our origins as we figure out where we are now. Lastly, it is a helpful reminder that the founders of our discipline discovered a strong but potentially dangerous method, one that needs to be practiced with care, compassion, ongoing self-reflection, and fundamental respect for the other. It is a method that encourages us to know more about ourselves as we practice our craft with our wounded patients. Wounded healers can potentially heal themselves as they heal others.

Previously published in *International psychoanalysis.net*, December 1, 2011, pp. 1–18.

References

Bair, D. (2003). *Jung: A Biography*. New York: Little Brown and Co. pp. 195–196, 713, n. 27.
Carotenuoto, A. (1982). *A Secret Symmetry: Sabina Spielrein between Jung and Freud*. New York: Random House.
Civington, C. and Wharton, B. (Eds.) (2003). *Sabina Spielrein: Forgotten Pioneer of Psychoanalysis*. East Sussex: Brunner-Routledge pp. 79–90.
Fisher, D. J. (2009). The Analytic Triangle. In *Cultural Theory and Psychoanalytic Tradition*. New Brunswick, NJ: Transaction pp. 79–90.
Hampton, C. (2002). *The Talking Cure*. London: Faber & Faber.
Heuer, G. (2011). *Sexual Revolutions: Psychoanalysis, History, and the Father*. London: Routledge.
Kerr, J. (1993). *A Most Dangerous Method*. New York: Knopf.
Lothane, H. (2000). Tender Love and Transference: Unpublished Letters of C.G. Jung and Sabina Spielrein. *International Journal of Psychoanalysis*, 80(6), 1189–1204.

Chapter 12

Peter Loewenberg's Contribution to Psychohistory and Psychoanalysis

What follows is a highly condensed biographical narrative of Peter Loewenberg's life and work. I am faithfully following his autobiographical essay, "A Life between Homelands" (2018). In A. W. Daum, H. Lehman, and J. J. Sheehan (Eds.), *The Second Generation: Emigres from Nazi Germany as Historians* (pp. 114–129). Oxford and New York: Berghahn Books.

Peter has lived an eventful and colorful life. To me, it has a novelistic form with recurring themes and motifs. I will not be discussing his pathbreaking scholarship because of the limitations of time. He has written three books and published over 70 scholarly articles: *Decoding the Past: The Psychohistorical Approach* (Knopf, 1984), his most important book; *Fantasy and Reality in History* (Oxford University Press, 1995); and with Nellie Thompson, *100 Years of the IPA: The Centenary History of the International Psychoanalytical Association 1910-2010, Evolution and Change* (Karnac, 2011).

This is not a eulogy. Peter is alive and well and going strong. He just recovered from his second vaccination shot, which threw him for a loop, but showed that his immune system was strong, illustrating his resilience. This past week, he has engaged in a lively debate about Freud's case history "Dora" online with members of the American Psychoanalytic Association, reminding them of the perils of present-centered thinking and the necessity of a historical consciousness.

He was born in Hamburg, Germany in August 1933, seven months after Hitler's seizure of power. His father Richard Loewenberg was a university psychiatrist with a humanistic background and a psychodynamic orientation. His mother Sophie worked as a public health nurse, converted to Judaism, and was an engaged socialist activist on the political left in the Weimar Republic. From his father, Peter inherited a passion for psychological insight, and from his mother a commitment to social justice.

The family left Germany and resettled in Shanghai, China in October 1933. Peter was six weeks old. This was the beginning of Peter's special and rich connection to China, which continues to this day. The Loewenberg family remained in Shanghai until 1937, leaving shortly after the Japanese invasion and moving to San Francisco. China was a life-saving refuge for his family against Hitlerian fascism, and currently China has become the space where

DOI: 10.4324/9781003488439-14

psychoanalytic practice and culture are thriving and growing, injecting new energy into our discipline.

At age four, he was separated from his parents who lived and worked in San Francisco, while Peter lived with two pediatrician families in Berkeley. He saw his working parents only on Sundays. This traumatic separation from loved ones caused great distress and pain for the young boy, exacerbating the loneliness of an only child. I believe this event was formative in Peter's subsequent development of sensitivity and compassion for those who lack parental support and who suffer from neglect and parental deprivation. The family eventually settled in Bakersfield where Peter attended public school, excelled at debating, and participated in student government. He attended the University of California, Santa Barbara, from 1953 to 1955, majoring in history.

Tragedy stuck the Loewenberg family in 1954 when his father Richard died of a stroke at age 56. His traumatic death triggered financial and emotional difficulties. Peter needed to find jobs to help support himself and his education. He worked as a short-order hamburger cook, a bellhop at a local hotel, pumping gas at a Shell station, and clerking in a law firm. He also found mentors and surrogate fathers, the two most important being Carl Schorske in Berkeley and the Los Angeles Psychoanalyst, Samuel Eisenstein, himself a refugee from Rumania and Italy.

Peter attended the University of California, Berkeley from 1955 to 1965, studying Central European History and European Cultural and Intellectual History. He was one of Schorske's first doctoral students. Berkeley in this period was a veritable hothouse of political experimentation and cultural effervescence. He learned as much outside the classroom and library as inside. An unbelievably exciting place, Berkeley exposed Peter to Marxism in all its varieties, to the sociology of Max Weber, to psychoanalysis, anarchism, the Free Speech Movement, cultural relativism, environmentalism, and conservation. Peter learned about the educational possibilities of study groups.

Peter attended the Free University of Berlin from 1961 to 1962. He witnessed the construction of the Berlin Wall. He was also in Germany in 1989 when he saw the coming down of the Berlin Wall and the destruction of the DDR. He has a knack for being present when major historical changes occurred.

From the brilliant and dialectically adept Carl Schorske, Peter imbibed a forthright and honest humanism. In a telling conversation with him, Peter expressed doubts about a psychoanalytic explanation for historical phenomena. Schorske replied, "Never give up the fundamental principles you believe in."

In graduate school, Peter developed an incisive critique of the historical profession, seeing the discipline's conceptual approach as naïve psychologically by assuming that historical actors were rational and self-interested. Peter realized that such explanations did not go deeply enough, that they overlooked the unconscious roots of human motivations, conflicts, and behavior. It was at that moment that he decided to pursue psychoanalytic training to learn the discipline from the inside and also to eventually work with patients.

As a history professor at UCLA, Peter began his analytic training at the Southern California Psychoanalytic Institute (SCPI) from 1967 to 1971 simultaneously with research into the psychodynamics of fascist leaders and followers, and the psychology of group process among the Nazis. Two articles appeared in the discipline's premier historical journal, *The American Historical Review*, thanks to the broad-mindedness and tolerance of Robert K. Webb, its editor; both articles were refereed by professional historians and psychoanalysts. "The Unsuccessful Adolescence of Heinrich Himmler" and "The Psychohistorical Origins of the Nazi Youth Cohort" both beautifully integrated the insights of depth psychology and historical, contextual analysis. I remember my intellectual excitement reading these two essays in the University of Wisconsin periodical room when I was a graduate student in history in 1971. Peter also published a masterly, insightful study of Theodor Herzl, the founder of Zionism, indicating the creative possibilities of fusing depth psychology with biography.

In 1966, he participated in the Bruin Granada Project in Mississippi, serving as a tutor in school integration. Peter has always had a clear commitment to civil rights and social justice. Having decided to pursue psychoanalytic training, Peter was greatly supported by Samuel Eisenstein who served as a personal mentor, friend, and guide. Peter's debt to Sam Eisenstein from SCPI can be seen in his naming his first son Samuel and by asking Eisenstein to give Josefine away as his bride in 1985. With Sam's help and assisted by Sigmund Gabe, Peter's former analyst, SCPI established a research training fellowship to help academics pay for training in psychoanalysis. Fellowship winners were given $10,000 a year for a three-year stipend. This marked the beginning of the training and eventual registration of the Research Psychoanalysts by the Medical Board of California. When Peter became Dean of SCPI in 2001, that stipend was doubled to $20,000 to cover four years of training. Academic researchers from UCLA, USC, Caltech, and California State universities received this award over the years.

Countless books and articles have resulted from this innovation in training the Research Psychoanalysts and from their immersion in psychoanalytic theory and practice. Such education, Peter argued, would expand the academic arsenal of research methodology by emphasizing the clinical dimension, while simultaneously enriching psychoanalytic discourse by introducing significant perspectives from other academic disciplines, in particular the humanities and social sciences. Peter exemplified the creative potential of having dual training, of working at the points of convergence of psychoanalysis and the allied fields in the humanities and social sciences. Analytic training, including a clinical training analysis, would alert the researcher to aspects of subjectivity, the inner world, the interpersonal domain, the role of defenses and self-deception, affectivity, transference, and countertransference dynamics, all of which come into play in research, writing, and teaching.

Several Research Psychoanalysts have become award winning authors and teachers at analytic institutes and universities. Here, once again, Peter was a forerunner. While teaching at analytic institutes, they have provided higher levels of rigor in the seminars, of questioning basic presuppositions, of reading texts in a sophisticated fashion, and of posing questions about psychoanalytic methods and applications. In short, the presence of the Research Psychoanalyst has improved the quality of institute education, made it intellectually more stimulating, more democratic, more supportive to its students, and more receptive to its younger members. The educational approach is closer to the university model than a technical training school or religious sectarianism. The spirit of encouragement, inclusion, and promoting young members is vintage Loewenberg, deriving from his value system and his way of being in the world.

Peter was also instrumental in helping to promote the first Research Psychoanalyst Law. This legislation was supported by Howard Berman, California State Assembly Majority Leader. It was signed into law by Governor Jerry Brown on September 30, 1977.

Psychoanalytic history has infamously been one of continuous bickering, acrimony, and outright splits, beginning with Freud's break with Adler, Stekel, and Jung. Peacemakers are exceptional and rarely successful. They are often despised. SCPI split from the Los Angeles Psychoanalytic Society and Institute in 1950. As Dean of SCPI, Peter personally orchestrated the eventual merger of the two adversarial institutes, healing an old breach that no longer made sense in the new century. He astutely realized that both institutes had more in common than what appeared to divide them. Under his effective guidance and with the assistance of the Director of Education from LAPSI, Mark Thompson, the two institutes merged in 2005. It is now called The New Center for Psychoanalysis, combining the strength of both institutes.

Without Peter's energy and vision, this merger would never have occurred. He risked his reputation, losing old friendships to promote and ultimately secure the merger. He was personally attacked in a manner distinctly psychoanalytic, that is, with a high degree of nastiness and personal venom. Ultimately, he accomplished the reunification of the two institutes with an amazing degree of patience, political finesse, and determination. NCP is currently a thriving psychoanalytic institute, with a strong theoretical and clinical curriculum, large assets, a lovely building, an outstanding library, and a world-class archive; at one time it offered a state sponsored Ph.D. program, which is now being contested by State bureaucratic regulations. Above all, it has become the most successful program for Research Psychoanalysis in the world. This success is one of Peter's most significant legacies. We all owe him a debt of gratitude.

With Robert Nemiroff and Nancy Chodorow, Peter helped to inaugurate the University of California Interdisciplinary Psychoanalytic Consortium (UCIPC) with annual meetings held at the Lake Arrowhead conference center (it is now called the UCNCPIPC Consortium). The first meeting was held in May 1993. The Consortium is important because it indicates the formal recognition of psychoanalysis in the curriculum and research agenda of the university. Open-mindedness and dialogic exchange embody the spirit of the Lake Arrowhead meetings. Informal workshops are privileged over lectures. Different generations intermingle. Clinicians and academics interact with mutual interest and curiosity. Informality prevails. We take our meals together, watch and critique a movie, occasionally dance the tango, take hikes around the lake, and have many informal but generative chats. Many young graduate students and junior faculty members have been inspired to pursue analytic training as a result of these Lake Arrowhead Consortium encounters. It is a key link to the university community and a significant source of recruitment.

Last but not least is Peter's involvement with China. He brought his enthusiasm, his political acumen, his desire to cut through the IPA's bureaucratic red tape and delay, and his thorough-going critique of its neo-colonial and arrogant attitudes toward China. Peter taught psychoanalysis on many trips to China, including visits to Shanghai, Beijing, Wuhan, Kunming, and Chengdu beginning in 2003. He chaired the IPA's China Program from 2007 to 2013. Psychoanalysis is currently growing more rapidly and widely in China than anywhere else in the globe. Peter always sensed that the Chinese were eager to receive the best of Western talk therapies. A typical Loewenberg aphorism: we Westerners can learn much from the Chinese, especially in terms of personal relations, public tact, sensitivity, and sensibility. For Peter, the penetration and diffusion of psychoanalysis in China has always been a two-way exchange, a reciprocal dialogue.

To summarize, Peter has lived a big life, a multi-dimensional life, a life of learning and teaching, of friendship and intimacy. He is a sophisticated cosmopolitan and internationalist. He has a zest for earthly explorations. He loves the mountains, especially the Sierras, and he relishes personal and interpersonal encounters. Peter appears to know everyone and with his wife Josefine has made an art out of entertaining with wonderful food and a warm ambiance. He has the most interesting and varied of friends visit his home. His fifty plus year friendship with Josh Hoffs blends professional interests in psychoanalysis as a practice with the confidentiality that only a long, intimate relationship can offer. Peter leads a productive, scholarly life, one of continuous curiosity, marked by encyclopedic knowledge in many areas; he rarely gets bogged down in narrow specialties, always prefers to be a generalist. He can also be ironic, opinionated, outspoken, and willing to take sharp political and cultural stands, letting his audience know what matters to him on issues of integrity and conscience. Peter also has a marvelous sense of humor, blending acerbic remarks with self-deprecation. After a lecture in the NCP auditorium by a distinguished analytic colleague, he marched down the aisle, locked eyes with me, summarizing the talk in one word: "psychobabble!"

I have been Peter's friend and colleague for 47 years. This relationship is one of the great gifts of my lifetime.

Previously published in *Psychohistory News*, Vol. 40, No. 2, Spring 2021, pp. 2–5.

Part III

Toward a Psychological Understanding of Resistance and Collaboration during Vichy France

Chapter 13

Reflections on the Collaboration and the Jewish Question

As I attended the exhibition at the Archives Nationales in Paris in late December 2014 on the French collaboration, I experienced powerful feelings of pain and anger, followed by puzzlement. "The collaboration" covers the years of the German Occupation of France from 1940 to 1945. It is remarkable that the exhibit was held at all, after decades of cover-up, silence, and apologies about it. Officially sponsored by the French government, this disturbing exhibition was accompanied by an excellent book/catalog published by the French Ministry of Defense and an evocative poster, which also serves as the cover of the book. It shows a black and white photograph of Marshall Philippe Petain in the upper right corner, gazing down on an upside-down color photograph of Hitler, shaded in red, signifying bloodiness and death. Reversing the old way of understanding the history of Vichy France, with the received opinion that the French took their orders from the Nazi occupiers, both this photo and exhibition radically demolish this view. Collecting over 600 sources arranged chronologically, including many unpublished documents, the book reveals factually the origins and horrors of the collaboration.

Vichy France is one of the most ugly and ignoble periods of contemporary French history. Superb documentary films exist on the period such as Marcel Ophuls' *The Sorrow and the Pity* (1969) which was banned from French movie theaters through the middle 1970s and from television until 1981. Tatiana de Rosnay published a novel, *Sarah's Key* (Rosnay, 2008), followed by a movie of the same name; although fictionalized, it poignantly captures the soul-destroying effects of the French Holocaust by following the impact of these events on the life and mind of an adolescent girl. The earliest first-rate scholarship on the subject came from American scholars of France, such as Stanley Hoffmann (Hoffmann, 1962) and Robert Paxton (Paxton, 1972). Despite French translations of their work, there was great resistance to accepting the enormity of Vichy's crimes and its complicity in the mass slaughter of the Jews. Michael Marrus and Robert Paxton published the standard work in the field *Vichy France and the Jews* (Marrus and Paxton, 1982). Yet there is still much mystification about the collaboration. This public showing and book perform the work of demystification.

I saw it in Paris three days after visiting the Anne Frank House in Amsterdam and rereading her diary, and ten days before the murderous attacks on *Charlie*

Hebdo and the assassination of four unarmed Jewish civilians in a Parisian kosher market. I was exceedingly aware of aspects of recent Jewish history, including the pervasiveness of anti-Semitism in France, Europe, and increasingly in America. It also converged with my own sensitivity to being a vulnerable Jew in an increasingly anti-Semitic world. The Jewish Question was no longer a settled matter, taking on an intensity and relevance in the here and now. This show took place within a context of rising anti-Semitism in France, some coming from the extreme Right, some deriving from the Left where there is a conflation of a critique of Israel's foreign and domestic policy with anti-Jewish attitudes. Anti-Zionism can often disguise its anti-Semitism.

The perception of Vichy France was once saturated with simplistic mythologies. After the victory of the Allies and the ouster of the Germans, there was the naïve view that all Frenchmen were in the Resistance. This was followed by a counter legend that all the French were collaborators. As usual, historical truth is more complex and ambiguous. Historians have discovered that there was a spectrum of opinion, varying degrees of political, ideological, and moral support for the regime. It moved from ultra collaboration, to active collaboration, to passive collaboration, the latter justified in the attempt to adapt to a time of crisis and shame precipitated by the rapid German victory in "the strange defeat" (in the words of historian Marc Bloch) and by the humiliations of the German Occupation. There was considerable apathy, hard to define as either collaboration or Resistance, perhaps best understood as an attempt to get by during adverse circumstances of Occupation and repression. The Resistance was also marked by a panorama of perspectives and engagement, moving from active to passive forms of resistance, including nonviolent and violent forms of opposition to the Vichy regime.

Fontaine and Peschanski (Fontaine and Peschanski, 2014) argue that a majority of the French population was opposed to the collaboration and were against the German occupation, but obviously with different levels of outrage and involvement. "…all indications, all sources show that the great majority of the French had quickly rejected the politics of collaboration from the occupier and from the collaborators" (Fontaine and Peschanski, 2014, p. 9). They reiterate that many Frenchmen were just trying to accommodate to the new political regime during this dark period, trying to make some money, to protect their families and businesses, to continue to exist with the least amount of stress and strain – in short, to survive. They use the fashionable term "resilience" to describe this phenomenon, not explicating its meaning in terms of physics or psychology. They write, "But the mass of the French were situated between the two extremes, in accommodation or in resilience" (Fontaine and Peschanski, 2014, p. 10). Undoubtedly, some saw the Vichy period as an opportunity to move socially upward; some were careerists seeking to improve their status socially and economically. More seriously, the political and military group that assumed power during the collaboration consisted of active and ruthless anti-Semites, who made it their policy without Nazi pressure to marginalize, round up, deport, and ultimately exterminate the Jewish population of France. The authors conclude that "…It is Vichy which is henceforth, in our memories, the central actor of the collaboration, even before the Parisian extremists and even the Germans" (Fontaine and Peschanski, 2014, p. 11).

The collaboration touched all aspects of French life: there was political collaboration, economic collaboration (including forced labor sent to Germany to assist in the German war effort), and collaboration by old sectors of the parties of order in France, including the Catholic Church. These collaborationists were unequivocally opposed to parliamentary democracy and to the practice and expression of human rights, civil liberties, and secularism in France. They specifically took aim at the separation of church and state, itself an outcome of the deep tradition of republican anti-clericalism, of not permitting the Catholic faith to intrude upon the public space of politics. These rights were won after hard-earned political struggles, often-revolutionary victories. It was the French Revolution that also emancipated the Jews, accelerating the process of assimilation. The collaboration systemically vilified and dismantled these victories. Vichy's authoritarian forces defended the traditional values of work, family, country, and piety, slogans that reflected its reactionary, anti-democratic politics and repressive mentality of law and order. They were also aggressively anti-Jewish in their rhetoric and ideology. Many of the French collaborated because they believed that Germany would win the war, wagering that German hegemony would prevail in the future of Europe and the world.

A triangular relationship existed between Vichy, Paris, and Berlin. The chief responsibility for the collaboration came from Vichy itself. The Vichy regime was the chief actor of the collaboration even before the actions and words of the Parisian extreme right-wing extremists, the French militia, and before the Germans tightened their grip on the French, demanding submission. German archival evidence proved that Vichy did not submit to the dictates of the German occupier. Rather it followed its own internal logic, creating its own momentum. Citing Paxton, our editors say, "using German archives demonstrates that the Vichy regime finds its origins in the long history of the French extreme Right; that the French state—the national Revolution that it put in place, the values it carries—have their own logic; that far from simple submission to the dictates of the occupier, it demanded collaboration" (Fontaine and Peschanski, 2014, p. 11). Vichy France directed the persecution and ultimately the murder of foreign and French Jews. In effect, Vichy France found its origins and value system in the long history of the French extreme Right. This had devastating consequences for the population of French Jews, who numbered 330,000 in 1940.

Vichy depicted the Jew as its priority enemy, as the cause of all evils in France. It justified this position with the use of pseudo-scientific language and with the half-baked ideas of racial theory. Ideology is not only a system of ideas but also a set of ideals, attitudes, and passions with an aim. The goal of the collaboration's anti-Jewish ideology was the arrest, deportation, and ultimately the extermination of its Jewish population.

The exhibition shows that these policies developed gradually but accelerated as the government solidified itself. State sanctioned anti-Semitism led to the

"Aryanization" of Jewish businesses and enterprises. Wealthy Jews were targeted, their property and possessions expropriated. Jews were forbidden to work in certain professions, including teaching, journalism, and law. There was an incarceration of foreign-born Jews, mostly of East or Central European origin, in the southern zone. Vichy authorities passed statutes ordering the systematic registration of Jews as a "race." Under the guise of "dejudaization," Jews were denounced as foreigners. Leading French publishing houses were Aryanized, including Gallimard, Calmann-Levy, and others. A museum exhibition called "The Jew and France" opened in Paris, drawing 250,000 visitors. It visualized the Eastern European Jew as being a hybrid of Asian and African. Jews were pictured as carriers of the plague, as parasites and rats, attempting to engulf the globe. One document portrayed the "Eternal Jew" in a grossly caricatured way, with particularly dehumanizing aspects of his personality; Jewishness became synonymous with facial ugliness, signaling his "open and fleshy mouth, thick lips, large ears, massive and protruding, strongly convex nose, large and flabby nostrils, flabby features" (Fontaine and Peschanski, 2014, p. 127).

Vichy authorities opened the Drancy detention camp with Jews being sent there in August 1941. This period saw a massive pillage of Jewish property, estimated at 100,000 artworks and 500,000 pieces of furniture. Editors were prohibited to publish books by English or Jewish authors, or texts devoted to Jewish subject matter. They were forbidden to publish "biographies, even by Aryan authors, consecrated to Jews" (Fontaine and Peschanski, 2014, p. 34). Jewish Synagogues were bombed and criminally attacked in 1941. In August 1941, 4,232 French and foreign Jews were taken to Drancy located in the northeastern suburb of Paris and subsequently deported to concentration camps in Germany and Poland. On July 16 and 17, 1942, 13,000 Parisian Jews were arrested, rounded up, and sent to the Velodrome d'Hiver (the Vel'd'Hiv). Amongst those deported were 4,000 children. They were subsequently sent to Auschwitz-Birkenau. Numbers are cold and impersonal. But they are factual and carry weight. In total, 76,000 French Jews were killed in Nazi concentration camps. 47,000 were gassed on their arrival at Auschwitz. (Adler, 1987).

The State-run collaboration organized and orchestrated the massive deportation of French Jewry in the summer of 1942. The regime was obsessed with its sovereignty and preoccupied with its notion of internal enemies. Vichy France targeted Free Masons, Communists, as well as Jews. These associations and the Communist Party and trade unions were accused of being cults and secret societies. Vichy conflated Free Masonry and Bolshevism with Jewishness, employing the Jewish star and Jewish facial stereotypes in its anti-Masonic and anti-Communist propaganda. The operative slogan of "Work, Family, and Fatherland" promoted the retrograde and authoritarian nature of Vichy's ideology. It extolled discipline, order, thrift, and courage against their enemies' value systems. Vichy associated its enemies with laziness, demagoguery, internationalism, democracy, parliamentary forms of government, and anti-militarism. Jews were supposed leaders in all these movements, influential in Communism, big business, and in the closed society of Free

Masonry. The assault on the Free Masons, Marxists, and Jews was equivalent to an attack on progressive and secular ideas, as well as a frontal attack on science and reason. Subsequent crimes against humanity could be legitimized with these bogus concepts. Vichy propaganda never considered the glaring contradiction that they marked Jews as both capitalists and communists.

During the black years of the collaboration, there was a coherent effort to organize many centers of information, education, and entertainment throughout France. Collaborators assumed partial control of the press, the radio, the movies, and the museums, issuing pamphlets, brochures, and controlling publishing houses. The dominant ideology of Vichy was a regression to an old-fashioned, late nineteenth-century form of French cultural nationalism, racism, and xenophobia that was distinctly fascist or proto-fascist in its biases. This ideology pandered to the anxieties and hostility of the constituency of Vichy, namely, the members of the lower and middle classes, conservative Catholics, and the aristocracy, all of whom had contempt for republican ideas, very few of whom had empathy toward Jews. There was a vast network of police complicity, the collusion of the legal system and courts, as well as the intimidating presence of fascist leagues and paramilitary militias. These armed militias copied Nazi uniforms, spewing fascist slogans and flashing fascist symbols. These leagues and their fascist theatrical paraphernalia functioned to harass and marginalize Jews, whipping up a collective racist hatred against the Jewish population.

Ideologically, the collaboration borrowed from the tradition of the Action Francaise. It was fundamentally anti-Jewish, exactly as it had been during the Dreyfus Affair. It borrowed many of its slogans and rhetoric from Edouard Drumont, author of *La France juive* [Jewish France] (Drumont, 1886). This violent propaganda, derived from profound anti-Jewish resentments, pictured Jews as the private enemy of France. They generated a simplistic narrative, referring to a "Jewish peril." Vichy sponsored tracts and posters calling for Jews to be deported to the frontier, banishing them from France. The only definitive solution to the Jewish question would be the "liquidation" of the French Jews. As Jews mythically enriched themselves, they supposedly used their money and influence to become powerful and to divide the country. As part of a campaign that demonized Jews, they were blamed for "invading" the country, pushing France toward war; anti-Jewish statutes were legitimized in the name of taking strong measures against a group that was "outside of the national community." Most perniciously, they pathologized Jews as non-French, uprooted, or alien. If the Jews were represented as a cancerous illness, this contrasted with eternal France and the mystical ideas of being rooted in French history and its golden, rural, pre-industrial past. The headline of the newspaper *Au Pilori* dated March 14, 1941, read "French or Jewish Earth? Israel everywhere. Death to the Jew!" (Fontaine and Peschanski, 2014, p. 78).

There is a legend that most committed French writers and intellectuals were on the Left. Vichy France illustrated that there was a tradition of engaged artists and intellectuals on the Right, often the extreme or fascist Right. These counter-intellectuals violated most of the canons of humanism, betraying the tradition of rational debate, scientific discourse, and fundamental respect and sensitivity to the rights of others, particularly minorities. Some of these writers were gifted; many of them lent their talents to defend French purity and to attack Jews in the most vicious terms.

By way of example, Lucien Rebatet's novel, *Les Decombres*, became a best seller in 1942, purchased by over 65,000 readers. In it, he proudly proclaimed his adherence to a tough and relentless form of French fascism, declaring his esteem for Hitler's "vast genius," wishing for the victory of Nazi Germany. Louis-Ferdinand Celine, celebrated author of *Journey to the End of the Night*, wrote virulently anti-Jewish tracts and brochures, in which anti-Semitism fused with racist theory. Celine spoke the language of the Nazi final solution, calling for "Jewish elimination." In *Les Beaux Draps* (In a Fine Pickle), Celine exclaimed: "Art that does not recognize the country! What stupidity! What a lie! What heresy! What a Jewish saw! Art exists only of Race and Country. This is the rock by which one constructs it!" (Fontaine and Peschanski, p. 75).

Drieu de la Rochelle assumed the editorship of the prestigious *La Nouvelle Revue Francaise*, the leading French literary journal. Robert Brasillach and Alphonse de Chateaubriant contributed incendiary anti-Jewish broadsides. Collaborationists depicted Jews as "terrorists," that is, an incoherent blend that included Bolsheviks, owners of capitalist trusts, and gangsters. Fascist-inclined collaborators were exhorted by hard-line Fascist intellectuals like Robert Brasillach, editor in chief of the journal *Je Suis partout*, to surpass the Germans in their cruelty, militarism, and aggressiveness, exhorting the French to become "more German than the Germans" (Fontaine and Peschanski, 2014, p. 241).

Vichy France published glossy magazines with young, athletic, and healthy looking French men and women, accompanied by texts drawn from racial theory, aspiring for "Aryan victory." Vichy propagandists showed Nazi inspired films throughout France, including "The Jew Suss," which was seen by one million spectators between 1941 and 1944. In the film, Jews appeared demonic. They were alleged to be power hungry, money hungry, morally corrupt, and nothing less than thieves and criminals. The authorities issued lists of prohibited books including those considered Communist, anglophile, or Jewish. The press demeaned Jews as an "epidemic," their presence in France constituted a "micro-invasion." Anti-Semitic caricatures reified Jews as ugly and grotesque, vulgar cigar smokers, with over-sized ears and large noses. In a particularly revealing poster sponsored by the French Legion of Fighters and Volunteers for the National Revolution, there is a catalogue of values and ideological positions that reduced collaboration into a simplistic dichotomy, one of good against evil. Those for the Vichy regime participated in a new crusade; naturally, they wore fascist style uniforms, pledged an oath of loyalty to France and Petain, held one arm raised upward in a fascist salute, and placed one knee on the ground as if praying. They were "against skepticism and for faith, against anarchy and for discipline, against democracy and for authority, against international capitalism and for French corporatism, against Bolshevism and for nationalism, against Jewish leprosy and for Christian

Civilization." The last opposition was most ominous: "Against the forgetting of crimes. For punishment of those responsible for crimes" (Fontaine and Peschanski, 2014, p. 217).

Because it is largely composed of primary documents, Fontaine and Peschanski's book often lacks complexity and nuance. They only provide a seven-page Introduction to a text that runs over 320 pages. This leads to a simplification of Vichy France, a rather black and white perspective on the epoch, one lacking in subtlety, tonality, and color. They do not sufficiently contextualize their sources, nor place the book into a larger historiographical framework dealing with prior work on the subject. Most egregiously, they omit any discussion of or even a bibliographical citation to Jacques Semelin's massive book, *Persécutions et entraides dans la France occupée* [Persecutions and Mutual Aid in Occupied France] (Semelin, 2014). In this text, the author argues that 75% of Jews in France were saved, escaping deportation and death, and 90% of French Jews survived, while foreign-born Jews experienced the highest death rate.

If the documents reiterate that Vichy France was fundamentally anti-Jewish, the book omits reference to parts of the French population, especially in the provinces, that were explicitly anti-Petainist and anti-German. Many French people did what they could do in the struggle against Vichy and the Germans. There were French Protestants who supported, hid, and rescued Jews. While the Catholic hierarchy was evidently collaborationist during this period, many local priests proved sensitive to the plight of Jews in hiding, specifically the dilemma of Jewish children. Based on a true story, Claude Berri's 1967 film *Le vieil homme et l'enfant* [The Old Man and the Child] poignantly illustrates the saving of a Jewish child by an old World War I veteran and Petainist. One wonders if the French populations' initial support of Marshall Petain, a former military hero, an elderly and reassuring figure, might illustrate Freud's thesis about the blindness, passivity, and conservatism of the masses, particularly its longing for a leader, catalyzed in moments of national crisis.

Similarly, the authors omit any reference to the activities of Left-wing intellectuals and independent writers, many of whom were sympathetic to the Resistance; no mention is made of the Jewish resistance to Vichy France and the occupation by the Nazis (Latour, 1981). They also omit any reference to the robust cultural activity that existed during the era, and the increasingly strong centers of disagreement, protest, and resistance within Vichy France (Wilkinson 1981, pp. 25–77).

The weakest part of the exhibition and book is the absence of a sustained analysis of the psychology of the collaboration, both individual and collective. To write about my reactions to the exhibit and book on the collaboration, I began to reflect on empathy and its limits. How is one to enter oneself into the minds and emotions of the collaborators, especially if one approaches the topic as a Jew, a self-identified member of the Left, a psychoanalyst, and an author of an intellectual biography of an anti-fascist French intellectual (Fisher, 1988). I tried to imagine how the collaborators came to their positions and made their choices, which were often brutal and murderous, irrational, blasphemous, and genocidal. I wondered how to maintain an empathic perspective on those who degrade, dehumanize, marginalize, and ultimately deport and exterminate their enemies. I was trained both as a historian and a psychoanalyst to privilege empathy as a way of understanding human motivation in context. Empathic understanding is a powerful way of gathering information, of grasping why individuals make their choices in these specific circumstances, even if they might not be the courses of action I would have made.

Camus incisively remarked that there was a little bit of the fascist in all of us. Empathy also implies recognizing one's own potential for violence and cruelty and for reification of the other. The concept of empathy, then, functions as an instrument of gathering data, of understanding complex human motives, not as a way of sentimentalizing the past. Empathic understanding need not be regarded as sanctioning this behavior or as minimizing the crimes and shameful behavior of the historical perpetrators. It involves decentering the observer or historian from what is being observed. What follows are some psychological ideas that may help illuminate the politics of vengeance and murder of the collaboration.

To begin with, the anti-Semitism of the Vichy regime and its supporters sprang from the resentment of French Jewish wealth and success. Success could be found not only in the business world but also in the areas of intellectual, scientific, professional, and cultural achievement. Of the French population of 330,000 Jews in France in 1940, there was a disproportionate number of high achievers compared to the majority of the French. Jewish talent and at times brilliance generated fears and irrational anxieties within the French, tapping into an existing sense of shame and inferiority concerning Jewish competition and excellence. This generated hostile envy with resentment projected outward onto the Jewish population.

Collaborationist propaganda blamed Jews for France's rapid and humiliating military defeat in 1940, for the existing social and political divisions, immediately stemming from the Popular Front era in the middle 1930s, where France was governed by a Socialist and Jewish Premier, Leon Blum. Some of these resentments went back to the era of the Dreyfus Affair, where the anti-Dreyfusards took their revenge on republican ideas and ideals, frontally attacking Jews. They attributed French poverty to Jewish wealth and greed. The collaboration could find unity in its negative image and callous insensitivity toward Jews, while offering social advancement and racial and national unity around a myth of ideal French rootedness. It also tapped into patriotic sentiment caused by the German occupation, playing to an appeal to national recovery, or more minimally surviving in an extreme situation. If the vast majority of France's population were apathetic – that is, non-collaborators – then the moral callousness and moral obliviousness of the population may have opened up material and professional gains for ordinary Frenchmen, many of whom hated and vilified the Jews for their apparent gifts, talents, and dominance.

These collaborationists could replace the so-called pushy, aggressive, and over-achieving Jews. But to do so, they needed a new morality and worldview that legitimized their discrimination, plunder, and policies of mass assassination. They linked envy of the Jew to the ideology of an old form of French racial anti-Semitism and Jew baiting, dating back to the political anti-Semitism generated during the Dreyfus Affair at the turn of the century, revived in a second wave of political and racial anti-Semitism during the polarization of the 1930s into Left and Right. The psychological mechanism used here is splitting, the division of the self into good and bad internal objects, and the projection out of the bad object onto a stereotyped, demonic, and evil other. The foreigner within became unconsciously externalized onto the Jew; the alien part of the self became projected onto the Jew as an object of hatred. This psychological dynamic of splitting and projection existed on a mass scale, becoming linked with an ideology of racial, authoritarian, and Catholic and Christian anti-Semitism. Clearly, this ideology was narrow, bigoted, and violent, but not to its proponents. It left no room for ambivalence, toleration of difference, or peaceful co-existence between distinct ethnic groups. It also left the perpetrators and their supporters with little sense of guilt about their actions.

The self-criticism and anxieties of the average Frenchman were concealed, while their embarrassment about their own limitations resulted in a massive social projection. Jewish excellence became transformed into Jewish vice. Jewish "chosenness," once associated with righteousness and justice, became inverted into a horror of all things Jewish. The roots of aggression during the collaboration were born of the dynamics of narcissistic vulnerability and shame. Frenchmen became inflated and exalted, while Jews were devalued and debased. Persecution, harassment, deportation, and murder were justified in the name of self-defense, the need to cleanse France in a pitiless way of pathology in the present to guarantee a future of health and prosperity. Lastly, the apathy and passivity of the general population allowed for, even facilitated, the ethnic and religious intolerance and crimes of the ardent collaborators. Moderates and so-called centrists postured as apolitical, preferring to evade or avoid any responsibility for the barbaric consequences of collaborationist attitudes policies.

In conclusion, we must assert that if Vichy France was fundamentally anti-Semitic, there were vast sectors of the French country and population that were not. This book demonstrates that the indifference and the complicity of the general population of France greatly fostered the crimes of the Vichy extremists. These extremists definitively held the levers of power, politically and culturally. The ultra anti-Semites of the collaboration exploited mercilessly the envy, jealousy, greed, and apathy of the wider population, leading to the mass murder of the Jews of France. The collaboration must now be viewed distinctly as a regime that committed genocide against an unarmed, already marginalized, embattled, and victimized civilian population. In short, the collaboration was grounded in collective genocidal sadism. It participated in crimes against humanity and yet it was not taking orders from the National Socialists of Berlin. The awful slogan, "the French [to become] more German than the Germans" became transformed into official policy and practice. Without the Allied victory, the collaboration would have meant further torment, mass death, and decimation of the French Jewish population.

Previously published in *Journal of Jewish Studies*, Vol. 67, No. 1, Spring 2016, pp. 216–220.

References

Adler, J. (1987) *The Jews of Paris and the Final Solution: Communal Response and Internal Conflicts, 1940–1944*. London: Oxford University Press.

Berri, C. (Director). (1967). *Le Vieil Homme et L'Enfant* [The Old Man and the Child] (Motion picture). France.

Drumont, E. (1886). *La France juive*. Paris: Flammarion.

Fisher, D. J. (1988). *Romain Rolland and the Politics of Intellectual Engagement*. Berkeley: University of California Press.

Fontaine, T. and Peschanski, D. (2014). *La Collaboration. Vichy. Paris. Berlin. 1940–1945.* Paris: Editions Tollandier.

Hoffmann, S. (1962). *In Search of France*. New York: Harper.

Latour, A. (1981). *The Jewish Resistance in France 1940-1944*. New York: Holocaust Library.

Marrus, M. R. and Paxton, R. O. (1982). *Vichy France and the Jews*. New York: Basic Books.

Paxton, R. O. (1972). *Vichy France: Old Guard and New Order*. New York: Norton.

Rosnay, T. (2008). *Sarah's Key*. New York: Macmillan.

Semelin, J. (2014). *Persécutions et entraides dans la France occupe* [Persecutions and Mutual Aid in Occupied France]. Paris: Le Seuil.

Wilkinson, J. (1981). *The Intellectual Resistance in Europe*. Cambridge, MA: Harvard University Press.

Chapter 14

To Resist and to Protect
A Critical Analysis of *Weapons of the Spirit*

The documentary, *Weapons of the Spirit* (1989), produced, written, and directed by Pierre Sauvage, tells an extraordinary story about the ordinary people of Le Chambon. Its events do not appear in standard historical works on the Holocaust. Even in Marrus and Paxton's *Vichy France and the Jews* (1982), they receive less than a page. Phillip Hallie's *Lest Innocent Blood Be Shed* (1978) focuses on Le Chambon, but his approach tends to be idiosyncratic and theological rather than historical and psychological.

Director Pierre Sauvage takes us to Le Chambon-sur-Lignon, a tiny village in south-central France, thirty-seven miles from St-Etienne. During the period of the Nazi occupation of France, Le Chambon became a safety zone for both foreign and French-born Jews; it is estimated that 5,000 Jews were protected, sheltered, and hidden by the approximately five thousand inhabitants of the surrounding area. While the Nazi Holocaust escalated in France, Central Europe, and Eastern Europe, the citizens of Le Chambon refused to name names, defiantly opposed all anti-Jewish policies, and valiantly resisted the Judeocide. Such active resistance was dangerous. In France, it was a time of indifference, betrayal, denunciation, and anti-Semitic excess, partly legitimized by the Nazi occupation, partly reflecting a deep thread of anti-Jewish and xenophobic sentiment in modern French history, epitomized in the policies and ideology of Vichy France. Both the French police and the government handed Jews over to the Nazis long before they were pressured to do so. Of the 350,000 Jews living in France in 1940, 76,000 perished in the Nazi genocide: many of the Jews rounded up in France went to their deaths in Auschwitz.

While statistics are cold and difficult to grasp, the film is warm, compassionate, and sensitive, avoiding sentimentality in its searching examination of resistance and its motivation. Sauvage explores historical and psychological themes while engaging in an intensely autobiographical drama. As a "Jewish baby" born in Le Chambon on March 25, 1944, Sauvage infuses the film with artistic and historical tensions that echo his own poignant search for his roots, his quest for his ethnic and human identity, and his preoccupation with how he and his family survived the Final Solution. His family told him late in life that he was Jewish; it had been a secret. The director's wish to celebrate the meaning of Le Chambon becomes particularly evident in a scene in which he interviews a pro-Vichyite Minister for

DOI: 10.4324/9781003488439-17

Youth. Sauvage asks the Minister some pointed questions about the origins and consequences of Vichy's anti-Jewish policies. He replies that he did not know the fate of 20,000 Jewish deportees, adding, "Some of my best friends are Jews." The activities of the citizens of Le Chambon stand up in sharp contrast to this empty and shallow speech.

Sauvage pursues a number of hypotheses to explain the decency of the Chambonnais. To begin with, the village was predominantly Huguenot; the plain and the conscientious Huguenots had a vivid memory of centuries of political and Catholic religious oppression in France, dating back to the Revocation of the Edict of Nantes in 1685. Recalling their own struggle to keep their faith and dignity intact, they resonated with the life and death dilemmas of the Jewish population. Reared on the Bible, dedicated to fundamental ethical precepts like caring for their neighbors, these Protestant villagers were ready to render help, even when it meant placing themselves in grave danger. To aid those in trouble was considered a customary, everyday event; it did not require elaborate theorizing or moral justification. They did not see themselves as heroes, just ordinary citizens doing the right thing.

Since members of the Catholic minority in Le Chambon also rescued Jews, one cannot account for this episode solely in terms of Protestant religious ideology and practice. There was also a significant tradition of pacifism, conscientious objection, and militant internationalism in the town – a tradition perhaps inspired by the diffusion of Gandhian ideas in French Protestant milieus in the late 1920s and through the 1930s. The town had two centers of pacifist resistance: a school with a distinctly nonviolent curriculum, which fostered a climate of study and political solidarity, and a man, Pastor André Trocmé, a Christian pacifist who organized opposition to the state. Trocmé preached pacifism at the outbreak of World War II; he subsequently called for non-obedience to Marshal Pétain and active forms of nonviolent resistance to the Germans. Through attributing "influence" to the pastor, Sauvage argues that the "conspiracy of goodness" occurred in Le Chambon spontaneously, naturally, without coherent leadership, reflecting a broad community consensus.

Ultimately, the film raises a profound if insoluble question, namely, how to account for the decency of Le Chambon in an era dominated by the implementation of the Final Solution, in an epoch typified by active and passive collaboration with Vichy's inhumane and brutal policies. We are moved by these generous acts, particularly by the villagers' apparently unheroic, unselfconscious, and unselfish ability to render service to the Jewish victims. Can individual and communitarian altruism be explained, historically and psychologically?

In watching the succession of interviews with the surviving villagers and peasants forty years after the events, the viewer is disarmed by the simplicity of faces, of dress, of personal presentation; these proud people remain reserved and self-contained, eager to behave in ways that are dignified and not shameful. Permitting himself a bit of license at the end of the film, Sauvage wonders if Le Chambon's refusal to collaborate actively in atrocities can be generalized to an attitude toward life that others could emulate. But Le Chambon was unique; most other communities, including Protestant communities, did not rescue Jews. During the massive trauma of the Holocaust, Le Chambon remained a significant but unusual island of peace (Zuccotti, 1993, pp. 227–231). Goodness and decency may be beyond historical and psychological understanding, possibly because sustained acts of sympathy and solidarity are so exceptional. It would be relatively facile to analyze the dynamics of decency by seeing it as psychopathology, to attribute acts of goodness to rescue fantasies, to identification with kind parents or caretakers, the need to be needed, or the rechanneling of hostile or aggressive urges into their opposites. But that would be cynical. And probably unjustifiable. We need more research to explicate goodness, to move us from memory to more reliable forms of knowledge. Samuel P. Oliner's book *The Altruistic Personality: Rescuers of Jews in Nazi Europe* (1988) is a step in the right direction.

Sauvage's attitude of gratitude and astonishment toward the village carries its own rewards, for this is a strong film that evokes powerful emotions and compels the viewer to ask puzzling questions. Sauvage agrees with Albert Camus, who, perhaps not accidentally, lived in Le Chambon from 1942 to 1943 while writing his seminal novel of resistance to fascism and to inhumanity, *The Plague*. Its heroes, like the villagers of Le Chambon, are plain-spoken and quietly courageous; they possess an uncanny knack for grasping the basic issues: "The essential thing was to save the greatest number of persons from dying and being doomed to unending separation, and to do this there was only one resource: to fight the plague. There was nothing admirable about this attitude; it was merely logical" (Camus, 1948). Director Sauvage clearly understands the same logic; the force of the struggle against plague microbes, within and without, animating the will to protect and to provide for a beleaguered Jewish population and demonstrating a resistance of the people of Le Chambon to the Nazis.

Previously published in *The American Historical Review*, Vol. 95, No. 4, October 1990, pp. 1136–1137.

References

Camus, A. (1948). *The Plague*. A. S. Gilbert (Trans.). London: Hamish Hamilton, 122.
Hallie, P. (1978). *Lest Innocent Blood Be Shed: The Story of the Village of Le Chambon and How Goodness Happened There*. New York: Harper Books.
Marrus, M. R. and Paxton, R. O. (1982). *Vichy France and the Jews*. New York: Basic Books.
Zuccotti, S. (1993). *The Holocaust, The French, and the Jews*. New York: Basic Books.

Part IV

Funeral Orations

Chapter 15

Father's Day

In June 1994, I made a Father's Day excursion, journeying from Los Angeles to Riverdale, New York, to visit with my ailing dad at the Hebrew Home for the Aged. Dad had always joked about the inequity that his birthday and Father's Day tended to coincide, robbing him of the double recognition (and doubling of presents) that he loved. Several weeks before my visit, he had suffered two "minor" strokes. If ever there was a misnomer in medical vocabulary, "minor" stroke is it: no stroke is minor, especially for someone who was 83 years old with a history of cardiovascular symptoms, Parkinsonian syndrome, incontinence, impaired ability to walk, depression, and senile dementia. The stroke produced some weakness on the left side; he was also exhibiting violent, agitated, and at times unmanageable behavior toward those attempting to assist him.

As I drove to the nursing home, several ironies occurred to me. My father had been a physician who specialized in cardiology and peripheral vascular disease, tending to treat an elderly population. The inevitable passage of time has reversed the physician–patient relationship, but without the patient having any realistic hope of healing himself, with no option of recovery. My dad knew nursing homes intimately from his medical training and practice; he consistently spoke of his hatred for them, even with well-run ones, finding them confining and depressing. He understood that once one entered a nursing home, one might not exit alive.

I experienced guilt about my limited caretaking for my dad. My bad conscience for not taking him to live with me and my family is considerable, even though space and circumstances do not realistically permit such an arrangement. I have a small home in Los Angeles, already overcrowded, with a toddler and infant both still in diapers. My father would require twenty-four-hour attention, several shifts of full-time aides. But to encounter him here as a nursing home resident seems unbelievable, slightly unreal. I berate myself for not doing more for him. The guilt, sadness, and self-reproaches often become unbearable.

I found my father sitting slumped over in a wheelchair in the lounge of the Hebrew Home, surrounded by magnificent art. The Hebrew Home in Riverdale prides itself on its extensive collection of paintings and prints; along the corridors, one finds original Picassos, Chagalls, and Ertes, as well as an excellent collection of Judaica. The beautiful paintings and lithographs provide a glaring contrast to the condition and appearance of the residents. In this bright, spacious room, I discovered rows of wheel chaired geriatric patients lined up against the perimeter, with one row in the middle, facing a picture window with a stunning view: a vast panorama opening up to the Hudson River, the Cloisters, the New Jersey Palisades, and the George Washington Bridge. The living corpses seemed oblivious to the spectacular view.

To enter this lounge, at least for the uninitiated, is to enter a grotesque spectacle. Wheelchair-bound individuals, many with contorted mouths, protruding tongues, twisted bodies, uttering bizarre sounds. The cries and wailing alternate with an equally eerie silence; sometimes the sounds are angry (protesting some food), sometimes poignant ("get me out of here"), sometimes incoherent.

Here, with my father, were strangers slouched over, some sleeping, some inert, staring, being attended to, not being attended to. The aides appear good-natured and professional, perhaps they are on good behavior for it is Father's Day, after all. I experienced disbelief thinking of my dad sitting in this setting for hours at a time. I wondered how the nurses, assistants, and staff accommodated to such an ambiance. I tried to conceive of how much my father suffered with the sights, sounds, and implications of this morbid scene. I was struck by how little interaction there was between patients – the absence of conversation, even trivial exchanges. The wheelchair brigade was predominantly a spectacle of silence, waiting, of existential inertia.

I was appalled by my father sitting there, even more disconcerted by his vacant look. For most of his life, my father had been so extraordinarily vital, so energetic, so expansive about life, now appeared absent. He had practiced medicine for more than fifty years, publishing thirty-five papers in the clinical literature, evincing a wide-ranging curiosity about people and the world. Here was a man who was once cheerful, exuberant, and deeply engaged with life – now he had vanished. Yet, he was physically present, and recognizable, at least externally. His posture typified his mental state: hunched over in this wheelchair, head perched on his chest, eyes closed. Dad was poised in a state of semi-deep, semi-consciousness. Maybe this somnambulistic state was adaptive, shielding him from the horrors of his daily situation, from an all too painful awareness of his deterioration, of little chance for recovery.

In our time together, he never initiated a conversation. He responded tersely to questions, a one-sentence answer at most, sometimes only a few words. He rarely made any requests. That troubled me – it was strangely out of character for him. Only activities that affected his physical needs bothered him. Prior to the stroke, he could get around with a walker. He now needed help to stand up, and he could barely walk a few steps. Those with walkers on his floor were the exceptions. To watch him walk so tentatively was profoundly sad for me; it recalled his former gait, his quickness of step, and his determination to get things done, to arrive at his destination. He required help to use the bathroom, to have his clothes changed. Chronic incontinence has necessitated diapers, but he resisted. Messiness prevailed, perhaps best encapsulated in the metaphor of incontinence.

I imagine the potential shame of his situation, how humiliated he may feel by his helplessness and dependence. As he sat lifeless and disabled, he seemed to have emigrated elsewhere. His blue eyes, once so sharp and animated, were dull. This once emotional and flamboyant man was deflated. He emitted no emotions.

His life at eighty-three had been reduced to the satisfaction of physical needs: sleeping, eating, and defecating. His full and complex life was compressed. All of his essential belongings fit in one room, in fact, reduced to one small closet, one chest of drawers. He showed no interest in people and utter indifference to financial affairs. A person who was characteristically fascinated by social and political events nationally and internationally, he had stopped reading the *New York Times*, and though he watched television, he appeared not to register what he saw. An avid sports fan, he seemed barely interested in watching a baseball game. I asked him if he was following the O.J. Simpson case, and he answered no, slightly disoriented.

He had lost all sense of time and of events and probably of place as well. He did not know that it was Father's Day. He could not remember his age, but vaguely recalled that he had just had a birthday. He still ate with a certain relish, but post-stroke food was not very appetizing, mostly pureed. He needed to be fed, even though he had some strength in his arms and hands.

I could not distinguish his regressive behavior from his physical disability. When I asked him less than an hour after lunch what he had eaten, he fumbled. He could not remember. He was resigned to this short-term memory loss by now, despite being confused by it. He good-naturedly said the meals were good.

Depression is not easily differentiated from dementia in the elderly. I was unable to discern which was predominant in my father's case. He had crossed over into a zone of mental deadness, emotional detachment, devitalization, and indifference. Some might call it dissociation or psychic numbness. He seemed unable to associate mentally or verbally. He appeared permanently exhausted, disconnected. I could not distinguish if he was truly sad, or simply not there. I certainly was a terribly sad observer, wishing I did not have to witness and experience his state. I tried to use my experience of him in decline as a way into understanding what he might be thinking, feeling, fantasizing, and associating.

Yet, he was alive and physically present, albeit disabled and diminished, but with no complaints, no requests, no demands, no desires, no sense of the future. With memory, interpersonal contact, and cognitive capacity impaired and probably irreparable, I wondered what human qualities remained. Then, he became momentarily alert. He smiled his winning and charming smile, his blue eyes twinkled, and his emotional isolation suddenly ruptured. However, it regrettably was transient, immediately followed by retreat, vacuity, and that numbing silence.

He even ventured a few sentences, the most resonant for me being his affirmation of love for me and my family. Perhaps this simple "I love you" articulated all that needed to be said, perhaps it hadn't been spoken enough and spontaneously when he and I were younger. He suddenly said, "You've got to fix me," implying an awareness of being broken, or deeply damaged. When asked how or where he needed fixing, he faltered, retreating into silence, unable to complete his thought.

Strokes, of course, do great and permanent damage to the brain. Those recovering from strokes often express anger and extreme emotional and depressive reactions, often displayed as reflexes. Although I did not witness this on Father's Day, my father was resisting touch on the part of the nursing staff, refusing help on the part of a devoted and deeply trusted loved one. Sometimes, he would bite. Sometimes his anger escalated into rage and his stubbornness became transformed into an out-of-control state, where four aides were required to restrain him in order to change his clothes. If I was impressed by this residue of physical strength in him, I was terribly saddened by his lack of conscious awareness of his aggressivity, or of what motivated his rage.

In the face of this awful extinction of my father's self, and my own sense of powerlessness and inadequacy as a loving bystander, exacerbated by the distance from L.A. to New York, my father's family reacted with an extreme degree of emotion, often impairing their perceptions and judgment. All of us knew that he wouldn't improve, that he wouldn't regain his previous competence, even recapture his former impairment prior to his stroke. None of us knew how long he would live. My knowledge about his condition was inadequate, nor did I know what to do with this abundance of guilt about my father, how to manage my despair about his loss of function and intellect, how to channel my sense of waste about the utter extinction of his sense of self, my grief at the loss of his vitality. I became incompetent and sad. I was numb to my own feelings, unable to process them. I sensed this in others, too.

One outlet for my family's helplessness and distress was to pressure and vilify one another; my youngest brother living in New York became inadvertently the target for much of the venting. He was burdened with many key decisions and responsibility for my father's care. Accusations flew, blame escalated, vituperation replaced empathic understanding, and emotional outbursts overwhelmed compassion for one another, and sensitivity to my father.

Family members, anguished over my father's state, exaggerated an already horrific situation. They lobbied for him to receive even more assistance and attention; they demanded a full-time companion. They vehemently insisted that he be made to feel more comfortable and argued that he needed to be spared the horrors of the lounge, although it was unclear that he registered any of these sensations. Although those recommendations were unsolicited, they demoralized us, depleting the already compromised energy and self-confidence of the immediate family, filling us with self-doubt.

The nursing home, with its well-trained administrative staff and "interdisciplinary" approach, reassured us appropriately that my father was currently obtaining optimal care and that any changes would be wasteful of resources, nontherapeutic, and a huge expenditure of money. Money, of course, was on everyone's mind (except my father's) and yet remained unspoken. My father anticipated his fate and put sufficient money in trust to finance these expenditures. The Hebrew Home for the Aged was one of the country's more expensive nursing homes; entry was difficult, waiting lists were long, and sometimes influential connections had to be used to secure a bed. It was extremely costly – $8,500 per month – and none of the expenses were tax deductible or reimbursed by third parties. Yet another irony, $102,000 annually to sustain my dad, whose quality of life was minimal and whose inner world had apparently vanished. I was skeptical about the use of this considerable sum of money to sustain his care for an indefinite period. I reproached myself for asking the question; even thinking the thought seemed self-centered and shameful.

While I was a bit relieved that my father probably did not realize his plight, I was puzzled by the ethical, social, and medical dimensions of pondering when enough care and attention was enough. These issues admitted no facile answers. My father left written instructions about his wishes for no heroic measures to maintain life when he was lucid and when he signed his living will. But his current status had become ambiguous. I was unable to strike a balance between a forbidden desire to hasten his death and a dread of perpetuating his tragic and empty life.

Father's Day 1994: a day to be present, to bear witness, to love, to be loved, to think thoughts about sickness, health, death, mortality; in short, a day to reflect, a day for self-examination. With my father there but gone, with him appearing not to care or to know anything (he frequently replied to a direct question by saying that he did not know), with symptoms of dementia mingling with depression, I speculated about what would happen, what ought to be done. Maybe things would get worse. Maybe he would hang on to life (to life?) longer. And what, if anything, was the meaning of this Father's Day with its no exit ugliness and geriatric grotesqueries, its unanswered existential questions. I was not sure. Normal mourning clearly begins before the death of a loved one, linear thinking about the terminal stage of the life cycle no longer made any sense, especially as one's parents aged and yet clung to life. Grief for the loss of the loved one preceded the organic end of life.

In my middle forties, I became a dad. I valued being remembered and affirmed on Father's Day; the day now had a resonance to me that it previously never had. But I still see my dad there slouched over, and I can't extrapolate any significance from his situation. Dad had consistently expressed his desire not to burden or disappoint me. He wanted to exit from life without oppressing his sons. He was a lifelong advocate of self-reliance. A negative freedom was still freedom, even if one's options have been exhausted. To reflect on him enduring his last days with at least that degree of dignity intact may be salutary in at least one way. Remembering him will strengthen me when I am faced with a similar context and choice.

My father died quietly eleven weeks after Father's Day, just prior to Labor Day. His body gave out, unable to resist a "minor" infection.

Coda

A recent letter in response to my essay denounces my insensitivity and immorality for publicly revealing the physical deterioration, loss of function, and increasing mindlessness of my father. The letter writer's morality, it seems, pivots on silence, or some elaborate intellectual rationalization for avoidance. But when confronting the bewildering dilemmas of our aging parents, we ought not to be evasive in the name of a principle of abstract prudence or supposedly dignified denial, even if justified by the "commandment" of honoring one's parents.

It is estimated that over two million five hundred thousand Americans live in nursing homes and assisted living facilities. Many are disabled, immobilized, demented, and suffering from mild to extreme forms of depression. Incontinence is a highly pervasive condition for the elderly, including those not under institutionalized care. It is neither a violation of privacy nor an attempt to humiliate the elderly sick to confront these problems honestly. My essay was designed to give candid emotional expression to the profound sadness, grief, and helplessness that my father's condition called up in my family and me while maintaining an enlightened and humane concern for those who, like my father, suffer, and ultimately die. Age, disability, and confinement unleash so many ambivalences on the part of the children, despite the understanding and gratitude one feels for our loved ones. Only when the real situation of the disabled elderly and our genuine reactions to their condition are confronted can authentic dialogue begin, and genuine grief work be processed.

Previously published in *Tikkun*, May/June 1995, pp. 69–72.

Chapter 16

Remembering Robert J. Stoller (1924–1991)

Robert J. Stoller, M.D.[1] evolved from having an ordinary, if distinguished, career in Psychiatry into an extraordinary, world-class thinker and researcher in psychoanalysis. From 1954 until his death, he served on the academic faculty at the Department of Psychiatry at the University of California School of Medicine in Los Angeles, where he was regarded as an outstanding teacher, sensitive supervisor, and first-rate theorist. Stoller's investigations into the areas of sexuality and gender formation sprang from a deep reservoir of intellectual and clinical curiosity, a wish to understand the aspects of sexual behavior and fantasy that were insufficiently explored by traditional psychoanalytic perspectives. Stoller articulated, defined, and illustrated concepts that are now widely current. These include the concept of core gender identity; the central importance of the interplay of biological determinants with very early family environment and the generation of psychological conflict; the critical importance of aggression in contributing to the excitement of sexual arousal, particularly in perverse patients, but active, in one degree or another, in all aspects of play, fantasy, and imaginative activity.

In recent years, Stoller combined his clinical skills with the research methods of anthropology and ethology. He employed these talents in endeavoring to comprehend aspects of Sambia culture in Papua, New Guinea, as well as the subcultures of sadomasochism and pornography in West Hollywood; in these studies, the psychoanalytic inquiry into individual sexuality and personal history expanded into and intersected with the realm of cultural structures and social mores. Uninterested in psychoanalytic politics or in abstract theoretical debates, Stoller enriched our knowledge by the force of his personality, by his use of direct and unpretentious language, while demonstrating the evocativeness and strength of psychoanalysis as a research tool and an instrument of creative thinking.

At first, I misjudged him as aloof, slightly inaccessible, and even a bit patrician. On the surface, he appeared self-confident, elegant in a buttoned down sort of way. It was easy to dismiss him and to disregard cavalierly the significant body of his work. Only later did I realize that his somewhat Olympian attitude toward conflict and ideological battles within psychoanalysis sprang from a deep self-discipline and a passionate commitment to his subject matter. Underlying the glibness, beneath the residues of cynicism, Bob was profoundly warm, compassionate, sensitive, funny, and ethical; above all, he was a man of high intellectual seriousness.

As we gradually became more intimate, as the professional contours of our relationship intersected with the personal, I discovered another human being, more textured, more dimensional, more surprising, and altogether more caring in style and in substance than he initially appeared. Both in his private life and in his scholarship, Bob was a thoroughly curious man, amazingly open to learning, tough-minded, and nonsentimental in his approach to knowledge, its assimilation, and transmission. He had a healthy skepticism toward intellectual fashions and therapeutic fads. Yet he was a skeptic who experimented with research methodologies, techniques of gathering data, and with innovative, interpretative strategies.

Bob was authentically committed to intellectual life in that he maintained a willingness to write and to exchange ideas candidly. He was a psychologically minded and ethical man who opposed moralizing, philosophizing, and metapsychologizing. Psychoanalytic therapy was for him a deeply relational activity, presupposing a consensual moral agreement between analyst and analysand, the freely suspended attention of the analyst being the counterpart of the analysand's free association; insight, understanding, and the surpassing of self-deception were the mutual goals. If he loathed the self-righteous posturing and doctrinaire generalizing of many psychoanalytic practitioners, his own style of research reveled in specificity; Bob never tired of the pertinent – sometimes bizarre – detail and of collecting fascinating pieces of clinical data, which he enjoyed organizing, assessing, and extrapolating the meaning from, meanings that often contradicted grand theories.

From his training analysis with Hannah Fenichel in the early and middle 1950s, Stoller absorbed the strengths and encountered the limitations of classica psychoanalysis; most significantly, he learned how to free associate. Bob regarded free association (along with the discovery of the transference) as Freud's most potent clinical tool: for him, free association was both a powerful method of inquiry and a path toward creative self-expression. He experienced the generative possibilities of free association as everyday pleasures, as integral aspects of clinical work, writing, teaching, and being alive. Bob always struck me as vibrantly, athletically alive, pulsating with ideas, perceptions, impressions, and opinions.

He was a free-spirited nonconformist who was thoroughly conversant with the conceptual foundations of psychoanalysis. He identified fully and playfully with psychoanalysis, and he took pride in his affiliation with the Los Angeles Psychoanalytic Society and Institute; he connected his home institute to a grand tradition of thinkers, thinking, and the promotion of advanced forms of psychoanalytic research and application. Yet he was decidedly critical toward mainstream psychoanalysis, both locally and in the American Psychoanalytic Association. (For that matter, he could be scathing about the "nonmainstream.")

He worried about the ossification of psychoanalysis in America, the mechanistic transformation of brilliant hypotheses into conservative attitudinizing, and the hardening of creative insights into rigid dogma; much of his writing, implicitly or explicitly, attempted to rethink established psychoanalytic pieties. Bob had contempt for received opinions from any discipline, including his own. As for the "scientific" status of psychoanalysis, he raised searching questions about what constituted data, truth, reliable knowledge, and the limits of the knowable. He was an empiricist and scientist who took seriously the truths of fiction.

Bob's iconoclasm, then, extended and updated a genuine psychoanalytic position of critical thinking; his capacity to think about thinking stubbornly positioned itself against the true believers in the field; Stoller opposed all tendencies toward religious belief and mystification. His stance worked against the despair and defeat of those practitioners who never presented their own work and who rarely challenged the clinical and theoretical basis of their discipline, thus stifling the growth of psychoanalysis, guaranteeing its mediocrity. At his best, Bob moved beyond flippancy and irreverence toward razor-sharp self-reflexiveness; he was gifted at looking at himself while looking at his patients and his colleagues, all part of a project to widen the scope of the discipline of psychoanalysis by pushing it to its limits.

Bob evolved into that extraordinary thing in America: a literate physician, a psychoanalytic stylist. He was profoundly invested in and devoted much time to his writing. Because he had no interest in committees or administration, he was undeflected by the bureaucratic sides of psychoanalytic or psychiatric education. He was among the minority of analysts who took joy in conceptualizing, whose ear was not only attuned to the beats and dissonances of psychodynamics but also to the music and rhythm of latencies in human speech. Bob's vehement opposition to psychoanalytic jargon and his aim to write in plain, felicitous English all derived, I believe, from his immense pleasure in the emergence of a distinct literary style. In discovering his voice, Bob expressed himself directly, cogently, corrosively, and yes, literarily.

I became close to Bob through participating in an ongoing study group composed primarily of Research Psychoanalysts from UCLA, USC, and Cal Tech. Bob, typically, was the only regular member of this group of clinically oriented academics from the humanities and social sciences who was medically trained; reversing standard practice in America, here the medical psychoanalyst was the outsider. Claiming repeatedly that he learned much from the dialogue with us, he considered himself, protesting too much, as uneducated. His self-denigration contrasted with a considerable knowledge outside of psychiatry and psychoanalysis; he was a highly cultivated man, who read widely and omnivorously; he was well traveled, cosmopolitan, and sophisticated. Within the framework of the study group, Bob functioned as a gifted listener, as someone who responded well to cogent (and often mordant) criticism, and who was never personally upset or angry, even when his theories or person were directly attacked.

Within this study group, he never played the prima donna, never the master thinker, never the monologist, even in the year that we structured our meetings around his seminal contributions to sex and gender. In recent years, he loved to raise probably unanswerable epistemological questions about knowledge in the manner of Montaigne: asking, What do I know? Yet, Bob very much desired to know. I can testify that Bob encouraged young scholars, exhorting them to expand their research and reflection, to move toward clarification and self-clarification. His discerning gaze penetrated intellectual dishonesty; his wit punctured arrogance. If he questioned the analytic researcher's ability to approximate "objectivity," he stressed that we be relentlessly honest about our own "subjectivity," that we lay bare our "biases." Although he expressed strong and coherent views, he was never cruel, tendentious, or needlessly harsh. In practice, he was generous with his time. He enjoyed evaluating work in progress and he had an exuberant, humorous, insightful way of alerting you to mistakes, drawing attention to exaggerations, and cajoling you to revise and deepen your thinking.

I had written a first draft of a paper on the psychoanalytic hermeneutics of Paul Ricoeur and Jurgen Habermas. Here is Bob's reaction to it, dated April 4, 1990:

Dear Jimmy:

As promised the other night, here are a few words on your hermeneutics.

First, I most enjoyed it, for, as is the case with everything you write, you educated me.

Second, I agree that psychoanalysis, when we are in the office with a patient, is all about interpretation and nothing else. But, as you and I know, the number of interpretations is not infinite, unless one allows for absurdities.

Third, I do not agree with those who feel that, though everything is meaning, meaning is not cause. To believe that is to stop being a therapist and become no more than a machine that receives messages.

Fourth, I distrust hermeneuticists' idea "Hermeneutic psychoanalysis is suspicious of consciousness." Take, for instance, your first sentence in that category (p. 6): "The art of interpreting begins with a stance that is aware of the multiple possibilities of false consciousness and remains suspicious about consciousness." But is not that art, that stance, that awareness, a consciousness that "is aware" and that "remains suspicious"? Who takes "a stance" if not a conscious creature?

The same holds for the whole of that category. I don't see how these hermeneutic folks do their hermeneuticizing from a state of unconsciousness. If they want to argue that there is no such thing as consciousness, that's fine though total damn foolishness, since it gives the lie to everything they do all day long. If your version of their suspiciousness is accurate, they should go back to the drawing board, for their enterprise has crashed.

Fifth, p. 10: "Truth consists in recognizing oneself with a degree of acceptance and without accusation." Why not accusation? What's wrong with a shot of accusation once in a while?

Again, p. 10: "Truth resides in the case histories …" Should not that read "Truth"? Is there any use of the word truth that would not benefit from enclosures within quotes?

Sixth, p. 11: "Psychoanalysis is linked to the disciplines and techniques of freedom." Isn't that utopian? If "psychoanalysis" is a term used to collectivize a body of people – psychoanalysts – then you may admit that your description on this page of "psychoanalysts" does not quite fit any psychoanalyst you have met. The disparity between perceived reality and impossible high hope defines utopia.

One last punch-in-the-nose for hermeneuticists (p. 3): "Hegel's aphorism that the true is the whole" is too holy, holey and unwholey. It drips with sentimentality.

See you soon, I hope.

Cordially, Robert J. Stoller, M.D.

Original thinkers are usually narcissistically invested in the correctness of their theories. Bob, on the contrary, was rarely defensive about his ideas and on more than one occasion I observed him grappling with a stinging ideological attack on his work on sexuality. After demonstrating that he could do it himself, he counseled me to pay attention to criticism, even polemics that really hurt; they often illuminated core conceptual problems, revealing unresolved ambiguities.

As an extraordinary individual talent, he wrote a number of books as a coauthor (with Colby, Herdt, and Levine); he seemed energized and revitalized by collaborative intellectual work. He and I ventured to explore the psychoanalytic implications of Michel Foucault's critical theory, particularly his writings on the history of sexuality. As a condition for our collaboration, Bob asked me to structure our readings together; whatever joint writings were to emerge from our effort, he generously insisted that my name was to appear before his – despite his seniority and name recognition. That project, sadly, went unfinished at the time of Bob's death, even though we had studied a vast number of Foucault's published writings and the secondary literature. Bob liked closure, but could tolerate delay and detour; he had every intention to complete what we had started. Now, I will have to dedicate it to his memory.

Stoller decentered the contemporary psychoanalytic approach to sexuality in at least two ways. First, by investigating the intricacies of so-called "deviant" sexuality, he radically widened the spectrum of our understanding of psychosexuality, enlarging the scope of what constituted sexual practice. In doing so, he demonstrated that the notion of "normal" sexuality was meaningless. Second, by studying patient populations like transsexuals, homosexuals, sadomasochists, and pornographers, that is, by focusing attention on those far removed from "normal" or neurotic practices, he transformed the concept of the "obscene" into one with significance both psychodynamically and in terms of the life history and fantasies of the individual. Rather than reciting old platitudes or warmed-over formulas about sexuality, Bob restored sexuality to its rightful subversive place in the psychoanalytic understanding of the individual. In the history of psychoanalytic thinkers on sexuality, Stoller's scholarship is second to none other than Freud.

His writings revolutionized the concept of primary femininity, while also uncovering the treacherous path of achieving masculinity for males. In pressing for answers to what constituted the exciting component of erotic arousal, Stoller emphasized the primacy of hostility and aggressivity in sexual scenarios. For supporting evidence, he ingeniously drew a wide gamut of sources and information, from pornography to fashion, to magazine advertising, to erotic daydreams, to data culled from his clinical practice. For Bob nothing "abnormal" or "perverse" was foreign to him; on the contrary, such phenomena were well worth inquiry and sustained thought. If the "obscene" was meaningful psychodynamically, not to be explained away by biology, or demonized by pathology, he erased the clear – normalizing – demarcation between the sleazy and non-sleazy, the prurient and nonprurient, and the acceptable and nonacceptable. Bob's work abolished the Victorian and Puritanical residues and binaries that had infiltrated psychoanalytic explanations of sexuality. He was an early pioneer and strong advocate against the pathologizing of homosexuality, perversions, and sexually active women. To the homophobes in his profession, Stoller insisted that homosexuality be seen in its plural form, not as one clinical complex with one underlying etiology. He was also skeptical about the "normalcy" of conventional heterosexuality.

Despite Bob's prominence, productivity, and apparent visibility in the Department of Psychiatry at the UCLA School of Medicine, for years he was in fact the only analytically trained tenured full professor on the faculty who identified himself as an analyst. He was marginalized in the department given its turn toward bio-behavioral forms of research and its disciplinary bias toward psychopharmacological and diagnostic practices.

Bob was similarly but more subtly isolated in the psychoanalytic community. Every seven or ten years, he witnessed a succession of fashions, each with a new promise and new enthusiasm, each with new gurus, almost always a displacement of attention away from the unconscious dimension of sexuality and erotics. Furthermore, Bob was never officially appointed to the faculty of the Los Angeles Psychoanalytic Institute, although he taught whenever it was requested of him. This was doubly ironic because he loved teaching and because he was an inspired and inspiring (and award-winning) teacher. Since he never wished to be a training analyst, he never became one. Lacking this status also meant a loss of prestige and honor among analytic clinicians. Many analysts viewed his patient population, with their severe personality disorders, as nonanalyzable; they tended to banalize Bob's work by regarding it as "interesting" descriptively, or by relegating Bob to the periphery of their universe by classifying him with the sexologists.

Bob's marginality pained him and liberated him. If he was hurt by the lack of recognition and the dismissals, it freed him up to research, reflect, and write. It seems strange to view a man of 66 as if he were in the full flowering of his productivity. But Bob had published two books in 1991, another was forthcoming before his death and he told me without bragging that he had enough material for five or six more books. Those books would have challenged, perplexed, stimulated, enchanted, and disenchanted his readers; they would have been hard to categorize. His death cut him off in his prime, absurdly taking him from us in a senseless automobile accident. We are left to transform his ruptured life into a completed one, to assimilate what was valuable in his work and method, and to preserve his pioneering and humane work by sustaining the vitalistic and critical core of his perspective.

Previously published in *The Psychoanalytic Review*, Vol. 83, No. 1, Winter, 1996, pp. 1–10.

Note

1 For a full bibliography of Robert J. Stoller's writings, see *Los Angeles Psychoanalytic Bulletin*, Winter, 1992, pp. 40–50.

References

Stoller, R. J. (1968). *Sex and Gender: On the Development of Masculinity and Femininity*. New York: Science House.
Stoller, R. J. (1973). *Splitting*. New York: Quadrangle Books.
Stoller, R. J. (1975a). *The Transsexual Experiment: Sex and Gender*, vol. II. London: Hogarth Press.
Stoller, R. J. (1975b). *Perversion: The Erotic Form of Hatred*. New York: Pantheon.
Stoller, R. J. (1979). *Sexual Excitement: Dynamics of Erotic Life*. New York: Pantheon.
Stoller, R. J. (1985a). *Observing the Erotic Imagination*. New Haven, CT: Yale University Press.
Stoller, R. J. (1985b). *Presentations of Gender*. New Haven, CT: Yale University Press.
Stoller, R. J. (1991a). *Pain and Passion: An Ethnography of Consensual Sadomasochism*. New York and London: Plenum Publishing.
Stoller, R. J. (1991b). *Porn: Myths of Our 20th Century*. New Haven, CT: Yale University Press.
Stoller, R. J. and Kenneth M. Colby (1988). *Cognitive Science and Psychoanalysis*. Hillsdale, NJ: The Analytic Press.
Stoller, R. J. and Gilbert Herdt (1990). *Intimate Communications*. New York: Columbia University Press.
Stoller, R. J. and I. S. Levine (1993). *Coming Attractions: The Making of an X-Rated Video*. New Haven, CT: Yale University Press.

Chapter 17

Eulogy for Joseph Natterson, M.D. (1923–2023)

Friendship is an extraordinary and precious thing. Joe and I were friends for 45 years. We celebrated the same birthday, though I was a quarter of a century younger. We played tennis at Roxbury Park. We were suite mates at 9911 W. Pico Blvd. for 15 years, sharing an office and a common waiting room. He referred patients to me and believed in my clinical acumen, helping me feel more confident about my therapeutic skills. He vehemently supported the presence of Research Psychoanalysts in the analytic community; he respected our knowledge base, our interest in ideas, and our engagement with theory, critical inquiry, research, and publication. We traversed rites of passage together, sharing moments of joy and sorrow, including the weddings of his children, a fiftieth wedding anniversary party, and the death of my spouse; we consulted one another on health matters and had several doctors in common. We had many festive dinners together, ones marked by good cheer, gossip, shop talk, and deeper reflections on politics and culture. Once at the Campanile Restaurant, Joe and I drank two martinis; I still don't know how either of us managed to drive home safely that evening. Joe was also warm and welcoming to my fiancé Sherry Rodriguez, very much opening his heart to her and her family.

Joseph Natterson was born in 1923 in Wheeling, West Virginia, the only son and youngest child of Anna and Sam Natterson. He was raised and educated in West Virginia, including going to West Virginia University and its Medical School. Joe had four older sisters. West Virginia had a tiny Jewish population in the 1920s and 1930s; being Jewish was not an easy or comfortable situation. Joe, however, was never deeply identified as a Jew and was without any semblance of Jewish ritual or observance. He was clearly aware of and opposed anti-Semitism. His parents were Marxists and members of the American Communist Party. From them, Joe inherited a deep respect for workers, believing in the dignity of labor, supporting labor unions, while being intensely class conscious and aware of class conflict. He had a profound affection for the Soviet Union, including an admiration for Stalin; Joe was in staunch opposition to the Cold War. In recent years, and much to my chagrin, he uttered praise for Putin, despite the invasion of Ukraine by Russian forces. On certain issues, Joe and I agreed to disagree without it interfering with our exchanges; some of our political differences reflected generational factors, him being a member of the Old Left and me closer to the

DOI: 10.4324/9781003488439-21

New Left, where I was suspicious of ordinary Marxism and critical of the dogma and banalities of Soviet Communism.

But most importantly it was dialogue and mutual concerns that brought us into intimate contact. Joe had an amazing intellectual curiosity and an openness to learn. He would alert me to the latest article in *The Nation* magazine or *The London Review of Books*, telling me I had to read these pieces and discuss them with him. He would do the same for books. He put me onto major tomes by Frankfurt School writers and critical theorists like Jurgen Habermas and Axel Honneth; he urged me to read Hans-Georg Gadamer. At our most intimate moments, Joe and I discussed our respective writings and clinical cases. As many of you know, he was a gifted and conscientious clinician with a busy and diverse practice. He was devoted to the liberation of his patients from paralyzing inhibitions, debilitating depression, negative self-images, and distorted self-esteem. Contemplating the clinical process in a career spanning seven decades, he emphasized the importance of the therapist's irreducible subjectivity, the significance of recognition in facilitating change and growth in our patients, and the patient's intrinsic right to love and be loved despite early and present difficulties in expressing their desire for mutual love. I was instrumental in the publication of his last book, *The Loving Self*, feeling honored when he requested that I write a Preface to it.

When I encountered problems with my patients, I consulted with Joe for his wisdom and subtle understanding of the clinical process. He was consistently generous, caring, affirming, and willing to be present and engaged. We both admired a small book by Adam Phillips and Barbara Taylor called *On Kindness*. Joe felt that Adam and he were effectively describing the same phenomena and curative value of the loving self and the individual's potential for expressing kindness. When I arranged a lunch for his wife Idell and Joe when Adam visited Los Angeles, they both were enchanted with Adam's aliveness and receptivity to their work and perspectives. Joe was beaming after this lunch.

As a thinker and master clinician over the decades, Joe evolved from a practitioner of classical psychoanalytic ego psychology to self-psychology, to his own innovative version of intersubjectivity, to his final grounding in contemporary relational psychoanalysis. To the non-clinicians in the audience, this means simply paying strict and sustained attention to the speech, emotions, and dimensions of self that emerged when two individuals meet regularly in a safe, comfortable, reliable setting, often for years; their task was a collaborative one, to co-construct meaning about the patient's inner world, to provide coherence about her present and past relationships.

Joe engendered trust by his compassionate and empathic attitude; he was curious about personality and complexity while being exquisitely attuned to micro-shifts in his patient's and his own feeling states. He insisted rightly that the therapist's interpretations constituted a loving version of understanding, that interpretation was fundamental to the clinical endeavor, and that interpretation could promote change, growth, and self-awareness. Toward the end of his life, Joe held that the person of the therapist was itself curative in the therapeutic dyad. Joe's clinical stance of being attuned, intuitive, and sensitive also went with an explicit commitment not to be intrusive or judgmental. He also tolerated not knowing and uncertainty without getting anxious or self-critical.

As the author of papers and a book on love, Joe was brave and non-sentimental about the things and people he loved. He loved the elegant and classy Idell and they were married for 67 years. He loved and was proud of his children, Amy, Paul, and Barbara, all of whom were distinguished in their own lives and careers. He loved learning. He loved to pun and was often puny, sometimes in ways that made me cringe, at other times amusing me. He loved art and often referred to masterpieces of art that moved him, like Picasso's "Guernica." He owned some beautiful paintings or lithographs by Picasso and Juan Miro.

Joe also loved the planet. And in the past decades, he was profoundly concerned about mother earth, the planetary crisis, and global warming, resulting from carbon emissions, overpopulation, and the greed and indifference of the ruling classes. He saw the crisis of the planet and ecological disaster as the most persistent existential threat to humanity, way more disastrous than nuclear holocaust. Joe loved rigorous intellectual and theoretical studies and was equipped with a fine and supple mind. He possessed a well-developed sense of humor and could let rip with a funny joke, one that was surprising, often packing a punch. Above all, Joe loved the idea and practices of freedom, underscoring the potentially liberating aspects of psychoanalytically informed therapy for struggling and suffering individuals. He practiced a socially informed psychoanalysis, one that promoted forms of progressive politics that could emancipate society from socioeconomic forms of inequality and cultures from asinine and ignorant approaches to racism, bias, and difference.

On my last visit to Joe several weeks ago, I observed sadly that he had become a faded version of the man I had known. He knew that he was not all right, wondering what had happened to his mind. He wanted to recover, hoping to return to work with his patients. Yet, he still had moments of lucidity. He predicted an event on the planetary level that would be emancipatory for humanity, but he was unclear what that event would be or how we could facilitate it. As I left, I asked him what I could do for him. He replied poignantly, "more contact and conversation." That for me was the real Joe, suddenly and transiently reemerging from the fog of memory loss and the tragedy of dementia.

So let's celebrate his life today, his desire for exchange and dialogue, his commitment to progressive change, and to individual and social emancipation from the crushing weight of illness, inhibition, oppression, and inequality.

I loved Joe. And I will dearly miss his smiling face and his caring telephone calls and our rich, relational visits. I felt thoroughly loved by him.

I was proud to call Joe Natterson my friend.

Previously published in *https://Internationalpsychoanlysis.net*, June 17, 2023.

Part V

Psychoanalysis and Political Engagement

Chapter 18

Trump as Symptom

Since the surprising results of the 2016 election, we must acknowledge the high degree of anxiety that liberals and progressives have felt before and after a Trump victory. We have never witnessed the media spectacle of all Trump, all the time. We have watched the rise and triumph of this media personality with both voyeuristic and exhibitionistic pleasures – and some of us with horror. My chapter is not about a historical or psychoanalytic investigation into the mind of Donald Trump, but rather an attempt to use historical and psychoanalytic perspectives to grasp the 46% of the electorate that voted for him, some of whom endorsing Trump vehemently, enthusiastically, and unequivocally.

They are the ones who would support him even if he were to go on Fifth Avenue and murder someone. They support him despite his history of unsavory business practices, evidence of sexual misconduct, and repeated, pathological patterns of lying. They endorse his presidency despite his ignorance about the specifics of foreign policy, governance, and the practice of politics as the art of compromise. They support him despite his contempt for democracy and for the separation of the branches of the government, his attacks on the judiciary and the Department of Justice, and his lack of acceptance of the separation of church and state. Trump taps into a deep discontent of certain sectors of American society, expressing a populist, paranoid mode of American politics. The task of my chapter is to empathize with the people who rally to him, but who feel alien to us. Hence, the title of my presentation is "Trump as Symptom."

Trump's primary constituency might be considered the uneducated white working class and underclass of America. In the election of 2016, his most zealous supporters were the people Trump called "uneducated" and whom Hillary Clinton referred to as "deplorable." Without patronizing this electorate, I want to approach their mentality and collective psychology as followers, which is ultimately more important than the leader.

Trump's core base is drawn from but is not exclusively the white working classes. It includes the wealthy and educated who want to protect their economic prerogatives and who agree with cutting taxes and oppose government regulation of banks, drug companies, and multi-national corporations. Some voted for him because they are antiabortion and want him to appoint very conservative

DOI: 10.4324/9781003488439-23

justices to the Supreme Court to replace Antonin Scalia and other liberal judges if vacancies occur. They resonate with his positions in the culture wars. Obviously, it extends to evangelicals, right-wing extremists, and some die-hard Republicans. Trump also appeals to those disenchanted voters who agree that the political system and the media are fundamentally bankrupt. His populist appeal stems from his ability to tap into their anxieties and grievances, their existential dread about the loss of jobs, resulting from globalization, the technological revolution and internet, and deindustrialization. They fear the loss of an already precarious social status, experiencing terror about the future for themselves and their families.

I do not see Trumpism as a coherent ideology with an incisive analysis of America's domestic or foreign policy challenges. It is too inconsistent and emotionally volatile to constitute a worldview. Its wide appeal may stem from its emotionality. Trump's grandiose message resonates with his constituency for four overlapping reasons: (1) misogyny and sexism; (2) racism; (3) xenophobia and nativism; and (4) repudiation of political correctness.

1 Misogyny. Trump's history of demeaning and denigrating women is well documented. But why does his rhetoric and actions elicit such strong support? Trump reduces women to objects, often to part objects. He has a predatory attitude toward them, shamelessly speaking of their beauty and aspects of their body, often in the most vulgar and crude terms. "Grabbing pussy" reflects an attitude that debases women. "Pussy power" is currently a rallying cry for those opposing his policies, a slogan of agency and integrity to those women who resist objectification. His sexism is strikingly evident in the campaign against Hillary Clinton, who was after all the first female candidate to be running on the top of the ticket of a major political party. It is difficult to imagine a more hostile slogan than "Lock her up!" He called her a "devil," implicitly advocating that others assassinate her. Michelle Obama eloquently exposed the underlying weakness and inadequacy of men who disrespect and humiliate women. Freud referred to this dynamic as psychic impotence, alerting us to a split in the male psyche between the intense idealization of females (ultimately of the mother) and the exaggerated and brutal need to devalue them as worthless or as whores.

There are many psychoanalytic insights into sexism, beginning with Freud's understanding of a basic psychic division in men between passionate lust and tender devotion. One disastrous result of this division is the angry and cruel debasement of women. From a relational point of view, the desire to dominate or be sadistic toward a woman, the need to maintain her exclusively as an exciting or enticing object, may indicate an underlying infantile dependency on the part of the male – a deep sense of threat, inferiority, and shame about the terror of masochistic submission to a stronger, tougher, highly evolved, and ambitious female. In short, this is a desperate attempt to secure an attachment to a female and to connect emotionally, even if it turns on the dynamic of dominating or shaming them.

2 Racism. Racism has a long and ignominious role in American history, dating back to Colonial America. It is always present, overtly or covertly. Populist demagogues have periodically been able to evoke hatred and manipulate the rage of racists. Trump's personal history, beginning with his father's real estate dealings, has been consistently bigoted toward blacks. His outrageous posturing about the guilt of the "Central Park Five," despite DNA evidence exonerating them, has been incendiary and extremist. Not least, he emerged politically as the spokesman of the Birther Movement, an attempt to portray Obama as un-American, to fictitiously identify him as African and/or Moslem. "Birtherism" tried to undermine the political legitimacy of his two electoral victories.

Trump launched his presidential campaign with the stereotyping of Hispanics as "criminals and rapists." His hostile slogan of "building a wall" and his rhetoric about deporting 11 million so-called illegal aliens all need to be designated as plainly racist. The same is true of his call for a ban on all Moslem immigration, codified in an unconstitutional Executive Order soon after his inauguration. Racism is inherent in his insensitivity to refugees from the Syrian Civil War, and his bombastic and unhistorical false allegation that Obama and Hillary Clinton were the founders of ISIS.

In the minds of his followers, these bans serve to counteract America's decline, to shore up its resources against evil agents. Trump's followers embrace these positions as if these simplistic and undemocratic solutions might restore America's grandeur, retrieving its exceptional place in the world. In short, talking harshly toward oppressed minorities and targeting displaced and insecure immigrants appeal to a constituency whose own fears and collective hysteria have been magnified and distorted in recent years. These reactionary and racist positions may also stem from a backlash to eight years of Obama's African-American Presidency.

Racism always turns on conspiracy theories. Analysts know that racist attitudes stem from deep internal splits. Projecting out the bad internal parts of the self ("objects" in the language of psychoanalysis) temporarily leaves the one who projects feeling good. Bad and unacceptable parts of the self are expelled into Mexicans, Muslims, and blacks, leaving a false sense of security and well-being. The moral panic of Trump's base is so extreme at the moment that the inherent, irrational racism of his message resonates so deeply. If the racist is fragile and fallible, he is only trying to protect and regulate a vulnerable sense of self. This fragility opens up the acceptance of apocalyptic and absolutist solutions, which have been echoing through Trump's rhetoric, campaign appearances, tweets, and policies as President.

If the system is rigged and if the entire political apparatus is corrupt, if every politician lies, then it is nonsensical to accept the results of the election – except if Trump won. Many Republican voters apparently agree with this illogical position. Ultimately, racism and the paranoid style of thinking that goes with it illustrate two primitive defenses: severe splitting of the self into good and bad objects and identification with the aggressor. Let's remember that paranoid modes of expression are not limited to patients certified as paranoid. Identifiable enemies – illegal aliens, Muslims, terrorists – can be targeted, marginalized, and ultimately expelled. This is a politics of crushing the largely imaginary enemy. At their best, these policies threaten American democracy and the rule of law. At its worst, it could unleash massive social unrest and violence.

3 Xenophobia and Nativism. Trump's words about restoring America's greatness go hand in hand with a persistent thread of American nativism and xenophobia. Trump's base identifies itself proudly and defiantly as white. Fear of the other is not just economic: anxieties about immigrants intensify their deepest fears about their safety and security. These are structural and existential fears, anxieties that make his base terrified. Trump's presidency feeds on the strengths and emotional intensity of xenophobia. It gives license to groups to express their deepest rage and resentments. In expelling their own bad internal objects, the Trump followers feel understood, exalted, and liberated by Trump's presence and his words. They accept these changsimplistic formulations, these black and white dichotomies, precisely because it permits them to rid themselves of unacceptable and disturbing aspects of their own inner world. It helps them to project out particularly intense anger and aggressiveness. It also permits them to evade personal responsibility and agency for their own destiny. Blaming the other is a powerful internal mechanism. It reflects fundamentally irrational and magical thinking, remaining oblivious to facts, evidence, or logical discussion. It does not readily modify itself by rational or scientific argument. Facts and truth have already been casualties of Trump's MAGA movement.

4 Repudiation of Political Correctness. Trump and his followers repudiate political correctness. His base is mesmerized by his unpredictability, his wacky performances, his vulgar gestures and humor; they are catalyzed by his unfettered language; and they are energized by his creation of chaos. They adore his attacks on political correctness, whether about women, blacks, Hispanics, Muslims, terrorists, intellectuals, and celebrities who oppose or mock him. Trump's speech is unfettered and unfiltered. He provokes fights with our allies such as Australia, Mexico, and the North Atlantic Treaty Organization (NATO), while saying positive things about Putin and other autocratic, anti-democratic regimes, many of which are anti-American. He and his followers seem to worship power and the deployment of power over all else. As a bad boy and bully, he speaks his mind with impunity. It is as if his wealth, celebrity status, and star power permit him to get away with palpably bad behavior, egregious ethical violations, scandalous and apparently criminal activity, and scatological forms of speech. For many in his base, this is unconsciously pleasurable; it permits them to externalize their resentments and grievances. They have felt shackled, suppressed, and devalued by decades of political correctness. This shame dynamic has been exacerbated by eight years with a despised black President, intensified by the country being on the cusp of another four years with a woman president and a Clinton to boot, for whom they have massive contempt. His presidency thrives on the intentional construction of chaos, verbal hand grenades, and Twitter bomb throwing.

So far, these patterns have inoculated him from rational debate and moral, political, or legal accountability. To have an empathic understanding of those vehemently opposed to political correctness, we need to acknowledge our bias against bias. Opponents of political correctness feel shame. They have been exposed and humiliated by the disdain and moral superiority directed at them, especially coming from the educated liberal and progressive elite who have little understanding of their everyday lives. Those targeted as politically incorrect feel condescended to and patronized. In the election cycle, they reacted with rage and resentment toward those who scorned them. Trump says outrageous and vicious things, feeding on the emotions they feel. That's why they listen to him and find him entertaining, fresh and enlivening, even reassuring. That's why they respond viscerally to his words and message, celebrating his manufactured grandiose image and his contradictory stance of being a martyr. He is simultaneously great and never wrong, but at the same time a victim of a "witch hunt," unfairly and unjustly targeted.

Political correctness is double-edged: on the one hand, it shows sensitivity to oppressed minorities or to vulnerable individuals; it can be an expression of compassion and attunement for the other. On the other hand, political correctness can be knee-jerk and inauthentic, lacking in substance and real engagement with the insecure and miserable lives of others, particularly the white uneducated people unfortunately designated as "deplorable." So much of Trump's constituency basks in his hatred of political correctness. They relish his expression of white privilege and his aggressive identification as white, strong, authoritative, omniscient, and omnipotent. Viewing Trump's campaign and presidency, we have witnessed a frightening and sad deterioration of political discourse, the rise of mean-spirited *ad hominem* arguments, the loss of civility, and the absence of any conversation about substantial issues of policy. The assault on political correctness could also fuel the fire of aggression, exacerbating the already severe political polarization and disenchantment with the democratic political process plaguing our country. Because of Trump's presence on the political scene and because of the complicity of the Republican Party with his shenanigans, there seem to be two Americas, red and blue, rural and urban, not connected by anything but mutual contempt and mutual antagonism.

In 1964, Columbia University historian Richard Hofstadter published an influential essay called "The Paranoid Style in American Politics." Written in the context of the Johnson/Goldwater election and fears about the rise of an extreme right-wing fringe, Hofstadter described a style of mind marked by "heated exaggeration, suspiciousness, and conspiratorial fantasy." We now know that the paranoid style extends to more than the disreputable fringes of the population; educated elites and the center have conspiracy theories too. Analysis of the paranoid style still has historical value and contemporary relevance precisely because it reflects attitudes and shared emotional states by more or less normal people, not those with profoundly disturbed minds. What is most enduring about Hofstadter's essay is his analysis of the projection of the self and of how that mechanism of projection can paradoxically lead to imitation of the enemy (what we would call identification with the aggressor). "The enemy seems to be on many counts a projection of the self: both the ideal and unacceptable aspects of the self are attributed to him. A fundamental paradox of the paranoid style is the imitation of the enemy."

The psychoanalytically informed historian can decode the fantasies and find patterns in those telling stories or spinning myths in American politics. Both historical consciousness and the psychoanalytic method prepare us to be deeply skeptical of paranoid ideas and conspiracy theories, to be aware of how the self can be split into good and bad internal objects. It teaches us to try to empathize with people and groups who seem radically different from us, like those drawn to Trump. It alerts us to how our own anxieties and vulnerable selves may influence our point of view. It helps us to be aware of our prejudice against prejudice. We must be aware of how we can become paranoid about paranoia, without minimizing the potential damage and destructiveness of the paranoid style. It is often hard to contain these anxieties, preferable to acknowledge them, beginning a cathartic process of emoting, critical analysis, and working through them.

Above all, a psychoanalytically informed historian can decode the fantasies and find patterns in those telling stories or spinning myths in American politics. Both historical consciousness and the psychoanalytic method prepare us to be skeptical of paranoid ideas and conspiracy theories, to be aware of how the self can be split into good and bad internal parts. It teaches us to try to struggle to be sensitive to people and groups who are radically different from us, like those drawn to Trump and other strongmen. It alerts us to how our own anxieties and vulnerable selves influence our point of view. It is preferable to acknowledge them, beginning a cathartic process of feeling, remembering, and working through the rigors of critical analysis and of self-reflection.

Above all, a psychoanalytically informed method may help us to maintain a reality-based understanding of contemporary American politics. It does so by reminding us that those who govern in America do so by advancing a fear-laden message, exercising power by expressing, often manipulating, existing anxieties and prejudices. These include defenses against misogyny, racism, and xenophobia, and attacks on political correctness. It may provide some clarity about how the language of the American dream provides a sense of identification, denying real class divisions, racial distinctions, and sexism. To demythologize the ideals of the American dream, particularly for Trump's core supporters, we must demonstrate that America is not the land of opportunity and that there is little upward mobility in this country. America is a land governed by powerful entrenched oligarchies without strong or viable political and intellectual resistance, and ultimately a threat to democratic forms of governance. American dream clichés deny the reality of downward mobility. We must be aware that the appeal to shared values masks the existence of deep class and cultural differences in America, the reality of economic inequality, and the existence of powerful discrepancies in education, sensibility, sensitivity, and value systems.

Lastly, we must be mindful that talk of American greatness, of things being "huge," of people being "incredible," of bombastic references to how rich and omnipotent

Trump is – all of this is empty speech, mendacious, factually inaccurate, and unhistorical. We know that his language and posturing resonate with an alienated, disenfranchised part of the population. These folks are inspired or activated by Trump's appeal to the little guy: to the one who is invisible and shamed, eager to embrace the culture wars, and reluctant to see reality in terms of social class or practical forms of politics. We need to be aware of the immense dangers to our democracy of this present blend of arrogance, stupidity, and transparent prejudice. Through historical and psychoanalytic understanding, let's see Trump as a symptom without denigrating his followers and without employing Trump's language to oppose Trump.

Previously published in *Clio's Psyche*, Vol. 24, No. 1, Summer 2017, pp. 8–15.

Chapter 19

Against the Separation of Children from Parents at the U.S. Border (with Van DeGolia)

The New Center for Psychoanalysis and psychoanalysts in general are alarmed by the Trump administration's policy of separating children from their parents at the United States border. We unequivocally oppose this policy.

As psychoanalysts, we respect the rights of individuals to seek safety and asylum in our country. Many of us come from families whose parents or grandparents immigrated to America. These human rights have a long and honorable history. Our country has historically been receptive to refugees fleeing violence and brutality. Individual families seeking refuge here ought to be warmly and hospitably welcomed, not criminalized or pathologized, not deported or interned in concentration camp-like detention centers.

Because of our clinical practices, we understand the devastating effects of breaking up families on both the children and the parents. Many children under 10 years of age may be permanently traumatized by these harsh policies, suffering deep, lasting psychological wounds. They will lose the safety and protection from their parents as they enter a new society. They may develop severe short-term and long-term symptoms, including nightmares and sleep disorders, eating disorders, and a spectrum of anxiety disorders, including abandonment terrors and panic attacks. Separation from parents may produce sadness and depression, a loss of self-regulation and self-esteem, a difficulty in trusting adults and authority figures, and a pervasive sense of psychic numbing, disorientation, derealization, and depersonalization, all damaging to an individual's sense of self.

Their parents will feel helpless and powerless to assist their children, particularly in a crisis situation of massive trauma and acute loss. As a result, the parents may also experience long-term aftereffects of shame and guilt about the separation from their children, blaming themselves for the abandonment, rather than holding the U.S. government accountable. But, more concerning, the parents may succumb to feelings of emotional fragmentation and develop symptoms of long-term PTSD, including dissociation, caused by having their children forcibly taken from them.

Psychoanalysis is grounded in a fundamental respect for the dignity and freedom of the individual. We affirm the potential of each individual's capacity for emotional and intellectual growth and fulfillment. We support policies that protect the integrity of the family, understanding its critical role in the psychological birth, development, and maturation of the individual. In the face of the forced separation of children from their families, healthy developmental pathways cannot occur and, at best, are likely to be derailed by the resulting shock and danger of these harsh separations.

We support the immediate reuniting of children with their parents. We oppose any and all policies that brutalize and dehumanize children. We vehemently oppose policies of putting children in cages. We oppose cutting off children from communication with their parents. We stand in opposition to the United States' policies of state-sponsored child abuse. We oppose the callousness of the administration's zero tolerance policies, seeing them as unethical, xenophobic, racist, and cruel.

Previously published in *New Center for Psychoanalysis webpage*, July 7, 2018.

Chapter 20

A Manifesto for Psychoanalytic Education with Sixteen Suggestions[1]

I want to thank The International Forum for Psychoanalytic Education for selecting me for this honor. It is unexpected and surprising. I especially want to express my appreciation to Tina Griffin and Larry Green for being facilitators.

Teaching has always been an important part of my professional identity and sense of self. It is one of the vocations that I love, along with psychoanalysis, writing, reading, sports, music, art, movies, and assorted other activities. I have been teaching for 56 years since 1968, when I served as a teaching assistant in my senior year of college at the University of Wisconsin. Because of my opposition to the War in Vietnam, I entered a master's degree program at New York University. After receiving the MA in Education in less than one year, I taught in an inner-city intermediate school in South Brooklyn, predominantly instructing a Hispanic and black population. Pedagogy bored me; it seemed mostly irrelevant to the creative dynamic that existed between interesting teachers and interested students, a relationship that promoted an intermediate space of playfulness and curiosity, privileging questioning and learning, acquiring knowledge and proficiency.

I received a doctorate in European cultural and intellectual history in 1973, then returned to Paris, France to participate for two years in a post-doctoral seminar on the "Geography of Marxism," directed by Professor Georges Haupt. I returned to America in 1975 and began teaching at various universities courses in European cultural history, French history, and critical theory. I mostly taught upper level undergraduates and graduate students.

I was drawn to psychoanalysis for a variety of powerful emotional and intellectual reasons. When I first read Freud, I felt he was describing my family and my own dynamics. I found reading him endlessly exciting, evocative, and disturbing; it was disturbing precisely in the sense that I desired to emulate his honesty, his awareness of complexity, his capacity to illuminate personality issues, and to investigate the forbidden issues of sexuality and aggression, of transference and resistance, of shame and guilt, and of dissociation and depersonalization. I was

---

[1] Remarks upon receiving the award for Distinguished Psychoanalytic Educator, International Forum for Psychoanalytic Education, November 7, 2020

DOI: 10.4324/9781003488439-25

captivated by Freud's literary and theoretical brilliance, how he wrote with utter candor, understanding how unconscious process subjectively affected him and others. I was first exposed to psychoanalytic thinking in my courses with Professor George L. Mosse at the University of Wisconsin; he assigned classical texts by Freud and Jung, though he presented a critical and debunking view of them.

I was fortunate to work closely, as an undergraduate and graduate student, with Mosse and Harvey Goldberg, two charismatic and entertaining lecturers. As a young man, I mistakenly associated inspiring teaching with lecturing, theatrical verbal performance with high level learning. Following the thrust of Mosse and Goldberg's lectures, I learned about the history of the right and left, of collectivities and mass movements, and the role of ideology in history, with an explicit grasp of how this would help clarify current trends in our own society and political universe. This was invaluable. I longed for a subversive history that shed light on the recent past while being simultaneously oriented to understand and radically transform the contemporary world. I became fascinated by the intersection of politics and cultural life.

My dissertation was on Romain Rolland and his version of being a responsible but committed intellectual in the period between the wars. Protest, dissent, opposition to the status quo, deep questioning of authority, and contestation of established norms and values became central to my project, as it was to Rolland and the circles of independent and non-conformist writers and artists clustered around him. I developed a style of thinking against the establishment, one of rebelliousness, of speaking out and questioning, especially on issues of social injustice and the unmasking of contradictions. My approach also reflected a radical point of view deeply embedded in the left-wing culture in the middle and late 1960s through the middle 1970s, best exemplified in our opposition to the War in Viet-Nam.

Demystification became my watchword. It is not surprising that when I taught seminars at a classically oriented psychoanalytic institute, I advocated for a contemporary point of view; and conversely, I defended classical or traditional perspectives at the contemporary psychoanalytic institute where I taught. This neither made me popular nor did it work to recruit disciples. I opposed discipleship and trendiness, thinking of them as infantile and intellectually immature; I much preferred honesty, seriousness, and independence, particularly of the kind that opposed "political correctness" or the consensus viewpoint in a small or large group.

Prior to leaving for Paris as an advanced graduate student, I organized (with my dear friend Richard Levine) a graduate seminar in Wisconsin. We studied with a practicing psychoanalyst to read systemically the writings of Freud. At that time there was only one analyst in Madison, Joseph Kepecs; he was a medically trained psychoanalyst who had graduated from the Chicago Psychoanalytic Institute. Joe was the first analyst I ever met; he was so different from Mosse and Goldberg. He was calm, laid-back, undaunted by criticism, confident in his knowledge of Freudian and post-Freudian theory, and, not least, clinically grounded. We read Freud chronologically from his early to late writings. Joe guided us through the intricacies of Freud's metapsychological and clinical writings.

I was blown away by how Kepecs taught the seminar. Although we had assigned readings, he came in with a smile and would say casually, "what do you want to discuss today"? I now realize that the way I have been teaching analytic seminars at various institutes for 35 years is deeply indebted to Kepecs' tone and method. Opening the seminar up to dialogue, inviting associations, and providing himself as a self-contained, reliable, and thoughtful presence proved to be just as rigorous as more organized approaches to the texts and issues; plus, it was more fun. Intense dialogue also worked against hierarchical and authoritarian tendencies in academia and establishment institutes of psychoanalysis.

We were so enthusiastic about learning about psychoanalysis with Kepecs that the seminar continued through the summer, where we studied seminal works by Wilhelm Reich, Herbert Marcuse, Norman O. Brown, R.D. Laing, Phillip Slater, and Franz Fanon. I was searching for an emancipatory form of psychoanalysis, something that ran against the prevailing norms of bourgeois respectability, middle-class conformism, fostering thinking against the current. This was the tail end of the 1960s and we were still enmeshed in the disastrous War in Viet Nam, trapped in a quagmire. Psychoanalytic humanism promised liberation from many of the external and inner constraints, both social conventions and individual repressions, we struggled against.

While I was doing archival research in Paris on Romain Rolland in the Archives Romain Rolland on Boulevard du Montparnasse, I discovered some unpublished letters between Freud and Romain Rolland, a Nobel Prize winning novelist with a vast public resonance. Although the correspondence was substantive and serious, these letters were incredibly intimate. I wrote an essay on their relationship and debates, some of which were private, others which spilled over into published texts such as Freud's *Civilization and Its Discontents*. In writing this essay, I had the audacity (some would say *chutzpah*) to psychoanalyze Freud based on my interpretation of their friendship and disagreements. I published this piece at age 29 without exposure to clinical training and without ever having been a patient. Unsurprisingly, the issues I uncovered in my analysis of Freud became some of the key themes in my personal analysis with Rudolf Ekstein that I undertook from 1979 to 1989 as part of my training at the Los Angeles Psychoanalytic Institute and Society (LAPSI).

Freud and Rolland debated the origins and meaning of the "oceanic feeling," a term Rolland coined to describe the emotions of unity or connection that he experienced in developing a mystical form of knowing about people, himself, and the world. He relied on intuition and emotional ways of communicating and connecting with other human beings, seeking out what united individuals, as opposed to what divided them. I realized subsequently that I was drawn into psychoanalysis precisely because the oceanic feeling was an affect. As a young man acculturated into American political culture, I had disavowed affective experience in my life. In my training in European cultural history, feelings were bracketed out. We were taught to keep subjectivity and emotion out of the process of doing history, of advancing a historical consciousness. Psychoanalytic humanism became for me a project to confront my own vulnerabilities, blind spots, and gaps in my formal and familial education. That project continues to this day. Incidentally, the essay on Freud and Rolland helped me to be accepted into psychoanalytic training at LAPSI and also introduced me to a sector of French psychoanalysis, when the piece was translated into French.

Here is a manifesto of sixteen suggestions for a radical method of psychoanalytic education, which may be helpful to my fellow teachers. It may also be pertinent for those of us who write. Think of them as proposals, provocations, food for thought, and catalytic agents:

1. Never be boring. Keep your audience in mind.
2. Respect the process in a seminar, be aware of the relationship between instructor and student, writer and reader, but don't fetishize the process. Good teaching is a transfer of energy between instructor and student.
3. Substance and scholarship matter, bring them into the classroom without being pedantic or overly scholastic. Avoid monologues. Emphasize dialogue and be non-defensive about criticism.
4. Psychoanalytic education is not a user's guide, or on how to do therapy. There is no one technique that encompasses the varieties of psychopathology that we experience in our clinical practice. Every analytic dyad is different. We need a vast armamentarium of approaches, flexibility, and elasticity in our attitude and methods. Good-enough clinical work presupposes the uniqueness and complexity of each patient, each transference-countertransference matrix, and consciousness of the specificity of each encounter in the analytic dyad.
5. Because content matters, beware of the dangers of intellectualizing, but never be anti-intellectual.
6. Try to fuse process and content, keeping in mind the relational components of an educational milieu, factoring in your students' readiness to learn and our own resistance to teaching.
7. Never forget that psychoanalysis is a humanism in that it inherits, updates, and surpasses a fundamental respect for human suffering, a respect for the integrity and wonders of the personality, a reverence for the rich, beautiful, and often ineffable domain of the inner world. Permit yourself to be selectively irreverent. Humor and wit often serve to balance arch seriousness and sterile didacticism.
8. Psychoanalysis needs to be aware historically and critically of the limits of rationality and humanism without embracing irrationality. We must rid from our method the antiquated and non-examined prejudices against thought implicated in the hegemonic web of colonialism, racism, classism, sexism, and the outright denigration of others who are different from us.
9. Remember that psychoanalysis was and continues to be a subversive method. Know the history of psychoanalysis, but try to modernize this subversiveness, making it compelling to a contemporary audience. Truly subversive methods mean resisting the temptations of intellectual and clinical superiority, of behaving in dogmatic or parochial ways, and of closing one's mind to innovations that may disturb our complacency and critiques that unmask our privileges.

10 Theory needs to be reinvented. To study and transmit theory, we must understand its relationship to practice, to how our students experience theory in the here and now. The dialectic of theory and practice searches for better clinical outcomes, trying to explain clinical impasses and transform clinical failures. Theory removed from practice can become rigid, reified, and even sacralized. It can be flat, sanitized, and dull. Theory can be transformed into ideology; it can distort and misinform. Theory can help contain the teacher's and student's anxieties about not knowing and uncertainty. Let's recast what Charcot said to the young Freud in the middle 1880s: "Theory is good, but it does not prevent facts from existing." Or, translating it more poetically, "Theory is ok, but it does not prevent one from existing." Let's try to fuse existing with theorizing.

11 Psychoanalytic education encourages critical thinking and critical analysis, not discipleship, not conformism, or blind obedience to a mainstream norm. Avoid idealization and devaluation of our founders, or local gurus, recognizing that idealization is always infantile and that devaluation stems from resentfulness and hostility, often from self-contempt. Respect and contextualize our pioneers, treating them with empathy and understanding of why they made their choices.

12 Critical thinking turns on a balanced blend of suspicion and trust in what one reads in the literature, hears from our patients, and identifies with our own analysts, supervisors, and teachers. Keep in mind the transferences are based on identification and counter-identification. Maintaining the tension of skepticism and trust will help to keep the discipline alive, promoting research, experimentation, and improvisation in our teaching (and our clinical practice).

13 Suspicion and trust must be a key component of our interpretations, including skepticism about the correctness or brilliance of our own point of view. This healthy suspicion works against definitiveness and arrogance, and disrespect of our patients and students. It is mindful of complexity, contradiction, and aspects of not knowing. Everything in psychic life is overdetermined. We need to be vigilant against reductionism, essentialism, over-simplification, and clichéd formulations. Learning opportunities in seminars are also multiply determined. Experienced instructors need to know, in the words of the Beatles, when to intervene and when just to let it be.

14 Critical thinking positions itself against slogans and facile assertions in our field, remembering the significance of play, paradox, and areas of incomprehension in the educational and clinical context.

15 Promoting critical thinking goes hand in hand with facilitating free association in our patients, students, and ourselves. Free associating in an ambiance where people gather to associate freely generates pathways to expansive, enlivened, and creative possibilities of learning. Free associating can develop into a life of the mind that is liberating, but it must be combined with a sense of limit and responsibility. Uninhibited freedom is not the goal in an educational setting.

16 We live in a world where cruelty, insensitivity, and unkindness appear ascendant, even triumphant. Within the context of a regression into barbarism,

psychoanalytic education must retain its fundamentally caring, provisional, and nurturing dimension. This constitutes not only a personal but also a political antidote to the political culture of right-wing authoritarianism and violent natioianlistic populism so prevalent in our body politic. We ought to also be vigilant about these tendencies among members of the left, particularly those who have abandoned dialectical thinking and who attempt to limit others from speaking or expressing their points of view. In struggling against barbarism, psychoanalysis ought to resist its own tendencies toward aggressiveness, devaluation, and dismissal, including of our own colleagues. An anti-authoritarian psychoanalysis is truly democratic and inclusive without being contemptuous of others or itself.

I would like to thank The International Forum for Psychoanalytic Education for presenting me with this award as a Distinguished Psychoanalytic Educator. It is an organization with an expansive and inclusive viewpoint that organizes events which make participants feel safe, comfortable, valued, seen, and heard. It is similar in spirit to the University of California Interdisciplinary New Center for Psychoanalysis Psychoanalytic Consortium, which I have been a member of for over 33 years. Both promote vigorous exchange, openness, experimentation, communication, and engaged dialogue on psychoanalytic themes, often broadly conceived. Both encourage innovative and improvisational presentations. We must enthusiastically endorse this approach. It can only do well for our field and our cause.

Recognition is of course better than misrecognition, or non-recognition. Being honored is preferable to being ignored. So, I receive this lovely honor in the spirit of gratitude and mutual appreciation. I do not feel that I have exhausted my conceptual ideas or that I do not have anything more to contribute as a teacher, writer, clinician, and supervisor. Hopefully, my "late" works will rejuvenate, reinvent, and extend the subversive intent of my previous educational ventures.

Previously published in *Internationalpsychoanalysis.net*, Summer, 2020.

Chapter 21

A Psychoanalyst Serves on a Jury

Few mental professionals serve on juries. This chapter narrates my personal experience of serving on a jury for nine consecutive business days. It makes no pretense to be an objective article. Because it was a particularly gruesome case, some of the details included may be difficult to read. After being chosen to serve and sworn in as a juror, I conducted a thought experiment. I decided to be a responsible juror, do my civic duty, carefully monitor the factual evidence and adhere to the rule of law and court procedures, and follow the judge's instructions. I tried to be rational, objective, and to sift and winnow through the facts of the case without bias or preconception. But simultaneously, I functioned as a practicing psychoanalyst, a participant observer. My goal was to strike a balance between a highly developed emotional capacity and considerable self-restraint, particularly regarding anger and fear. I permitted myself to freely associate, practice a stance of freely suspended attention, maintain an analytic attitude. I paid careful attention to the affect states and demeanor of the witnesses, attorneys, and judge and my own feeling states. I was aware of transference and countertransference matrixes and above all explicitly conscious of my own subjective states throughout the process. I took over 36 pages of notes, not trusting my own memory. And in writing this essay, I consulted various documents provided during the trial. As far as I know, there is nothing approximating this in the analytic literature. As such, I hope to contribute to an ongoing dialogue between very different disciplines, with distinct ways of arriving at truth, distinct methods of procedure and settings, and different tasks and goals. I have changed the names of all the participants in the interests of privacy, not confidentiality. A trial is a public hearing, very different from an analytic session. Legally and ethically, one is not required to withhold or change the names.

    I have often thought about Lacan's paradoxical remark that the psychoanalytic process was about the analyst's resistance; I wondered if it applied to me in this setting. When I am summoned to serve on jury duty by the Superior Court of the State of California, County of Los Angeles, I do everything in my power to resist serving. I do not want to miss valuable time with my patients, many of whom are vulnerable and regressed. I am concerned about the considerable loss of income. I am reluctant to have my ordinary, privileged life disrupted, with its regular features and established routines, even though I have never been selected to serve on a jury and do not know what to expect. I have no idea how intense and disturbing psychologically the experience might be, underestimating its potentially traumatizing and dysregulating effects.

I pass the morning of being summoned sitting and waiting. One dimension of my experience of serving on a jury is predominantly about waiting. Waiting and feeling powerless, as in Beckett's *Waiting for Godot*, whose opening line, "nothing is to be done," captures my feeling state throughout the process. Researching a paper on another project, I read a volume by the German poet Rilke, *Love and Other Difficulties*. One passage captures my imagination: "Love consists in this: that two solitudes protect and touch and greet each other." I know it is a bit ridiculous to be reading Rilke on love in the courthouse. Throughout the process, I realize that serving on a jury is contradictory, both an absorbing and absurd experience.

My luck runs out midway in the afternoon. I am randomly called for a jury panel. When I am brought into court for jury selection, I am asked several personal questions, including my profession. I answer that I am a psychoanalyst. Judge Greg Dickenson jokes that he could use my services. His Honor has a good sense of humor. I reply that I will leave him my card. When he asks what differentiates a psychoanalyst from a psychologist or psychiatrist, I pretentiously answer that we are better trained and that there is more rigor in our clinical approach. I find myself defensive and ill at ease, strangely tongue-tied and inarticulate. As potential jurors, we are under oath. It is a disorienting and novel experience for me.

The case under consideration is called the People Versus Majestic King of Shaka. I cannot grasp or hold onto his name. I find myself either forgetting it or turning "majestic" into "domestic." This recurs even as I write these pages. These slips of the tongue are meaningful, the lapses subject to much self-reflection. The charges are overwhelmingly serious. And heinous. Mr. Shaka is accused of two counts of rape, two counts of sodomy, two counts of forceful sexual penetration by a foreign object, including fingers, one count of kidnapping, and one count of armed robbery.

Mr. Shaka is sitting in the court as I arrive. He is a handsome black man, probably in his late 20s or early 30s. I later learn that is 43. He appears calm, sitting with folded hands. He wears civilian clothing. The victim is a 20-year-old Asian woman, referred to as Hanako Y. Her surname is never given. I do not know if this is her correct name. It may be a pseudonym used to protect her identity. Majestic King of Shaka apparently destroyed Hanako's domestic and personal security, just as his trial would disrupt to a far lesser extent my domestic, professional, and psychological tranquility for an indeterminate period.

When asked if there are any personal biases or past experiences that might influence my impartiality in the case, I state a strongly held point of view about structural racism in America, specifically in Los Angeles. I have major doubts about the Los Angeles Police Department, particularly their treatment of "people of color," as I put it. I refer to the Rodney King beating and to the continual history of racial profiling and police brutality against black males. I add that I have reservations about the legal system's capacity to be fair in dispensing justice to African Americans. My response creates a stir in the courtroom, including those already selected in the jury box. Although I did not utter the words Black Lives Matter, they were on my mind.

The prosecuting attorney, Ms. Johnson, questions me about my statement. She asks if I am aware that the victim in this case is also a person of color. I reply that her question is "very smart." She thanks me, emphasizing that it is an "earnest" question. I know I am in trouble. After a beat of silence, I tell her I think I can be impartial about the facts of this case. Did I set myself up, or possibly did I secretly and unconsciously want to be called to serve on a jury? I am elected and sworn in. For the next eight business days, my sense of self becomes partially transformed into juror number eleven.

I immediately become anxious about what to tell my patients. After some reflection, I opt to disclose to them that I have jury duty. I might have to contact them the night before an appointment, an antithetical way of practicing and contrary to my work within the analytic frame.

I begin to understand that I no longer have control over my time. I lose the customary rhythms of my life. Until the trial is concluded, the judge will determine major aspects of the structure of my day, including when to report, break, take lunch, resume, and adjourn for the day. There is something infantilizing about this arrangement. The orderly, ritualized, and privileged existence of a psychoanalyst's life is temporarily altered.

The loss of control over my time generates a good deal of uneasiness for the next week and a half. I realize viscerally that analysts need the analytic frame as much as our patients to contain their own uncertainties and anxieties. Time management helps us to keep a lid on the messiness of the analytic process. It assists in managing the lack of understanding in the handling of the unknown and uncertainty of the clinical process. It also helps us monitor and reflect upon the intrusion of our own personal lives into the analytic frame. Co-constructing time agreements with our patients is a critically important component of how we function at an optimal level. The regulation of time is an essential component of what we provide to our patients and ourselves. It generates reliability, sets limits, and provides a holding environment. We analysts are also held by these time constraints and by our patients.

Serving on a jury in Superior Court in downtown Los Angeles every day generates realistic fears and unrealistic anxieties. I observe that the setting is not particularly safe. Before entry into the lobby of the courthouse, one must line up and pass through a metal detector. I question my own paranoid ideation about the danger, but, then again, there are also plenty of police around, armed, and appearing vigilant.

Before the opening statements, the judge offers a listening strategy, advising the jury members to "be a sponge." He urges us to "keep an open mind." Analysts of course are professional listeners. I adopt the sponge metaphor but decide to engage in a thought experiment. I will listen to the case psychoanalytically, namely, with freely suspended attention during the proceedings. I attempt to take in the preconscious and unconscious components of the trail, allowing myself to free associate and to maintain freely hovering attention during the proceedings. I focus on the factual truth of the evidence, paying attention to the legal procedures and to the presentation of the facts. But I am equally fascinated by the unconscious dynamics and communications in the process of the trial, in addition to registering my own subjective and emotional experiences. I listen carefully to latencies in speech patterns and to unconscious dynamic interactions. I attend to non-verbal communication and try to trust my intuition. I try to strike a delicate balance between emotional attunement to the proceedings and to its cast of characters and the need for emotional self-restraint.

Regarding the charges, the judge instructs the jury to approach them as a "roadmap," not proof. The judge reiterates that the defendant has pleaded not guilty. We must presume his innocence unless the evidence proves his guilt "beyond a reasonable doubt." Guilt or innocence is to be decided on the truth and accuracy of the evidence. Jurors will have to determine inconsistencies and conflicts in the evidence, to detect witnesses who lie, or who tell partial truths.

Analysts are trained to relinquish judgment, to listen to our patient's free associations with an attitude of openness, receptivity, and caring, while a juror is enjoined to evaluate and to judge. This places me in a paradoxical position, a position between two disciplines and two methods of arriving at "truth": to judge and to be non-judgmental; to attempt to have empathy for both perpetrator and victim and other participants in the trial; to be skeptical about the truth value of what is presented in the various narratives and also to be trusting; and not least to be both suspicious and trusting of one's own certainty in arriving at the truth in this case. I attempt an experiment in hermeneutics drawing on the discipline and discourse of the legal system and my own version of psychoanalysis. I also try to remain skeptical about my own interpretive conjectures, never thinking I have arrived at some definitive or irrefutable truth.

The opening statements are a duel of two narratives. From the beginning to the end, the prosecuting attorney presents a clearer and more coherent story line. Perhaps it is because she argues a stronger case, not necessarily because she is a more able litigator.

Hanako Y. is a 20-year-old Japanese student, who journeys to Los Angeles to study English, hip-hop music, and dance. She lives in the guesthouse of a Russian American family, who traditionally house students. She meets a young black man called Leo at a bus stop on Fairfax Avenue in the West Hollywood neighborhood of the city, not far from her residence. They exchange telephone numbers and message texts. Her competence in English is unclear, but she communicates with some degree of proficiency. They meet a week after their initial encounter, ostensibly to go to a movie. Instead, they travel far away, taking two buses and one train, arriving at The Baldwin Hills Motel Inn. It is located in South Los Angeles, a predominantly black neighborhood.

After purchasing alcohol, Hanako gives Leo $100.00 to pay for several hours in the motel. The room costs $30.00. He then pockets seventy dollars. She willingly consents to go to the room and buy alcoholic beverages. As I listen to this narrative, I question the credibility of the plaintive, who appeared happy to pay for a motel room and buy alcohol. I speculated about Hanako's psychic reality, particularly her risky behavior, and her extreme foolishness and naïveté about accompanying this stranger to a distant motel. I speculated about some of her feelings of excitement and erotic fantasies.

When Leo begins to have aggressive sex with her, she protests and says no. He savagely beats her, strangling her to the point of unconsciousness. He pummels her body and punches her in the face, severely injuring her upper lip and her eyes, leaving her lips red and swollen and her eye shut. Fearful for her life, Ms. Y. submits. Leo rapes and sodomizes her. He then takes Hanako into the shower and washes her himself. He also washes her clothing. After the shower, he repeats the beatings, raping, and sodomizing her a second time. My initial reaction to hearing this was one of horror, contemplating how degrading and humiliating this must have been to this young woman.

After they check out of the motel three or four hours later, they walk to a nearby ATM machine, where Hanako is unable to withdraw money. Leo then steals her Nixon watch and takes ¥ 25,000, approximately $225.00. He also takes two of her cell phones. There is no DNA evidence, presumably because of the shower and Leo's use of a condom. When Ms. Y. reaches home that evening, the host family, shocked and responsive to the emergency, calls 911. She is taken to the emergency room at the UCLA Hospital in Westwood. She is then examined and treated by the UCLA Rape Treatment Center in Santa Monica that same evening.

The defense attorney, Mr. Silverman, offers a less compelling narrative. Acknowledging the seriousness of the charges, he argues that the sex between the two was consensual. He denies that Mr. Shaka beat Ms. Y. He tells the jury that Mr. Shaka is a homeless, male prostitute. I am astonished by this fact. It generated all kinds of strange images and associations. It was very far from my own frame of reference, foreign to my own lived experience. Mr. Silverman claims that the defendant has no motive or intent to rape Ms. Y. He blames the beating on the father of the host family, alleging he treated her "badly" and that he was "mean" to her. Lastly, he raises questions about Ms. Y.'s virtue, saying she is "not a "wallflower," that she is in an "open relationship" in Japan, and that she is a world traveler, not a "naïve" or "doe-eyed" young woman. Mr. Silverman implies that Hanako is promiscuous and that this encounter in the motel is part of a larger pattern of impulsive, sexual behavior, of sexually acting out. I was skeptical about this assertion. It appeared as if he was blaming the victim.

As I heard both opening statements, I speculated that the case might turn on the credibility of the victim versus the apparent perpetrator, reducing itself to a "he said/she said" contest. The evidence, compelling and irrefutable, will quickly dispel my initial impression.

The first witness is the police officer who responded to the 911 call, taking Ms. N. to the emergency room. He describes her as a victim of "gruesome attacks." The officer finds her to be "terrified," speaking in a whisper, trembling, and crying.

The next witness is the nurse from the UCLA Rape Treatment Center. She describes Ms. Y.'s emotional state, focusing on her difficulties in speaking, how she was shaking and wailing, hiding her face with her hair. She mentions the visible signs of strangulation and how Ms. Y. could not open her left eye. She reports genital and anal injuries, including bleeding and tearing. The photos projected on a screen of Ms. Y.'s beaten face are powerful and horrific to look at. It will be hard to refute the photographic evidence. We are not presented with photos of Ms. Y.'s vaginal or anal injuries, a small effort to protect the privacy and integrity of her body after such a brutal violation. In the face of such jarring and disorienting evidence, hearing the gruesome details makes me guilty of observing vicariously a sexually violent transgression. I realized afterward that I felt contaminated and somehow responsible, an attitude built into the psychic response of any participant in the trauma of sexual violence, even a bystander or juror after the fact. I understood my confusion, disorientation, and guilty self-doubt in being part of an audience to these terrifying events. My visceral reaction combined empathy and pity for the victim. I was disgusted by the story. Given the strength of my emotions, I realize I dissociated. Self-protectively, I monitor myself for any voyeuristic, prurient, or perverse interests in the sexual dimensions of the case. I cannot find any.

I assumed that the next witness will be the most significant and dramatic in the trial. It is Hanako Y. She appears with a victim's advocate, sitting next to her in the witness chair, and a Japanese translator. She is a petite and pretty, soft-spoken woman. Her words are barely audible. She is clearly fragile. I notice that she holds a towel on the witness stand. She is teary-eyed during much of her testimony, reliving the lurid events of the day she was assaulted. Her use of a transitional object underlines the depth of her trauma, how she feels vulnerable returning to Los Angeles to face her perpetrator, to re-experience the events of her rape, reliving her bodily and mental assault. Grasping a towel may be a way to hold onto a severely compromised, even an annihilated sense of self, and a method of finding comfort or maintaining a connection to a relatively secure object. The victim's advocate may have also played a similar role in creating a holding environment for her.

When asked to identify Leo, she points to the defendant Mr. Shaka. Testifying that she initially found him "sweet," they spoke of hip-hop music and dance. She believed she could "trust" him. The jury is shown a photo of Mr. Shaka and Hanako entering a bus on the day of the assault. She appeared unafraid, voluntarily agreeing to board the bus. We can see a watch on her left wrist. The photos and timeline are crucial to the prosecution's establishment of a fact pattern. Only retrospectively did I realize that I felt terrorized about seeing and hearing about photos of these destructive sexual practices.

The analytic part of me wondered what her thoughts, feelings, and fantasies were in agreeing to this encounter with Mr. Shaka. What was the nature of her desire at this moment? Did she understand the implicit risk and danger and possible excitement of accompanying Mr. Shaka to a motel? Perhaps she wanted to party with a "sweet" man who posed as a hip-hop specialist; perhaps she wished to enact some sexual activity; perhaps she found him exotic and cool, someone who could relate to her musical and cultural interests. Likewise, I wondered about the sexual and aggressive fantasies and desires for dominance of Mr. Shaka in bringing her to a motel. Unfortunately, the exploration of fantasy is not an integral component of legal inquiry. I am left to fantasize about their respective fantasies.

When she is inside the motel room and Mr. Shaka becomes aggressively sexual, Ms. Y. protests, "what are you doing?" As she resists his advances, he gets angry. She says this with tears in her eyes. He punches her when she protests. He engages in a lot of hitting, pummeling her, and placing his hands on her neck. As she is being choked, she finds herself unable to breathe. She sees spots. She blacks out temporarily. I observe that Ms. Y. tells her story with a degree of silence and multiple pauses, usually with tears in her eyes. During much of her testimony, she rocks and hides her face. I imagined how shamed she was by having to testify, how psychologically damaging her court appearance might be. For a woman, especially a young woman, I cannot think of anything more terrifying and debasing than rape. I assumed her testimony would expose her, making her feel intense embarrassment, perhaps verging on humiliation.

Her cultural and psychological background as an Asian woman may intensify these dynamics of exposure, shame, and fear of humiliation. I also wondered on the positive side if she might be empowered by coming forward and providing her point of view. Her words, demeanor, and affect seemed profoundly genuine to me.

We are later told that Hanako had not told her mother about the rape, corroborating my speculation about her shame dynamics. She shared some of the details of the assault with friends. I worry that the trial and its aftereffects might retraumatize her. I doubt that she has received or will receive psychological treatment after her violent ordeal. This tragic prospect of non-treatment made me sad for her; I speculated about how this horrifying violence would affect her throughout her lifetime, possibly with shattering consequences. Having treated victims of rape, I know how difficult it was to understand and work through these traumas, including all the confusion and self-blame associated with the rape and its aftermath. I slowly comprehend that I, too, felt disoriented and guilty about observing these brutal events as a juror. Once again corroborating Lacan's notion about the analyst's resistance to his own internal process, I withdrew into a psychic shell of denial, avoidance, and emotional numbing.

The testimony becomes more graphic and more atrocious. It is hard to listen to. If it is invasive and nightmarish to the jurors, it must be devastating to Ms. Y. Aspects of her testimony reappeared verbatim in my dreams during the period of the trial. I saw the photos of her swollen and bloodshot eyes and injured neck, visible signs of her suffering. It is as if the latent content transformed itself into the manifest content in these dream scenarios. My dreams disturbed me, but I considered them vitally important, as compelling evidence of the severity of her sexual assault and robbery. She speaks of how Mr. Shaka took off her clothes, touching her breasts and vagina, inserting fingers in her vagina and rectum. The more she says no, the more he hits her. With her body in excruciating pain and fearing for her life, she stops resisting. Mr. Shaka takes her to the shower, washing her body and her clothing. He steals her wallet, two cell phones, and a total of $300.00 in cash. After the shower, he rapes and sodomizes her again.

Upon leaving the motel room, the two walk to an ATM near the motel. There is a photo of them at the ATM machine with a specific time. This photo will be very damaging to Mr. Shaka's defense. She is wearing sunglasses and a hoodie, even though it is evening, apparently to cover up the wounds. The jury can clearly see the injury to her face and upper lip, which is swollen. It looks grotesque. It was painful to look at these hideous photos. After taking her possessions, he sends her home. Ms. Y. says that she continues to have problems hearing in her left ear for months after the beating and that she also needs to protect her injured left eye. She denies that anyone else other than Mr. Shaka attacked her, specifically that the father of the host family ever laid his hands on her.

The trial is an elaborate chess match, played out on a slow or bizarre clock. Jury time is surrealistic, perhaps best rendered in the early Dali painting, "The Persistence of Memory." Time melts or bends and becomes like the way one experiences it in a dream or a state of reverie. There are lots of rhetorical games, objections, delays, sidebars, and the inevitable apology by the judge for the delays. The judge says he is sorry for yet another 35-minute stoppage, saying, "It won't happen again." This repeated line is no longer funny, just lame. I was increasingly annoyed by these delays and excuses. I felt powerless in regulating jury time. It was infantilizing and disrespectful to us as jurors.

I am struck by my alternating and paradoxical feelings about the judge. He sits high above us on the bench in the chamber, wearing a black robe, issuing opinions, and making pronouncements. The attorneys are obsequious, overly formal, and accommodating to him, requesting his permission to approach a witness or to gather themselves when searching for a fact or document, or picking up the thread of their argument. One day the judge rather than the clerk comes out to the hallway. He takes attendance and then ushers the jury into the courtroom. He is not wearing a robe, his sleeves are rolled up, and his tie is loosened. He is disheveled. His Honor is short of stature, just an ordinary guy – a human being. Even a bit of a schlep. Then back in court five minutes later, the idealized fantasy of his power gets triggered again. He is the one wielding power. He has knowledge and authority. He is the father protector, the ultimate arbiter. He is law. And as jury members, we were his obedient (and at times resentful) servants.

Mr. Silverman's cross-examination turns on the notion that Hanako voluntarily consented to have sex with Mr. Shaka. There are intrusive questions about whether Mr. Shaka ejaculated and whether he used his penis or fingers inside her vagina and anus. He suggests that Ms. Y. is colluding with the prosecution, in effect not telling her own version of the story.

In feeling myself into Hanako's mind and emotions, I experienced this line of questioning as profoundly invasive. I found myself deeply split about the defense attorney: emotionally, I viewed him to be offensive, dishonest, and often out of line; intellectually, I have empathy for his plight. He was given this case with the facts and evidence exceedingly favorable to the prosecution. He is a public defender, probably receiving little or no compensation for his work. What options did he have in such a difficult legal situation with bad facts and incriminating evidence?

I presumed that he put aside his own personal antipathy for Mr. Shaka, to implement his ethical and professional obligation to advocate zealously on his behalf, quite possibly bracketing out his sense that Mr. Shaka was guilty of these heinous crimes. Empathy for Mr. Silverman meant that I had to put aside my own visceral distress at him for asking questions he asked, arguing the points he asserted. I realized reluctantly that Mr. Silverman was doing his job. (I remembered the value system of defense attorneys I had worked with in therapy who taught me these basic principles.) Mr. Shaka has the right to a rigorous defense. He asserts that Ms. Y. has received pressure from the police and the prosecutor to stay in America. He alleges that her paid round-trip fare from Japan to Los Angeles, including payment for her hotel, is a free vacation rather than a psychological ordeal of facing her perpetrator and having to testify publicly. Yet, I ultimately decided his questioning of the witness was an impingement on her sense of self, another act of violence against her, potentially retraumatizing, almost as debasing of this fragile female witness as the forcible acts of rape, sodomy, and kidnapping.

After all the drama of Hanako's testimony, something even more astonishing occurs. Mr. Shaka has taken the stand to testify. He is no longer wearing civilian clothing, but rather the county jail's clothing of bright orange. Both his arms and legs are in shackles. The judge tells us distinctly that we are not to be influenced by Mr. Shaka's being in constraints. Being in constraints has legally nothing to do with his guilt or innocence in the case.

However, I found myself speculating about why he took the stand in the first place, thinking he would only incriminate himself more deeply than the previously damaging evidence and timeline. Only a fool, a desperate person, or someone delusional would take the stand in such a serious trial. I wondered why he didn't try an insanity defense because he appears so deranged. Perhaps he had a prior conviction record and this putative "third strike" might send him to prison for a long sentence. Perhaps he may be at odds with his defense attorney, who realized he might be a disastrous witness, counseling him against testifying. Seeing him shackled also makes me think about his tendencies toward violence. Perhaps he had been aggressive over the weekend, or that morning, needing to be restrained. Despite the judge's instructions, how could I as a juror disregard observing what goes on in front of my eyes? This seems to be an impossible task. As an analyst, I pay attention to empirical facts and to the reality before my eyes. Seeing Mr. Shaka shackled and in prison clothing makes an indelible impression on me. I try to maintain compassion for him without denying my own fears, my experience that this guy really frightened me. Possibly, this feeling suggests an unconscious racism on my part, partly due to the relative absence of black individuals in my immediate life; perhaps the fears were embedded in deeper terrors about the dangers of black skinned individuals, terrors about the dangers of the black body. Returning to issues of race and the legal system, I speculate privately if a white prisoner would be shackled and treated the same way. Observing him dressed in orange and constrained made me wonder if the legal system had already objectified, profiled, and demonized him, pronouncing its verdict on him as being yet another violent, black criminal.

I find myself searching for a reassuring label. Listening to Mr. Shaka's testimony on his own behalf, I reflected on his sense of self. Who is this soft-spoken, handsome black man? We analysts know that proper names are critically important in developing a sense of self. Who is the real person who introduces himself to Hanako as Leo, whose real name is Tyrone Gresham, and whose assumed name is Majestic King of Shaka? Is he psychotic? Borderline on the psychotic edge of borderline? A multiple personality? Is he identified as a royal African warrior fighting against systemic white racism and colonial oppression? I tend to dismiss diagnostic categories as reductive and simplistic, not able to shed light on a complex personality. There is no leisure for me to have my habitual analytic assumption that if I wait patiently, the paradoxes of the personality will emerge, saturated with contradictions and multiple meanings. I wondered also about his dependence on alcohol and drugs, if his substance abuse massively changes his personality, bringing out an enraged and cruel side.

I was curious about his early childhood. Was he molested, abused, or abandoned during his childhood in Nebraska? All the above? What about the damaging effects of poverty, racism, lack of education, and living homeless on the streets on this man's history and internal world? Could he be rehabilitated? None of these analytic questions about his history, life cycle, or his intra-psychic or inter-personal makeup will be answered. I will never know much about his own life history. But as a psychoanalyst, it was my wish to know. My responsibility. This was a preliminary step in wanting to understand and help him. But perhaps he was beyond help? Serving on this jury made me reluctantly aware of my powerlessness, my awareness that there would be no second chance for a psychoanalytic influence on the outcome. This was poignant and tragic, as I understood that all the central actors involved in this court trial would suffer, possibly never be the same. Paradoxically, it is Mr. Shaka himself who might serve an extremely long sentence if convicted, who might never be released, might never have a second chance, ever a chance for redemption. And I reluctantly became aware of my complicity in his eventual incarceration.

In his own words, Mr. Shaka's lifestyle as a homeless male prostitute "speaks for itself." He admits that "I've been living a foul lifestyle since I have been out here just to survive." He identifies as a black male who is marginalized and persecuted by white society. Women find him irresistible and "magnetic," he declares grandiosely. He totally denies raping or beating up Ms. Y. He insists that the entire encounter is consensual and that she agrees to "get drunk and hang out" with him. She wants to go to the hotel with a "brother." She clearly lacks innocence, knowing she is going to have "physical relations." Although there is no mention of payment for his sexual services, she understands quite well that they are going "to kick it" – Mr. Shaka's violent term for hanging out together and having sex. Sex for him is an aggressive activity, a means to establish his dominance and authority.

Mr. Shaka is reluctant to speak more explicitly about what happened in the hotel room because "there are ladies in the courtroom." According to him, there was simply passion between two adult individuals. "She did not push me away. There were no screams. She did not tell me to stop." Admitting they had "rough sex," he adds that "I'm a brother," implying that he is not particularly gentle and can be aggressive as a sex partner. Twice he claims, "I didn't make her do anything." There is something circular and self-justifying in his words. He is disavowing responsibility and putting it all on Hanako.

When shown photos of her facial injuries, he says that her lip is bruised from a "blow job." This injury is to be expected when there is a "small girl and a black man." He states that he had sex with her only one time, pulling her hair, smacking her "butt," but "never touched her face." He denies stealing her money or possessions, saying that she gave him the money. Ms. Y. never says stop, never mentions he was hurting her, and never says to "get off me." There is no rape, he repeats. He is not into "pain," implying that he does not engage in sadomasochistic sex acts. Above all, he treated her like a "gentleman." If he had raped or sexually assaulted her, he would have left the city. Hearing his testimony, I was shocked by his misogyny, appalled by his need to behave destructively toward her as a woman.

As Ms. Johnson's cross-examination takes on a confrontational tone, it is also riveting. Because he has taken the stand, his prior convictions for robbery and selling drugs in Nebraska are brought into the record. As the prosecutor asks more pointed questions, Mr. Shaka gets more aggressive. This is the same pattern that occurs in his recorded interview with the two female detectives. When his self-esteem is wounded or he is accused of aggression, he strikes back, gets defensive, projects, displays paranoid ideation, and becomes verbally insolent and violent. He can suddenly become scary. He rages. The defense attorney is silent; Mr. Shaka's defense is an absolute denial in the face of overwhelming evidence. There is no admission of regret, or of a sense that he has gone too far. There seems to be a rigid stance that it is not culturally permissible for a defiant "African prince" at war with white colonialism and racism to admit to excessive violence or cruelty. Mr. Silverman somewhat pathetically does not try to mitigate the crimes, perhaps eliciting some form of mercy at the sentencing or appeal, possibly resulting in a lighter sentence.

Before she concludes, Ms. Johnson asks the judge to rule that Mr. Shaka has been stonewalling, lying, and "non-responsive." Shaka replies, "black people get thrown into jail," just as he worries that he will be another Mike Tyson in the transcript. Earlier in his interview, he had called himself the "Eddie Murphy" of Santa Monica Boulevard, his territory as a male prostitute in West Hollywood. He is omnipotently identified with black celebrities, particularly with notorious bad boys, who have been persecuted. Possibly his megalomania offsets his image of himself as small, inadequate, worthless, poor, marginal, and defective, as totally insignificant, possibly as someone who was neglected, maltreated, and abandoned. He reminds the jury that there is no DNA evidence, no witness, and claims that the detective and lawyer told witnesses what to say. He throws out another bombshell, asserting that he has no confidence in Mr. Silverman and that he "tried to get rid of my attorney five times." Mr. Shaka ends his testimony on another paranoid note, saying that people call him "aggressive because of a conspiracy of women against me." I theorized about his bad-enough mother, wondering if she was abusive, sexually molesting, negligent, or abandoning. Or all of the above.

During the closing statements, there is another unforeseen event. Mr. Shaka is nowhere present in the courtroom. The judge tells us that he has "voluntarily chosen not to be here." We are instructed not to be influenced by his absence in determining his innocence or guilt. I am skeptical about his disappearance, wondering if the judge was misstating the truth. Meanwhile, in the room adjacent to the courtroom, I can hear what sounds like Mr. Shaka's voice, screaming, insisting that he has the right to be present at his trial. There is no official explanation for these outbursts.

Several police officers enter the courtroom, checking their guns into a lockbox or cabinet. As they go into the adjacent room to quiet down the enraged individual, the closing arguments move forward. This is a crazy context to hear the summaries, making it difficult to focus and enter a reflective space. Meanwhile, everyone but the jurors proceed as if nothing is happening, business as usual. For me and the other jurors, it is incredibly jarring, even menacing. Violence may be unleashed in the courtroom. Though things settle down after five or so minutes, it seems much longer. The episode ends when the extra police officers reenter the courtroom, retrieve their weapons, and slowly exit.

Ms. Johnson asserts that the defense has misled the jury with many mistruths. She reiterates that Ms. Y. was raped, sodomized, and assaulted, submitting to the violence after a severe beating. If she had fought back, she would have received yet another beating. She went to the motel with her perpetrator out of youth, naiveté, and trust. She argues that Ms. Y. did not consent to sex during these assaults and that she had "no fight left in her" after the attacks began. What is more, Hanako belongs to "an obedient, non-confrontational culture," but even then, she did the best she could.

While his summary includes a rhetorical acknowledgment of Ms. Y.'s "pain and traumatized story," Mr. Silverman underscores how she agreed voluntarily to go to the hotel room, consenting to have sex with Mr. Shaka. Trying to inject doubt and uncertainty into our deliberations, he points out various "different stories" in the proceedings pertaining to the same events. He tells the jurors not to believe Ms. Y.'s account because the events of that afternoon are "fixed" in her mind. Even though she believes what she says happened, it "doesn't mean it happened the way she said." On the other hand, Mr. Shaka chose to testify and to speak to the police without an attorney present, implying that he has nothing to conceal and that he is honest and transparent. The defense counsel again minimizes her bodily injuries and the permanence of her wounds. He reiterates that there is no DNA evidence. Although Mr. Shaka is "rough around the edges," jurors ought not to turn him into a "bogey man," projecting their biases onto him. We are asked to vote not guilty, on the grounds that both the sex and the trip to the ATM were consensual.

When I had previously inquired about what to expect about the deliberation phase of jury duty, I was told universally that this would be the most fascinating part of the jury process. My experience was entirely different in this case. My heightened expectations are almost immediately dashed. The jury deliberations are anticlimactic. As the jury adjourned into the deliberation room behind the courtroom, I was struck by the freezing cold of the room. This adds to an ambiance of discomfort, mirroring the already disorienting experience of the trial. Now the final hours of serving on the jury take on a distinctly claustrophobic dimension.

As one of the oldest members of the jury panel and having been referred to by the judge as "doctor," I expected to be voted the foreman. This prospect generated some anticipatory anxiety, as I was emotionally shaken by the trial and did not want to adjudicate a group process, which I think may be contentious. Fortunately, a young man in his late 30s or early 40s, without previous jury experience, volunteers to be foreman. He emerges as a competent leader, one who facilitates the group dynamic without being impatient or authoritarian. He moves our discussion forward but allows for group conversation.

The jury panel represents a cross section of contemporary Los Angeles in its diversity; it is pluralistic, varied in terms of age, social class, ethnicity, and personality. There are African Americans, Hispanics, Asians, and Caucasians on the jury. There is a female black bus driver, several retired people, individuals in high technology, in the entertainment industry, some housewives, and someone in real estate. Some jury members speak too much; others are mostly silent; many are in between. Some are annoying. Others make pertinent remarks about the fact patterns and evidence in the case.

All in all, we vote unanimously guilty on all charges, except the second charge of sodomy. There is a sense that the second attack of sodomy, after the shower, could not be proven. The vote is nine to three that it occurred, with the three dissenters saying that they believed it happened, but the evidence did not support it "beyond a reasonable doubt." There is a lengthy, and in my mind, tedious discussion, about the robbery at the ATM. I have no doubts about Mr. Shaka's guilt on all the charges. For me, it was an open and shut case.

During our four and one-half hours of deliberation, there is considerable compassion for Ms. Y., sensitivity to her horrendous ordeal, and above all a consensus about how she may have been afraid for her life. While waiting for an official transcript of the testimony, I ask the group if anyone has any empathy for Mr. Shaka. One outspoken juror gives a qualified yes, realizing that conviction on all charges would mean a very long sentence. But my question does not generate much group discussion. Perhaps we are exhausted, and a bit burnt out on the process. I certainly was fatigued, wanting the trial process to end, wanting to exit from the bubble of serving as a juror, wanting to return to my "normal life."

Serving on a jury is not conducive to psychological reflection or sustained empathic understanding of the perpetrator. This trial put me in a slightly dissociated state, one of psychic numbing. Most of the jurors, me included, may have found him dangerous, possibly capable of further violent crimes, maybe murder. I realized after further reflection that service on the jury put me into a defensive and cut-off state of mind. I never stopped to consider my complicity in a system that might result in long incarceration for a black inmate. My inner emotional turmoil was so extensive that I was unable to understand my resistance to thinking about these consequences, my inability to understand my shame and guilt in participating in this process. The jury achieved an early consensus about his guilt, wanting him removed from the streets, deprived of his freedom. And I was a willing participant in that deliberation.

Knowing that I am a psychoanalyst, one juror privately tells me that she is unable to sleep and that the trial is disturbing her emotionally, adversely affecting her functioning. She wants to know "how long" her disturbance will last. I tell her candidly that I do not know and that it depends on many contingent factors, including her capacity for self-protection and her prior history of trauma. Wishing to be of help, I relate to her that I am also suffering from the psychological confusion and vulnerability of serving on this jury. I can only assume that serving on this jury panel was a heavy burden on my fellow jurors, that many were consumed by the trial, living the past nine days in a bubble just as I did. While many of us were upset by the disruption of our daily routines, some may have experienced their service as a welcome excitement, as something novel to participate in.

I conjectured that other members of the jury also experienced the same ambivalence about the legal system and its inefficiencies, feeling the same frustrations about the intrusion of the process into our daily lives as I did. In this, the psychoanalyst is no different from the electrician, store clerk, or student. Both then and now, I believe that we took our job seriously, followed the judge's instructions, and carefully considered the facts of the case and the relevant law. In short, we undertook a sincere effort to be rational and logical and to get the right result through a process of intelligent deliberation. While I began the process with a suspicion about the collective wisdom of a randomly selected group of citizens to dispense justice, I left the trial with a sense that justice had been served. But my experience also corroborated that the system of justice is itself quite brutal and dehumanizing. Mr. Shaka's punitive prison sentence will verify this.

I am left perplexed about the social dilemma of how to protect innocent civilians from harm and violence in a society that is more dangerous than most of us want to know. The guilty verdict did not quite serve as an adequate ending to the case and did not provide closure for me. Mr. Shaka is a dangerous predator and clearly guilty of all the charges. I continue to wonder if he is an absolute, irredeemable menace to society, an untreatable, incurable, and unreachable psychopath, saturated with hatred and rage, and possibly incapable of dialogue about his crimes and possible rehabilitation. Shouldn't Mr. Shaka, even after his heinous crimes, be forever worthy of a second look? I don't know if this is the expression of the guilt of a white, progressive male, someone who has benefitted from white privilege, about the incarceration of yet another black male, or if this is a cogent and humane sentiment.

Race or ethnicity never once is raised in our deliberations either about the defendant or the victim. We approach the matter solely as a matter of one individual apparently doing massive harm to another human being. I am surprised and educated by this. I raise the issue during deliberations of hearing Mr. Shaka's voice and screams outside the courtroom, wondering privately if a white man would have been treated the same way. One outspoken member of the jury claims it was not Mr. Shaka's voice; another said that the judge would not have permitted it if it were illegal; still, another reminded us that the judge mentioned that Mr. Shaka requested that he not be present. It remains unclear why he was not in the courtroom. In retrospect, I questioned whether I ought to have pushed harder on his absence, relating it to race. During deliberations, I regret not asking for the judge to clarify the reasons and meaning of his absence in the courtroom. With more distance and self-reflection, I realized that I am feeling some guilt about Mr. Shaka receiving such a long and harsh sentence.

I think to myself about trial by jury: such a strange system, so random, so anonymous, so outside the norms and rhythms of most of our lives. Yet somehow efficacious, at least in this specific case. There is a generalized sense that justice has been served and that we have done our job. This is exactly my view of the matter, without being self-congratulatory.

As we enter the courtroom, Mr. Shaka is present, still in shackles, surrounded by six cops. First, the judge reads the verdicts, then the clerk, and then each juror is polled about each individual count. I am not sure if another incident will occur, if violence or some verbal outburst will occur after the reading of the guilty verdicts. Mr. Shaka is convicted of all counts against him, except count five, the second sodomy charge, which is dismissed because of the hung jury. It is unclear what he or his lawyer thinks: both are silent. I cannot read their facial expressions or body language. There is no incident during the reading of the verdicts.

Before dismissing the jury, Judge Dickenson thanks us for our "time and effort." He hopes that it has been "quality weeks" for us. He explains that his humor is designed to "ease things for the jurors." He knows that the trial has ripped us from our lives, "exposing you to things you don't want to be exposed to." He mentions the diversity of our jury cohort with some sense of pride. Revealing that he has been a judge for thirty years, he pronounces that the American legal system is not "a perfect system, but it is the best." Does he make these remarks after every trial? Some of it is hackneyed, some true; some cliché-ridden, some idealistic. The judge is not sure if we have had "a pleasant experience," or one, which we might refer to with expletives. Lastly, and for me somewhat ominously, he ends on a note of reality: after one year, we will all be eligible to serve on another jury panel. I ironically think to myself: precisely what I don't need!

Concluding remarks

As a psychoanalyst serving on a jury, I was aware of many parallels and contrasts between the legal method of seeking the truth and the analytic. Like Hanako Y., whose watch was stolen, there had been theft of my time. Like the victim whose cash was stolen, I lost considerable money during the nine days of service. Like Hanako who had been violated and intruded upon, my own tranquility had been impinged upon. My sleep and dreams were disturbed, my routine disrupted, and my orderly, privileged life momentarily altered. Furthermore, being on the jury plunged me into an arena of horror and cruelty that was unwanted, so real that it was surreal. Of course, I also don't want to exaggerate the parallel process analysis. Hanako's psychological experiences were vastly more devastating than my own and will probably continue to trouble her for the long term. My defensive and adaptive capacities remain functional and reliable.

Nevertheless, to generalize from my own experience, the legal system and courts may underestimate the vicarious traumatic effects of certain criminal cases on the jurors. Despite the costs and practicality, it might be advantageous if there were mechanisms for jurors to process and a safe space to decompress from these experiences. The legal system ought to provide a specialist in secondary trauma to help jurors explore, express, elaborate, and work through the effects of serving on such criminal juries. I propose that one to five psychotherapy sessions might be appropriate and helpful, moving the juror beyond catharsis. It might not have to be conducted by a psychoanalyst, but rather a psychotherapist who is acquainted with the legal system and who has worked with traumatized patients. In a self-exploration of my subjective experience of serving on this jury, I discovered evidence of shock, emotional upset, and at times severe dissociation and emotional imbalance. Perhaps my experiences were to some extent universal.

I remember another passage by Rilke from the book I was reading on day one of my jury service: "I hold this to be the highest task for a bond between two people: that each protects the solitude of the other." In immersing myself in a case of rape, sodomy, sexual assault, robbery, and kidnapping, I entered a universe that was the opposite of love. Ms. Y.'s solitude was unprotected by these sadistic acts of violence against her, with aggression masking itself as sex. These acts were anything but love. They were a negation of love. In fact, for all the participants in this trial, there has been no healing, little therapeutic or reflective goals, nothing reparative. Ironically, it is Mr. Shaka who will experience the real "solitude," ostensibly "protected" by the State, but not with any loving or healing intentions.

Psychoanalysts need to create an artificial, private, and relatively formal environment to do their therapeutic work. We need a setting of comfort, security, stability, and reliability, creating a safe zone, designed for reflection, introspection, and a long-term increasingly intimate conversation. Working within our frame is vastly different from the framework of a court trial. The psychoanalytic setting is an island of peace, facilitating the patient's free associations and allowing for the analyst to think deeply in a sustained, caring, and receptive manner, to engage in reverie and to co-construct shared moments of intense bonding and mutual understanding.

The experience of the trial both radically interfered with and heightened my need to protect the solitude of my patients and my own. This is a vital and ongoing task, as Rilke specified. Protecting the boundaries of the psychoanalytic situation becomes indispensable in providing a framework for the work – and the intimacy – to unfold.

I have written this essay because I feel an urgency to work through the awful, brutal, and shocking experience of serving on this jury. The essay form provided me the freedom to explore my observations and inner reality, to acknowledge the discomforting and guilt-inducing aspects of the experience. I did not and do not contest the verdict, which I consider to be correct, especially given the facts and evidence lopsided in favor of the prosecution. Serving on the jury became part of my self-analysis.

Writing the essay encourages me – and hopefully the reader – to embrace the contradictions and ambivalence of participating in certain extreme situations like a rape/sodomy trial with an undercurrent of race. I remain troubled by the experience and disturbed by the entire process, including a post-trial period of relief and some guilt about collaborating with a brutal and dehumanizing legal system. I clearly experienced secondary trauma by serving on this jury. Part of the intent of this essay was to work through and process that trauma. I wrote it to rediscover my pleasure and capacity to do psychoanalytic work again. Lastly, writing this essay has enabled me to recover aspects of my own shattered solitude, permitting some repair and inner healing.

Coda

Punishment was not consciously part of the jury deliberation process. But one cannot bracket it out from our unconscious inner conflicts. I subsequently learned that Majestic King of Shaka was sentenced to life imprisonment in March 2016 with no possibility of parole. He was given sentences of six years to life imprisonment to run consecutively; that is, he must finish one sentence before starting the next. The longest of the terms was life with no parole on count seven, specifically for kidnapping with the intent to rob, kill, or rape. The Court of Appeal upheld the trial court's sentence in May 2017: "The court found that the crime involved great violence and bodily harm, the victim was particularly vulnerable, appellant had engaged in violent conduct indicating he was a danger to society, appellant had served a prior prison term." Incidentally, Mr. Shaka did not raise any issues in his appeal about his being absent from the courtroom. This suggests that his absence was possibly voluntary. In thinking about the very difficult choices that jurors make to carry out justice, I as a psychoanalyst only belatedly grasped that this traumatic experience that I participated in would result in permanent incarceration for the perpetrator. I underestimated how pervasive my guilt was, how deeply conflicted I was and remain because of this harsh sentence. Lastly, I wondered if a white perpetrator would have received a life sentence with no parole for similar crimes.

Previously published in *The Canadian Journal of Psychoanalysis*, Vol. 28, No. 2, Fall, 2020, pp. 277–298.

Part VI

Epilogue

Chapter 22

The Intellectual Itinerary of a Psychoanalyst

David James Fisher Interviewed by Paul Elovitz

David James Fisher was born on November 24, 1946, in Brooklyn to Martin Milton Fisher, an internist and peripheral vascular specialist with a practice in New York City, and Bess Kaufman Fisher, a housewife and mother. He is the oldest of three sons in a non-observant Jewish liberal professional middle-class family. When he was seven, the family moved to the suburbs, and he graduated from New Rochelle High School in 1964. He graduated as a history major from the University of Wisconsin-Madison in 1968. At New York University, he earned an MA in education (1968) and in history (1969), where he worked with intellectual historian Frank Manuel and French historian Leo Gershoy. For his doctoral degree in 1973, he returned to the University of Wisconsin where George L. Mosse was his major professor. Important influences were the European cultural and intellectual historian Mosse, historian of socialism and social movements Harvey Goldberg, and Professor of French Literature and Camus scholar Germaine Bree. At the Sixieme Section of the Ecole pratique des hautes etudes, he attended the postdoctoral seminar of Georges Haupt, a historian's historian and specialist in the history of socialism and communism. His psychoanalytic education occurred at the Los Angeles Psychoanalytic Institute and Society, 1980 to 1988, renamed the New Center for Psychoanalysis. He was analyzed by Rudolf Ekstein, Ph.D., supervised by Morton Shane, M.D., Maimon Leavitt, M.D., and Melvin Mandel, M.D.; his psychotherapy supervisors were Mel Lansky, M.D., and Jeffrey Trop, M.D.

As a historian, he has published three books: *Bettelheim: Living and Dying* (2008); *Cultural Theory and Psychoanalytic Tradition* (1991, 2009); and *Romain Rolland and the Politics of Intellectual Engagement* (1988, 2004). He edited the posthumously published book by Karen Fund, *Surrogate: How a Woman Named Sandra Made Me a Mother* (2020). In his valuable contributions to scholarship, he has shown a remarkable openness to writing about his own feelings, thoughts, and emotional and intellectual growth because of his life experience and psychoanalysis. In addition to these books, Dr. Fisher has authored over 50 journal articles and book chapters on contemporary French cultural history and the history of psychoanalysis, including essays on Freud, Lacan, Foucault, Sartre, Fenichel, Spielrein, and Stoller. He has published essays on the history of the psychoanalytic free clinics, the power structure and ideology of analytic institutes, and the technical and theoretical issues involved in working with erotic countertransference. A recent essay on Peter Loewenberg deals with the history of the University of California Interdisciplinary Psychoanalytic Consortium and the critical importance of the clinical training of Research Psychoanalysts.

Fisher has worked as an Associate Editor of North America for *The International Journal of Psychoanalysis* (IJP), on the advisory board of the journal *Society*, as Associate Editor of the journal *Humanities in Society*, and as the editor of *The Los Angeles Psychoanalytic Bulletin*. He has lectured extensively, speaking in France, Canada, and Great Britain, as well as at a number of prominent universities, including the California Institute of Technology, MIT, the University of Washington, Brandeis University, and Emory University. In addition, he has lectured at the Shanghai Mental Health Center and the Fudan University in Shanghai, China. Dr. Fisher is the father of two children, Benjamin D. Fisher, living in Los Angeles, and Chloe B. Fisher, living in Chicago and completing her degree in clinical psychology at the Chicago School of Professional Psychology. He practices psychoanalysis and psychoanalytic psychotherapy in Los Angeles.

Paul Elovitz (PE): What brought you to psychological history?
David James Fisher (DJF): I do not identify myself as a psychohistorian. I became interested in psychohistory in graduate school after having developed a deep intellectual interest in Freud and the seminal impact of psychoanalytic theories on the cultural history of the twentieth century. George Mosse always taught texts by Freud in his Western Civilization survey courses and in his upper-level courses in Modern European cultural history. He also introduced us to Jung's thoughts and to Jung's complicity with aspects of National Socialist ideology.

During the year 1968–1969 while at New York University, I had the privilege of studying European intellectual history with Frank Manuel. That was the year he published his psychoanalytic biography of Newton, which was incredibly stimulating to me. His approach to the history of ideas almost always included a subtle analytic understanding of the various thinkers on his syllabus, including utopian thinkers. As a graduate student at the University of Wisconsin from 1969 to 1973, we graduate students had an interest in psychohistorical perspectives and, above all, the writings of Erik Erikson. We were also interested in many of Peter Loewenberg's articles published in *The American Historical Review*. I never entirely embraced the methodology of psychohistory. It was important in my itinerary of moving from European cultural history to the practice of psychoanalysis. I would call myself a fellow traveler of psychohistory. If labels must be used, I am a cultural historian with a psychoanalytic perspective and an analyst who thinks historically. I define myself as a psychoanalyst. I have been practicing for over 45 years and it is a critical aspect of my professional identity. I remain fascinated by applied psychoanalysis and have written pieces on the psychology of literary texts, films, and art.

PE: How do you define psychohistory?

DJF: I am not sure how to define psychohistory. It would depend on which historian was practicing it. Perhaps it is the attempt to integrate both the historical and psychoanalytic approaches in understanding events, crises, and choices individuals make in a specific context. Psychohistory presupposed the primacy of psychology as the motivating force in history. In exploring the character structure of various personalities in history, psychohistories privilege the understanding of drive and defense if they embrace a conflict model; of trauma and dissociation if they embrace a deficit or relational model; or of grandiosity and self-devaluation if they embrace a self psychological or intersubjective model. Contemporary psychohistorians may be reluctant to pathologize their subjects, emphasizing the creative and transformational possibilities of individual experience. They would insist on the concept of over-determination in terms of reflecting on the psychological motives of individuals in frameworks not of their choosing. Each of these approaches can add a crucial dimension of understanding missing from conventional historical accounts. The latter tend to posit a rationalism, pragmatism, and self-interest on the part of historical actors that appears naïve to those grounded in depth psychology. I also think good psychohistorians may contribute to the understanding of collective behavior and group psychology, to what the French call "mentalite."

PE: When and why did you develop an interest in French and Western European history, which led you to becoming fluent in both?

DJF: I was always interested in history. I did well in social studies and had an aptitude to remember narratives and to analyze historical phenomena. It stoked my curiosity. It still does. I like to tell and to listen to stories. I developed an early interest in my own family's history, in Jewish history, and in the history of Western European cultural and intellectual life which seemed pertinent (the word we used then was relevant) to understanding and then changing history in the present. I became fascinated by the history of revolutions from the French Revolution to the Russian Revolution, the history of socialism and communism, and to ideas and cultural movements that were subversive. Psychoanalysis, at least early psychoanalysis, appeared to fit this model. I initially saw it as a way of challenging aspects of bourgeois morality and conformism, of middle-class respectability and hypocrisy; it helped me to develop a more profound grasp of the individual's unconscious dynamics, his or her sexuality, fantasies, and affective states. It was critically important in understanding trauma and the role of deficit and vulnerability in the inner world of the individual. It opened access to the dynamics of narcissism, of primitive states of resentment and envy, sadism and masochism, and the deepest longings and insatiable desires of the individual. I was impressed with how the early generations of analysts beginning with Freud would challenge some of the standard clichés about reason, self-interest, morality, and conventional ways of thinking about the individual in society.

Psychoanalysis also resonated with my own personal dynamics and with an imperative to understand my family. Reading Freud helped me to understand my family system and myself. Studying and transmitting contemporary analytic literature does the same. I am currently teaching seminars at the English Object Relations School. This opens vast insights into the inner world of my patients and my own, to the arena of the internal object, to the dynamics of countertransference, and to the significance of the analytic dyad.

As to fluency in French and Western European cultural history, I would be more modest about it. I have a certain base of knowledge. I have not always been able to keep up with the literature since I transitioned to a full-time analyst. I have preferred to investigate a given author or theme, say Sartre or the theme of anti-Semitism, in depth rather than focus on a general overview. I have privileged depth over surface. This was true of my training as a classical psychoanalyst, where depth is emphasized. As a cultural historian, it was the decisive influence of culture or ideology on the minds and behavior of individuals. Only recently in thinking about the approaches of Foucault and Lacan (and certain contemporary painters and artists) have I been able to appreciate the importance of surfaces. The unconscious is present on the surface, in language, and in obvious modes of communication. We don't have to plunge to the depths. We just need to open our ears, minds, eyes, and hearts to be receptive to it.

PE: Why did you choose to write about Bettelheim, Lacan, and Rolland?

DJF: I choose to write about Romain Rolland for both political and intellectual reasons. Rolland was curiously a hero to two of the professors I most esteemed, George Mosse and Harvey Goldberg. Mosse was my major professor and a fabulous lecturer and distinguished scholar with a vast knowledge of early modern and modern European history. He has an uncanny, generative knack for raising fabulous questions, questions that generate areas of research and investigation. I believe he supervised over twenty-nine doctoral dissertations. Goldberg was a highly valued European social historian at the University of Wisconsin, a scholar with a photographic memory and an unparalleled orator – an oratorical genius. Rolland was one of the exceptional and earliest writers to oppose the Great War. I came to him in the context of opposition to American involvement in the War in Viet Nam. I was unconsciously looking for someone who had the courage and insight to protest the war, go against the prevailing nationalist, militarist, and imperialist forces of that period. He was influential in developing a pacifist and Gandhian point of view, his biography of Gandhi putting the Mahatma on the cultural map not only in Western Europe but also in America and Asia. I was preoccupied, probably obsessed, by the theme of the responsibility of the intellectual. Noam Chomsky wrote an influential essay with that title, published in *The New York Review of Books*. Rolland was such a responsible intellectual, speaking truth to power and conscience to power. I also found his evolution from internationalist to pacifist to anti-fascist to fellow traveler of communism worth researching and pondering. I guess I was trying to find out the deeper motivations and limits of the engaged intellectual stance. Obviously, many of my generation of baby boomers, who came into consciousness in the 1960s, were deeply educated and inspired by Camus and Sartre. This was clearly the case for me. I saw Rolland as a precursor to Camus and Sartre. (They did not, but it did not bother me.) Other committed intellectuals stamped their imprint upon me in the 1960s, including Herbert Marcuse, R. D. Laing, C. Wright Mills, and Franz Fanon.

I came to Lacan in my years of living in Paris in the middle 1970s. I was alienated from America, from American politics, and in some ways all things American. I participated in a post-doctoral seminar with the social historian Georges Haupt, on "the geography of Marxism." Marxism was beginning its eclipse, though we were unaware of it. We studied the penetration and diffusion of Marxism into Western Europe and the world from Kautsky to the present. When I write about the history of psychoanalysis, I still borrow from the methodology of Haupt's seminar, now looking at the resistance to and adaptation of analytic ideas and practices. This plays into my interest in the history of psychoanalysis and the history of sexuality. My Paris years coincided with the structuralist moment in France, the age of Barthes, Levi-Strauss, Foucault, Lacan, and Derrida.

My former wife, Clarice Fisher, became interested in Lacan, reading carefully and annotating Lacan's medical doctoral thesis, a case study of a paranoid patient. Lacan was lecturing in Paris; in fact, his lecture hall was a happening scene, a place for the "tout Paris," including some of his patients. I regret never having gone to hear him lecture. I told myself I wouldn't be able to understand his French (which was probably true). But I think I was going against the current by not attending his lectures. He was popular, so I decided I wouldn't be part of the crowd idealizing and worshipping him. There is a funny vignette about encountering a young Parisian couple in the summer of 1975, who asserted that Lacan's texts, his *Ecrits*, were now "the revolution." That is, that the cultural revolution of the 1960s was over and that Lacan's understanding of language and the linguistic unconscious was the heir to the emancipatory potential of the human sciences. I thought of them as somewhat ridiculous, but their words stuck with me. When I returned to America, I started to study Lacan more closely. Sherry Turkle's book on Lacan, *Freud's French Revolution*, stoked my curiosity. After many years of teaching Lacan at analytic institutes, I think there is much merit and brilliance in many of his ideas, as well as a lot of wildness, irresponsibility, and nonsense in his technique and practice. Lacan's version of psychoanalysis postures against the exploration of meanings and is against understanding or insight. But he remains a major part of my analytic repertoire and I still hear his words and counsel as useful counters to thinking conventionally and being smug about my own insights and understanding of my patients. I believe I was the first person to deliver a formal paper on Lacan at the meetings of the American Psychoanalytic Association in 1980. My discussants were Stuart Schneiderman and Stanley Leavy; Sherry Turkle was also in attendance.

With Bettelheim, the story is more complicated and more ambivalent. I first heard his name mentioned in Mosse's lectures. Mosse always put his students on to writing that was controversial, textured, and penetrating. I remember seeing Bettelheim interviewed on the Dick Cavett television show in the late 1960s. I found him outrageously arrogant and authoritarian. He was extremely dismissive of the anti-war students and of the entire social and political movement to end the War in Viet Nam, questioning those who advocated radical change. I said out loud to my friends, if this is the voice of psychoanalysis, then psychoanalysis is now the enemy. Things changed when I started to study his works, above all his early writings on Nazi concentration camps, including his own incarceration. I was moved and found areas of agreement with his essay, *Freud and Man's Soul*, resonating with his empathy and to his portrait of a humanistic, soulful Freud. I think his fairy tale book, *The Uses of Enchantment*, is a masterpiece of applied psychoanalysis, one of the classics in the literature. It is a rare sample of the wisdom literature of psychoanalysis. I remember sending him several of my publications; he replied quickly and in a friendly and supportive manner. He was both receptive to and critical of my writings on Freud's *Civilization and Its Discontents* and Freud's relationship and debates with Romain Rolland.

When Bettelheim moved to Los Angeles in the late 1980s, I wrote, asking him if he was open to a visit. He immediately called me, and we developed an intense, mutually affectionate friendship. I saw him often, had meals with him, took him to concerts, and got him to talk about his life and the history of psychoanalysis. He offered to send me patients. I convinced him to go into therapy with a local German speaking colleague for his depression and suicidal thoughts. I went to him for advice on intimate matters. He was the most naturally empathic and attuned man I have ever met. He could also be harsh, cruel, and go directly to my unconscious conflicts with amazing clarity and insensitivity. A man who carried many residues of shame, he could be shaming. In short, he was a complicated man. And a difficult man. He once told me he regretted that I did not know him as a younger man. A recurring theme of our conversations was suicide, his intention to not go on existing and desire to take his life. I was in my middle 40s during the two brief years of this friendship. I was just beginning to start my family. I would leave these discussions about suicide exhausted and sometimes numbed off. But they were unbelievably intimate, however paradoxical that may sound. They were part of my maturational process and I cherish their memory.

I believe my Bettelheim book, a book of collected essays on him, was an attempt to work through my ambivalence about him and about male paternal figures. I have been drawn to powerful, charismatic, brilliant, and flamboyant Central European father figures. I was fortunate enough to develop an understanding of these idealizing transference dynamics in my training analysis with Rudolf Ekstein, a Viennese analyst and philosopher. Incidentally, I learned what topics to avoid with Bettelheim. For example, I never spoke to him about the 1960s, about the student radicals of that era, of the project to fuse Freud and Marx. Yet our conversations were rich and thought-provoking. I believe another motive to write about him was to oppose the mindless current of Bettelheim bashing that occurred after his suicide. He was no longer around to answer. I tried to write a balanced and nuanced account of the man and his writings. I hope his work will be revived and that students, scholars, and clinicians will take another look at Bettelheim. There is a great deal of substance and nuance in his writings. It is too easy to dismiss him as a patient abuser and bully. My writings on him after his death also constituted the work of mourning.

PE: Of which of your works are you most proud?
DJF: I am most proud of two pieces of writing. The first is one published in my late twenties on the relationship and debates between Freud and Romain Rolland ("Sigmund Freud and Romain Rolland: The Terrestrial Animal and His Great Oceanic Friend"). This essay is based on archival work I did in the 1970s at the Archives Romain Rolland in Paris on Boulevard du Montparnasse, Rolland's former apartment. It deals with the private and public aspects of their debate on what Rolland called the "oceanic feeling" spilling over into Chapter One of Freud's magnificent and ambiguous *Civilization and Its Discontents*. It also contextualizes and explicates Freud's 1936 paper, "A Disturbance of Memory on the Acropolis," written to honor Rolland's 70th birthday. This is a beautiful text, brimming with insight and self-analysis of the 80-year-old Freud, still at the peak of his analytic power. Besides having discovered some unpublished letters from Freud to Rolland and Rolland to Freud, the essay concludes with a section psychoanalyzing Freud based on their friendship and arguments. Quite audacious for a kid still in his 20s!

The paper also alerted me to the power and importance of affects, given that the oceanic feeling was a feeling, which in that period of my life I tended to disavow. What I discovered in my analysis of Freud became the dominant issue in my 10-year training analysis with Ekstein. I did not recognize it at the time. This essay was published in a French translation in a psychoanalytic journal called *Topique: Revue freudienne* and in *American Imago*. Its publication helped to get me accepted for analytic training, marking the beginning of my transition from a historian to a practicing psychoanalyst. I realized one could go only so far in psychoanalyzing others until I had been analyzed and before undergoing psychoanalytic training. A follow-up essay, "Reading Freud's *Civilization and Its Discontents*," offered my own critical analysis of the oceanic feeling from the point of view of the dynamics of narcissism and the ways in which the oceanic feeling may veil powerful feelings of anger and aggression.

A second favorite paper is called "Father's Day 1994." It is about my last visit to my father at a nursing home three months prior to his death. I tried to write something deeply intimate about his depressed and demented condition without recourse to analytic jargon or academic prose. It helped me during a period of intense mourning, writing becoming a form of grief work. It is revealing about my own state of mind during that period, disclosing the subjective states of feeling helpless in witnessing the decline and death of an elderly parent. This piece has been republished several times. It reverberates with an audience unlike anything else I have written. It is an emotionally honest and authentic piece of writing dealing with a significant rite of passage in my life and obviously in others.

PE: What are you working on now?

DJF: I am currently working on a critical analysis of an early autobiographical song by Leonard Cohen, "Famous Blue Raincoat." I examine the tenderness and sorrow in the song, the role of psychic splitting, and the alternation between omnipotence and sad, nihilistic, and suicidal feelings. It is about Leonard Cohen's difficulties in loving. Listening to Cohen's songs has become a source of joy and stimulation to me, even though he has been part of my psychic playlist since the 1960s. I hope to write about it without jargon and in a direct fashion with respect for the composer and yet include a direct expression of my subjectivity and feelings. I plan to send it to *The International Journal of Psychoanalysis* for publication. I also have a case study of a narcissistic patient who had a pattern of lying in his intimate life. It is someone I treated for over 15 years, making it an interesting study of the false self/true self opposition. I recently presented it in China, where the Chinese clinicians showed a genuine interest in working with narcissistic patients.

PE: What is your primary affiliation?

DJF: Psychoanalysis is my primary affiliation I teach and supervise at two analytic institutes. I have been a training and supervising analyst at ICP for the past 34 years. I am on the Board of Directors at NCP. I recently won an award I am quite proud of: Best Faculty Teacher for 2015. My primary responsibility is to my patients and to the psychoanalytic cause, which I still see as a sociopolitical and cultural movement.

PE: What special training was most helpful in your doing psychohistorical work?

DJF: Formal, clinical psychoanalytic training has been fundamental in my life. I believe it is vital for those doing psychohistory, or psychoanalytically informed history. Without it, the issues of personality remain abstract and intellectualized. Psychohistorians without clinical training and without having had the experience of a long character analysis can sound wild, non-empathic, and lacking in the capacity to understand fragile persons often in vulnerable or precarious circumstances. I deal with "The Question of

Psychohistory" and these themes in an essay in my book, *Cultural Theory and Psychoanalytic Tradition*. It is a detailed discussion of Peter Gay's *Freud for Historians* and Peter Loewenberg's *Decoding the Past*. I also published a detailed analysis of Manuel's *A Portrait of Isaac Newton* in that same book; it is called "Narcissistic Themes in a Psychobiography of Isaac Newton."

PE: Have you published, or do you plan to publish, an autobiography or any autobiographical writings?

DJF: I have published several autobiographical studies. You know the titles. In part, everything I write is autobiographical. I only write about things that I care about, things that have meaning or multiple meanings for me. I have gotten away from "objective history," even though I was trained in that discourse. I was always suspicious about it. But I am also suspicious about overly subjective forms of writing. Trusting and suspicious. I am also trusting and suspicious of my own interpretive work with patients, but often not suspicious enough.

PE: Which books were important to you in your development?

DJF: The most important psychohistorical books for me include:

Frank Manuel, *A Portrait of Isaac Newton* (which I have written about)
Erik Erikson's *Gandhi's Truth*, particularly his chapter "An Open Letter to the Mahatma," dealing with his countertransference in a powerful and poignant manner.
Maynard Solomon's *Beethoven*, a beautiful analytically oriented biography, on a figure I revere and whose music I find inspiring.
Vamik Volkan's *Nixon*, about which I have been highly critical, a text to be studied for what not to do in terms of psychohistory.
Bettelheim's *The Uses of Enchantment* for a subtle and incisive approach to the psychology of fairy tales and the importance of the relational experience of parents reading to their children. The book is less a historical study than a reading of the fairy tale literature from the point of view of an astute analytic literary critic with vast knowledge of the developmental psychology of children and the dilemmas of parents.

PE: In your experience and life, are high achievers more identified with their fathers?

DJF: Regarding identification with the fathers and high achieving, I am not sure about this. I haven't studied the question or examined the research findings. I would like to write a paper on the role of fathers in the formation of psychoanalysts, with particular emphasis on how many of us had fathers as physicians. It would be fascinating to know about these early identifications. There are five or six individuals who fit this description in Los Angeles alone; that is, analysts whose fathers were doctors – caretakers.

PE: Please tell us about the University of California Interdisciplinary Psychoanalytic Consortium and how it furthers applied psychoanalysis (psychohistory).

DJF: I have written on the University of California Interdisciplinary Psychoanalytic Consortium, in my piece on Loewenberg, published recently in *Clio's Psyche*. I have been attending these conferences for over 34 years. At NCP, we are trying to get this annual conference at Lake Arrowhead funded. It has been highly successful in terms of encouraging academics who use analytic methods in their research and stimulating graduate students to present their work and to consider formal analytic training. The UCIPC brings together academics and clinicians in an informal and relaxed fashion, fostering dialogue and critical exchange. It gathers three generations of students and professors, apprentices, and master clinicians. Many of us have presented early drafts of works at the conference. Early versions of my papers on Stoller and erotic countertransference, as well as my Leonard Cohen paper, originated at the Lake Arrowhead Conference Center, the "magic mountain," our private name for this lovely spot in the San Bernardino Mountains. It is a wonderful and unique association. We need more like it. Many graduate students and junior faculty members attend the Lake Arrowhead conference and subsequently enroll in psychoanalytic training at NCP. It is another form of outreach to the universities in Southern California.

PE: Who was important in your development as a student of psychosocial phenomena? Did Erik Erikson have an impact on you?

DJF: I have been fortunate to have had many male mentors. I believe that I unconsciously sought them out. These have included George Mosse, Harvey Goldberg, Frank Manuel, Michel de Certeau, Robert Stoller, Peter Loewenberg, Bruno Bettelheim, and Rudolf Ekstein. Germaine Bree was a female role model and mentor. I have written about all of them. They continue to influence me, to help me organize my thoughts, and to make me feel safe and protected when I don't understand something clinical or intellectual or political, which is quite often. I have been fortunate in my choice of and experiences with these ego ideals. They have been generous, caring, and nurturing to me in periods when I needed their assistance. One downside: it may have impeded my ability to find my own voice, my own unique way of understanding. It may account for a long period of my apprenticeship and susceptibility to imitation, which I continue to struggle against. I now believe that these identifications and counter-identifications exist in some complicated dialectical relationship, informing my clinical work and my writing. It is not so easy to disentangle these identifications. I am also increasingly critical of hero worshippers, knowing full well I have been one of them. This began as a child with my love of the Brooklyn Dodgers, the "Boys of Summer" team. My earliest heroes were

Duke Snyder, Jackie Robinson, Roy Campanella, Carl Erskine, and Sandy Koufax. Perhaps I have never entirely grown up in terms of those dynamics. Perhaps it continues to keep me young, playful, vital, and open to new experiences. It has changed as I became a parent, mentor, and transference figure to others. It is still strange to be idealized by others. I am becoming more comfortable with it, seeing its healing qualities and its potential to center, hold, and contain vulnerable individuals, while simulating thinking and creative activity.

Previously published in *Clio's Psyche*, Vol. 22, No. 3, December 2015, pp. 168–180.

Index

abandonment terrors 5, 21, 190
abstinence 12, 13, 63
adaptation 29
ad hominem argument 105, 128, 187
adolescence 21, 28, 38, 144
Adorno, T. 55, 90
aesthetics, aestheticians 19, 100
aggression xii, xiii, xiv, xv, xvi, xx, 57, 67, 69, 81, 82, 95, 129, 137, 157, 171, 187, 192, 208, 213, 223; external and internal forms of xiii; psychopathology of xx; sexual arousal xiv; sexuality and xii
Aichhorn, A. 89
Aimee (Lacan's patient) 118, 120
Alexander, F. 102, 103
The Altruistic Personality: Rescuers of Jews in Nazi Europe (1988) 161
ambivalence xiii, xviii, 5, 62, 63, 75, 81, 94, 103, 157, 170, 211, 213, 222
American Historical Review, 144,161
American Psychoanalytic Association 100, 101, 103, 104, 123, 126, 142, 172, 222
analyst's resistance 198, 204
analytic disputes 112
analytic institutions *see* psychoanalytic institutes
analytic thinking 114
analytic transference 37
anti-authoritarian psychoanalysis 197
anti-Semitism xv, 42, 67–69, 81, 92, 94, 96, 115, 118, 127, 136, 139, 140, 150, 151, 154, 155, 156, 157, 220
anti-Zionism 150
anxiety disorders 190
Arlow, J. 101
Arnold, M. 31
Ashbery, J. 51
atheism 93

attunement 13, 24, 103, 124, 126, 187, 201
Aubry, J. 115
Austro-Marxist assumptions 86
authoritarianism 18, 37, 51, 101, 105, 116, 128, 133, 197
autochthony 54

Bail, B. 104, 110
Barthes, R. 31
Belle (case history of) xiv, 3, 6, 16, 18
Bellow, S. 43
Benjamin, W. 90, 218
Bergstrom, J. 83
Berlin Poliklinik 96
Berman, H. 145
Bernfeld, S. xvi, 85, 89
Bettelheim, B. xxii, 24, 96, 127, 217, 220, 222, 223, 225, 226
Bevan, A. 41
Bion, W. 32, 53, 55, 57, 104
Bleuler, E. 132
Bloomsbury Group 40, 132
Blum, L. 156
Boehm, F. 96
Bonaparte, M. 93, 116, 119, 120
Borderline patients 207
Bornstein, B. 86
Boston Psychoanalytic Institute 100
Brandchaft, B. 103, 104
Braque, G. 122
Brasillach, R. 154
Bree, G. 83, 217, 226
Brenner, C. 101
Breton, A. 115
Breuer, J. 66, 68, 69, 71, 72, 74, 78, 81, 132, 137
Breuer, M. 79
British Psychoanalytic Society 33, 36

Brown, J. 145
Brown, N. O. 194
Burgholzli Psychiatric Clinic 130

Campanella, R. 227
Camus, A. xx, 156, 161, 217, 221
Caretaker 5
Cartesian 55, 64, 118
case history 5, 6, 8, 10, 13, 15–19, 65, 66, 118, 142
castration anxiety 73
Catholics xvii, 153
Cecily (case history) 74–76
Celine, L.-F. 153, 154
Central Europe 88
Character Analysis (1933) 91
Charcot, J.-M. 68, 77, 98, 196
Chicago Psychoanalytic Institute 100, 106
child analysis 88
children, separation from parents xxi, 191–192
China xiv, 142, 146, 218, 224
Chodorow, N. 145
Clift, M. 67
clinical data 88, 101, 128, 172
clinical skills 171
clinical training analysis 144
Clinton, H. 183, 184
collaboration xiv, 24, 65, 66, 70, 88, 127, 130, 134; with fascism 92, 154, 161
communism 95, 152, 217
Compte, A. 125
confidentiality xvii, 18, 24, 50, 89, 90, 99, 120, 146, 198
conformism xvii, 126, 194, 219
containing 57
contemporary psychoanalysis 31
context xix, xv, 11–14, 68–69, 74, 77, 80, 82, 94
Cooper, David 76
counteraccusations 104
counter identification 29
countertransference xviii, 11, 132
couple relationship 72
creativity 4, 56, 88, 101, 103, 109, 121, 126
critical theory 53, 117, 175, 178, 192
critical thinking 43, 93, 94, 107, 125, 128, 173, 196
Cronenberg, D. xviii, 130, 138, 139
cultural criticism 86
cultural nationalism xix
Czermac, M. 122, 123

Dadaism 117
"*A Dangerous Method*" (film) 130–141
Danto, E. 85–87, 89, 91, 92, 94
daydreams 3, 4, 6, 7, 9, 12, 17, 176
debasement of women 184
de Beauvoir, S. 64–66
de Clerambault, G. 118
defenses xiii, 5, 6, 10, 17, 58, 121, 144, 185, 188
definitive interpretations xv
De Gaulle, C. 116, 122
depression xii, xx, 93, 165, 167, 169, 170, 179, 190, 222
de Rosnay, T. 149
desire: countertransference desire 15; erotic desire 6; for mutual recognition 21
destructiveness 131
determinism xvi, 62, 76
Deutscher, I. 42
development and developmental stages 10
discipleship xvii, 107, 126, 193, 196
dissociation xiii, xx, xxi, 122, 130, 141, 167, 190, 192, 213, 219
dream approach, of James Grotstein: adopt Bion's writing style 55; autochthony (self-creation) 54; Bion's concept of O 57; dream continuous and discontinuous associations 53; dual-track thinking 56; evocative dream 53; Kleinian-Bionian of psychoanalysis 58; manifest content 54; occult writings/esoteric traditions 55; paradoxes 55; pre-modernist, modernist, and postmodernist camps 52; psychoanalysis 57; psychoanalytic methodology 54; psychoanalytic theory 53; transcendent position 57–58; unconscious, concept of 56, 57; version of postmodernism 52
dreams 10, 19, 35, 44, 54, 56, 65, 73, 78, 80, 128, 135, 137, 138, 176, 204, 212
Dreyfus Affair 115, 127, 153, 156, 157
Drumont, E. 153
Dylan, B. 43

early childhood development xv
early psychoanalysis xviii
ego psychology xvii, xiv, xv, 22, 23, 89, 100, 102, 119, 179
Eisenstein, S. 144
Eissler, K. 100, 101
Eitingon, M. 85, 91, 93
Ekstein, J. 30

Ekstein, R. xiv, xiv, xv, 21, 24, 25, 26–30, 194, 217, 223, 226
elderly population: age, disability, and confinement 170; chronic incontinence 166; depression 167; Hebrew Home 167; helplessness and dependence 166; optimal care 167; physical disability 167; physical needs 167; physician–patient relationship 165; sadness, grief, and helplessness 170; self-reliance 169; strokes 167
Ellis, H. 124
Elovitz, P. xxii
Emerson, R. W. 31
emotionality 184
empathic understanding 156, 168, 187, 210
empathy xxi, 71, 89, 106, 116, 153, 155, 156, 196, 201, 203, 205, 206, 210, 222
Enlightenment 94, 125
Erikson, E.H. xxii, xiv, xv, xvii, 21–25, 57, 218, 225, 226; identity and the life cycle 22; individual personality, analytic comprehension of 22; transitional object 22–24
erotic countertransference xiv, 11, 14, 15, 17, 218, 226
erotic daydream 3, 6, 9, 12, 176
erotic desire 6
erotics and sexual excitement xiv, xx; abandonment 5; arrogance and omniscience 19; conscious barriers 13; countertransference 12, 13; dirtiness 7; erotic countertransference 17; gender identity 6; genital orgasms 9; humiliation 3; loveliness 7; orgasm 7; primal sexual and masturbatory fantasies 17; primary femininity, concept of 17; sadomasochism 8; sexual arousal 8, 9, 12; sexual display and provocations 14; sexual fantasies 7; sexual practice 7; sexual quality 14; subjective functioning 7; transference 9; unconscious barriers 13
Erskine, C. 227
essays 32, 33, 39, 213–214
ethics xii, 18, 103, 107, 125
exhibitionism 7, 8, 11, 13, 14
existential xix, 22, 62, 63, 69, 70, 101, 166, 169, 180, 184, 186
existential-Marxist 63
experimentation 78, 87, 88, 95, 132, 143, 196, 197

Fairbairn, R. 53, 103, 126
The Family Idiot 62
Fanon, F. 194
fantasy xii, xiv, 3, 5–9, 11, 15–17, 23, 62, 82, 135, 138, 140, 172, 187, 204
fascism 92
fashion 8, 68, 73, 176
fathers 23, 29, 81, 225
Father's Day xx, 165–170
Fechner, G. 124
fees (psychoanalytic fee structure) 92
femininity (primary femininity) 4, 5, 17–18
Fenichel, H. 4, 90, 171, 172
Fenichel, O. xvi, 4, 85, 86, 90, 102, 103, 172, 217
Ferenczi, S. 32, 90, 127, 138
fetishism 30
Fifth International Psychoanalytic Congress 91
Fisher, D. J. 217–227
Fisher, M. M. 165–170
Flaubert, G. 62, 72, 118
Fleiss, W. 65, 78–81
Flemming, J. 105
Foot, M. 41
Forrester, J. 17
Foucault, M. 89, 116, 175, 217, 220, 221
France, V. xix, 149, 150
free association 30, 71, 73, 74, 81, 82, 99, 127, 172, 201
free clinics: clinical case presentation 89; clinical data 88; clinical experimentation 88; Freud initiated 91; history of 89; mental health services 87; primitive mental disorders 90; psychoanalytic technique 89
freedom 62, 63
French collaboration: anti-Jewish ideology 151; France, Vichy 150–152, 154, 157; information, education, and entertainment 153; mass assassination 156; new political regime 151; parliamentary democracy 151; process of assimilation 151
French Revolution 151
Freud, A. 89, 93, 100
Freud, J. 80–81
Freud, S. xv, xiv, xviii, 4, 26, 31, 39, 40, 44, 50, 54, 90, 95, 98, 102, 117, 118, 120, 130, 132, 133, 137, 192, 193; anti-Semitism 68–70; bonds of paternity 76–83; *Civilization and Its Discontents* 194; and classical

psychoanalytic formulations 17; discovery of Oedipus complex 82; donation for free clinic 93; Dream Book 54; fictional biography 77; fictional biography of 63; free clinic 91; *The Freud Scenario* 67; illusions and self-deceptions 139; interaction with Jung 137; interactions with patients 70–75; liberalism 93, 94; libido theory 138; literary and theoretical brilliance 193; long-term self-analysis 73; metapsychological and clinical writings 193; metapsychology 62, 63, 86, 101; politics and sexuality 86; psychic determinism 63; psychic role of father 81; psychoanalytic intersubjectivity 74, 83; psychoanalytic technique 133; psychology of unconscious 82; psychopathology xviii; self-analysis xvi, 74; self-confidence and self-assurance 79; sexual and social revolution 95; sexual aetiology, theory of 78; sexual desire, understanding of xvi; social dilemmas 82; speech and commitment 91; *Studies on Hysteria* 66; topographical model 63; transferential relationship with Fleiss 79–80; unconscious, conception of 62; work with Karl von Schroeh 71
Freudianism 117
The Freud Scenario 62, 63, 82
Freund, J. 93
Friedlander, K. 86
Fromm, E. xvi, 85, 86, 90

Gabe, S. 144
Gadamer, H.-J. 179
Gay, P. 83
gender equality 86
gender identity 6, 17, 172
genocide 157, 159
gentleness 10, 74
Gero, G. 86
Gide, A. 116
Goethe, J.W. 23, 29, 125
Goldberg, H. 193, 217, 220
Greenson, R. 4, 15, 66, 86, 102–104, 106, 110–112
Gross, H. 133
Gross, O. 133, 134
Grotjahn, M. 86, 95, 96

Grotstein, J. 52–58, 83, 106; dream approach of *see* dream approach, of James Grotstein
guilt 165, 214
Gyomroi, E. 86

Habermas, J. 174, 179
Hale, N. 98
Hamilcar 80
Hampstead Clinic 33–34
Hampton, C. 130
Hannibal 80
Haupt, G. 192, 217, 221
healthy sexuality 86
Hegel, G. 56, 119, 124, 175
Hegelianism 117
Heidegger, M. 53
hermeneutic psychoanalysis 174
hermeneutics 174, 201
Herzl, T. xix
history of psychoanalysis 85–86, 98, 129
Hitschmann, E. 85
Hoffer, W. 89
Hoffmann, S. 149
Hofstadter, R. 187
holding environment 12
homosexuality xx, 63, 118, 176
homosexuals 175
Honneth, A. 179
Hopkins, L. 36
Horkheimer, M. 90
Huguenot (French Protestants) 160
humanism 195
human rights 190
humiliation 3, 150, 204
Huston, J. xvi, 61, 62, 64–67
hypocritical sexual attitudes and practices 133
hysteria 65, 66, 68, 70, 130, 132, 185

identity 23
identification 29
individuation 24
imagination 5, 53, 54, 81
incoherent discourse xvii
inhumane policies xxi
intellectualization xxii
International Psychoanalytic Association (IPA) xvii, 103, 115
interpretation 7, 9, 10, 13, 14, 16, 18, 19, 32, 45, 54, 62, 81
The Interpretation of Dreams 54, 80
intersubjective 56, 64, 70, 72, 76, 79–83

introspection 85, 213
Isakower, O. 100

Jacobson, E. 86, 96
Jacoby, R. 86, 87
James, H. 40
Jewishness xv, 40–41, 42, 43, 63, 69, 116, 140, 152
Jewish self-hatred 153
Jones, E. 65
Jouve, P-J. 117
judge, as authority 200, 201
Jung, C.G. xviii, 38, 96, 130–134, 141; anti-Semitism 136; archetypes 136; Aryan psychology 136; collective unconscious 136; interaction with Freud 137; mutual analysis 134; mystical leanings 137; mysticism 136; sexual repression 134
Jung, E. 140
jury service 213

Kaufman, C. 67, 217
Kepecs, J. xxi, 193, 194
Kernberg, O. 112, 113
Kerr, J. 130
Khan, M. 35, 36, 50
kidnapping 199, 206, 213
kindness 12, 32, 71, 179
Kirsner, D. xvii, 98–107; *see also* psychoanalytic institutes
Klein, M. 45, 88, 102, 131
Kleinian approach 45, 51, 88, 104–105
Kleinian development 109, 112
Kleinian theory 104–105, 112, 131
Kohut, H. 99, 126
Kojeve, A. 118
Koufax, S. 227
Kraft-Ebbing, R. 124
Kris, E. 100
Kris, M. 93, 100
Kristeva, J. 53
Kurzweil, E. 98

Lacan, J. xvii, 32, 53, 56, 57, 98, 114–123, 131, 204, 217, 220–222; characterological and ideological affinities 120; clinical experience 120; intellectual and clinical framework 116; intellectual biography of 115; medical thesis 118, 120; psychoanalytic discourse 114; unorthodox practice of psychoanalysis 121

Laing, R.D. 76, 194
Lake Arrowhead Interdisciplinary Psychoanalytic Consortium 145, 146
language 6, 7, 13, 17, 54–55, 57, 63, 104, 105, 114, 117–123, 127, 129, 131, 132, 151, 154, 185–186
Lantos, B. 86
Laplanche, J. 37
lay analysis 22, 88, 102, 126
Le Chambon-sur-Lignon 159
Les Decombres 154
Levine, R. 193
liberalism 94
libido theory 138
life cycle xiv, xv, 21–23, 25–30, 135, 169, 207
life imprisonment 214
Loewenberg, P. xxii, xix, 83, 127, 142–146, 218, 226; analytic training 144; Bruin Granada Project 144; debt to Sam Eisenstein 144; education 143; energy and vision 145; involvement with China 146; learning and teaching 146; life and work 142; psychoanalysis trip to China 146; psychoanalytic history 145; UCNCPIPC Consortium 145
Loewenberg, R. 142–143
Loewenstein, R. 116, 119–120
Los Angeles Psychoanalytic Institute and Society (LAPSI) 100–106, 109–113, 126, 145, 194–195
love affair 134–136
loss 23

Madame Bovary 72
Mahler, M. 100
Mailer, N. 43
Majestic King of Shaka 199, 207, 214
Makari, G. xviii, 124–129
Mann, D. 14
Manuel, F. xxii, 218, 225
Mao, Tse-Tung 114, 122
Marcuse, H. 86, 90, 194
Markowitz, R. 86
Marrus, M. 149, 159
Marx, K. xvi, xvii, 63, 91, 106, 223
Marxism 92, 117
masochism 10, 11, 17, 219
Mason, A. 55, 106, 109, 110
The Mass Psychology of Fascism (1933) 92
masturbatory fantasies 17
Maurras, C. 118
McDougall, J. 19

McGuire, I. 104
metaphysical 52, 138
metapsychology 62, 63, 86, 101
Meynert, T. 68, 70, 71, 78, 81
Michels, R. 13
Middle School, or Independent School xiv, 32
Mill, J.S. 94
Miller, H. 19, 32
Miller, J.-A. 117
Mills, C.W. 100
mindful adaptation xiii
mindlessness xiii
Minotaur 56
Miro, J. 180
misogyny xxi, 184, 188, 208
Mitchell, J. 43
modern urban civilization 133
monogamy xv, 46, 47, 91, 92, 138
Monogamy (1996) 46
Monroe, M. 66, 103, 111
Montaigne, M. 19, 173
Mosse, G. L. 83, 193, 217, 218, 220, 222, 226
mourning 24, 47, 77, 129, 169, 223, 224
Mozart, W.A. 27
Müller-Braunschweig, C. 96
mysticism 55, 136, 139
mystery 8

narcissism 6, 58, 116, 219, 223
The Nation 179
nativism 184, 186
Natterson, J. xx, 83, 178–18
navel of the dream 54
Nemiroff, R. 145
Newton, I. 218, 225
New Age xiii
New York Psychoanalytic Institute 100, 101
Nietzsche, F. 31, 32, 53, 124
Non-Jewish Jews 42
Nye, R. 83

Obama, M. 184
object relations xiv, xv, 27, 53, 102, 112, 113, 131, 220
oceanic feeling 57, 94, 194, 223
Oedipus complex 65, 82, 127
Oliner, S.P. 161
On Kindness 179
Ophuls, M. 149
oral testimony 105
overinterpretation 44–45

panic attacks 190
pansexualism 134
paradox xii, xvi, 7, 18, 32, 45, 55, 56, 63, 125, 188, 196, 207
paradoxes 55
paranoia 88, 101, 112, 118, 188
paranoid patients 120, 221
paranoid style in American politics 187–188
Paris 117
Pater, W. 31
patriarchal society 83, 133
Paxton, R. 149, 159
penetration xviii, 13, 88, 146, 199, 221
penis envy 17
personalities 29
personality issues 192
perversion xx, 124, 176
Petain, P. 149
Phillips, A. xv, 31–51, 179
physician–patient relationship 165
Piaget, J. 131
Picasso, P. xxiii, 122, 166, 180
Pinchas-Levy 40
The Plague xx, 161
"*Playing and Reality*" by Winnicott xv, 33, 38, 39
polemical 6, 32, 94, 115, 128, 138
political correctness 186–187
Pollock G. 106
Pontalis, J.-B. 67, 77, 82
pornography 46
postmodernism 52
post-traumatic stress disorder (PTSD) xxi, 190
power structure xvii, 100, 217
primary femininity xiv, 17, 175
privacy 18, 34, 89, 137, 170, 198, 203
psychic numbness 167
psychoanalysis xxiii, 22, 35, 36, 42, 43, 109, 141, 171, 191; in academia and establishment institutes of 194; codification and bureaucratization of 105; contemporary China xix; critics of 89; cultural artifacts xiii; defined 175; dissociative and defensive strategies xiv; early history of 133; French psychoanalysis 115, 116, 195; history of 98; intense trauma and loss xiii; internal conflict xiii; and Marxism 92; mindlessness xiii; normalcy and pathology xii; pan-sexualism xvii; rationality and humanism 195; sexuality

and aggression xii; social adjustment and domination xviii; subversive method 195; theory and practice 196; trust and suspicion xiii
psychoanalyst 33
psychoanalytic community 176
psychoanalytic education: critical thinking and critical analysis 196; radical method of 195; substance and scholarship 195
psychoanalytic hermeneutics 7, 19, 174
psychoanalytic humanism 194
psychoanalytic institutes: cultural studies 98; intellectual independence 99; issues of ethics and practice 107; prestige in 107; professional advancement in 99; skeptical intelligence and radical self-reflection 99
Psychoanalytic International 86
psychoanalytic metapsychology 63
psychoanalytic psychotherapy 33
psychoanalytic research 111
psychoanalytic therapy 171
psychoanalytic writing 31, 49
psychological astuteness 24
psychopathology xvii
psychotic patients 52, 123
public intellectual xv, 32

racism xix, xxi, xxii, 41, 69, 82, 94, 184, 185, 188, 199, 206–208
Rangell, L. 103, 104, 106, 110–112
rape xxii, 199, 203, 204, 206, 208, 213, 214
Rashomon phenomenon 101–102, 106, 109–110
Rathenau, W. xix
Reason and Violence 76
Rebatet, L. 154
recriminations 104
regression 10, 22, 29, 153, 196
Reich, A. 86, 91, 92, 100
Reich, W. xvi, xvii, 86, 89–92, 94, 96, 194
Reinhardt, M. 66
Reinhardt, W. 66, 67
relationship xv, 10, 23, 24, 55, 56, 65, 72, 76, 79, 94, 103, 132–137, 140, 194, 196
religious commitment 29
Renner, K. xix
Renoir, A. 11
repression xvi, 64, 79, 92, 125, 132, 134, 150
repudiation of political correctness 184
Research Psychoanalysis xix, 145

Research Psychoanalyst 144, 145
resistance xix, xx, 6, 10, 11, 13, 17, 32, 71–74, 91, 98, 128, 129, 138, 150, 155, 159–161, 198
revelation xvi, 57
reverie xvi, 53, 57, 205, 213
Ricoeur, P. 174
Rilke, R.M. 199, 213
Robinson, P. A. 86
Rodman, R. 47
Rodriguez, S. 178
Roheim, G. 86
Rolland, R. xxii, 57, 94, 116, 193, 194–195, 220–223
Rosenfeld, H. 104
Roth, P. 43
Roudinesco, E. xvii, 98, 115, 122
Russian Revolution 87, 128, 219

sadism xix, 131
sadness 165
sadomasochism xiv, 7, 8, 171, 175, 208
sadomasochists 175
Sarah's Key 149
Sartre, J.-P. xvi, 61–83; and Huston 64–67; portrait of Freud *see* Freud, S.; and psychoanalysis 61–64
Sartre and Psychoanalysis 62
Sauvage, P. xix, 159–161
Schorske, C. 125, 127, 143
Schweitzer, C. 61
science xviii, 55, 68, 70, 74, 78, 95, 125, 129, 144, 146, 153
secondary trauma xxii, 213, 214
secularism 93
Segal, H. 104
self-analysis 74, 78, 81, 136
self-criticism xii, 157
self-esteem 190
self-psychology 179
self-reflection xv, xvi, 11, 12, 25, 57, 73, 99, 129, 141, 188, 199, 211
self-reflective disciplines 85
self-regulation, loss of 190
self-reproaches 165
self-revelation xvi
Semelin, J. 155
senile dementia 165
separation anxieties xv, 47
sexism 184
Sex-Pol 92
sexual desire 119
sexual enactments xiv

sexual enlightenment 93
sexual excitement xx, 6–11, 14, 15, 19
sexual expressiveness 92
sexuality 5, 6, 47, 131, 175; and gender xiv, 48
sexual jealousy 47
sexual liberation 82
sexual monogamy 92
sexual practice 175
sexual rights, of women 133
sexual suppression 92
short session xvii, 119, 121
Siegfried fantasy 135, 140
Simmel, E. 85, 90, 95, 102
Slater, P. 194
Snyder, D. 227
Social Amnesia (1975) 86
social democracy 87, 92, 94
Social Democratic ideology 86
social emancipation 180
socialism 42, 217, 219
social justice xx
social reform 93
Society for Psychoanalytic Medicine of Southern California 102
socioeconomic inequalities xx
The Sorrow and the Pity (1969) 149
Spielrein, S. xviii, 128, 130–135, 138–141, 217
Stoller, R. J. xiv, xx, 3, 5, 15, 16, 171–177; classical psychoanalysis 172; contemporary psychoanalytic approach 173; primary femininity, concept of 175; psychoanalytic therapy 172; religious belief and mystification 173; sexuality and gender formation, investigation of 171
Stolorow, R. 83
Strachey, J. 36, 37, 49, 50
Strauss, J. 27
stroke xx, 143, 166, 167, 168
strokes 167
structuralism xvii
subversive xiii, xv, xvii, xviii, xxi, 19, 32, 82, 85, 86, 92, 115, 118, 124, 126, 129, 175, 193, 195, 197, 219
super-ego 17, 56, 64, 82
supervision xv, xvii, 33, 88, 89, 136
surrealism xvii, 116, 117, 119
Surrealism 117
suspicion and trust xiii, 19, 105, 117, 139, 196, 211
symptom xiii, xvi, xxi, 7, 66, 73, 77–79, 130–131

Tandler, J. 86, 87
Tavistock Clinic 33–34
Taylor, B. 41, 179
technique xiii, xiv, xxi, 9, 10, 12, 13, 62, 73, 78, 89, 90, 93, 94, 99, 101, 102, 107, 114, 121, 123
theory: critical theory 53, 117, 175, 178, 192; Kleinian theory 104; libido theory 138; object relations theory 112; sexual aetiology 78
Tizard, J. 50
tolerance 93
topographical model 63
training analyses 37
transcendent position 57–58
transference xviii, xxii, 9, 10, 11, 12, 15, 17, 18, 24, 29, 30, 37, 54, 56–58, 71–72, 192
transference and countertransference 29, 195
transformation xii, 8, 48, 131, 133, 172
transitional objects and generativity xiv, xv, 21–30, 203
translation xv, 49, 50, 65, 67, 223
transsexuality 175
transsexuals 175
trauma xiii, xxi, xxii, 7, 23, 48, 57, 75, 102, 131, 132, 141, 161, 190, 203, 211, 213, 214
Trotsky, L. 42
Trump, D. xxi, 96, 183–189
truth 18
Truth and Reconciliation Commission 113
Turkle, S. 98

UCLA Department of Psychiatry 15
uncertainty xii, xv, 18, 23, 53, 72, 74, 125, 129, 180, 196, 200, 209
unconcealment 57
unconscious 16, 18, 19, 32, 51, 53, 56, 57, 62–64, 66, 67, 73, 78–80, 82, 106–107, 118, 119, 125–127, 135–139, 200–202
uncritical thinking 107
unknown and unknowable xxiii, 14, 18, 52, 55, 56, 100
"The Uses of an Object" (Winnicott) xv

Vichy France 149–157
Vienna 22, 23, 26, 67–70
Vienna Ambulatorium 96
Vienna Society of Psychoanalysis 96
Viennese Psychoanalytic Society 132
Viennese Social Democrats 86

violence 82, 95, 138, 156, 203, 204
von Freund, A. 93
von Schroeh, K. 71–73
voyeurism 13

Wagner, R. 132, 135
War in Viet Nam 192–193
Weapons of the Spirit (1989) xix, 159–161
"Weapons of the Spirit." (Sauvage) 159
Webb, R. K. 144
Wexler, M. 103, 106, 110
"*Who is the Dreamer Who Dreams the Dream*" (Grotstein) xvi, 52
Wilde, O. 31

Winnicott, D.W. xv, xvi, 12, 21, 22, 24, 26, 27, 30, 31, 33, 36–40, 44, 45, 47, 48, 50
wisdom and wisdom literature 25, 222
Wolff, T. 138, 140
"*The Words*" (Sartre) 76
wounded healer xviii, 141
writer and writing 32, 49

xenophobia xix, xxi, 86, 115, 184, 186, 188, 184, 186

Y. (Hanako) 199, 201–206, 209, 210, 212
Yeats, W. B. 58
York, S. 67
Young, N. 43

Milton Keynes UK
Ingram Content Group UK Ltd.
UKHW031501071224
451979UK00015B/155